SOCIAL PROBLEMS 96/97

Twenty-Fourth Edition

Editor

Harold A. Widdison
Northern Arizona University

Harold A. Widdison, professor of sociology at Northern Arizona University in Flagstaff, holds degrees in Sociology and Business Administration from Brigham Young University and Case-Western Reserve University. Employed as an education specialist with the U.S. Atomic Energy Commission, he was awarded a Sustained Superior Performance Award. As a medical sociologist, Dr. Widdison is actively involved in his community with the local medieal center's neonatal committee, a founding member of Compassionate Friends, a member of the board of directors of the Hozhoni Foundation for the mentally handicapped, and a consultant on death, dying, and bereavement.

Annual Editions
A Library of Information from the Public Press

Cover illustration by Mike Eagle

Dushkin Publishing Group/
Brown & Benchmark Publishers
Sluice Dock, Guilford, Connecticut 06437

The Annual Editions Series

Annual Editions is a series of over 65 volumes designed to provide the reader with convenient, low-cost access to a wide range of current, carefully selected articles from some of the most important magazines, newspapers, and journals published today. Annual Editions are updated on an annual basis through a continuous monitoring of over 300 periodical sources. All Annual Editions have a number of features designed to make them particularly useful, including topic guides, annotated tables of contents, unit overviews, and indexes. For the teacher using Annual Editions in the classroom, an Instructor's Resource Guide with test questions is available for each volume.

VOLUMES AVAILABLE

Abnormal Psychology
Africa
Aging
American Foreign Policy
American Government
American History, Pre-Civil War
American History, Post-Civil War
American Public Policy
Anthropology
Archaeology
Biopsychology
Business Ethics
Child Growth and Development
China
Comparative Politics
Computers in Education
Computers in Society
Criminal Justice
Developing World
Deviant Behavior
Drugs, Society, and Behavior
Dying, Death, and Bereavement
Early Childhood Education
Economics
Educating Exceptional Children
Education
Educational Psychology
Environment
Geography
Global Issues
Health
Human Development
Human Resources
Human Sexuality

India and South Asia
International Business
Japan and the Pacific Rim
Latin America
Life Management
Macroeconomics
Management
Marketing
Marriage and Family
Mass Media
Microeconomics
Middle East and the Islamic World
Multicultural Education
Nutrition
Personal Growth and Behavior
Physical Anthropology
Psychology
Public Administration
Race and Ethnic Relations
Russia, the Eurasian Republics, and Central/Eastern Europe
Social Problems
Sociology
State and Local Government
Urban Society
Western Civilization, Pre-Reformation
Western Civilization, Post-Reformation
Western Europe
World History, Pre-Modern
World History, Modern
World Politics

Cataloging in Publication Data
Main entry under title: Annual Editions: Social problems. 1996/97.
    1. United States—Social conditions—1960.—Periodicals. I. Widdison, Harold A., *comp.*
II. Title: Social problems.
309′.1′73′092′05   73-78577   ISBN 0-697-31732-3
HN51.A78

Twenty-Fourth Edition

Printed in the United States of America

Printed on Recycled Paper

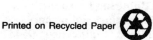

To the Reader

In publishing ANNUAL EDITIONS we recognize the enormous role played by the magazines, newspapers, and journals of the *public press* in providing current, first-rate educational information in a broad spectrum of interest areas. Within the articles, the best scientists, practitioners, researchers, and commentators draw issues into new perspective as accepted theories and viewpoints are called into account by new events, recent discoveries change old facts, and fresh debate breaks out over important controversies.

Many of the articles resulting from this enormous editorial effort are appropriate for students, researchers, and professionals seeking accurate, current material to help bridge the gap between principles and theories and the real world. These articles, however, become more useful for study when those of lasting value are carefully *collected, organized, indexed,* and *reproduced* in a *low-cost format,* which provides easy and permanent access when the material is needed.

That is the role played by *Annual Editions.* Under the direction of each volume's *Editor,* who is an expert in the subject area, and with the guidance of an *Advisory Board,* we seek each year to provide in each ANNUAL EDITION a current, well-balanced, carefully selected collection of the best of the public press for your study and enjoyment. We think you'll find this volume useful, and we hope you'll take a moment to let us know what you think.

Welcome to *Annual Editions: Social Problems 96/97.* When Democrat Bill Clinton was elected president in 1992, he expressed great optimism for social reform, based on what appeared to be an end to political gridlock. However, his campaign promises to eliminate welfare as we know it, to "reinvent" government, and to provide health care for every American have been much more difficult to achieve than he envisioned. During the first two years of Clinton's presidency, both houses of Congress comprised a Democratic majority, which many believed should have enabled him to make major changes. However, significant numbers in his own party did not share his vision of what the future could and should be. At the conclusion of 1994, Congress shifted to a Republican majority with its "Contract with America," which ended the president's chances to achieve his campaign promises. To complicate matters, the specter of domestic terrorism turned into a reality with the April 1995 Oklahoma City bombing. This edition of *Annual Editions: Social Problems 96/97* has been revised to reflect the significant events, concerns, and problems emerging or highlighted during the past year.

As in the past, hundreds of articles have been reviewed in preparing this edition. In some cases it was very difficult to select which, among the numbers of very good articles, would be included in this edition. In other cases, we have had to search for quality materials for inclusion. I wish to thank those individuals who took the time to seek out and send in materials for consideration. Your efforts made my task much easier. The criteria used in selecting materials to include in the book are timeliness, quality, content, relatedness to the other articles, and readability. Some articles were very good, but the technical nature of the materials made them of little use to most readers. A superabundance of articles dealing with welfare reform, poverty, family and parenting issues, crime, drugs, terrorism, and the quality of life were discovered. What we were not able to find were articles that were current and readable in the areas of aging, sex (other than AIDS and related issues), religion, and global concerns. As a result, some areas may not be covered as well as they should be, and your help in locating quality materials in these areas would be appreciated. To make room for newer materials, some excellent articles that had become dated had to be deleted. It is hoped that their replacements are of comparable quality.

This edition begins with two articles examining various theories of social problems. Following this introductory section are seven units. Unit 1 clusters articles concerning the basic unit of society—the family—including the changes it is experiencing and the implications of these changes for the individual and society. Unit 2 looks at the causes and impact of crime, delinquency, and violence on the American society, and what, if anything, can be done to control them. This unit has been expanded to include materials on terrorism and the significance it can and is having locally and internationally. Unit 3 examines problems associated with access to and quality of health care. Unit 4 discusses issues, trends, and public policies impacting on poverty and inequality. Unit 5 explores the implications of mass immigration on the American society, the desirability of cultural pluralism, and the advisability of affirmative action. Unit 6 looks at some of the major problems facing cities and their ability to provide their residents with a high "quality" of life. Unit 7, the final unit, examines global issues that transcend national geographic boundaries.

To assist the reader in identifying topics or issues covered in the articles, the *topic guide* lists various topics in alphabetical order and the articles in which they are discussed. A reader doing research on a specific topic is advised to check this guide first.

Most of the authors of the articles express serious concern about the troubled state of America's cities, families, economy, and deteriorating position as a world power, as well as concern about the condition of Earth's environment, but they have not given up. They also suggest strategies to help the family, reduce crime, make cities safer, improve the environment, and so forth.

If you have suggestions for articles or topics to be included in future editions of this series, please write and share them. You are also invited to use the postage-paid form provided on the last page of this book for rating the articles. Your ideas and input would be appreciated.

Harold A. Widdison
Editor

Contents

Introduction

Two introductory articles summarize the three major theoretical approaches to studying social problems: symbolic interactionism, functionalism, and conflict.

Unit
1

Parenting and Family Issues

Four selections examine how the socially stabilizing force of the family has been assaulted by the dynamics of economic pressure, and unemployment.

The concepts in bold italics are developed in the article. For further expansion please refer to the Topic Guide and the Index.

Unit 2

Crime, Terrorism, and Violence

Six articles discuss the extent and significance of crime and delinquency in today's society.

Unit 3

Health and Health Care Issues

Seven articles address society's aging, health, and health care issues.

The concepts in bold italics are developed in the article. For further expansion please refer to the Topic Guide and the Index.

Unit

4

Poverty and Inequality

Seven selections examine how inequality affects society
and the institutions of education, women's rights, the
economy, and welfare.

The concepts in bold italics are developed in the article. For further expansion please refer to the Topic Guide and the Index.

Unit 5

Cultural Pluralism and Affirmative Action

Five selections discuss various aspects of cultural pluralism: that it has been minimized, that diverse differences promote unity, and that diversity is the sign of social maturity.

The concepts in bold italics are developed in the article. For further expansion please refer to the Topic Guide and the Index.

Unit 6

Cities, Urban Growth, and the Quality of Life

Nine articles examine the current state of cities in the United States and various other countries.

The concepts in bold italics are developed in the article. For further expansion please refer to the Topic Guide and the Index.

Unit 7

Global Issues

Six articles discuss common human social problems faced by people worldwide. Topics include the environment, drugs, and cultural misunderstanding.

Topic Guide

This topic guide suggests how the selections in this book relate to topics of traditional concern to students and professionals involved with the study of social problems. It is useful for locating articles that relate to each other for reading and research. The guide is arranged alphabetically according to topic. Articles may, of course, treat topics that do not appear in the topic guide. In turn, entries in the topic guide do not necessarily constitute a comprehensive listing of all the contents of each selection.

Introduction

Before initiating any analysis of social problems, it is always useful to agree on what it is that is being talked about. Things that are symbolic or seem to represent a serious social problem to one group might be seen by others as a symptom of a much larger problem, or even as no problem at all.

Two articles are included in this section that explore the complexities of social problems. While some individuals take a very simplistic black-and-white approach in defining social problems and, in turn, what must be done to eliminate them, sociologists realize how complex and intertwined social problems are in all aspects of social life. But even sociologists do not agree as to the best approach to take in the study of social issues.

Harold Widdison and H. Richard Delaney, in the first article, introduce the reader to sociology's three dominant theoretical positions and give examples of how those espousing each theory would look at specific issues. The three theories—symbolic interactionism, functionalism, and conflict—represent three radically different approaches to the study of social problems and their implications for individuals and societies. The perceived etiology of problems and their possible resolutions reflect the specific orientations of those studying them. As you peruse the subsequent articles, try to determine which of the three theoretical positions the various authors seem to be utilizing. Widdison and Delaney conclude this article by suggesting several approaches students may wish to consider in defining conditions as "social" problems and how they can and should be analyzed.

The second article explores how social problems are born, that is, why some issues, actions, or behaviors become defined as significant social problems while others do not. Nathan Glazer believes that the logic underlying the symbolic language is the critical factor in determining if an individual concern will eventually evolve into a societal-level social problem.

The introduction of this book of readings with a discussion of this type is desirable in order to help readers understand the social and sociological aspects of problems and issues plaguing modern society. The other articles included in this edition range from living in single-parent families to the pending destruction of the world's environment. The reader should ask why the issue addressed in each article is a social problem. Is it a case of rights in conflict, a case of conflicting values, or a consequence of conflicting harms? To find out, the reader might first skim over each article to get a general idea of where the author is coming from—that is, the author's theoretical position—and then reread the article to see just what the author indicates is the cause of the problem and what can or should be done to resolve or eliminate it.

SOCIAL PROBLEMS:

Definitions, Theories, and Analysis

Harold A. Widdison and H. Richard Delaney

INTRODUCTION AND OVERVIEW

When asked, "What are the major social problems facing humanity today?" college students' responses tend to mirror those highlighted by the mass media—particularly AIDS, child abuse, poverty, war, famine, racism, sexism, crime, riots, the state of the economy, the environment, abortion, euthanasia, homosexuality, and affirmative action. These are all valid subjects for study in a social problems class, but some give rise to very great differences of opinion and even controversy. Dr. Jack Kevorkian in Michigan and his killing machine is one example that comes to mind. To some he evokes images of Nazi Germany with its policy of murdering the infirm and helpless. Others see Kevorkian's work as a merciful alternative to the slow and agonizing death of individuals with terminal illnesses. In the latter light, Kevorkian is not symbolic of a potentially devastating social issue, but of a solution to an escalating social problem.

The same controversy exists at the other end of life—specifically, what obligations do pregnant women have to themselves as opposed to the unborn? Some individuals see abortion as a solution to the problems of population, child abuse, disruption of careers, dangers to the physical and emotional health of women, as well as the prevention of the birth of damaged fetuses, and they regard it as a right to self-determination. Others look at abortion as attacking the sanctity of life, abrogating the rights of a whole category of people, and violating every sense of moral and ethical responsibility.

Affirmative action is another issue that can be viewed as both a problem and a solution. As a solution, affirmative action attempts to reverse the effects of hundreds of years of discrimination. Doors that have been closed to specific categories of people for many generations are, it is hoped, forced open; individuals, regardless of race, ethnicity, and gender, are able to get into professional schools, and secure good jobs, with the assurance of promotion. On the other hand, affirmative action forces employers, recruiting officers, and housing officials to give certain categories of individuals a preferred status. While affirmative action is promoted by some as a necessary policy to compensate for centuries of exclusion and discrimination, others claim that it is discrimination simply disguised under a new label but with different groups being discriminated against. If race, sex, age, ethnicity, or any other characteristic other than merit is used as the primary criterion for selection or promotion, then discrimination is occurring. Discrimination hurts both sides. William Wilson, an African American social scientist, argues that it is very damaging to the self-esteem of black individuals to know that the primary reason they were hired was to fill quotas.

Both sides to the debate of whether these issues themselves reflect a social problem or are solutions to a larger societal problem have valid facts and use societal-level values to support their claims. Robin William Jr. in 1970 identified a list of 15 dominant value orientations that represent the concept of the good life to many Americans:

1. Achievement and success as major personal goals.
2. Activity and work favored above leisure and laziness.
3. Moral orientation—that is, absolute judgments of good/bad, right/wrong.
4. Humanitarian motives as shown in charity and crisis aid.
5. Efficiency and practicality: a preference for the quickest and shortest way to achieve a goal at the least cost.
6. Process and progress: a belief that technology can solve all problems and that the future will be better than the past.
7. Material comfort as the "American dream."
8. Equality as an abstract ideal.
9. Freedom as a person's right against the state.
10. External conformity: the ideal of going along, joining, and not rocking the boat.
11. Science and rationality as the means of mastering the environment and securing more material comforts.
12. Nationalism: a belief that American values and institutions represent the best on earth.
13. Democracy based on personal equality and freedom.
14. Individualism, emphasizing personal rights and responsibilities.

Written by Harold A. Widdison and H. Richard Delaney for *Annual Editions: Social Problems.* © 1995 by Dushkin Publishing Group/Brown & Benchmark Publishers, Guilford, CT.

15. Racism and group-superiority themes that periodically lead to prejudice and discrimination against those who are racially, religiously, and culturally different from the white northern Europeans who first settled the continent.

This list combines some political, economic, and personal traits that actually conflict with one another. This coexistence of opposing values helps explain why individuals hold contradictory views of the same behavior and why some issues generate such intensity of feelings. It is the intent of this article and the readings included in this book to attempt to help students see the complex nature of a social problem and the impact that various values, beliefs, and actions can have on them.

In the next segment of this article, the authors will look at specific examples of values in conflict and the problems created by this conflict. Subsequently the authors will look at the three major theoretical positions that sociologists use to study social problems. The article will conclude with an examination of various strategies and techniques used to identify, understand, and resolve various types of social problems and their implications for those involved.

As noted above, contemporary American society is typified by values that both complement and contradict each other. For example, the capitalistic free enterprise system of the United States stresses rugged individualism, self-actualization, individual rights, and self expression. This economic philosophy meshes well with Christian theology, particularly that typified by many Protestant denominations. This fact was the basis of German sociologist Max Weber's "The Protestant Ethic and The Spirit of Capitalism" (1864). He showed that the concepts of grace (salvation is a gift—not something you can earn), predestination (the fact that some people have this gift while others do not), and a desire to know if the individual has grace gave rise to a new idea of what constitutes success. Whereas, with the communitarian emphasis of Catholicism where material success was seen as leading to selfishness and spiritual condemnation, Protestantism viewed material success as a sign of grace. In addition, it was each individual's efforts that resulted in both the economic success and the spiritual salvation of the individual. This religious philosophy also implied that the poor are poor because they lack the proper motivation, values, and beliefs (what is known as the "culture of poverty") and are therefore reaping the results of their own inadequacies. Attempts to reduce poverty have frequently included taking children from "impoverished" cultural environments and placing them in "enriched" environments to minimize the potentially negative effects parents and a bad environment could have on their children. These enrichment programs attempt to produce attitudes and behaviors that assure success in the world but, in the process, cut children off from their parents. Children are forced to abandon the culture of their parents if they are to "succeed." Examples of this practice include the nurseries of the kibbutz in Israel and the Head Start programs in America. This practice is seen by some social scientists as a type of "cultural genocide." Entire cultures were targeted (sometimes explicitly, although often not intentionally) for extinction in this way.

This fact upsets a number of social scientists. They feel it is desirable to establish a pluralistic society where ethnic, racial, and cultural diversity exist and flourish. To them attempts to "Americanize" everyone are indicative of racism, bigotry, and prejudice. Others point to the lack of strong ethnic or racial identities as the unifying strength of the American system. When immigrants came to America, they put ethnic differences behind them, they learned the English language and democratic values, and they were assimilated into American life. In nations where immigrants have maintained their ethnic identities and held to unique cultural beliefs, their first loyalty is to their ethnic group. Examples of the destructive impact of strong ethnic loyalties can be seen in the conflict and fragmentation now occurring in the former Soviet Union, Czechoslovakia, and Yugoslavia.

James Q. Wilson (1994:54–55) noted in this regard:

> We have always been a nation of immigrants, but now the level of immigration has reached the point where we have become acutely conscious, to a degree not seen, I think, since the turn of the century, that we are a nation of many cultures. I believe that the vast majority of those who have come to this country came because they, too, want to share in the American Dream. But their presence here, and the unavoidable tensions that attend upon even well-intentioned efforts at mutual coexistence, makes some people—and alas, especially some intellectuals in our universities—question the American Dream, challenge the legitimacy of Western standards of life and politics, and demand that everybody be defined in terms of his or her group membership. The motto of this nation—*E pluribus unum*, out of the many, one—is in danger of being rewritten to read, *Ex uno plures*—out of the one, many."

THEORETICAL EXPLANATIONS: SYMBOLIC INTERACTION, FUNCTIONALISM, CONFLICT

In their attempts to understand social phenomena, researchers look for recurring patterns, relationships between observable acts, and unifying themes. The particular way in which researchers look at the world reflects not only their personal views and experiences, but their professional perspective as well. Sociologists focus on interactions between individuals, between individuals and groups, between groups, and between groups and the larger society in which they are located. They try to identify those things that facilitate or hinder interaction, and the consequences of each. But not all sociologists agree as to the most effective/appropriate approach to take, and they tend to divide into three major theoretical camps: symbolic interactionism, functionalism, and conflict theory. These three approaches are not mutually exclusive, but they do represent radically different perspectives of the nature of social reality and how it should be studied.

Symbolic Interaction

This theoretical perspective argues that no social condition, however unbearable it may seem to some, is inherently or objectively a social problem until a significant number of politically powerful people agree that it is contrary to the public good. Scientists, social philosophers, religious leaders, and medical people may "know" that a specific action or condition has or will eventually have a devastating effect on society or a specific group in society, but until they can convince those who are in a position to control and perhaps correct the condition, it is not considered a social problem. Therefore it is not the social condition, but how the condition is defined and by whom, that determines if it is or will become a social problem. The social process whereby a specific condition moves from the level of an individual concern to a societal-level issue can be long and arduous or very short. An example of the latter occurred in the 1960s when some physicians noticed a significant increase in infants born with severe physical deformities. Medical researchers looking into the cause made a connection between the deformities and the drug thalidomide. Pregnant women suffering from severe nausea and health-threatening dehydration were prescribed this drug, which dramatically eliminated the nausea and appeared to have no bad side effects. But their babies were born with terrible deformities. Once the medical researchers discovered the connection, they presented their findings to their colleagues. When the data were reviewed and found to be scientifically valid, the drug was banned immediately. Thus a small group's assessment of an issue as a serious problem quickly was legitimized by those in power as a societal-level social problem and measures were taken to eliminate it.

Most situations are not this clear-cut. In the mid-1960s various individuals began to question the real reason(s) why the United States was involved in the war in Southeast Asia. They discovered data indicating that the war was not about protecting the democratic rights of the Vietnamese. Those in power either ignored or rejected such claims as politically motivated and as militarily naive. Reports from the Vietcong about purported U.S. military atrocities were collected and used as supportive evidence. These claims were summarily dismissed by American authorities as Communistic propaganda. Convinced of the validity and importance of their cause, the protesters regrouped and collected still more evidence including data collected by the French government. This new information was difficult for the U.S. government to ignore. Nevertheless, these new claims were rejected as being somewhat self-serving since the Vietcong had defeated the French in Indochina and presumably the French government could justify its own failure if the United States also failed.

Over the years the amount of data continued to accumulate augmented by new information collected from disenchanted veterans. This growing pool of evidence began to bother legislators who demanded an accounting from the U.S. government and the Department of Defense, but none was forthcoming. More and more students joined the antiwar movement, but their protests were seen as unpatriotic and self-serving—that is, an attempt to avoid military service. The increasing numbers of protesters caused some legislators to look more closely at the claims of the antiwar faction. As the magnitude of the war and the numbers of American servicemen involved grew, the numbers of people affected by the war grew as well. Returning veterans' reports of the state of the war, questionable military practices (such as the wholesale destruction of entire villages),

complaints of incompetent leadership in the military, and corrupt Vietnamese politicians gave greater credibility to the antiwar movement's earlier claims and convinced additional senators and representatives to support the stop-the-war movement, even though those in power still refused to acknowledge the legitimacy of the movement.

Unable to work within the system and convinced of the legitimacy of their cause, protesters resorted to unconventional and often illegal actions, such as burning their draft cards, refusing to register for the draft, seeking refuge in other countries, attacking ROTC (Reserve Officers' Training Corps) buildings on college campuses, and even bombing military research facilities. These actions were initially interpreted by government officials as criminal activities of self-serving individuals or activities inspired by those sympathetic with the Communist cause. The government engaged in increasingly repressive efforts to contain the movement. But public disaffection with the war was fueled by rising American casualties; this, coupled with the discontent within the ranks of the military, eventually forced those in power to acquiesce and accept the claims that the war was the problem and not the solution to the problem. Reaching this point took nearly 15 years.

For the symbolic interactionist, the fact that socially harmful conditions are thought to exist is not the criterion for what constitutes a social problem. Rather the real issue is to understand what goes into the assessment of a specific condition as being a social problem. To the symbolic interactionist, the appropriate questions are, (a) How is it that some conditions become defined as a social problem while others do not? (b) Who, in any society, can legitimate the designation of a condition as a social problem? (c) What solutions evolve and how do they evolve for specific social problems? (d) What factors exist in any specific society that inhibit or facilitate resolution of social problems?

In summary, symbolic interactionists stress that social problems do not exist independently of how people define their world. Social problems are socially constructed as people debate whether or not some social condition is a social problem and decide what to do about it. The focus is on the meanings the problem has for those who are affected by it and not on the impact it is having on them.

Functionalism

A second major theory sociologists use to study social problems is functionalism. Functionalists argue that society is a social system consisting of various integrated parts. Each of these parts fulfills a specific role that contributes to the overall functioning of society. In well-integrated systems, each part contributes to the stability of the whole. Functionalists examine each part in an attempt to determine the role it plays in the operation of the system as a whole. When any part fails, this creates a problem for the whole. These failures (dysfunctions) upset the equilibrium of the system and become social problems. To functionalists, anything that impedes the system's ability to achieve its goals is, by definition, a social problem. Unlike the symbolic interactionists, the functionalists argue that a social problem is not contingent on someone's assessment that it is a problem. Serious social problems may exist without anyone being aware of the detrimental effects they are having on various members of society or on society itself. Functionalists examine the stated objectives, values, and goals of a group; observe the behaviors of the members of the group; and assess how their behaviors impact on the abilities of the group to achieve its goals.

Many times the stated objectives (what sociologists call the "manifest functions") produce results that were not desired nor intended (what sociologists call "latent functions") and are in fact working against the group's abilities to accomplish its goals. Sociologists attempt to make the members of the group aware of the consequences of specific behaviors. For example, in an attempt to help single mothers of infants to provide for their children adequately, the American government created Aid to Families with Dependent Children (AFDC), a program designed to provide single women with enough money to feed, clothe, and house their children. This program was motivated by the Judeo-Christian philosophy that society is obligated to care for those who cannot care for themselves. In this regard the program has been a success. But it also has had a dark side in that it has discouraged the establishment of stable households with a father present, since two-parent families do not qualify for aid. If a woman marries or is known to be living with a man, she loses her eligibility and her benefits. As a result, males have been pushed to the periphery of the family. Many lower-class, unskilled males cannot earn as much as a single mother under AFDC. It does not mean that men are not around, only that they are discouraged from becoming permanent fixtures in these families. As a result, a program designed to help families ended up altering the structures of families and in the process created a whole new social problem.

Functionalists also argue that if a behavior or social institution persists, it must be meeting some need within the society. Merely defining a behavior as a problem does not assure its demise. To eliminate any behavior researchers/society must first find out what functions it is serving and then make the behavior dysfunctional, which in turn will cause the behavior to disappear. As poverty, crime, and inequality exist and persist in all societies, the task of the social scientist is to discover how and why. In this regard most individuals would argue that poverty is not desirable and should, if possible, be eliminated. Yet, as discussed by Herbert J. Gans in his article "The Uses of Poverty: The Poor Pay All," poverty benefits a significant portion of society. The incentive to eradicate poverty is neutralized by specific benefits to the nonpoor. Five of the 13 functions Gans identified are as follows:

1. Poverty ensures that society's "dirty work" will be done. Poverty functions to provide a low-wage labor pool that is willing, or rather unable to be unwilling, to perform dirty work at low cost.
2. Because the poor are required to work at low wages, they subsidize a variety of economic activities that benefit the affluent.
3. Poverty creates jobs for a number of occupations and professions that serve or "service" the poor, or protect the rest of society from them, such as social workers, police, and prison staff.
4. The poor buy goods others do not want, thus prolonging the economic usefulness of such goods—that is, day-old bread, fruit, and vegetables that would otherwise have to be thrown out, secondhand clothes, and deteriorating automobiles and buildings.
5. The poor, being powerless, can be made to absorb the costs of change and growth in American society. Urban renewal and expressways, for example, have typically been located in poor neighborhoods.

Although not explicitly stated by Gans, the poor cannot afford the ever-spiraling costs of health care and become those upon which the fledgling physician can practice his or her profession. As part of the learning process, mistakes are common and the poor are thus likely to have a lower level of medical expertise. Many medical, dental, and nursing schools are located within the inner city. In exchange for free or greatly reduced fees, poor people become guinea pigs to help student nurses, doctors, and dentists become experienced enough to practice on the more affluent.

The functionalists examine conditions, behaviors, and institutions in an attempt to try to understand the functions being met by these specific phenomena. To eliminate any of these problems the associated behaviors have to become dysfunctional. But because many of the functional alternatives to each problem would be dysfunctional for the affluent and powerful members of society, there is an incentive for the behavior to persist.

In summary, functionalists emphasize the interrelationship of the various parts of a system and believe that changes in one part will have significant implications for other parts. Any particular social problem is only a part of a larger whole. This means that in order to understand a social problem, one must place it in a broader context. A social problem is a consequence of the way a social system is put together.

Conflict Theory

Those social philosophers adhering to the conflict perspective view life and all social interaction as a struggle for power and privilege. They see every person and every group as being in competition for scarce and valued resources. They believe that even though people occasionally may have to cooperate with each other or even form alliances, they are still essentially in conflict. As soon as the alliance is no longer beneficial, conflict will often ensue. Unlike the functionalists who see the elements of a society as harmoniously working together and contributing to the whole, conflict theorists view all the parts as being in competition with each other. They see the guiding principle of social life as disequilibrium and change, not equilibrium and harmony. But, like the functionalists, they argue that social problems can and do exist independently of people's assessments of them. They argue that whether people are aware of it or not, they are enmeshed in a basic struggle for power and survival. Each group in society is attempting to achieve gains for itself that must necessarily be at the expense of other groups. It is this consistent conflict over limited resources that threatens societal peace and order.

Whereas the functionalists try to understand how different positions of power came into existence (Davis & Moore 1945), the conflictists show how those in power attempt to stay in power (Mills 1956). The conflict theorists see social problems as the natural and inevitable consequences of groups in society struggling to survive and gain control over those things that can affect their ability to survive. Those groups that are successful then attempt to use whatever means they must to control their environment and consolidate their position, thus increasing their chances of surviving. According to conflict theorists, those in power exploit their position and create poverty, discrimination, oppression, and crime in the process. The impact of these conditions on the exploited produces other pathological conditions such as alienation, alcoholism, drug abuse, mental illness, stress, health problems, and suicide. On occasions, such as that which occurred in Los Angeles in the summer of 1991 when policemen were found innocent of the use of excessive force in the beating of Rodney King, the feelings of helplessness and hopelessness can erupt as rage against the system in the form of violence and riots or as in Eastern Europe as rebellion and revolution against repressive governments.

The conflict theorists argue that drug abuse, mental illness, various criminal behaviors, and suicide are symptoms of a much larger societal malaise. To understand and eliminate these problems, society needs to understand the basic conflicts that are producing them. The real problems stem from the implications of being exploited. Being manipulated by the powerful and denied a sense of control tends (a) to produce a loss of control over one's life (powerlessness), (b) to lead to an inability to place one's productive efforts into some meaningful context (meaninglessness), (c) not to being involved in the process of change but only in experiencing the impact resulting from the changes (normlessness), and (d) to cause one to find oneself isolated from one's colleagues on the job (self-isolation). Conflictists see all of these problems as the product of a capitalistic system that alienates the worker from himself and from his or her fellow workers (Seeman 1959).

To protect their positions of power, privilege, prestige, and possessions, those in power use their wealth and influence to control organizations. For example, they manipulate the system to get key individuals into positions where they can influence legislation and decisions that are designed to protect their power and possessions. They might serve on or appoint others to school boards to assure that the skills and values needed by the economy are taught. They also assure that the laws are enforced internally (the police) or externally (the military) to protect their holdings. The war in the Persian Gulf is seen by many conflict theorists as having been fought for oil rather than for Kuwait's liberation.

When the exploited attempt to do something about their condition by organizing, protesting, and rebelling, they threaten those in power. For example, they may go on a strike that might disrupt the entire nation. Under the pretext that it is for the best good of society, the government may step in and stop the strike. Examples are the air-traffic-controllers strike of 1987 and the railroad strike in 1991. In retaliation the workers may engage in work slow-down, stoppage, and even sabotage. They may stage protests and public demonstrations and cast protest votes at the ballot boxes. If these do not work, rebellions and revolutions may result. Those in power can respond very repressively as was the case in Tiananmen Square in China in 1989, threaten military force as the Soviet Union did with the Baltic countries in 1990, or back down completely as when the Berlin Wall came down. Thus reactions to exploitation may produce change but inevitably lead to other social problems. In Eastern Europe and the former Soviet Union, democracy has resulted in massive unemployment, spiraling inflation, hunger, crime, and homelessness.

Sometimes those in power make concessions to maintain power. Conflict theorists look for concessions and how they placate the poor while still protecting the privileged and powerful. The rich are viewed as sharing power only if forced to do so and only to the extent absolutely necessary.

Robert Michels (1949), a French social philosopher, looked at the inevitable process whereby the members of any group voluntarily give their rights, prerogatives, and power to a select few who then dominate the group. It may not be the conscious decision of those who end up in positions of power to dominate the group, but, in time, conscious decisions may be made to do whatever is necessary to stay in control of the group. The power, privilege, and wealth they acquire as part of the position alters their self-images. To give up the position would necessitate a complete revision of who they are, what they can do, and with whom they associate. Their "selves" have become fused/confused with the position they occupy, and in an attempt to protect their "selves," they resist efforts designed to undermine their control. They consider threats to themselves as threats to the organization and therefore feel justified in their vigorous resistance. According to Michels, no matter how democratic an organization starts out to be it will always become dominated and controlled by a few. The process whereby this occurs he labeled the "Iron Law of Oligarchy." For example, hospitals that were created to save lives, cure the sick, and provide for the chronically ill, now use the threat of closure to justify rate increases. The hospital gets its rate increase, the cost of health goes up, and the number of individuals able to afford health care declines, with the ultimate result being an increase in health problems for the community. Although not explicitly stated, the survival of the organization (and its administrators) becomes more important than the health of the community.

In summary, the conflict theoretical model stresses the fact that key resources such as power and privilege are limited and distributed unequally among the members/groups in a society. Conflict is therefore a natural and inevitable result of various groups pursuing their interests and values. To study the basis of social problems, researchers must look at the distribution of power and privilege because these two factors are always at the center of conflicting interests and values. Moreover, whenever social change occurs, social problems inevitably follow.

Conflict and Functionalism: A Synthesis
While conflict theorists' and functionalists' explanations of what constitutes the roots of social problems appear to be completely

contradictory, Dahrendorf (1959) sees them as complementary. "Functionalism explains how highly talented people are motivated to spend twenty-five years of study to become surgeons; conflict theory explains how surgeons utilize their monopoly on their vital skills to obtain rewards that greatly exceed that necessary to ensure an adequate supply of talent." (See also Ossowski 1963; van de Berghe 1963; Williams 1966; Horowitz 1962; and Lenski 1966 for other attempts at a synthesis between these two theoretical models.)

SOCIAL PROBLEMS: DEFINITION AND ANALYSIS

Value Conflicts

It is convenient to characterize a social problem as a conflict of values, a conflict of values and duties, a conflict of rights (Hook, 1974), or a social condition that leads to or is thought to lead to harmful consequences. Harm may be defined as (a) the loss to a group, community, or society of something to which it is thought to be entitled, (b) an offense perceived to be an affront to our moral sensibilities, or (c) an impoverishment of the collective good or welfare. It is also convenient to define values as individual or collective desires that become attached to social objects. Private property, for example, is a valued social object for some while others disavow or reject its desirability; because of the public disagreement over its value, it presents a conflict of values. A conflict of values is also found in the current controversy surrounding abortion. Where pro-life supporters tend to see life itself as the ultimate value, supporters of pro-choice may, as some have, invoke the Fourteenth Amendment's right-to-privacy clause as the compelling value.

Values-versus-Duties Conflicts

A second format that students should be aware of in the analysis of social problems is the conflict between values and obligations or duties. This approach calls our attention to those situations in which a person, group, or community must pursue or realize a certain duty even though those participating may be convinced that doing so will not achieve the greater good. For example, educators, policemen, bureaucrats, and environmentalists may occupy organizational or social roles in which they are required to formulate policies and follow rules that, according to their understanding, will not contribute to the greater good of students, citizens, or the likelihood of a clean environment. On the other hand, there are situations in which, we, as a individuals, groups, or communities, do things that would not seem to be right in our pursuit of what we consider to be the higher value. Here students of social problems are faced with the familiar problem of using questionable, illogical, or immoral means to achieve what is perhaps generally recognized as a value of a higher order. Police officers, for example, are sometimes accused of employing questionable, immoral, or deceptive means (stings, scams, undercover operations) to achieve what are thought to be socially helpful ends and values such as

removing a drug pusher from the streets. Familiar questions for this particular format are, Do the ends justify the means? Should ends be chosen according to the means available for their realization? What are the social processes by which means themselves become ends? These are questions to which students of social problems and social policy analysis should give attention since immoral, illegal, or deceptive means can themselves lead to harmful social consequences.

Max Weber anticipated and was quite skeptical of those modern bureaucratic processes whereby means are transformed into organizational ends and members of the bureaucracy become self-serving and lose sight of their original and earlier mission. The efforts of the Central Intelligence Agency (CIA) to maintain U.S. interests in Third World countries led to tolerance of various nations' involvement in illicit drugs. Thus the CIA actually contributed to the drug problem the police struggle to control. A second example is that of the American Association of Retired Persons (AARP). To help the elderly obtain affordable health care, life insurance, drugs, and so forth, the AARP established various organizations to provide or contract for services. But now the AARP seems to be more concerned about its corporate holdings than it is about the welfare of its elderly members.

RIGHTS IN CONFLICT

Finally, students of social problems should become aware of right-versus-right moral conflicts. With this particular format, one's attention is directed to the conflict of moral duties and obligations, the conflict of rights and, not least, the serious moral issue of divided loyalties. In divorce proceedings, for example, spouses must try to balance their personal lives and careers against the obligations and duties to each other and their children. Even those who sincerely want to meet their full obligations to both family and career often find this is not possible because of the real limits of time and means.

Wilson (1994:39,54) observes that from the era of "Enlightenment" and its associated freedoms arose the potential for significant social problems. We are seeing all about us in the entire Western world the working out of the defining experience of the West, the Enlightenment. The Age of Enlightenment was the extraordinary period in the eighteenth century when individuals were emancipated from old tyrannies—from dead custom, hereditary monarchs, religious persecution, and ancient superstition. It is the period that gave us science and human rights, that attacked human slavery and political absolutism, that made possible capitalism and progress. The principal figures of the Enlightenment remain icons of social reform: Adam Smith, David Hume, Thomas Jefferson, Immanuel Kant, Isaac Newton, James Madison.

The Enlightenment defined the West and set it apart from all of the other great cultures of the world. But in culture as in economics, there is no such thing as a free lunch. If you liberate a person from ancient tyrannies, you may also liberate him or her from familiar controls. If you enhance his or her freedom to create, you will enhance his or her freedom to destroy. If you cast out the dead hand of useless custom, you may also cast out the living hand of essential tradition. If you give an individual freedom of expression, he or she may write *The Marriage of Figaro* or he or she may sing "gangsta rap." If you enlarge the number of rights one has, you may shrink the number of responsibilities one feels.

There is a complex interaction between the rights an individual has and the consequences of exercising specific rights. For example, if an individual elects to exercise his or her right to consume alcoholic beverages, this act then nullifies many subsequent rights because of the potential harm that can occur. The right to drive, to engage in athletic events, or to work, is jeopardized by the debilitating effects of alcohol. Every citizen has rights assured him or her by membership in society. At the same time, rights can only be exercised to the degree to which they do not trample on the rights of other members of the group. If a woman elects to have a baby, must she abrogate her right to consume alcohol, smoke, consume caffeine, or take drugs? Because the effects of these substances on the developing fetus are potentially devastating, is it not reasonable to conclude that the rights of the child to a healthy body and mind are being threatened if the mother refuses to abstain during pregnancy? Fetal alcohol effect/syndrome, for instance, is the number-one cause of preventable mental retardation in the United States, and it could be completely eliminated if pregnant women never took an alcoholic drink. Caring for individuals with fetal alcohol effect/syndrome is taking increasingly greater resources that could well be directed toward other pressing issues.

Rights cannot be responsibly exercised without individuals' weighing their potential consequences. Thus a hierarchy of rights, consequences, and harms exists and the personal benefits resulting from any act must be weighed against the personal and social harms that could follow. The decision to use tobacco should be weighed against the possible consequences of a wide variety of harms such as personal health problems and the stress it places on society's resources to care for tobacco-related diseases. Tobacco-related diseases often have catastrophic consequences for their users that cannot be paid for by the individual, so the burden of payment is placed on society. Millions of dollars and countless health care personnel must be diverted away from other patients to care for these individuals with self-inflicted tobacco-related diseases. In addition to the costs in money, personnel, and medical resources, these diseases take tremendous emotional tolls on those closest to the diseased individuals. To focus only on one's rights without consideration of the consequences associated with those rights often deprives other individuals from exercising their rights.

The Constitution of the United States guarantees individuals rights without clearly specifying what the rights really entail. Logically one cannot have rights without others having corresponding obligations. But what obligations does each right assure and what limitations do these obligations and/or rights require? Rights for the collectivity are protected by limitations placed on each individual, but limits of collective rights are also mandated by laws assuring that individual rights are not infringed upon. Therefore, we have rights as a whole that often differ from those we have as individual members of that whole.

For example, the right to free speech may impinge in a number of ways on a specific community. To the members of a small Catholic community, having non-Catholic missionaries preaching on street corners and proselytizing door-to-door could be viewed as a social problem. Attempts to control their actions such as the enactment and enforcements of "Green River" ordnances (laws against active solicitation), could eliminate the community's problem but in so doing would trample on the individual's constitutional rights of religious expression. To protect individual rights, the community may have to put up with individuals pushing their personal theological ideas in public places. From the perspective of the Catholic community, aggressive non-Catholic missionaries are not only a nuisance but a social problem that should be banned. To the proselytizing churches, restrictions on their actions are violations of their civil rights and hence a serious social problem.

Currently another conflict of interests/rights is dividing many communities, and that is cigarette smoking. Smokers argue that their rights are being seriously threatened by aggressive legislation restricting smoking. They argue that society should not and cannot legislate morality. Smokers point out how attempts to legislate alcohol consumption during the Prohibition of the 1920s and 1930s was an abject failure and, in fact, created more problems than it eliminated. They believe that the exact same process is being attempted today and will prove to be just as unsuccessful. Those who smoke then go on to say that smoking is protected by the Constitution's freedom of expression and that no one has the right to force others to adhere his or her personal health policies, which are individual choices. They assert that if the "radicals" get away with imposing smoking restrictions, they can and will move on to other health-related behaviors such as overeating. Therefore, by protecting the constitutional rights of smokers, society is protecting the constitutional rights of everyone.

On the other hand, nonsmokers argue that their rights are being violated by smokers. They point to an increasing body of research data that shows that secondhand smoke leads to numerous health problems such as emphysema, heart disease, and throat and lung cancer. Not only do nonsmokers have a right not to have to breathe smoke-contaminated air, but society has an obligation to protect the health and well-being of its members from the known dangers of breathing smoke.

These are only a few examples of areas where rights come into conflict. Others include environmental issues, endangered species, forest management, enforcement of specific laws, homosexuality, mental illness, national health insurance, taxes, balance of trade, food labeling and packaging, genetic engineering, rape, sexual deviation, political corruption, riots, public protests, zero population growth, the state of the economy, and on and on.

It is notable that the degree to which any of these issues achieves widespread concern varies over time. Often, specific problems are given much fanfare by politicians and special interests groups for a time, and the media try to convince us that specific activities or behaviors have the greatest urgency and demand a total national commitment for a solution. However, after being in the limelight for a while, the importance of the problem seems to fade and new problems move into prominence. If you look back over previous editions of this book, you can see this trend. It would be useful to speculate why, in American society, some problems remain a national concern while others come and go.

The Consequences of Harm

To this point it had been argued that social problems can be defined and analyzed as (a) conflicts between values, (b) conflicts between values and duties, and (c) conflicts between rights. Consistent with the aims of this article, social problems can be further characterized and interpreted as social conditions that lead, or are generally thought to lead, to harmful consequences for the person, group, community, or society.

Harm—and here we follow Hyman Gross's (1979) conceptualization of the term—can be classified as (a) a loss, usually permanent, that deprives the person or group of a valued object or condition it is entitled to have, (b) offenses to sensibility—that is, harm that contributes to unpleasant experiences in the form of repugnance, embarrassment, disgust, alarm, or fear, and (c) impairment of the collective welfare—that is, violations of those values possessed by the group or society.

Harm can also be ranked as to the potential for good. Physicians, to help their patients, often have to harm them. The question they must ask is, "Will this specific procedure, drug, or operation, produce more good than the pain and suffering it causes?" For instance, will the additional time it affords the cancer patient be worth all the suffering associated with the chemotherapy? In Somalia, health care personnel are forced to make much harder decisions. They are surrounded by starvation, sickness, and death. If they treat one person, another cannot be treated and will die. They find themselves forced to allocate their time and resources, not according to who needs it the most, but according to who has the greatest chance of survival.

Judges must also balance the harms they are about to inflict on those they must sentence against the public good and the extent to which the sentence might help the individual reform. Justice must be served in that people must pay for their crimes, yet most judges also realize that prison time often does more harm than good. In times of recession employers must weigh harm when they are forced to cut back their workforce: Where should the cuts occur? Should they keep employees of long standing and cut those most recently hired (many of which are nonwhites hired through affirmative action programs)? Should they keep those with the most productive records, or those with the greatest need for employment? No matter what employers elect to do, harm will result to some. The harm produced by the need to reduce the workforce must be balanced by the potential good of the company's surviving and sustaining employment for the rest of the employees.

The notion of harm also figures into the public and social dialogue between those who are pro-choice and those who are pro-life. Most pro-lifers are inclined to see the greatest harm of abortion to be loss of life, while most pro-choicers argue that the compelling personal and social harm is the taking away of a value (the right to privacy) that everyone is entitled to. Further harmful consequences of abortion for most pro-lifers are that the value of life will be cheapened, the moral fabric of society will be weakened, and the taking of life could be extended to the elderly and disabled, for example. Most of those who are pro-choice, on the other hand, are inclined to argue that the necessary consequence of their position is that of keeping government out of their private lives and bedrooms. In a similar way this "conflict of values" format can be used to analyze, clarify, and enlarge our understanding of the competing values, harms, and consequences surrounding other social problems. We can, and should, search for the competing values underlying such social problems as, for example, income distribution, homelessness, divorce, education, and the environment.

Loss, then, as a societal harm consists in a rejection or violation of what a person or group feels entitled to have. American citizens, for example, tend to view life, freedom, equality, property, and physical security as ultimate values. Any rejection or violation of these values is thought to constitute a serious social problem since such a loss diminishes one's sense of personhood. Murder, violence, AIDS, homelessness, environmental degradation, the failure to provide adequate health care, and abortion can be conveniently classified as social problems within this class of harms.

Offenses to our sensibilities constitute a class of harm that, when serious enough, becomes a problem affecting moral issues and the common good of the members of a society. Issues surrounding pornography, prostitution, and the so-called victimless crimes are examples of behaviors that belong to this class of harm. Moreover some would argue that environmental degradation, the widening gap between the very rich and the very poor, and the condition of the homeless also should be considered within this class of harm.

A third class of harms—namely impairments to the collective welfare—is explained, in part, by Gross (1979:120) as follows:

> Social life, particularly in the complex forms of civilized societies, creates many dependencies among members of a community. The welfare of each member depends upon the exercise of restraint and precaution by others in the pursuit of their legitimate activities, as well as upon cooperation toward certain common objectives. These matters of collective welfare involve many kinds of interests that may be said to be possessed by the community.

In a pluralistic society, such as American society, matters of collective welfare are sometimes problematic in that there can be considerable conflict of values and rights between various segments of the society. There is likely to remain, however, a great deal of agreement that those social problems whose harmful consequences would involve impairments to the collective welfare would include poverty, poor education, mistreatment of the young and elderly, excessive disparities in income distribution, discrimination against ethnic and other minorities, drug abuse, health and medical care, the state of the economy, and environmental concerns.

BIBLIOGRAPHY

Dahrendorf, R. (1959). *Class and class conflict in industrial society.* Stanford, CA: Stanford University Press.

Davis, Kingsley, & Moore, Wilbert E. (1945). Some principles of stratification. *American Sociological Review, 10,* 242–249.

Gans, Herbert J. (1971). The uses of poverty: The poor pay all. *Social Policy.* New York: Social Policy Corporation.

Gross, Hyman. (1979). *A theory of criminal justice.* New York: Oxford University Press.

Hook, Sidney. (1974). *Pragmatism and the tragic sense of life.* New York: Basic Books.

Horowitz, M. A. (1962). Consensus, conflict, and cooperation. *Social Forces, 41,* 177–188.

Lenski, G. (1966). *Power and privilege.* New York: McGraw-Hill.

Michels, Robert. (1949). *Political parties: A sociological study of the oligarchical tendencies of modern democracy.* New York: Free Press.

Mills, C. Wright. (1956). *The power elite.* New York: Oxford University Press.

Ossowski, S. (1963). *Class structure in the social consciousness.* Translated by Sheila Patterson. New York: The Free Press.

Seeman, Melvin. (1959). On the meaning of alienation. *American Sociological Review, 24,* 783–791.

Van den Berghe, P. (1963). Dialectic and functionalism: Toward a theoretical synthesis. *American Sociological Review, 28,* 695–705.

Weber, Max. (1964). *The protestant ethic and the spirit of capitalism.* Translated by Talcott Parsons. New York: Scribner's.

William, Robin Jr. (1970). *American society: A sociological interpretation,* 3rd. ed. New York: Alfred A. Knopf.

Williams, Robin. (1966). Some further comments on chronic controversies. *American Journal of Sociology, 71,* 717–721.

Wilson, James Q. (1994, August). The moral life." *Brigham Young Magazine,* pp. 37–55.

Wilson, William. (1978). *The declining significance of race.* Chicago: University of Chicago Press.

CHALLENGE TO THE READER

As you read the articles that follow, try to determine which of the three major theoretical positions each of the authors seems to be using. Whatever approach the writer uses in his or her discussion suggests what he or she thinks is the primary cause of the social problem/issue under consideration.

Also ask yourself as you read each article, (1) What values are at stake or in conflict? (2) What rights are at issue or in conflict? (3) What is the nature of the harm in each case, and who is being hurt? (4) What do the authors suggest as possible resolutions for each social problem?

How Social Problems Are Born

Nathan Glazer

Nathan Glazer is co-editor of The Public Interest.

How do we get more attention, more public action, for a problem we consider important? More important, how do we get the right kind of public attention and action, right in scale, and right in the kinds of solutions the public is willing to accept and fund?

Contemporary social scientists are skeptical about the possibilities of achieving such a rational ordering of things. Consider the following from the sociologist Joseph Gusfield:

> Human problems do not spring up, full-blown and announced, into the consciousness of bystanders. Even to recognize a situation as painful requires a system for categorizing and defining events. . . . "Objective" conditions are seldom so compelling and so clear in their form that they spontaneously generate a "true" consciousness. Those committed to one or another solution to a public problem see its genesis in the necessary consequences of events and processes; those in opposition often point to "agitators" who impose one or another definition of reality.

This passage is taken from Gusfield's *The Culture of Public Problems: Drinking-Driving and the Symbolic Order* (University of Chicago Press, 1981) and he exhibits in it a common approach in today's social sciences to the issue of how we make social problems out of social conditions, which may be crudely summarized as: It's all in the head. We need a system of defining and categorizing events before we know we have a problem. When most of us agree we do have a problem—when a social condition has been changed into a problem—we interpret this as a case of the problem having become worse, or a case of increasing empathy and sympathy on the part of the public for those suffering. Paradoxically, we often recognize that we have a problem when the condition we are responding to has improved. Recall how the problem of "poverty" burst upon us in the early days of the Kennedy administration. John Kenneth Galbraith had just published *The Affluent Society,* and Michael Harrington had published *The Other America,* but as we now know poverty had been declining all through the forties and fifties.

So our first explanation of how a condition has become a problem may not hold—the problem may not have become worse. Our second, that we have become wiser or more understanding or more sympathetic to the plight of others, is flattering to us, but Gusfield does not give us that credit. It is our categories, rather than reality, that have changed. As we look further into his study of drinking-driving in the book from which I have quoted, we find it is rife with discussions of symbolism, dramaturgy, rhetoric, metaphor, and the like. "The Fiction and Drama of Public Consciousness," one chapter title announces. "The Literary Art of Science: Drama and Pathos in Drinking-Driver Research," another reads.

This is not a case of individual idiosyncrasy. Much of the writing by leading social scientists on how we fix upon social problems, on how they get on the agenda of public attention, is skeptical as to the kind of simple and direct relation we might imagine: the problem gets worse, or we become more sensitive to it. More likely, an interest group of some sort, an advocacy group, has taken it up and made it a matter of public concern. The arts of publicity are more relevant than the findings of science.

Thus, in Gusfield's *The Culture of Public Problems,* devoted to the problem of the drinking driver—one would think a serious enough issue to deserve direct attention—we will find rather more references to the literary critic Kenneth Burke than to any scientist or social scientist.

The issue for Gusfield is not only the social construction of public problems, which do indeed have many dimensions, among which the determination of fact, of the existing situation, is only one, but the social construction of science itself, a rather popular theme among social scientists and advanced literary critics these days.

THE ROLE OF RHETORIC

There is undoubtedly a degree of overkill in Gusfield's approach but there is something to learn from it too, as we consider how we get the right kind of public attention for an issue of importance. One problem to which Gusfield points is that we move very rapidly from the problem itself, which may be both undeniable and important, to the arts of publicity and attention-getting, and, as he argues, these arts also affect almost immediately the very facts that we use to get attention and that are the bedrock of our initial concern. Thus, if we examine the facts which we use as the basis to claim attention, public money, funds for research, we see that the facts themselves become shaped by the need to compete with other claims, other problems, for which the arts of publicity are also employed.

Half of the 50,000 deaths a year from automobile accidents are attributed regularly, we are told, to drink on the part of the driver. When we examine this oft-repeated statistic, according to Gusfield—and he goes into the source of the figure in detail—it turns out that it is hardly solidly based, that many questions can be raised about it. Similarly with the statistic on how many Americans have serious drinking problems—a common figure of 9 or 10 million was used when Gusfield was writing his book in the early

1980s; its sources are murky and uncertain, and of course depend on what we mean by drinking problems.

It is not only in the case of drinking-driving and alcoholism that the first necessary step in defining a problem—finding out just what the scale of the problem is—immediately gets mixed up with the necessary requirements of the next steps in getting attention for it, bringing it to the notice of necessary publics. And so we are familiar with disputes right now about the scale of date rape on campus, as well as with the prior question of just what date rape is. Similarly with child abuse, and many other public issues.

Is Gusfield only playing games when he asks just how do the authorities decide that an accident was based on drinking, and other questions which undermine the statistic that half of all automobile accident fatalities are owing to drinking? Of course drinking-driving is a serious problem, so why does he bother us with the figures used in making a case to congressional committees or attracting publicity or funds? But his approach does alert us to a number of things of importance. First, that rhetoric, drama, the arts of gaining access to the mass media or congressmen, are implicated at the very beginning in all our efforts to gain attention to social problems. Second, that there is no easy way of scaling social problems from the point of view of how "important" they are. In the passage I reprinted from his *The Culture of Public Problems,* he placed the words "objective" and "true" in quotation marks. Third, that because this is so there is the constant danger of overkill, over-dramatization, the constant possibility that those most gifted in the arts of publicity and drama will engross a larger share of funds and attention than *their* problem warrants. (I leave aside for the moment the question of whether we can decide on any objective basis how much money or attention one problem deserves as against another, or the methods by which we might decide. Whatever our answer, we would probably all agree that some problems seem to have gained an inordinate amount of attention compared to others of apparently similar or greater scale. This has been argued in the case of AIDS. Very likely the attention AIDS gets is in part related to the number of people in the arts and fashion and publicity who are affected.)

It is revealing that Gusfield titled an earlier book, on the temperance move-

ment, *Symbolic Crusade,* and it is clear that the use of the term "crusade" is meant to suggest to us that a movement that tried to deal with a problem that was serious enough at the time, and that may be as serious today, was overdone, excessive, shrill, in some ways more than the problem called for. (After all, it led, astonishingly, to the passage of a constitutional amendment banning alcoholic drinks.) The use of the word "crusade" today implies that we are confronted with something that is rather too grand, too much, for its object, and the word tends to evoke skepticism of the cause to which it is attached, rather than inspiring greater commitment to the cause. What, after all, in our laid-back contemporary world, used to horrors of all sorts, deserves a "crusade," with its religious implications? (We seem happier with the word "war," as in war against poverty, and war against drugs, headed by a czar rather than a pope.)

THE KNOWLEDGE PROBLEM

Gusfield does I believe emphasize too much the social construction of problems rather than their objective realities (and I am not using quotation marks, as he did around "objective"), but his work draws our attention to a surprising fact about social scientists' examination of the question of how a social condition becomes a social problem: There is a considerable degree of skepticism of how we go about it, or indeed how we can go about it in a democracy in which the mass media inevitably shape public perception and knowledge.

One finds the same in another social scientist, the late Aaron Wildavsky, who devoted a considerable part of his enormous energy and great talents to the study of how society deals with risk. Wildavsky gave more credit to the objective realities than Gusfield does, but he doubted they could play a major role in determining how we allocate our resources in dealing with risk. While he dealt primarily with environmental risks, he would have said the same thing about social risks and social problems. But despite his much greater respect for science and scientists and their ability to determine the degree of danger from various environmental risks (had he been speaking about social problems he might well have approached Gusfield in skepticism), he also believed that any hope of matching our resources to our problems by taking account of the scale of the danger they posed was probably a vain one. The problems were primarily political, and when Wildavsky said political he meant also cultural, tied up with our interests, our values, our perceptions, which brings him not far from Gusfield.

"What would be needed," he and Mary Douglas asked in their book *Risk and Culture,*

> to make us able to understand the risks that face us?—Nothing short of total knowledge (a mad answer to an impossible question). The hundreds of thousands of chemicals about whose dangers so much is said are matched easily by the diversity of the causes of war or the afflictions of poverty or the horrors of religious and racial strife. Just trying to think of what categories of objects a person might be concerned about is alarming. Indeed, it might be better for mental health to limit rather than expand sources of concern. Since no one can attend to everything, some sort of priority must be established among dangers. . . . Ranking dangers . . . so as to know which ones to address and in what order, demands prior agreement on criteria. There is no mechanical way to produce a ranking.

Scientists may come together on this (less likely social scientists) but there is no way of making their agreement public policy: We are not a nation of philosophers and kings. The issue then becomes political, with everything involved in that term. Douglas and Wildavsky quote some other authorities on risk:

> Values and uncertainties are an integral part of every acceptable-risk problem. As a result, there are no value-free processes for choosing between risky alternatives. The search for an "objective method" [again, in quotation marks] is doomed to failure and may blind the searchers to the value-laden assumptions they are making.

Another quotation from a different source:

> Not only does each approach fail to give a definitive answer, but it is predisposed to representing particular interests and recommending particular decisions. Hence, choice of a method is a political decision with a distinct message about who should rule and what should matter.

Scientists may agree on what risks should be addressed, in what order, with what resources, but even that is not assured, and when it comes to social prob-

lems and social scientists agreement is even less likely. Popular passions will be aroused, they will affect what politicians and administrators do, and one can only hope that knowledge—authentic knowledge, solidly based, scientifically established, something I still believe in despite the assault on its possibility we have seen in the newer trends in the humanities and social sciences—will play some role in determining what legislators and administrators do.

So in almost all transitions from social condition to social problem we are in the grip of passions, interests, perceptions, values that are not going to be affected much by what the scientists tell us. Gusfield called the fight for temperance a "crusade," Aaron Wildavsky uses the term "sectarian," with its religious connotations, to describe those who devote themselves to getting the public and government to pay attention to what they conceive of as major risks, and he uses the term not as an epithet but as a carefully constructed concept which for him describes the character of the people and groups who have done so much to alert us to environmental risks.

Despite the fact that there is a great deal that we can learn from the work of Gusfield and Wildavsky on how social conditions become social problems, I will separate myself from the full scope of their arguments. I believe that there are objective ways of determining the scale of a problem, even if all our efforts are somewhat corrupted by our political attitudes, by human failings that affect even scientists, and other factors; and that while we have undoubtedly seen cases in which the attention to a problem and the resources devoted to it can properly arouse skepticism, there are indeed conditions which hardly need to be "socially constructed," which spring to our eyes and appeal to our human sympathies and simply demand attention, and for which there would appear to be only one central question to consider: What to do about it. Yet we must be alerted to the issues the social scientists raise when we consider pragmatically how to make a social condition a social problem.

THE CASE OF PROHIBITION

Our two authors have tended to concentrate on issues which have in some way been misconstrued owing to interests and passions, perceptions and

values, they do not share. Thus, temperance was initially raised as a moral problem, a problem of making people better. This was in time joined by other considerations: temperance would fight poverty among workingmen, making them better workers, fathers, husbands. Eventually the method chosen to make them better was that of depriving them of the means for bad behavior. We consider Prohibition a great failure, but it did (according to the best authority) reduce the consumption of alcohol by half.

It is not clear how the problem of excessive alcohol consumption might have been better construed at the time; it could not easily have been construed differently from what it was in a largely rural and small-town, Protestant and evangelical America, fearful of the rising numbers of immigrants and Catholics, of the growth of the big cities with their wider range of acceptable behavior, their greater tolerance. We now see the crusade as mistaken, because we see the problem of alcohol consumption, when it becomes a problem, as one of mental health, and its incidence and impact have declined, at least in public perception, perhaps in reality. That decline has much to do with our viewing alcohol—as so much else—in the context of health rather than sin, as we have seen the decline of the theological ethic, and the rise of the therapeutic ethic. (The decline in alcoholism may also be connected with changes in taste and fashion, from hard liquor to wine, from wine to water.)

Just as Gusfield's temperance crusaders are seen as motivated by the fight against sin, evil, bad behavior, when they might have chosen (and in time their successors did) a more effective way of viewing the problem, Wildavsky's environmental crusaders are viewed as sectarians, impassioned, moving from one topic that arouses their indignation to another, incapable of placing in the balance the goods the technologies they oppose have brought, or comprehending the impact on lives and economies of the measures they demand. Religion has now been replaced by a suspicion of science and technology, a suspicion of big organizations, whether industrial firms or government, even though government is called upon to restore the ecological balance (but the distrust of government is such that it is primarily the courts and judges who are depended on to keep government in line in enforcing the rules and regulations).

TOBACCO, A SUCCESS STORY

Despite the rather sour tone adopted by many of our best social scientists toward crusaders and sectarians and indeed toward the passion for reform in general (a tone we may trace, perhaps, to Richard Hofstadter's *The Age of Reform*), we live in a society afflicted with problems that are hardly imaginary, hardly the result of misperceptions inspired by the passions of crusaders and sectarians. And we have seen successes in transforming conditions into problems in which we do not sense that crusaders and sectarians are driving forces, but rather scientific understanding and pragmatic policymakers. Perhaps the largest success (partial it is true), is the decline in tobacco consumption, and the decline in its social acceptance. While the battle against smoking is not without its sectarians, the costs of smoking to health are undeniable and ever more solidly documented, and the efforts that have been devoted to reducing its incidence have been balanced and, in time, effective.

Interestingly enough, the effort to reduce the consumption of tobacco has not been conducted, as so many others have, by means of major federal legislation, giving responsibility to a major federal agency, new or old, operating under law and issuing detailed regulations. Nor do we have a single major reform organization devoted to the cause of eradicating smoking—there is no equivalent to the Women's Christian Temperance Union, the Anti-Saloon League, the major environmental organizations. There are anti-tobacco crusaders, but they are local rather than national, hardly organized, and their effectiveness has been in getting local restrictive legislation, and in getting large organizations to set rules limiting the areas where smoking is permitted. At the national level, there have been warnings rather than prohibitions, the voluntary—though under pressure—banning of advertising on TV, the local pressure against billboards.

The campaign for the reduction of smoking has thus been characterized first by the fact that it was initiated by almost unambiguous scientific findings, announced by high medical authority, rather than by mass pressure from a mass organization; second that it has been conducted more on the local level than on the national; third that it has been characterized more by voluntary concessions, as in the case of advertising, than by national prohibition.

I have been trying to understand just why the campaign against smoking has been successful to the degree it has, so much more successful than the campaign against drugs for example, and why its characteristics have been so instinctive, but it has not been easy to get light on this matter. Seeking for some understanding on the shelves of the Widener Library at Harvard, I discover to my surprise that there is very little on the subject. "Smoking" comes in the Library of Congress cataloguing system between "drink" and "drugs," and while one finds shelf upon shelf of material on these two subjects, on smoking, there is almost nothing, a few disparate volumes. I wonder whether this is because we prefer studying failure rather than success; or because the limited degree of national coercive action means there is less to study; or because tobacco is inherently less glamorous than drink and drugs. But it kills as many people and if we have an example of success, even partial success, it should be worthy of study.

I am sure that to the smoker my assessment of the moderate nature of the campaign against smoking, compared to the crusade against drink, or the war against drugs, is too benign. Yet it is my impression there is something to be learned from the smoking story as we try to understand the more effective ways in which we convert social conditions into social problems. One thing to be learned, for example, is that moderation in the campaign, the willingness to accept slow but steady progress, may prevent a major backlash. In the case of drinking, the backlash was the repeal of the Eighteenth Amendment. Much had been learned from Prohibition and one important thing that had been learned was that it was better to leave the matter to the states and the localities. As a result, drink disappeared from the national agenda, and an issue that had troubled American political life for generations was domesticated. Excessive drinking became a medical and health problem, not a moral or legal problem.

BACKLASHES

The war against drugs has not yet met such a backlash, but it may in the campaign for legalization. There are incredible problems around legalization, but there are incredible problems around our efforts to eradicate drug use, too, and we may well find in time that questions will be raised about why we spend billions ineffectively in trying to eliminate the sources of drugs and in trying to eradicate dealing in drugs, why so large a proportion of our criminal justice resources—in police, judges, prosecutors, courts, jails, prisons—is devoted to the attempt to wipe out drug use.

We may shortly find another case of backlash in the case of child abuse. The story of child abuse is also one of a case, as in smoking, in which reform starts from the top, rather than as a result of mass pressure from crusaders or sectarians, and in which doctors rather than movement people play the central role, at least at the beginning. The story is an interesting one. It begins with interest in sponsoring research on the issue of child abuse in the Children's Bureau in the then-Department of Health, Education, and Welfare. They funded the work on this subject of Dr. C. Henry Kempe, a pediatrician who specialized in immunology, and who noted that the interns and residents he supervised were more interested in diagnosing rare blood diseases in the children under their care than in noting physical injuries to the children. Dr. Kempe wanted to draw attention to this problem. In one of his first efforts to report on the physical abuse of children, he organized a seminar at an academic meeting on the physical abuse of children. We are told by Barbara J. Nelson, who has researched this story, that

fellow members of the program committee suggested that a title such as physical abuse which emphasized legally liable and socially deviant behavior might make some members wary of attending the seminar. Kempe agreed, renaming the seminar the "Battered Child Syndrome." In one stroke he labeled the problem in a manner which downplayed the deviant aspects while highlighting the medical aspects. From an agenda-setting perspective the effect of the label cannot be overestimated.

In 1962 Kempe published an article under that title in the *Journal of the American Medical Association*. The rest is history. The mass media took up the phrase and the issue (scarcely a case of a situation that had become observably worse, but rather one for which the right label had been found) became a national one, a classic case of how a social condition becomes a social problem. The Children's Bureau proposed a model child abuse reporting statute in 1963, and by 1967 every state had passed a reporting law. Laws were revised over time to become ever stronger. To the physical abuse of children, attractive enough to the mass media, was added concern for their sexual abuse, and we may well have now reached a stage where considerably more is reported and even prosecuted than exists, and we may be on the verge of a backlash against the attention and resources devoted to the problem, a common stage in the history of such "victories."

Of course it is inevitable, what with changing cycles of attention and fashion, that at one point there will be great attention to a social problem, at a subsequent point much less, with very little change in the problem itself. But what most impresses when one considers the range of problems with which the mass media, scientists, social scientists, legislators, voluntary organizations, all deal, is that no problem is fully neglected. This is not surprising in a democracy where everything is open, every issue has its advocates, and the mass media are ever ready to exploit a problem which has been lying fallow and relatively neglected. There are entrepreneurs of problem-making, problem-enhancing, at all levels: professionals in given areas, who see a problem others do not, such as battered children; bureaucrats seeking to maintain old missions, expand into new missions, as in the case of the Children's Bureau; legislators who leap into an area in which there is no or little legislation and try to make it their own, as Congressman Mario Biaggi did in the case of child abuse; scientists, natural and social, who see opportunities for research; editors and journalists, seeking new and interesting topics; advocacy organizations, some single-mindedly dealing with one clientele, one issue, others seeking to expand into new issues as old ones lose interest and salience. We see the change in perception starting in some cases through some administrative or bureaucratic action at the top, in others being initiated by an outside advocacy group, in others seemingly launched on the public stage by a single book, e.g., Rachel Carson's *Silent Spring,* Ralph Nader's *Unsafe at Any Speed.* The number of enterprises of this sort that have failed (including I am sure many books as good as Nader's and Carson's and trying to draw attention to a

problem as serious as the effect of pesticides on the environment or automobile safety) are far more numerous than the few that have achieved remarkable success.

There is one factor in the potential success of such enterprises that has not been much noted. I think the scale and steadiness of public response to the entrepreneurs of problem-making depends not only on the seriousness of the problem, on the degree to which it impinges directly on public perception, the degree to which it agitates and concerns the public, but on whether any effective action to deal with it is visible. Consider what is called the "urban crisis," the problem of the inner cities. One may argue with the term, it is not well-defined, and contains within itself a host of other problems. It was once high on the public agenda, in the 1960s and 1970s, and then declined, despite steady study, publications, popular books, advocacy groups, special academic programs, and I would conclude this was for one reason: There was nothing to be done, or at least nothing much to be done. Other problems present clear targets, things to be done, even if they will fail: prohibit drink, ban smoking in enclosed spaces, interdict drugs. We learn from the experience, even if slowly and poorly, and eventually we learn there is not much to be done: people will drink and take drugs, there will be cycles of greater or lesser use, and moderate impact is all we can hope for.

We are now at a moment in which great attention is being given in the mass media to a specific problem that can be considered part of the "urban crisis," gun violence, the use of guns in situations, whether of fights among youths or of robbery, in which they were until recently less available or less used, with an accompanying high rate of homicide particularly affecting young black males (who are also those who are using the guns), bystanders, shopkeepers, taxicab drivers. We are now seeing efforts by those in the field of public health to try to recast the problem as a public health one. Thus, it is likened to an "epidemic," which it certainly is, as the word is popularly used, but public health people wonder whether equating it to epidemics such as tuberculosis or AIDS will give us more insight into what is happening, or direct more attention and more effective attention to it, or suggest more tools with which to deal with it.

The model for the campaign against

gun violence that is now developing is the successful reduction of smoking, or of driving under the influence of drink. The public health model calls for such actions as proper tracing of the incidence of the condition, relating it to other social conditions, developing campaigns of information and modes of treatment, devising techniques of education or publicity which change habits—which, for example, would make the possession and use of guns reprehensible. Undoubtedly we will be hearing and seeing a good deal more about this in the coming months, perhaps years. Any such effort, if we take as a model the case of driving under the influence of drink, or smoking, must be long-range. The campaign will take forms we cannot imagine now, and we cannot know whether we will achieve the relative success of our efforts to reduce smoking and drinking-driving, or the relative failure of our efforts to reduce the use of drugs.

But one contrast comes to mind and suggests a caution: smoking and drinking-driving were not matters in which incidence was concentrated in one social class, one ethnic or racial group. One could argue the same with gun violence, if one concentrates on the possession of guns, and the overall incidence of deaths from guns, and if one places in the same statistical category suicides from the use of an available gun, hunting accidents, domestic violence which climaxes with shooting. These kinds of deaths from guns are old matters, and there has not been, I think, any marked change in recent years. The gun violence that is now the subject of so many newspaper and TV stories is a different matter, concentrated in the inner city, affecting largely one major minority group—young blacks—even though it is also present generally and affects almost everybody.

Is anything gained by lumping this phenomenon into a general category of "gun violence," and considering it under the category of public health? I think not. It is one thing to change behavior, through publicity appeals, through campaigns that change popular attitudes toward a behavior from acceptance to disapproval, when that behavior is found throughout the society, and when those to whom one is appealing are representative of the society in general. It must be a different matter when one deals with behavior that is encapsulated in a specific social group. Consider one consequence of cre-

2. How Social Problems Are Born

ating a general category of "gun violence." One possible approach, the one most popular today in the mass media and among political leaders, is: Make it harder to get guns. This is likely to work among the middle classes and among groups who presently hold guns legally. It is likely to be completely ineffective among the groups whose very behavior has raised the issue to the high pitch of current concern, the young people who are killing each other in the urban ghettoes, and more occasionally (but often enough) killing others. It suggests to us that it is still important to consider just what the problem is, and we move in rather ineffective directions if we frame it improperly. Is the problem "gun violence," or is it rather the larger one of the complex of social problems in the inner cities that we still have no effective means of attacking? Can the problem of gun violence be effectively isolated from this larger complex and reduced? It seems to me doubtful, but many efforts are under way, from Jesse Jackson's exhortations to the attempt to reframe the issue as one of public health to the campaign of Jay Winston of the Harvard School of Public Health to get anti-gun messages into TV programs. And we will learn from these efforts whether gun violence is more like smoking or more like drugs.

Parenting and Family Issues

Throughout history the family has been the most effective and primary transmitter of values, beliefs, and behaviors, for good or ill. But the American family has been under increasing assault since the 1960s. Some individuals argue that it is not so much an assault as it is a restructuring of an antiquated social institution. Single parents, couples with no children, single individuals, unmarried people living together, homosexual couples—almost any and all combinations of persons living under a common roof are now classified by some as a "family."

Questions raised by the articles in this unit include: (a) Just what is a family? (b) What impact is the "new" family structure having on its members, especially the children? (c) What impact are other social institutions having on the family? (d) How does what is happening in the family impact on other institutions? (e) What can and should be done to strengthen the family? (f) What must be done to reconnect fathers with the family?

The essay "Fount of Virtue, Spring of Wealth: How the Strong Family Sustains a Prosperous Society" examines the role that strong families play in a prosperous society. Cross-cultural anthropological studies reveal that there are links between violence, poverty, drug abuse, health (both physical and mental), educational accomplishments, and family stability.

The essay "Honor Thy Children" looks at the problems facing children who are raised in families without fathers. Various strategies to reconnect fathers to their families are identified, evaluated, and discussed.

"Growing Up against the Odds" documents a significant link between the rate that "traditional" families are breaking down and the increase in every type of social pathology. Robert Royal concludes that if children are to

have a meaningful chance for successful and fulfilling lives, the traditional family must thrive, not merely survive.

In "Why Leave Children with Bad Parents?" implications of programs that stress parental rights and/or family preservation over the welfare of children are focused. In attempting to keep families intact, social welfare agencies aggressively encourage the return of abused children to their abusive parents even when no evidence exists that the parents will not repeat the abuse.

Looking Ahead: Challenge Questions

What personal experiences have you had with problems in your family?

Is the current high divorce rate good or bad for society?

How do the problems facing children of single parents differ from those who have two parents?

Is it possible and/or desirable to try and preserve the traditional family?

Under what conditions should abused children be returned to their abusive parents?

In what major ways are the lives of children in peril, especially children in troubled families?

What are the consequences of being forced to survive in families living on welfare?

How possible is it to reconnect many fathers with their families?

In what ways would the approaches of symbolic interactionists, functionalists, or conflict theorists differ in the study of family issues?

What conflicts in rights, values, and duties seem to underlie each issue?

FOUNT OF VIRTUE, SPRING OF WEALTH

How the Strong Family Sustains a Prosperous Society

Charmaine Crouse Yoest

Charmaine Crouse Yoest is a Bradley fellow at the University of Virginia and a public policy consultant. She is former deputy director of policy at the Family Research Council, a Washington-based study institute.

"Daddy," I asked, "will you have to go to war?"

At that point, the Vietnam War, for me, consisted primarily of television footage of helicopters and soldiers in the jungle. I was terrified that my father would be called to go to war and die at any moment.

"No, honey," he replied, "the military doesn't draft men who are in school."

Still not understanding why men had to fight and die in wars, I pressed on. "But what if you did have to go? Would you really go?"

"Yes, I would. Sometimes men have to fight to protect the people they love," he explained. "If a burglar wanted to break into our house, I would fight to keep your mom and you and your brother safe."

As he talked, I understood: There are things that are worth dying for. For my dad, like many other people, the list begins with family.

That night my father taught me the integral connection between family and country—that there are times when the burglar is another country and the house our families live in is our country.

And so it is with most of the lessons children need to learn as they grow and mature—they are best taught and modeled in the context of family. Children are the future citizens of any nation. For this reason, societies have a stake in whether children are raised to become good citizens rather than bad ones.

President Theodore Roosevelt wrote: "Sins against pure and healthy family life are those which of all others are sure in the end to be visited most heavily upon the nation." Sociologist Urie Bronfenbrenner, in outlining the needs of children, provides a compelling rationale for the state's interest in preserving the family as the primary context for cultivating healthy children and seeing them develop into productive citizens.

> The informal education that takes place in the family is not merely a pleasant prelude, but rather a powerful prerequisite for success in formal education from the primary grades onward. This empowering experience reaches further still. As evidenced in longitudinal studies, it appears to provide a basis, while offering no guarantee, for the subsequent development of the capacity to function responsively and creatively as an adult in the realms of work, family life, and citizenship.[1]

Quite simply, the family lays the foundation. As increasing bodies of research attest, our families are the fertile ground from which children acquire the patterns, habits, lessons, and values that, in our increasingly interdependent society, affect us all.

From a societal viewpoint, the family is important because of its role in shaping good citizens. Fundamentally, the state

---

1. Urie Bronfenbrenner, "What Do Families Do?" *Family Affairs* (New York: Institute for American Values, Winter/Spring 1991), 4.

This article originally appeared in *The World & I*, August 1994, pp. 359-375. Reprinted by permission of *The World & I*, a publication of The Washington Times Corporation. © 1994.

President Theodore Roosevelt wrote: "Sins against pure and healthy family life are those which of all others are sure in the end to be visited most heavily upon the nation."

needs stability, achievement, and loyalty from its citizens, and families foster these three qualities.

THE STATE'S NEED FOR STABILITY IN ITS CITIZENRY

There can be no more graphic testimony to a society's need for law and order than the smoldering images of riot-torn Los Angeles. Events like the L.A. riots, New York City's "wilding" episode, and the depredations of Jeffrey Dahmer overshadow the complex policy discussions over the merit of various government spending programs and actions, and they are a keen reminder that, above all else, society is meant to protect its citizens. Although we rarely do it consciously, each of us gives up a measure of individual rights and autonomy in order to live within the bounds of community. We do so with the expectation of greater stability and security than we would have on our own. Thus, while we chafe at the delay in stopping at intersections when the light is red, few of us begrudge that infringement on our personal freedom because of the safety and order it brings to our daily travels.

Some do, however; there are more and more individuals claiming their right to become a law unto themselves. While running red lights is a relatively minor breach of the community contract, the daily escalation of violence in our country attests to increasing instability and weakening of the social order.

Respect for authority and willingness to accept personal limits are character traits upon which social order is built. The lessons that build that kind of private discipline, so important to public stability, are best taught in the home. Kay James,

former assistant secretary at the U.S. Department of Health and Human Services (HHS), tells a true story about two young boys growing up in a poverty-stricken neighborhood.

One day while roaming the neighborhood, the two boys broke into the local school and stole several chickens from the cafeteria refrigerator. Both boys then proudly took their bounty home to their mothers for dinner that night.

The first mother cried out in delight: "Boy, I don't know where you got this, but we sure are going to eat good tonight!"

The second boy came home to a different response. "Son," his mother asked, "I know you don't have a job, and you don't have money. Where did you get those chickens?"

When she heard the details, she took the chickens by the feet and started pummeling her son with them. She backed him into a corner, and with one hand still holding the birds and the other pointed right in his face, she said, "Boy, I will starve before I let one of my children bring stolen food into this house!"

That was all she said before she turned and opened the back door and flung those chickens into the backyard. "If you want to help out around here," she declared, "you can get a job."[2]

Kay recounts that several years later the first mother was left grieving beside the casket of her son, shot to death in a drug deal. The second woman was Kay's own mother. Both she and her brother learned

---

2. Kay James, *Never Forget* (Grand Rapids, Mich.: Zondervan Publishing House, 1993), 46.

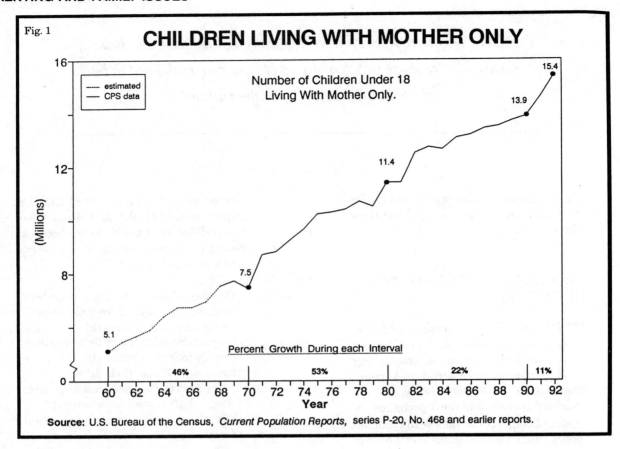

Fig. 1

CHILDREN LIVING WITH MOTHER ONLY

Number of Children Under 18 Living With Mother Only.

- - - - estimated
——— CPS data

(Millions)

Percent Growth During each Interval

46%   53%   22%   11%

Year

Source: U.S. Bureau of the Census, *Current Population Reports,* series P-20, No. 468 and earlier reports.

an enduring and valuable lesson in honesty and respect for authority that night.

Many children today are not being taught respect for any authority—in part because of the increase in father absence. The active involvement of fathers in the raising and disciplining of children, particularly young boys, is crucial. Myriam Miedzian, author of *Boys Will Be Boys: Breaking the Link Between Masculinity and Violence*, stated in testimony before the U.S. House of Representatives that "raising a son without a nurturant father in the home significantly increases the likelihood of the boy becoming violent."[3] She added that this is true even in other cultures:

Cross-cultural anthropological studies indicate that violent behavior is often characteristic of male adolescents and

adults whose fathers were absent or played a small role in their son's early rearing. For example, anthropologists Beatrice Whiting's and John Whiting's study of children in six cultures revealed that those tribes in which the father was most loosely connected with the family and had least to do with the rearing of children, were the most violent. These findings are corroborated by other studies.[4]

Is it any wonder, then, that violence is increasing in our society when the number of children in single-parent, female-headed homes has increased 202 percent since 1960? Today, nearly one-third—28 percent—of all children are born into single-parent homes (see figure 1). In the black community, it has reached as high as 68 percent.

Unfortunately, because of the disparity between the white and black communities in the percentages of single-parent

3. Myriam Miedzian, testimony to the Select Committee on Children, Youth, and Families, U.S. House of Representatives, "Babies and Briefcases: Creating a Family-Friendly Workplace for Fathers," June 11, 1991, 1.

4. Miedzian, "Babies and Briefcases," 3.

"Cross-cultural anthropological studies indicate that violent behavior is often characteristic of male adolescents and adults whose fathers were absent or played a small role in their son's early rearing."

homes, there has developed a mistaken perception that increased levels of crime in some communities is a racial issue rather than one of family structure. A study by Douglas A. Smith and G. Roger Jarjoura, published in 1988, disproved this fallacy:

Many studies that find a significant association between racial composition and crime rates have failed to control for community family structure and may mistakenly attribute to racial composition an effect that is actually due to the association between race and family structure.[5]

The research points to a strong correlation between the increasing numbers of children growing up in single-parent homes and the rising levels of violence and crime in our country. One reason is the appalling number of adolescent boys who live on the streets and whose need for belonging, identity, camaraderie, and security that should come from family is filled by gangs. Leon Bing, author of *Do or Die*, talked with two fourteen-year-old gang members, "Sidewinder" and "Bopete," in a youth detention center:

Bopete: "Sometimes I think about not goin' back to banging' when I get outta here. I play in sports a lot here, and I . . ."

Sidewinder's laugh interrupts. "Sound like a regular ol' teenager, don't he? I sound like that, too, after the drive-by. I got shot twice in the leg . . . and when that happen I didn't want to bang no more, either. Makin' promises to God, all

like that. But when it heal up . . ." He is silent for a moment; then, "I tell you somethin'—*I don't feel connected to any other kids in this city or in this country or in this world. I only feel comfortable in my 'hood. That's the only thing I'm connected to, that's my family. One big family—that's about it.*" (emphasis mine)

"In my 'hood, in the Jungle, it ain't like a gang. It's more like a nation, everybody all together as one. Other kids, as long as they ain't my enemies, I can be cool with 'em." Bopete lapses into silence. "I'll tell you, though—if I didn't have no worst enemy to fight with, I'd probably find somebody."

Sidewinder picks it up. "I'd find somebody. 'Cause if they ain't nobody to fight, it ain't no gangs. It ain't no life. I don't know . . . it ain't no . . ."

"It ain't no fun."

"Yeah! Ain't no fun just sittin' there. Anybody can just sit around, just drink, smoke a little Thai. But that ain't fun like shootin' guns and stabbin' people. *That's* fun."[6]

The family also promotes societal stability by providing men with a proper channel for their sexuality and providing appropriate role models for adolescent boys of a stable, healthy masculinity. Without the nuclear family of husbands and wives, mothers and fathers, to provide these crucial social functions, a vacuum of enormous and devastating proportions is developing. Miedzian quoted the classic work of sociologist Walter Miller:

Miller pointed out that the extreme concern with toughness and the frequent

5. Douglas Smith and G. Roger Jarjoura, "Social Structure and Criminal Victimization," *Journal of Research in Crime and Delinquency* 25 (February 1986), 27–52.

6. Leon Bing, *Do or Die*, as quoted by William Tucker, "Is Police Brutality the Problem?" *Commentary* 95 (January 1993), 26.

"Anybody can just sit around, just drink, smoke a little Thai,"
a gang member said. "But that ain't fun like shootin'
guns and stabbin' people. That's fun."

violence in lower-class culture probably originates in the fact that for a significant percentage of these boys there is no consistently present male figure whom they can identify with and model themselves on. Because of this they develop an "almost obsessive . . . concern with 'masculinity'" which Miller refers to as "hypermasculinity."[7]

Little boys, as they grow toward manhood, must make a break from the feminine role modeled for them by their mothers and establish their own masculine identity. With a father in the home, they can do this relatively painlessly by imitating their dads; when they become men, they can find masculine roles in becoming husbands and fathers themselves. But in our society today, far too many boys are growing up without that male role model and entering an adult society that has ceased to value and support marriage.

In his book *Men and Marriage*, George Gilder champions marriage as an indispensable social construct for the appropriate channeling of male sexual aggression into creativity. "Without a durable relationship with a woman," explains Gilder, "a man's sexual life is a series of brief and temporary exchanges, impelled by a desire to affirm his most rudimentary masculinity."[8]

He goes on to make the case that this male impulse, biologically based though it is, results in a destabilizing influence on society. And, ultimately, it is not fulfilling for men themselves. In the end, looking for meaning in life and given impetus through societal constructs, a man will marry: "The man's love . . .

offers a promise of dignity and purpose. For he then has to create, by dint of his own effort . . . a life that a woman could choose. Thus are released and formed the energies of civilized society. He provides, and he does it for a lifetime, for a life."[9]

A civilized society, a stable society— the antithesis of the mayhem engendered by the new "evolving" family forms—is precisely the objective. Family, based on the fundamental marital union, is the foundation for a strong nation.

As society experiments and individuals reject the responsibilities of family, we all pay a price. Sen. Daniel Patrick Moynihan sounded this alarm in a 1965 article that was greeted with widespread approbation. Three decades later, daily headlines confirm his prescience:

From the wild Irish slums of the nineteenth century eastern seaboard, to the riot-torn suburbs of Los Angeles, there is one unmistakable lesson in American history: a community that allows a large number of young men to grow up in broken families, dominated by women, never acquiring any stable relationship to male authority, never acquiring any set of rational expectations about the future—that community asks for and gets chaos. Crime, violence, unrest, disorder—most particularly the furious, unrestrained lashing out at the whole social structure—that is not only to be expected; it is very near to inevitable. And it is richly deserved.[10]

7. Miedzian, "Babies and Briefcases," 2.
8. George Gilder, *Men and Marriage* (Gretna, La.: Pelican Books, 1992), 14.

9. Gilder, *Men and Marriage*, 290.
10. Daniel Patrick Moynihan, *Family and Nation: The Godkin Lectures, Harvard University* (San Diego, New York, London: Harcourt, Brace, Jovanovich, 1986), 9.
11. Alan Carlson, *Family Questions: Reflections on the American Social Crisis* (New Brunswick and Oxford: Transaction Books, 1988), 7.

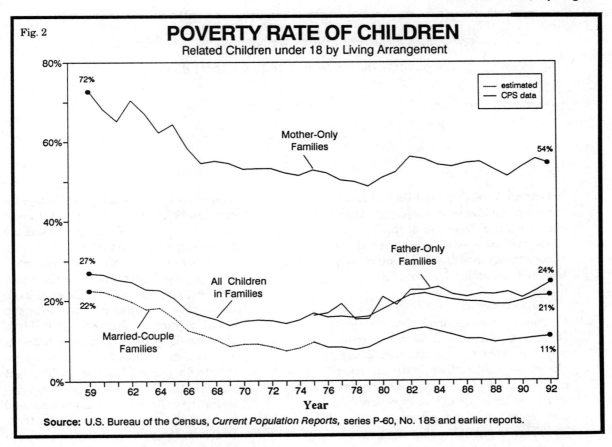

Fig. 2

POVERTY RATE OF CHILDREN
Related Children under 18 by Living Arrangement

- - - - - estimated
——— CPS data

72%

Mother-Only Families

54%

Father-Only Families

24%

All Children in Families

27%

22%

Married-Couple Families

21%

11%

Year

Source: U.S. Bureau of the Census, *Current Population Reports,* series P-60, No. 185 and earlier reports.

THE FAMILY AND ECONOMIC STABILITY

The family fosters stability through its role in character formation. Stability has other facets, however. Among these is economic stability.

The White House Conference on Children in 1970 came to the conclusion that "society has the ultimate responsibility for the well-being and optimum development of all children."[11] Like many ideas that at first glance pass muster, this one contains a kernel of truth: When a child has been abandoned or abused, someone must step in to care for that child. But it is essential to recognize that this is merely a remedial action; the family is the first line of defense and provision of our children. Nevertheless, it has become increasingly common to hear terminology that reflects the philosophy inherent in the White House Conference statement. Some refer to "society's children," but even more often we hear, "America's children." In many

cases, this is an innocent turn of phrase; in others, it reflects a lack of recognition of the primacy of the parental responsibility for children.

But what relevance do parental rights and responsibilities have in the context of economic stability? Headlines scream, "Numbers of American Children in Poverty Rising," and some public opinion brokers draw the erroneous conclusion that economics is the major factor in producing poverty.

The truth is that not all American children have shared equally in the rising poverty rates. Children in single-parent homes are five times more likely to live in poverty than children in two-parent homes (see figure 2). Additionally, children in two-parent homes move more easily out of poverty through fluctuations in the economy; children in single-parent homes live in more persistent poverty despite improvements in economic conditions.

The strong correlation between family structure and poverty among children is consistently overlooked or downplayed

*Children in single-parent homes are five times more likely to live
in poverty than children in two-parent homes.*

by policymakers. Of course, some children in two-parent homes live in poverty. However, with a differential of this magnitude—*five times*—the importance of the nuclear family in providing basic economic essentials for children should be unquestioned.

The inescapable difficulty of raising children alone is even more clear if we look at the poverty levels of children living with only their fathers: These children are less likely than children living with only their mothers to live in poverty, but they are *still twice as likely* to live in poverty as children in two-parent homes.

There is a striking contrast between the changes in the poverty levels of children living with only their mothers and children in two-parent homes. With improvements in the economy in the past, the poverty level of children in two-parent families has dramatically dropped; at the same time, the poverty level of children in single-parent homes has steadily increased with very few fluctuations. During the 1975 and 1982 recessions, more children became impoverished, with a subsequent drop occurring during the recovery in families with married parents.

By meeting children's and other family members' most basic economic needs so effectively and efficiently, the family functions as a stabilizing bulwark. Its absence leaves gaping holes. Just look at the last three decades in our country—welfare dependency has increased dramatically in the wake of unprecedented family breakdown. The majority of women receiving Aid to Families with Dependent Children (AFDC) are not married to the fathers of their children. Fifty-three percent of all AFDC recipients have "no marriage tie." The second most prevalent reason for AFDC payments, 38.5 percent, is divorce or separation. The group

most likely to become long-term (ten years or more) AFDC recipients are women who are single mothers. Marriage remains the No. 1 escape route from the welfare rolls.

When parents shirk their responsibility to provide financially for their own children, everyone suffers. Even though the government has stepped into the breach to provide subsistence for children abandoned by their fathers, a bureaucratic safety net has proved a poor substitute for paternal provision. The fact remains, the family is society's best vehicle for the self-reliance of individuals and the care of children. Even the centrist-Democrat Progressive Policy Institute, in its *Mandate for Change* document, states: "It is no exaggeration to say that a stable, two-parent family is an American child's best protection against poverty."[12] Research clearly demonstrates this truth. The U.S. Department of Health and Human Services found that in 1985–86 "the poverty rate for married teens living with husband and children was 28% compared with 81% for unmarried teen mothers living alone with their children."[13]

THE ROLE OF THE FAMILY IN PHYSICAL AND MENTAL HEALTH

Another facet of societal stability is the general level of health of its population. In an era of high-tech medical care, health is an area where the family has a significant, but little recognized, effect. Yet research

12. Elaine Ciulla Kamarck and William Galston, "A Progressive Family Policy for the 1990s," *Mandate for Change* (New York: Berkley Books, 1993), 157.
13. Gilbert Crouse and David Larson, "Cost of Teenage Childbearing: Current Trends," *ASPE Research Notes: Information for Decision Makers*, U.S. Department of Health and Human Services (August 1992).

demonstrates another, slightly surprising, contribution the family makes to its members: Children in stable, two-parent homes are healthier than other children, and adults who are married are healthier than those who are not.

The National Commission on America's Urban Families released its *Families First* report in January 1993, saying that: "In sum, problems of psychological distress and poor mental health, which carry profound social as well as personal consequences, are among the most pervasive and most damaging consequences of current family fragmentation in the United States."[14]

There is increasing recognition that divorce is a prime contributor to health problems for both adults and children. However, skeptics have claimed that the ill effects of divorce on children can actually be attributed to the negative predivorce environment of the home and that divorce is an improvement for those children. While it is certainly true that the nature of the marital relationship has a profound effect on children, one study cited by the Urban Commission indicates that divorce may not be the best solution for a contentious home. A 1991 study compared two sets of troubled boys, the first from divorced homes and the second from intact homes. After a five-year follow-up, the researchers found that the former group of boys had higher rates of both substance abuse and mental health problems than the latter.[15]

One of the most influential studies to be done in recent years was the 1991 report by Deborah Dawson of the National Center for Health Statistics based on the 1988 National Health Interview Survey on Child Health, which was a survey of seventeen thousand children nationwide. On the positive side, Dawson found "overall good health of the child population." However, she found that after controlling for social and demographic characteristics, "children who had experienced the separation of their natural parents . . . were more likely than other children to

have had an accident, injury, or poisoning in the preceding year."[16]

But the most startling results came when Dawson turned to the emotional and psychological health of children: "Children living with formerly married mothers were more than three times as likely as those living with both biological parents to have received treatment for emotional or behavioral problems in the preceding twelve months."[17]

She found an elevated score for children living with stepparents and never-married mothers, as well. Finally, in looking at the "overall behavioral problem score," she found that children living with their biological parents once again scored better. "This pattern was repeated in the scores for antisocial behavior, anxiety or depression, headstrong behavior, hyperactivity, dependency, and peer conflict or social withdrawal," reported Dawson.

Adults as well as children are affected. Researchers at Yale and the University of California at Los Angeles have found that marriage is a significant buffer against the stresses of life for adults. Among both blacks and whites, men and women, being married correlates with a lower rate of psychiatric illness. They concluded, "The loss of a spouse through death, divorce, or separation is especially predictive of ill health."[18]

HOW THE FAMILY PROMOTES INDIVIDUAL ACHIEVEMENT

The greatest wealth a society has is its citizens. To thrive, a country needs the productivity of motivated citizens who press forward to achieve. The mystique of the "American work ethic" springs out of the innumerable individual accomplishments and innovations that have, collectively, made the United States the great nation that it is.

14. *Families First*, Report of the National Commission on America's Urban Families (Washington, D.C.: January 1993), 29.

15. William Doherty and Richard Needle, "Psychological Adjustment and Substance Use among Adolescents before and after a Parental Divorce," *Child Development* 61 (April 1991), 332–35; as cited in *Families First*.

16. Deborah Dawson, "Family Structure and Children's Health: United States, 1988," U.S. Department of Health and Human Services, Public Health Service, Centers for Disease Control, National Center for Health Statistics (June 1991), 7.

17. Dawson, "Family Structure," 3.

18. David Williams, David Takeuchi, and Russell Adair, "Marital Status and Psychiatric Disorders among Blacks and Whites," *Journal of Health and Social Behavior* 33 (1992), 140–57; as cited in *The Family in America* (Rockford, Ill.: The Rockford Institute, October 1992).

Children in stable, two-parent homes are physically and mentally healthier than other children, and adults who are married are healthier than those who are not.

This, too, begins in the family. One very accomplished professional woman remembers hearing her father, Mr. Stone, say to his family on many occasions, "We Stones are hard workers!" The repetition left an indelible impression. It is this unique ability of the family to encourage the development of character in its members that makes it invaluable in preparing young people to be positive contributors to society. Values that are essential in the work force—discipline, respect for authority, perseverance—most often are forged in the family crucible.

Family also provides motivation. The historian and family expert, Alan Carlson, has said, "The family contains within its bounds the necessary positive incentives which make human beings behave in economically useful ways."[19] In echoes of Gilder, the point is that both men and women will strive harder to achieve and provide for those they love than they will for themselves.

And, as any teacher in any school across our nation will attest, the family is an irreplaceable foundation for education. The data underscore a family's integral role in preparing children for learning. More specifically, just as crime, health, and poverty are affected by family structure, the research leaves no doubt that children in two-parent families have a significant advantage in formal education. According to a U.S. Department of Education study of twenty-five thousand students, after controlling for socioeconomic status, race, and sex:

[Students] from single-parent families were still more likely to fail to perform at the basic proficiency levels. They were

about one-quarter to one-third more likely to perform below the basic reading and math levels and were more than two and a half times as likely to drop out of school as were students from two-parent families.[20]

(Additionally, Deborah Dawson found that children in single-parent homes were 40–75 percent more likely to repeat a grade and 70 percent more likely to be expelled from school.)

Although there are several factors contributing to the worsening state of American education, we cannot afford to turn a blind eye to the effect single parenthood is having on the readiness to learn, and the ability to learn, of millions of young children. If our country is to stay competitive, it cannot afford to have poorly educated citizens and workers. In particular, as we move into an increasingly sophisticated, highly technical economy, we will need equally sophisticated workers.

THE FAMILY'S PART IN FOSTERING LOYALTY

My brother and I as kids used to belt out the *Battle Hymn of the Republic* with childish enthusiasm . . . "Mine eyes have seen the glory of the coming of the Lord," building to a crescendo on the "Glory, Glory Hallelujahs." We loved that part, drawing out the emphasis on the high note with questionable musical effect. The song is indelibly linked in my mind with the laughter of my grandfather,

19. Carlson, *Family Questions*, xvi.

20. "Characteristics of At-Risk Students in NELS: 88," U.S. Department of Education, National Center for Education Statistics, 13–14; as cited in *Families First*.

Gloria Steinem stated that "family is content, not form." This rationalization accompanied the sixties' changes in individual behavior—changes that gave rise to skyrocketing rates of divorce and out-of-wedlock births.

a proud Marine and World War II veteran, who took great joy in teaching us patriotic songs. Now, many years after his death, the song tends to evoke for me, not laughter, but a wistfulness mixed with a deep and abiding pride in the heritage of courage and patriotism he gave us.

Like many veterans, my grandfather did not talk much about his war experiences. He did not have to. The mere fact of his service gave testimony to his devotion to his country. Semper Fi! No school civics lesson could compare with the example of patriotism set by my grandfather.

Years later, the last notes of Taps sounded over Arlington National Cemetery as the chaplain stepped over to hand my mother-in-law the folded flag. My father-in-law had died after a full life, surviving service in two wars. Beyond our circle of friends and family, up the hill as far as the eye could see, were row after row of rounded white tombstones, standing in mute testimony to the men and women who were dedicated to the defense of our country.

One last, essential need a country has of its citizens is devotion. Our Constitution says our Founding Fathers had come together to "provide for the common defense." The gravestones in Arlington Cemetery represent devotion to country. Where does that kind of sacrifice, that bravery, come from? What made so many willing to die?

Why were they willing? For love of country, surely. But that love and devotion is most often predicated upon the fact that the country hosts what we hold most dear: our families.

'LOVE THE ONE YOU'RE WITH . . .'

What kind of social construct produces a good citizen? Many view the sweeping changes occurring in families as a benign social progression. In the last few decades, more and more people have joined the chorus of voices saying, "All you need is love." According to this viewpoint, family structure simply does not matter very much. Gloria Steinem, for instance, has stated that "family is content, not form." This rationalization accompanied the sixties' and seventies' changes in individual behavior—changes that gave rise to the skyrocketing rates of divorce and out-of-wedlock births. Partly causal factor and partly retrospective rationale, the cries of "family is what you make it" provide both a blazing path for those seeking individual self-actualization and an explanation for those seeking a context for their own bewildering circumstances. Unfortunately, the theory does not match up too closely with reality.

One man, now a successful professional in his midtwenties with a beautiful wife and a well-adjusted life, still vividly remembers the effect the loss of his father in a car crash had on him as a young teenager. He hears the public debate over family structure with strident voices claiming that single-parent families are "just as good" as two-parent homes and compares those claims to his own experience.

"Do they mean," he asks, "that my dad's death just didn't matter? How can

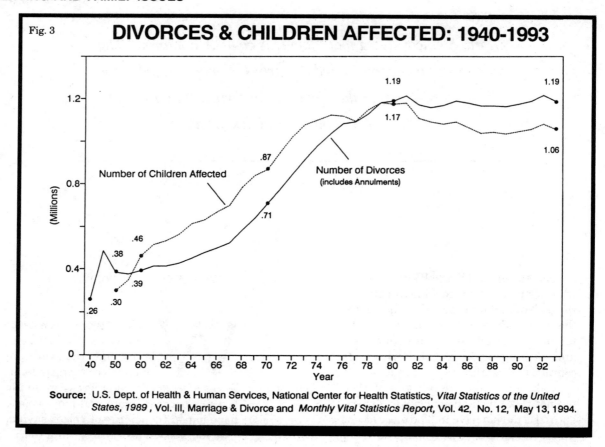

Fig. 3

DIVORCES & CHILDREN AFFECTED: 1940-1993

Number of Children Affected

Number of Divorces (includes Annulments)

.26 .30 .38 .39 .46 .71 .87 1.19 1.17 1.19 1.06

(Millions)

Year

Source: U.S. Dept. of Health & Human Services, National Center for Health Statistics, *Vital Statistics of the United States, 1989* , Vol. III, Marriage & Divorce and *Monthly Vital Statistics Report*, Vol. 42, No. 12, May 13, 1994.

they imply that growing up without my father was irrelevant?"

Another woman struggled through her parents' divorce as a teenager. As an adult, she built her own successful life—until she began contemplating marriage herself. Then, her parents' experience became a barrier, as it does for many children of divorce. Today, even with an adoring, devoted fiancé, she says she struggles with feelings of insecurity. "How do I know," she wonders, "that he won't leave me like my father left my mom?"

Even though the personal anecdotes are piling up and are supported by an ever-increasing body of social science research, many authorities in our society deny the intrinsic importance of the family. *Time* magazine, in a special issue devoted to "Beyond the Year 2000," claimed that "the very term nuclear family gives off a musty smell." Leslie Wolfe, executive director of the Center for Women Policy Studies, said in that issue in an article entitled: "The Nuclear Fam-

ily Goes Boom": "The isolated nuclear family of the 1950s was a small blip in the radar. We've been looking at it as normal, but in fact it was a fascinating anomaly."

The real surprise in Wolfe's statement is that she did not come right out and use the overworked sobriquet of "Ozzie and Harriet" as a target in her sneer at the 1950's. Typically, those attacking the nuclear family exercise no such self-restraint. In a 1989 report, Daniel Seligman of *Fortune* reported that:

we sidled up to Nexis the other day and nonchalantly asked how many news stories in 1989 included the phrase "Ozzie and Harriet." Startling answer: 88 stories. Usual context . . . A politician was onstage reciting the news that the traditional nuclear family—the kind symbolized by the Nelsons during their marathon stint on black-and-white TV—was dead or dying.[21]

21. Daniel Seligman, *Fortune*, July 17, 1989; as cited in "Catching the Reruns: Ozzie, Harriet, and the Media," *Family Affairs* 2 (New York: Institute for American Values, Summer/Fall 1989), 13.

*Almost one hundred years after Nietzsche declared that "God is dead,"
his intellectual descendants, in perhaps a natural succession of
thought, are crying, "The family is dead."*

Almost exactly one hundred years after Friedrich Nietzsche declared that "God is dead," his intellectual descendants, in perhaps a natural succession of thought, are crying, "The family is dead."

Stephanie Coontz, who has written a book titled *The Way We Never Were: American Families and the Nostalgia Trap*, is one such pessimist. Perhaps her entire thesis—and that of the ideological movement she represents—can be summed up by this statement:

Although there are many things to draw on in our past, there is no one family form that has ever protected people from poverty or social disruption, and no traditional arrangement that provides a workable model for how we might organize family relations in the modern world.[22]

Predictably, she joins the chorus attacking sitcom straw men: "1950's family strategies and values offer no solution to the discontents that underlie contemporary romanticization of the 'good old days.' Contrary to popular opinion, 'Leave it to Beaver' was not a documentary."[23]

The depth of the philosophical disagreement on the family can be seen in a further look at Senator Moynihan's statements on family. Despite his early and courageous recognition of the consequences of family breakdown, he, too, denies the existence of a specific "form" that is recognizable as *family*:

It would be enough for a national family policy to declare that the American government sought to promote the stability and well-being of the American family;

. . . and that the President, or some person designated by him, would report to the Congress on the condition of the American family in all its many facets—not of THE American family, for there is as yet no such thing, but rather of the great range of American family modes in terms of regions, national origins, and economic status.[24]

This debate over the value of the family and its place in society is nothing new. Nevertheless, at times, we retread ground that has proven sterile in the past, unwisely failing to learn from history.

Sociologists tell us that an almost inescapable component of the growth of modernity is a corollary rise in individualism. This has certainly been true in our own society. And individualism has had a marked effect on family life. Problems arise when "the sacredness of the family" is replaced by "the sacredness of the individual."[25] Harvard sociologist Carle Zimmerman has identified cycles of two or three generations where individualism has replaced an emphasis on family,[26] including eight major periods in Western history in which the family was viewed as old-fashioned. In each of these times, society began valuing the individual over the concerns of the family as a unit. The results in each instance led to societal decay.

Examples of the failure of individualism include the Greek and Roman societies in the third century B.C. and the fourth century A.D., respectively. Greek society in the third century B.C. engendered the collapse of the patriarchal family, leading to an emphasis on the indi-

22. Stephanie Coontz, *The Way We Never Were* (New York: Basic Books, 1992), 5.
23. Coontz, *The Way We Never Were*, 29.

24. Moynihan, *Family and Nation*, 11.
25. Don McNally, "The Family in History," *Vanguard* (September/October 1980), 13.
26. McNally, "The Family in History," 13–14; citing Carle Zimmerman, *The Family of Tomorrow* (1949) and Christopher Dawson, *The Dynamics of World History*.

Judith Stacey, author of Brave New Families, *says: "The 'family' is not here to stay. All democratic people, whatever their kinship preferences, should work to hasten its demise."*

vidual and devotion to public life that resulted in late marriages and small families. The final cultural breakdown led to Roman conquest. The Roman Empire in the fourth century A.D. made the same mistake, resulting in its fall.[27]

GOVERNMENT'S INFLUENCE ON THE FAMILY

As we approach the twenty-first century, the family and the government are in an uneasy alliance in America. Forward movement, however, has become a wobble rather than a smooth progression as the balance between family and government has been shaken askew. A battle rages—sometimes quietly, sometimes with guns blazing—as those who would increase the power of government jockey for position with those who resist in favor of family autonomy. David Blankenhorn, in looking at these combatants, gives this analysis:

There is a particularly sterile argument about the role of government. The traditional argument between left and right has been over the size of government. The conservatives want less, the liberals want more, and that's the perennial argument. The debate regarding families is not really, should government be smaller or larger. What matters is the relationship of public policy to family well-being. What is the distribution of costs and benefits to families and what is the message of public policy about what

we value and what we devalue about the importance of family in this society.[28]

The central question remains: Do we value families? While their role in strengthening society should be undisputed, it is not. The family is indispensable in the formation and continuity of a strong and stable society. Even in the face of those who view the family as irrelevant, the family stands on its own, with its own intrinsic strength. So much so, in fact, that some recognize the superiority of family over government in accomplishing societal goals.

The real battle is with those who see the family as competition and threat. Witness Judith Stacey, author of *Brave New Families*: "The 'family' is not here to stay. Nor should we wish it were. On the contrary, I believe that all democratic people, whatever their kinship preferences, should work to hasten its demise."[29]

Although Stacey's sentiments are based on the overarching philosophy of individualism, her conclusions fall in line with those who have, throughout history, seen the interests of family as diametrically opposed to those of society—and come down on the side of an omniscient, paternalistic government. Plato, Marx, Hitler, Stalin—all in their own way recognized the strength of the family. But rather than viewing that strength as a basis upon which to build a thriving, vital society, they sought to control and dampen its vibrancy.

History has proven the bankruptcy of opposition to the family. The way forward for individuals and for the nation is in rebuilding and reemphasizing the family. The society that does so will, in the doing, become stronger.

---

27. McNally, "The Family in History," 13–14; citing Carle Zimmerman, *The Family of Tomorrow* (1949) and Christopher Dawson, *The Dynamics of World History.*

28. David Blankenhorn, "The Relationship of Public Policy to Family Well-Being," *American Family* (August 1988), 3.

29. As cited by David Popenoe, "The Controversial Truth: Two-Parent Families Are Better," *New York Times,* 16 Dec. 1992, 21.

HONOR THY CHILDREN

Nearly 2 of every 5 kids in America do not live with their fathers. Now, a movement is growing to repair the damage and reconnect dads to their children

Dad is destiny. More than virtually any other factor, a biological father's presence in the family will determine a child's success and happiness. Rich or poor, white or black, the children of divorce and those born outside marriage struggle through life at a measurable disadvantage, according to a growing chorus of social thinkers. And their voices are more urgent because an astonishing 38 percent of all kids now live without their biological fathers—up from just 17.5 percent in 1960. More than half of today's children will spend at least part of childhood without a father.

These new critics challenge the view that external forces like street crime, lousy schools and economic stress lie behind the crisis in families. The revised thinking is that it's the breakdown of families that feeds social ills. "Fatherlessness is the most destructive trend of our generation," argues David Blankenhorn, author of a provocative new book *Fatherless America: Confronting Our Most Urgent Social Problem.*

U.S. News poll of 1,000 adults designed by Celinda Lake of Lake Research and Ed Goeas of the Tarrance Group and conducted by Market Facts' TELENATION survey Feb. 10–12, 1995. Margin of error: Plus or minus 3 points.

The absence of fathers is linked to most social nightmares—from boys with guns to girls with babies. No welfare reform plan can cut poverty as thoroughly as a two-parent family. Some 46 percent of families with children headed by single mothers live below the poverty line, compared with 8 percent of those with two parents. Raising marriage rates will do far more to fight crime than building prisons or putting more cops on the streets. Studies show that only 43 percent of state prison inmates grew up with both parents and that a missing father is a better predictor of criminal activity than race or poverty. Growing up with both parents turns out to be a better antidote to teen pregnancy than handing out condoms. Sociologists Sara McLanahan and Gary Sandefur say in their recent book, *Growing Up With a Single Parent,* that young women who were reared in disrupted families are twice as likely to become teen mothers. Social scientists have made similar links between a father's absence and his child's likelihood of being a dropout, jobless, a drug addict, a suicide victim, mentally ill and a target of child sexual abuse.

Bringing the issue into sharp focus are some brutal realities. Only 51 percent of kids still live with both biological parents. There were some 1.2 million divorces last year, about 53 percent of which involved minor children. In addition, 68 percent of black children and 30 percent of all kids are born outside of marriage. There are places in America where fathers—usually the best hope to socialize boys—are so rare that bedlam engulfs the community. Teachers, ministers, cops and other substitute authority figures fight losing battles in these places against gang members to present role models to preteen and teenage boys. The result is often an astonishing level of violence and incomprehensible incidents of brutality.

Americans know this and increasingly yearn for children to have more protection. Fully 71 percent of those surveyed by *U.S. News* said it is "very important" for "every child to have his or her father living at home" and nearly 8 in 10 think both fathers and mothers should spend more time with their kids. Some 58 percent say it should be harder for couples with children to get a divorce. That's a position Vice President Al Gore wouldn't endorse. But in an interview with *U.S. News*, the administration's leading spokesman on the fatherhood issue laments the number of parents who won't "tough out" troubled marriages.

Most Americans reject the harshest solution advocated by some conservatives: encouraging unwed mothers to put their children up for adoption by two-parent families. Seventy percent of those in the *U.S. News* survey said that when children are born to single mothers, it is "preferable for them to be raised by their mothers" than in a two-parent adoptive family.

It seems simple enough to say every child needs a father. But must Daddy be a biological, married and in-residence paterfamilias, as Blankenhorn and his allies insist? These "new traditionalists" argue that the odds are overwhelming against a divorced dad or a father substitute. For proof, they argue that 18 million children should be entitled to $34 billion more in child support from noncustodial parents (about 90 percent of whom are fathers). Even the lucky child who sees his or her dad at least once a week—just 1 child in 6—often winds up with a "treat dad" for weekend movies, not a father to offer constant guidance and discipline.

It even turns out that the fairy tales contain germs of truth about stepparents. Youngsters in stepfamilies do no better, and often fare even worse, than children in homes headed by a single parent, according to several recent studies. Stepparents often bring needed income, but that advantage is offset by the emotional rivalries among parents and children in stepfamilies.

Finally, the new traditionalists dispute the idea that kids are worse off when stuck in their parents' lousy marriages. Divorce can increase an adult's happiness, but it is devastating to a child, says psychologist Judith Wallerstein, who has studied her child clients since 1971. One third report moderate or severe depression five years after a divorce. The hurt may remain hidden for years. They often grow up wary of love, marriage and family, and over a third have little or no ambition 10 years after their parents part. "Divorce is not just an episode in a child's life," notes Wallerstein. "It's like a natural disaster that really changes the whole trajectory of a child's life."

Blankenhorn, founder of the New York-based Institute for American Values, says action must be taken to slow family breakups. The "logic" of his argument, he says, may lead to steps like ending no-fault divorce and encouraging more single mothers to give up children for adoption. (Adoptive parents are the exception to his preference for biological ones.) He also urges that access to sperm banks be denied to unmarried women.

Blankenhorn and his allies are struggling against another group—call them fatherhood "reinventors"—who say it is wrongheaded to stigmatize absent fathers. Millions try to be good dads, And most children of divorce, despite the added

risks, turn out fine. Besides, reinventors argue, high divorce rates result from irreversible cultural shifts that are best to accommodate rather than battle—like the economic independence of working women who no longer get stuck in abusive marriages. Reinventors say the solution is to build a network of support to help all fathers including separated fathers or father figures, be involved in children's lives. Family-friendly workplaces, parenting classes and wider visitation rights are among the answers. Says Richard Louv, author of *Father Love:* "We need all the fathers we can get."

These skirmishes show that fatherhood itself is in transition. Inside marriage, there is confusion as fathers are no longer a family's clear-cut breadwinner, the traditional role of a patriarch. Some blame "feminism," like the evangelical Christian Promise Keepers, a burgeoning grass-roots movement that wants to bring a million men to Washington next year to proclaim their desire to be "godly" leaders of their families. Yet, others thank feminism for showing them a more satisfying model of parenting.

Unfortunately, even the most earnest attempts to strengthen fatherhood, whether they come from traditionalists or reinventors, seem destined for limited success. A close look at such efforts suggests just how hard it will be to find policies to decrease divorce or to make AWOL fathers less distant.

CAN WE RECONNECT FATHERS?

In Cleveland's Hough neighborhood, social worker Charles Ballard meets young men who have attended scores of funerals but few, if any, weddings. There are children, he says, who grow up not knowing the proper finger for wearing a wedding ring. But the 58-year-old Ballard—abandoned by his own father at age 3 and a father himself at 17—has overcome inner-city Cleveland's bleak economic and emotional landscape to teach poor fathers that the key to being a man is to be a good father.

Since 1982, Ballard's Institute for Responsible Fatherhood and Family Revitalization has worked to reconnect over 2,000 absent fathers with their children. Ballard does it through an intensive social-work approach—visiting the homes of his clients and referring them to parenting classes, drug abuse programs or GED courses. But Ballard's approach is also radical. He turns on its head the usual assumption that men cannot be responsible parents if they cannot find jobs. Convince young men first of the importance of being good fathers, Ballard argues, and they are then motivated to finish school and find work. Social workers have long known that teen mothers are

most likely to complete school, get off drugs or find a job when they see it as a way of protecting their child.

Alonzo Warren proves the point. The unemployed 31-year-old father of six children by six different women was referred to Ballard when he went to the county seeking custody of his 9-year-old son, who was in the care of a relative. Although Warren's new job, cooking hamburgers at a nearby fast-food restaurant, pays just the minimum wage, his steady source of income puts him in a stronger position to persuade county social workers to allow him overnight visitations with his son as well as to do more to support his other young children. "All the guys I know, even though we're not living with our kids, not a single day goes by when we don't worry about them," says Warren. "Even with our faults, they need us."

A study by Case Western Reserve University political science professors G. Regina Nixon and Anthony King shows that Ballard's one-on-one program, which lets fathers take the initiative in solving their own problems, gets some often astonishing results. Ninety-seven percent of the men began providing financial support for their children; 71 percent did not have any more children outside of marriage; only 12 percent had full-time work when they entered, but 62 percent found such work and 12 percent got part-time jobs. There was one glaring shortcoming: The program had less impact on marriage rates. Just 1 in 5 of the participants married. Although the study sample was small, the results persuaded the Ford Foundation to give Ballard a $400,000 grant to try to replicate his success in 14 other cities later this year.

Still, there are questions as to whether what works in Cleveland will work elsewhere. Ballard is a charismatic visionary whose day-to-day presence may be decisive. And other localities may balk at Ballard's insistence that his staffers neither drink nor smoke nor be homosexual.

Other experiments around the country show that it is not easy to match scarce jobs to unskilled workers. Parents' Fair Share, a multimillion-dollar federal demonstration program that began in nine cities in 1992, requires noncustodial fathers of children on welfare to attend employment training when they cannot afford to pay child support. Early results showed that, overall, only 22 percent of those referred to the program reported any employment. But peer support training sessions did appear to rekindle the fathers' desire to do right by their kids.

Other fathers similarly yearn for more of a role in their kids' lives. Many men, particularly those in fathers' rights groups, push for joint custody. Although these arrangements remain rare, 90 percent of fathers in them pay child support, which is about triple the national average. Men who feel they have a significant role in the lives of their sons and daughters spend more time with them and pay more child support. Still, three quarters of mothers oppose joint custody, which complicates their own parenting by giving ex-husbands decision-making power.

SHOULD DIVORCE BE HARDER?

It is still a mystery why divorce rates doubled in the decade after the early 1960s. But Illinois State Rep. Bernard Pedersen blames the introduction of no-fault divorce laws that let an unhappy spouse end a marriage unchallenged. So Pedersen, wed 45 years himself, proposed a law that would let marrying couples choose to put fault back in divorce. The effort failed. So did attempts in states like Florida and Washington, indicating that although it might cut the number of divorces, Americans have no interest in returning to the days when wives hired private detectives or even a surrogate blond to catch philandering husbands.

Instead, most efforts have focused on teaching divorcing parents to get along for the sake of the kids. In a soft voice, 8-year-old Kaitlyn talks of her pain when her parents separated. "I felt really sad because I thought it was something that happened to other people," she says, nervously swinging her legs, which do not reach the hotel ballroom floor under her chair. She is one of several children, ages 8 to 28, who tell their stories to groups of Maryland parents seeking divorce. Often the soft sobbing of a parent is the only other sound in the room.

The sessions are a part of the most popular trend in family courts today: parenting courses for divorcing adults. Not intended to stop divorce, the classes simply show parents how to put their children's needs first. Connecticut and Utah require them for all divorcing adults, and more than 100 courts elsewhere do the same. (One Chicago court, however, ruled it unconstitutional to force unwilling parents to attend.) Studies show that parents come away more aware of divorce's impact on their youngsters, but there is no proof yet that fathers increase the frequency of their visits or support payments.

And courses that typically last two to six hours can do little to change a lifetime of problems, notes psychologist Sanford Braver. "They do a good job of selling the idea that for the sake of the children, it's important to get along," says the Arizona State University professor, who surveyed such programs. "But getting parents to put aside hurts and jealousies and carry it

off is another matter." Divorced dad Ed Cushman, 52, and his daughter Lora, 24, tell parents to "never give up" trying to get along. Ed dropped by the pizza parlor where Lora worked every week for a year until she would open up to a reconciliation. Both agree their relationship is better now than before the divorce. Still, father and daughter, who participate in panels sponsored by the Children of Separation and Divorce Center in Columbia, Md., repaired their relationship only after years of counseling.

Edwin Smithers of Connecticut says a similar class improved his parenting, too. However, his wife and three daughters moved across country and now, Smithers says, it is his stepsons who benefit from his new skills. He thinks the same classes, earlier, might have saved his marriage. "Parent training should be required, the way we require driver's training before you get a driver's license," he says.

CAN MARRIAGE BE TAUGHT?

"God hates divorce," says Michael McManus, citing Scripture (Malachi 2:16). Churches, says the author of *Marriage Savers,* can best take the lead in reversing the divorce rate. McManus has persuaded ministers in 28 cities to require engaged couples to undergo lengthy relationship counseling before marriage—three quarters of Americans marry in churches—and to train older couples to mentor the younger ones about how to resolve conflict. Amy and Jeff Olson took the marriage preparation course McManus runs at the Fourth Presbyterian Church in Bethesda, Md., and credit it with getting their marriage off to a firm start by resolving their differences over money management.

The Catholic Church has long practiced such premarital counseling. And it prohibits divorce. So it is not surprising that Massachusetts, the second-most-heavily-Catholic state, has the lowest divorce rate. McManus thinks the fact that some 75 Peoria, Ill., ministers adopted his idea has something to do with the fact that the number of divorces there fell from 1,210 in 1991 to 984 in 1994. But he notes that couples in Peoria often avoid such counseling by going to a minister who does not require it. Churches can also help long-married couples strengthen relationships. Yet the Marriage Encounter weekend retreats, which once attracted 100,000 couples a year, now get only 15,000. McManus attributes that to spouses' reluctance to probe trouble spots in their marriages.

Conservatives tend not to trust schools to teach family values. Largely unnoticed, however, is that high schools have become the new academies of parent training. Such classes are already a grad-

uation requirement in at least eight states, including California, Delaware, Michigan, New Jersey, New York, Tennessee, Vermont and Virginia, notes Jan Bowers of the Home Economics Education Association. And, another surprise, it is being taught in home economics classes. Home ec, now called family and consumer science, is not cooking and sewing anymore. Nor is it just for girls: Boys make up 42 percent of the students.

Two years ago, rural Anna, Ohio (population 1,164), made parenting class a requirement for high school students. Although these boys may be many years from fatherhood, teacher Joanne Ansley notes that lessons in discipline or child development come in handy to the basketball star who coaches a youth team or the 16-year-old whose baby brother asks so many annoying questions.

Small-town Anna has its share of big-town problems. Town ministers welcomed the parenting curriculum, in part, to stop early pregnancies. Students get a smack of reality when drawing up family budgets or visiting the nearby Wilson Memorial Hospital to watch a film on childbirth. "A lot of people in Anna marry and have kids right out of high school, but the course helped me realize just how big of a responsibility fatherhood is," says Tony Albers, 17, who says he now plans to finish college and wait "at least until I'm 25" to start a family.

Blankenhorn, however, doubts that fatherhood can be taught. It is a complicated, lifelong endeavor. "Parenting is not like plumbing or carpentering," he says. "It's not a set of techniques. It depends on a human identity." Some boys seem too young to take the lessons seriously, and there is a good deal of adolescent horseplay on any given day in class. Moreover, precedents are not encouraging. Sex education was also intended to change behavior. But classroom lessons, no matter how well taught, are often forgotten in real-life situations, as is clear from rising teen pregnancy rates.

CAN WE SUPPORT FATHERHOOD?

Valente Jimenez knows plenty about machines. He is a mechanic who fixes air-conditioning units for the Los Angeles Department of Water and Power. After his wife gave birth, a company nurse instructed Jimenez how to work a device he didn't know much about: a breast pump. The company lent the electric breast pump, one of 90 it bought for its employees—80 percent of whom are men.

"Management sees this as an investment, as a good business strategy," notes company work-family specialist Kimberlee Vandenakker. She cites reduced job turnover and absenteeism since LADWP began its fathering program. Among other services to dads: LADWP lends beepers to expectant fathers working on power lines and other remote job sites; it sets up mentoring sessions with other fathers; it started a child-care center and offers unpaid paternity leave.

Most companies remain reluctant to offer such programs to mothers, much less to fathers. And men are even more reluctant to ask for father-friendly policies, says James Levine of the Families and Work Institute, who calls LADWP's program "the single best" for dads. Under the new federal family-leave law, many working fathers are eligible for 12 weeks of unpaid parental leave, but it is the rare man who takes it. Moms usually prefer to be the one to take off, Levine says, because it is expected, they need to recover physically or breast-feed, or because their husbands bring home bigger paychecks.

At LADWP, most who take advantage of the fathers' policies come from white-collar jobs. Supervisors have more flexible schedules, and there is still the "macho" factor for some blue-collar workers. Jimenez's family was surprised when he agreed to care for his baby while his wife, Jeanne, took a four-day trip to visit family in Texas. Jimenez said the example of other fathers at work convinced him. "I come from a Hispanic family, and we didn't do that kind of stuff," he says. "But this program has opened my eyes."

Virtually all sides in the debate now agree that such changes in attitudes are the first and best hope for repairing fatherhood. The campaign to fight fatherlessness will be waged over a long period, much the same way campaigns worked to convince drivers that they should not drink or smokers that cigarettes ruin health. Government programs won't have nearly the impact as numberless one-on-one encounters over a lifetime between men and kids. Both the White House and House Republicans, for example, want to give parents a $500-per-child tax credit. While money helps, most family experts say there is no evidence that such policies directly influence decisions as personal as marriage and childbearing. Of course, there are partisan stakes in this fight. The *U.S. News* poll found that Americans trust Republicans more than Democrats—37 to 32 percent—to help make families stronger.

But most see the issue in transcendent terms. As Hillary Rodham Clinton told *U.S. News* last week: "It's difficult for fathers to put aside their own aspirations about their own lives," but one who can "put his child first . . . is giving a great gift to a child." Real progress will come only when there is renewed conviction, as Blankenhorn argues, that "being a loving father and a good husband is the best part of being a man."

BY JOSEPH P. SHAPIRO AND JOANNIE M. SCHROF WITH MIKE THARP IN LOS ANGELES AND DORIAN FRIEDMAN

Growing Up against the Odds

Despite billions of federal dollars, America's children face an uncertain and bleak future.

ROBERT ROYAL

Robert Royal is vice president of the Ethics and Public Policy Center, Washington, D.C.

Childhood used to be a time of relative security and innocence in America. Most children passed their lives in stable families that, despite their economic ups and downs, provided their .young members with the kind of affection and discipline needed to become mature and responsible adults.

Neighbors, churches, and schools reinforced family lessons. Sex, drugs, and violence were only a distant threat. And children were given a chance to develop physically, emotionally, intellectually, and spiritually before entering the hard, adult world that all of us eventually must face.

It certainly is no longer the case for far too many young people, whose future is America's future. The kind of childhood that many people now living can still remember did not just happen naturally. It was a civilizational achievement.

Prior to relatively modern times, children were basically regarded as young adults. Though they were not often exposed to the kinds of social pathologies children commonly encounter today, they were set to work as soon as they were able and received little formal schooling except at the higher social levels. For mostly agrarian, premodern societies, this system worked well enough. It promoted stability and social integration for the young, but it also entailed almost complete social immobility.

Modern societies have provided unprecedented social and economic opportunities for ever-wider groups of people. But they imposed some new requirements on families and children. Childhood in early bourgeois democracies became easier in many ways.

Children went to school instead of to the fields. Childhood development—with its suddenly proliferating special dimensions—took on new importance. Early life experiences became far more crucial to the new open societies since they could no longer rely on automatic training of children for work or their moral formation as responsible citizens. Yet the risks were amply rewarded.

What several historians have called the "invention of childhood"—the cultural creation of a period specially set aside from practical worries—meant a liberation for millions of children in the middle and lower classes to grow into the productive and prosperous adults their talents and ambitions suited them to be.

Some scholars have tried to dispute the sometimes overidyllic picture that has been painted of Victorian and early twentieth-century family life. To a certain extent, they are right to do so. No doubt, families during those times suffered from the full range of human sins and weaknesses. But as families operating under modern conditions, and as special enclaves for children being prepared for full participation in adult life—with its high demands for good work habits, vocational skills, and general knowledge—they were generally far healthier and effective socializing institutions than what we often are forced to call families today.

It used to be fashionable among radicals to criticize families for their narrow bourgeois values and patriarchal oppression. Now that we have had the full experience of what the absence of the limited but necessary bourgeois values and disciplines can mean for children's lives in modern societies, bourgeois respectability does not seem so bad, particularly given the frightening alternatives that have emerged.

Typically, what we now have are children growing up not only outside bourgeois exhortations to productivity, regular work habits, and religiosity, but children forced to grow up before they have had any real formation at all.

There is a difference between giving a young child the responsibilities of tending sheep (rigorous, but no moral danger) and exposing a young child to the now common dangers of drugs, sex, and violence (for many, the premature death of childhood). Premodern children, even if they were treated harshly by modern standards, still existed within the horizon of the adult world of responsibility and realism. But postmodern children often confront adult problems without benefit of adult supervision or sufficient emotional and moral maturity to make good decisions on their own.

Decline, by the numbers

What has all this meant? Many different things. But there are some concrete measures of what has happened to children in recent decades that show us to be, if not in a full social crisis, at least in the grips of something quite alarming.

In a now-famous story, *U.S. News & World Report* a few years ago went back to teacher surveys in the 1940s and discovered that the most serious public school disciplinary problems then in their order of importance were: talking out of turn, gum chewing, making noise, running in the halls,

Major Problems

* By the year 2000, 40 percent of all American births are expected to occur out of wedlock.

* Since 1960, the rate at which teenagers take their own lives has more than tripled.

* About 20 percent of teenage girls will have at least one abortion by age 20.

* Of all age-groups, children are the most likely to be poor.

cutting into lines, improper dress, and littering.

In 1990, a similar teacher survey revealed the most serious problems to be: drugs, alcohol, pregnancy, suicide, rape, robbery, and assault—this during one of the greatest expansions of expenditures on education at all levels in the history of America and perhaps the world. Whatever had happened for the good in those 50 years, some unprecedented evil had happened to the environment of schoolchildren.

That societal shift had effects outside of school as well. Take suicide. For most of us, childhood and adolescence were times of happiness and exuberance, but also inevitably times of stress, of finding out who we are and where we fit into the world. These stresses have led to suicide attempts at any age, either because of personal or social problems or medical conditions.

The medical conditions, we may assume, are less of a problem than ever before. Yet teenage suicide rates have gone from 3.6 per 100,000 in 1960 to 11.3 in 1990. Young males are far more likely—five times more likely—to commit suicide than young females.

But young males do not only direct lethal violence toward themselves. Rates of arrests of

juveniles for violent crimes (mostly males) have closely paralleled the suicide rate, more than tripling between 1965 and 1990. Murders by young blacks doubled over the same period.

A factor that may explain a good portion of these phenomena is that 70 percent of juveniles in long-term correctional facilities grew up in homes without fathers. Compared with the murder, mayhem, and disorder of "alternative" families, the rigors of the old "patriarchal" family were mere kid stuff.

But absent fathers are far from being the only alarming parental problem. Somewhere between six and seven million schoolchildren come home every day to a house with no adult present at all—many in far from ideal, inner-city neighborhoods. Various problems naturally stem from this lack of supervision. One of the worst is that many teenage pregnancies, according to good survey data, get started in those after-school hours.

Like the other juvenile pathologies, rates of teen pregnancy and abortion have been soaring. In 1972, already a high year relative to previous decades, almost 5 out of every 100 teenage girls got pregnant in America. By 1990, the rate had zoomed to almost 10 out of 100. Put in concrete figures, probably more than a million unmarried American teenagers get pregnant every year, and of those about 40 percent have abortions.

When this yearly toll is added up and the consequences tallied for the whole of American society at any given moment, it is easy to see why illegitimacy, school dropout rates, young women in poverty as heads of households, violent crimes, and drug use by undisciplined youths—all mutually reinforcing and self-perpetuating pathologies—have become the most nationally pressing social problems.

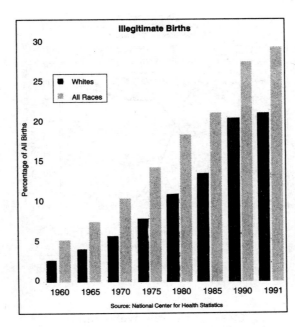

Illegitimate Births

Whites
All Races

Percentage of All Births

1960 1965 1970 1975 1980 1985 1990 1991

Source: National Center for Health Statistics

By the time we get down to an inner-city woman who has to bring up one or more children—sometimes adolescent boys who need the presence of a father—in a rough neighborhood and add that she probably has to work long hours to support the family, all elements are present for a variety of mishaps.

This is not meant to be criticism of poor black women or women on welfare. It is a mere description of the challenges and potential failures that anyone, white or black, Hispanic or Asian, faces when the supplementary systems of families have disappeared. Statistical surveys have shown that children from all races and ethnic groups placed in the same circumstances of family breakdown and poverty tend to exhibit the same problems.

Causes and effects

The causes of all this are complex—but not so complex that we cannot discern and try to do something about them. Family breakdown is probably the area most Americans now agree poses the greatest threat to public life.

With a divorce rate of nearly 50 percent and illegitimacy rates of about 22 percent for whites and 68 for blacks (for a national average of around 30 percent), most children now come into the world with a handicap unprecedented in any culture on earth at any period of human history: no stable family to speak of. All the attempts to redefine and expand the notion of family in order to avoid stigmatizing people cannot get around this plain fact.

Radical feminists and advocates of alternative life-styles have tried, for example, to make it appear that the rise of the euphemistically designated "female-headed household" is a perfectly viable alternative to old patriarchal, male-headed, two-parent families. This is, at best, dangerously misleading.

Certainly many single women are heroic and successful parents and should be com-

mended for their achievements. But they should not be recommended as models for others, not yet parents, to imitate. Nor can the risky business of single parenting be simply equated with two-parent or extended families. The documented results just do not support the contention.

Every pathological tendency in the culture has been visited on our children at earlier and earlier ages in recent decades. And we can see from the data that all social classes have been affected by it to a greater or lesser extent. The general breakdown in public morals, for example, has led to cheating in school at massively higher levels than ever before.

Paradoxically, cheating seems to be more widespread among middle- and upper-class children than among their poorer counterparts. Aside from that exception, the poorer and more vulnerable sectors of the society have been hit the hardest by social pathologies—as is always the case. Wealthier people living in more stable communities just have more layers of correction and insulation built into the social fabric.

Riding the Third Wave

This breakdown could not have come at a worse time in American history. When America was still a predominantly agricultural or industrial nation, there were many jobs for men and women with limited or minimal skills. Lack of formal training in school or even an ability to read were not serious disqualifications for a host of honorable ways to earn a living.

Today, the mainstream of the economy requires literacy and specialized skills. One sign of where we are headed: A report in April 1995 documented that only about one-third of high school graduates are proficient in reading. The next third are below proper levels, and the final third are functionally illiterate.

Without some effort to redress this problem through remedial programs or other means, two-thirds of the teenagers graduating from high school every year in America will be unsuited for the primary work force.

Alvin and Heidi Toffler have recently described the new information society in which we are now living as the Third Wave, replacing the Second Wave of the industrial society, which in turn had replaced the First Wave of agricultural societies. They and their most famous admirer, House Speaker Newt Gingrich, are optimistic that the Third Wave will provide new opportunities that will naturally lead the young into a new age.

The Tofflers also regard the old nuclear family as appropriate for Second Wave industrialization, but—far too blithely—as only one of many viable family forms for the Third Wave. They may be right that other kinds of "families" will be common in the brave new world aborning. All the evidence we have so far, however, indicates that the welfare state cannot substitute for the family.

"Alternative" families, even at best, are equally unlikely to do well by children except for some rare and very lucky individuals. No amount of Third Wave opportunities alone, especially absent nurturing families across the social spectrum, will offset the continuing damage being done to children at present.

Some social critics, such as the writer Mickey Kaus in his provocative book *The End of Equality,* have argued more plausibly that, without some major changes, we may be on our way to a two-tiered society:

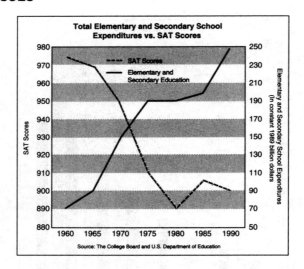

Total Elementary and Secondary School Expenditures vs. SAT Scores

- - - - SAT Scores
—— Elementary and Secondary Education

SAT Scores

Elementary and Secondary School Expenditures (in constant 1989 billion dollars)

Source: The College Board and U.S. Department of Education

those from relatively intact families who are literate and participate in the social and economic mainstream, and a large mass of virtually illiterate proletarians who will be forced into low-paying, menial jobs largely without benefits like health-care insurance and retirement plans.

An America where two-thirds of the work force is a distant second class economically is not the America the Founding Fathers or our contemporary public culture would think tolerable. Nor is it likely to remain stable for long.

Restoring childhood and adulthood

Many of the people who fail in modern societies as adults do so because they never had the time and place to be children. Our kind of society makes high

What we now have are children growing up not only outside regular work habits, and religiosity, but children forced to grow up before they have had any real formation at all.

demands and provides high rewards for adults.

But adulthood, except for retraining as society and the economy change, is usually not an optimum time for learning the things we usually learn better as children. Paradoxically, in the time of protection and innocence, we learn responsibility and common sense.

The habits of our first two decades have to carry us for the rest of a lifetime. Unless we find a way to make childhood possible again—either through a moral regeneration that restores the family or (far less likely) through alternative institutions—not only will we be destroying our children's present and future, but we may be concocting a dismal prospect for ourselves as well.

Why Leave Children With Bad Parents?

Family: Last year, 1,300 abused kids died—though authorities knew that almost half were in danger. Is it time to stop patching up dead-end families?

MICHELE INGRASSIA AND JOHN MCCORMICK

THE REPORT OF DRUG PEDdling was already stale, but the four Chicago police officers decided to follow up anyway. As they knocked on the door at 219 North Keystone Avenue near midnight on Feb. 1, it was snowing, and they held out little hope of finding the pusher they were after. They didn't. What they discovered, instead, were 19 children living in horrifying squalor. Overnight, the Dickensian images of life inside the apartment filled front pages and clogged network airwaves.

For the cops that night, it seemed like a scavenger hunt gone mad, each discovery yielding a new, more stunning, find. In the dining room, police said, a half-dozen children lay asleep on a bed, their tiny bodies intertwined like kittens. On the floor beside them, two toddlers tussled with a mutt over a bone they had grabbed from the dog's dish. In the living room, four others huddled on a hardwood floor, crowded beneath a single blanket. "We've got eight or nine kids here," Officer John Labiak announced.

Officer Patricia Warner corrected him: "I count 12." The cops found the last of 19 asleep under a mound of dirty clothes; one 4-year-old, gnarled by cerebral palsy, bore welts and bruises.

As the police awaited reinforcements, they could take full measure of the filth that engulfed this brigade of 1- to 14-year-olds. Above, ceiling plaster crumbled. Beneath their feet, roaches scurried around clumps of rat droppings. But nothing was more emblematic than the kitchen. The stove was inoperable, its oven door yawning wide. The sink held fetid dishes that one cop said "were not from that day, not from that week, maybe not from this year." And though the six mothers living there collected a total of $4,500 a month in welfare and food stamps, there was barely any food in the house. Twice last year, a caseworker from the Illinois Department of Children and Family Services (DCFS) had come to the apartment to follow up reports of serious child neglect, but when no one would let her in, the worker left. Now, it took hours to sort through the mess. Finally, the

police scooped up the children and set out for a state-run shelter. As they left, one little girl looked up at Warner and pleaded, "Will you be my mommy?"

Don't bet on it. Next month the children's mothers—Diane Melton, 31; Maxine Melton, 27; May Fay Melton, 25; Denise Melton, 24; Casandra Melton, 21, and Denise Turner, 20—will appear in Cook County juvenile court for a hearing to determine if temporary custody of the children should remain with the state or be returned to the parents. Yet, for all the public furor, confidential files show that the DCFS is privately viewing the 19 children in the same way it does most others—"Goal: Return Home."

Why won't we take kids from bad parents? For more than a decade, the idea that parents should lose neglected or abused kids has been blindsided by a national policy to keep families together at almost any cost. As a result, even in the worst cases, states regularly opt for reunification. Even in last year's budget-cutting frenzy, Congress earmarked nearly $1 billion for family-preservation programs over the next five years. Yet there is mounting evidence that such efforts make little difference—and may make things worse. "We've oversold the fact that all families can be saved," says Marcia Robinson Lowry, head of the Children's Rights Project of the American Civil Liberties Union. "All families *can't* be saved."

Last year there were 1 million confirmed

cases of abuse and neglect. And, according to the American Public Welfare Association, an estimated 462,000 children were in substitute care, nearly twice as many as a decade ago. The majority of families can be repaired if parents clean up their acts, but experts are troubled by what happens when they don't: 42 percent of the 1,300 kids who died as a result of abuse last year had previously been reported to child-protection agencies. "The child-welfare system stands over the bodies, shows you pictures of the caskets and still does things to keep kids at risk," says Richard Gelles, director of the University of Rhode Island's Family Violence Research Program.

Nowhere has the debate over when to break up families been more sharply focused than in Illinois, which, in the last two years, has had some of the most horrific cases in the nation. Of course, it's not alone. But unlike many states, Illinois hasn't been able to hide its failures behind the cloak of confidentiality laws, largely because of Patrick Murphy, Cook County's outspoken public guardian, who regularly butts heads with the state over its aggressive reunification plans. The cases have turned Illinois into a sounding board for what to do about troubled families.

The Chicago 19 lived in what most people would consider a troubled home. But to veterans of the city's juvenile courts, it's just another "dirty house" case. In fact, Martin Shapiro, the court-appointed attorney for Diane Melton, plans to say that conditions could have been worse. He can argue that Melton's children weren't malnourished, weren't physically or sexually abused and weren't left without adult supervision. He's blunt: "Returning children to a parent who used cocaine—as horrific as that might seem—isn't all that unusual in this building." If only all the cases were so benign.

What Went Wrong?

ON THE LAST NIGHT OF JOSEPH Wallace's life, no one could calm his mother's demons. Police say that Amanda Wallace was visiting relatives on April 18, 1993, with 3-year-old Joseph and his 1-year-old brother, Joshua, when she began raving that Joseph was nothing but trouble. "I'm gonna kill this bitch with a knife tonight," Bonnie Wallace later told police her daughter threatened. Bonnie offered to keep the boy overnight, but Amanda refused, so Bonnie drove them to their apartment on Chicago's impoverished West Side. It's unclear what forced Amanda's hand, but authorities tell a harrowing tale: at about 1:30 a.m., she stuffed a sock into Joseph's mouth and secured it with medical tape. Then she went to the kitchen, retrieved a brown extension cord and wrapped it around Joseph's neck several times. She carried her

son to the living room, stood him on a chair, then looped the cord around the metal crank arm over the door. In the last act of his life, Joseph waved goodbye.

Amanda Wallace, 28, has pleaded not guilty to charges of first-degree murder. No one ever doubted that Amanda was deeply troubled. When Joseph was born, she was a resident at the Elgin Mental Health Center in suburban Chicago, and a psychiatrist there warned that Amanda "should never have custody of this or any other baby." Three times, the DCFS removed Joseph from his mother. Yet three times, judges returned him to Amanda's dark world. Six months after the murder—which led to the firing of three DCFS employees—a blue-ribbon report blasted the Illinois child-welfare system, concluding that it had "surely consigned Joseph to his death."

Even in the most egregious instances of abuse, children go back to their parents time and again. In Cook County, the public guardian now represents 31,000 children. Only 963 kids were freed for adoption last year. But William Maddux, the new supervising judge of the county's abuse and neglect section, believes the number should have been as high as 6,000. Nationwide, experts say, perhaps a quarter of the children in substitute care should be taken permanently from their parents.

But it's not simply social custom that keeps families together, it's the law. The Adoption Assistance and Child Welfare Act of 1980 is a federal law with a simple goal—to keep families intact. The leverage: parents who don't make a "reasonable effort" to get their lives on track within 18 months risk losing their kids forever. The law itself was a reaction to the excesses of the '60s and '70s, when children were often taken away simply because their parents were poor or black. But the act was also one of those rare measures that conservatives and liberals embraced with equal passion—conservatives because it was cheap, liberals because it took blame away from the poor.

By the mid-'80s, though, the system began to collapse. A system built for a simpler time couldn't handle an exploding underclass populated by crack addicts, the homeless and the chronically unemployed. At the same time, orphanages began shutting their doors and foster families began quitting in droves. The system begged to know where to put so many kids. It opted for what was then a radical solution: keeping them in their own homes while offering their parents intensive, short-term support—child rearing, housekeeping and budgeting. But as family-preservation programs took off, the threat of severing the rights of abusive parents all but disappeared. What emerged, Gelles argues, was the naive philosophy that a mother who'd hurt her child is not much different from one who can't keep house—and that with enough supervi-

sion, both can be turned into good parents.

In hindsight, everyone in Chicago agrees that Joseph Wallace's death was preventable, that he died because the system placed a parent's rights above a child's. Amanda could never have been a "normal" parent. She had been a ward of the state since the age of 8, the victim of physical and sexual abuse. Between 1976 and Joseph's birth in 1989, her psychiatrist told the DCFS, she swallowed broken glass and batteries; she disemboweled herself, and when she was pregnant with Joseph, she repeatedly stuck soda bottles into her vagina, denying the baby was hers. Yet 11 months after Joseph was born, a DCFS caseworker and an assistant public defender persuaded a Cook County juvenile-court judge to give him back to Amanda, returning him from the one of the six foster homes he would live in. The judge dispatched Amanda with a blessing: "Good luck to you, Mother."

Over the next two years, caseworkers twice removed Joseph after Amanda attempted suicide. But a DCFS report, dated Oct. 31, 1992, said she had gotten an apartment in Chicago, entered counseling and worked as a volunteer for a community organization. And though the report noted her turbulent history, it recommended she and Joseph be reunited. Joseph Wallace was sent home for the last time 62 days before his death, by a judge who had no measure of Amanda's past. "Would somebody simply summarize what this case is about for me and give me an idea why you're all agreeing?" the judge asked. Amanda's lawyer sidestepped her mental history. Nevertheless, the DCFS and the public guardian's office signed on. When Amanda thanked the judge, he said, "It sounds like you're doing OK. Good luck."

Murphy says that deciding when to sever parents' rights should be obvious: "You remove kids if they're in a dangerous situation. No one should be taken from a cold house. But it's another thing when there are drugs to the ceiling and someone's screwing the kids." Ambiguous cases? "There haven't been gray cases in years."

No one knows that better than Faye and Michael Callahan, one of the foster families who cared for Joseph. When Joseph first came to them he was a happy, husky baby. When he returned after his first stretch with Amanda, "he had bald spots because he was pulling his hair out," Faye says. By the third time, she says, Joseph was "a zombie. He rocked for hours, groaning, 'Uh, uh, uh, uh'." The fact that he was repeatedly sent home still infuriates them. Says Michael: "I'd scream at those caseworkers, 'You're making a martyr of this little boy!'"

See No Evil, Hear No Evil

EARLY LAST THANKSGIVING, ARETHA McKinney brought her young son to the emergency room. Clifford Triplett was semiconscious, and his body was pocked with burns, bruises and other signs of abuse, police say. The severely malnourished boy weighed 17 pounds—15 percent less than the average 1-year-old. Except Clifford was 5.

This wasn't a secret. In a confidential DCFS file obtained by NEWSWEEK, a state caseworker who visited the family last June gave a graphic account of Clifford's life: "Child's room (porch) clothing piled in corner, slanted floor. Child appears isolated from family—every one else has a well furnished room. Child very small for age appears to be 2 years old. Many old scars on back and buttocks have many recent scratches." In April, another caseworker had confronted McKinney's live-in boyfriend, Eddie Robinson Sr., who claimed that Cliff was a "dwarf" and was suicidal—neither of which doctors later found to be true. Robinson added that Cliff got "whipped" because he got into mischief. "I told him that he shouldn't be beat on his back," the caseworker wrote. "Robinson promised to go easy on the discipline."

It's one thing to blame an anonymous "system" for ignoring abuse and neglect. But the real question is a human one: how can caseworkers walk into homes like Clifford's, document physical injury or psychological harm and still walk away? A Cook County juvenile-court judge ruled last month that both McKinney and Robinson had tortured Clifford (all but erasing the possibility that he'll ever be returned to his mother). But caseworkers are rarely so bold. In Clifford's case, the April worker concluded that abuse apparently had occurred, but nine days later another found the home "satisfactory." Says Gelles: "Caseworkers are programmed by everything around them to be deaf, dumb and blind because the system tells them, 'Your job is to work to reunification'."

Murphy charges that for the past two

SAONNIA BOLDEN

"The amount of stress and frustration has been reduced. Sadie appears to have a lot more patience with her children and she continues to improve her disciplinary techniques." The same day the worker wrote this, Sadie's daughter Saonnia died after boiling water was poured on her. An autopsy uncovered 62 injuries, many recent.

FROM CASEWORKER REPORT ON SAONNIA BOLDEN

years, Illinois has made it policy to keep new kids out of an already-clogged system. "The message went out that you don't aggressively investigate," he says. "Nobody said, 'Keep the ----ing cases out of the system'." But that, he says, is the net effect. "That's just not true," says Sterling Mac Ryder, who took over the DCFS late in 1992. But he doesn't dispute that the state and its caseworkers may have put too much emphasis on reunification—in part because of strong messages from Washington.

The problems may be even more basic. By all accounts, caseworkers and supervisors are less prepared today than they were 20 years ago, and only a fraction are actually social workers. Few on the front lines are willing, or able, to make tough calls or buck the party line. In the end, says Deborah Daro, research director of the National Committee to Prevent Child Abuse, "the worker may say, 'Yeah, it's bad, but what's the alternative? I'll let this one go and pray to God they don't kill him'."

In most cases, they don't. Nevertheless, children who grow up in violent homes beyond the age of 8 or 10 risk becoming so emotionally and psychologically damaged that they can never be repaired. "The danger," says Robert Halpern, a professor of child development at the Erikson Institute in Chicago, "is not just the enormous damage to the kid himself, but producing the next generation of monsters."

Clifford Triplett is an all-too-pointed reminder of how severe the injuries can be. He has gained eight pounds, and his physical prognosis is good. But there are many other concerns. "When he came, he didn't know the difference between a car and a truck, the difference between pizza and a hot dog," says his hospital social worker, Kathleen Egan. "People were not introducing these things to him." Robinson and McKinney are awaiting trial on charges of aggravated battery and felony cruelty. McKinney's attorney blames Robinson for the alleged abuse; Robinson's attorney declined to comment. Clifford is waiting for a foster home. A few weeks ago he had his first conversation with his mother in months. His first words: "Are you sorry for whipping me?"

Band-Aids Don't Work

ACCORDING TO THE CASEWORKER'S report, 2½-year-old Saonnia Bolden's family was the model of success. Over 100 days, a homemaker from an Illinois family-preservation program called Family First worked with Sadie Williams and her boyfriend Clifford Baker. A second helper—a caseworker—shopped with Sadie for shoes and some furniture for her apartment; she evaluated Sadie's cooking, housekeeping and budgeting. She even took her to dinner to celebrate her progress. On March 17, 1992, the caseworker wrote a report recommending that Sadie's case be closed: "Due to the presence of homemaker, the amount of stress and frustration has been reduced. Sadie appears to have a lot more patience with her children and she continues to improve her disciplinary techniques."

What the Family First caseworker evidently didn't know was that, just hours before she filed her report, Saonnia had been beaten and scalded to death. Prosecutors claim that Williams, angered because her young daughter had wet herself, laid the child in the bathtub and poured scalding water over her genitals and her buttocks. Williams and Baker were charged with first-degree murder; lawyers for Baker and Williams blame each other's client. Regardless of who was responsible, this wasn't

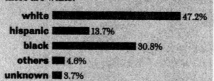

Race of Foster Children

Contrary to public opinion, foster care is not dominated by minorites. Nearly half the kids there are white.

white	47.2%
hispanic	13.7%
black	30.8%
others	4.6%
unknown	3.7%

SOURCE: AMERICAN PUBLIC WELFARE ASSOCIATION

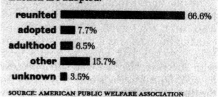

Where Do Children Go?

Two thirds of children who leave foster care are reunited with their parents; only a fraction are adopted.

reunited	66.6%
adopted	7.7%
adulthood	6.5%
other	15.7%
unknown	3.5%

SOURCE: AMERICAN PUBLIC WELFARE ASSOCIATION

A One-Man Children's Crusade

Twenty years ago, an angry young lawyer named Patrick Murphy wrote a book that exposed an injustice: state social workers too often seized children from parents whose worst crime was poverty. Today Murphy is the scourge of a child-welfare system that too often leaves kids with their abusive, drugged-out parents. He has not made the about-face quietly. In many cities, confidentiality laws protect caseworkers and judges from public outcries when their bad decisions lead to a parent's murder of a child. In Chicago, Murphy calls blistering press conferences to parcel out the blame. To those who say he picks on parents who are poor, black and victimized, he hotly retorts: "So are their kids."

Murphy is the Cook County (Ill.) public guardian, the court-appointed lawyer for 31,000 abused and neglected children. He's also a self-righteous crusader. last year, campaigning to rein in one "family preservation" program, Murphy sent every Illinois legislator color autopsy photos of a little girl scalded and beaten to death after caseworkers taught her family new disciplinary skills. It's a loner's life, poring over murder files and railing at fellow liberals who think the poor can do no wrong. "A lot of people hate my guts," Murphy shrugs. "I can't blame them."

His views on family reunification changed because child abuse changed. Drugs now suffuse 80 percent of the caseload; sexual and physical assaults that once taxed the imagination are now common. Murphy believes that most families should be reunited—but the child-welfare agencies waste years trying to patch up dead-end families when they should be hurrying to free children for early adoption. Murphy, 55, blames such folly on bleeding hearts like himself, who once lobbied for generous social programs without working to curb welfare dependency and other ills.

Now children of troubled families must pay the price—sometimes with their lives. "We inadvertently pushed a theory of irresponsibility," he says. "And we created a monster—kids having kids."

To Murphy's critics, that smacks of scorn for the less fortunate. "He's a classic bully," says Diane Redleaf of the Legal Assistance Foundation of Chicago, who represents parents trying to win back their kids. "Thousands of poor families are *not* torturing their children." Redleaf has drafted legislation that would force Murphy to get a judge's order each time he wants to speak about a case. That would protect children's privacy—and give the system a convenient hiding place. Murphy will fight to keep things as they are. His is the only job, he says, in which a lawyer knows that his clients are truly innocents.

J.M.

---

the first assault. The autopsy on Saonnia's visibly malnourished body found 62 cuts, bruises, burns, abrasions and wrist scars, among other injuries. Eleven were still healing—meaning they probably happened during the time the homemaker was working with the family.

Since Illinois's Family First program began in 1988, at least six children have died violently during or after their families received help. In many other instances, children were injured, or simply kept in questionable conditions. Such numbers may look small compared with the 17,000 children in Illinois who've been in the program. But to critics, the deaths and injuries underscore the danger of using reunification efforts for deeply troubled families. Gelles, once an ardent supporter of family preservation, is adamant about its failures. "We've learned in health psychology that you don't waste intervention on those with no intention of changing," he argues.

A University of Chicago report card issued last year gave the Illinois Family First program barely passing grades. Among the findings: Family First led to a slight *increase* in the overall number of children later placed outside their homes; it had no effect on subsequent reports of maltreatment; it had only mixed results in such areas as improving housing, economics and parenting, and it had no effect on getting families out of the DCFS system. John R. Schuerman, who helped write the report, says it's too simplistic to call Family First a

failure. Still, he concedes that the assumption that large numbers of households can be saved with intensive services "just may not be the case."

Nevertheless, in the last decade, family-preservation programs have become so entrenched there's little chance they'll be junked. Health and Human Services Secretary Donna Shalala carefully sidesteps the question of whether it's possible to carry the reunification philosophy too far. Asked where she would draw the line in defining families beyond repair, she diplomatically suggests that the answers be left to child-welfare experts. "Nobody wants to leave children in dangerous situations," says Shalala. "The goal is to shrewdly pick cases in which the right efforts might help keep a

family together." So far, not even the experts have come up with a sure way to do that.

Where Do We Go From Here?

POLICYMAKERS BELIEVE THAT IF THEY could just remove the stresses from a family, they wouldn't have to remove the child. But critics argue that the entire child-welfare network must approach the idea of severing parents' rights as aggressively as it now approaches family reunification. That means moving kids through the system and into permanent homes quickly—before they're so damaged that they won't fit in anywhere. In theory, the Adoption Assistance Act already requires that, but no state enforces that part of

---

CLIFFORD TRIPLETT

"I talked to him [Eddie Robinson, Cliff's mother's boyfriend] about Cliff and the old scars on his back. Robinson said . . . Cliff had a tendency to get into a lot of mischief," the caseworker noted. "This is why Cliff was whipped—however I told him that he shouldn't be beat on his back. Robinson promised to go easy on the discipline. (Said he wasn't doing the whipping.)"

FROM CASEWORKER REPORT ON CLIFFORD TRIPLETT

the law. Illinois is typical: even in the most straightforward cases, a petition to terminate parental rights is usually the start of a two-year judicial process—*after* the 18-month clean-up-your-act phase.

Why does it take so long? Once a child is in foster care, the system breathes a sigh of relief and effectively forgets about him. If the child is removed from an abusive home, the assumption is that he's safe. "There's always another reason to give the parent the benefit of the doubt," says Daro. "They lose their job, the house burns down, the aunt is murdered. Then they get another six-month extension, and it happens all over again. Meanwhile, you can't put a child in a Deepfreeze and suspend his life until the parent gets her life together."

In the most blatant abuse and neglect cases, parents' rights should be terminated immediately, reformers say. In less-severe cases, parents should be given no more than six to 12 months to shape up. "You have social workers saying, 'She doesn't visit her child because she has no money for carfare'," says Murphy. "But what parent wouldn't walk over mountains of glass to see their kids? You know it's a crock. You have to tell people we *demand* responsibility."

And if parents can't take care of them, where are all these children supposed to go? With just 100,000 foster parents in the system, finding even temporary homes is difficult. For starters, reformers suggest professionalizing foster care, paying parents decent salaries to stay home and care for several children at a time. Long range, many believe that society will have to confront its ambivalence toward interracial adoptions. Perhaps the most controversial alternative is the move to revive orphan-

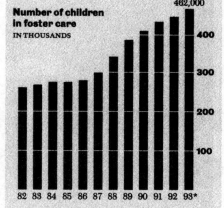

Number of Foster Children

The dramatic rise in the number of children needing foster care began in 1986, coinciding with the start of the nation's crack epidemic.

Number of children in foster care
IN THOUSANDS

462,000

*YEARS ARE FISCAL YEARS. 1993 IS AN ESTIMATE.
SOURCE: AMERICAN PUBLIC WELFARE ASSOCIATION

ages, at least for teenagers, who are the least likely to be adopted. One of the fiercest supporters is Maddux, the new supervising judge of Cook County's abuse section. Maddux, 59, says that his own family was so desperately poor they once lived in a shanty with two rooms—one of which was an old car. When the family broke up, he and his younger brother went to live at Boys Town, Neb. He believes that many foster children today could benefit from the nurturing-yet-demanding atmosphere of group living. "I wasn't raised in a family after the age of 12," Maddux says. "I didn't miss it. Thousands of kids at Boys Town knew that being in a destitute, nonfunctioning family was a lot worse than not

being in a family." In Illinois, some are taking the idea seriously—among the proposals is turning closed military bases into campuses for kids.

Ironically, Illinois could wind up with one of the best child-welfare systems in the nation. Pressed by public outrage over Joseph Wallace's death, state legislators last year passed a law that puts the best interest of children ahead of their parents'. Foster parents will be given a voice in abuse and neglect cases. And the DCFS is beefing up caseworker training, so that those in the field will learn how to spot dangerous situations more quickly.

Some of the toughest changes are already underway in Cook County. The much-criticized Family First program has been replaced with a smaller, more intensely scrutinized family-preservation project known as Homebuilders. And the county's juvenile-court system has been expanded so that there are now 14 judges, not eight, hearing abuse and neglect cases; that cuts each judge's caseload from about 3,500 to about 2,000 children per year. But reform doesn't come cheap. The DCFS budget has tripled since 1988, to $900 million, and it could top $1 billion in the next fiscal year.

Whether any of this can save lives, it's too soon to tell. In its report on Joseph Wallace's death, the blue-ribbon committee was pessimistic. "It would be comforting to believe that the facts of this case are so exceptional that such cases are not likely to happen again," the panel wrote with a dose of bitterness. "That hope is unfounded." The temptation, of course, is to blame some faceless system. But the fate of children really lies with everyone—caseworkers, supervisors, prosecutors, judges—doing their jobs.

Crime, Terrorism, and Violence

The probability is becoming greater that every American will at some time in his or her life be subjected to a criminal act and that act will involve some degree of violence. With the ever increasing crime rate, especially in major cities, confidence in law enforcement is declining, and citizens feel forced to arm themselves and turn their homes into minifortresses. What must be done to make our streets safe to walk, our highways safe to drive, and our homes safe from unwanted intrusions? These are the concerns addressed by articles in this unit.

The April 19, 1995 bombing in Oklahoma City and the awareness that this was not the malicious act of a foreign terrorist shocked and further heightened the fears of many Americans. Terrorism was something that happened in the Middle East, not in America. This section has been expanded to include several articles that focus on what happens when extremists and terrorists strike close to home.

George Lardner, in "Getting Serious about Crime," argues that it makes little sense to arrest offenders if the arrest is not associated with serious punishment. Attempts to rehabilitate these serious offenders do not work, and, contrary to some reports, the cost society must bear to imprison these individuals is far less than the cost society must bear for their subsequent criminal activities.

"Ethics, Neurochemistry, and Violence Control" looks at the allure of a quick fix for violence. Medical scientists have been searching for a genetic link to violence that

can be chemically controlled. Stephen Post questions the validity of such a notion because he believes that violence is a complex interaction of many social, psychological, and biological factors. Therefore, any chemical attempt to control behaviors should be viewed with suspicion and caution.

What should be done, what can be done, and how to determine the difference is hotly debated in "Terrorism in America." Orrin Hatch, senior senator from Utah, argues that we must take decisive action and take it now. Doug Bandow, a senior fellow at the Cato Institute, cautions that the anger and anguish associated with the bombing in Oklahoma City must not result in a draconian overresponse.

In the next essay "Enemies of the State," Jill Smolowe looks at the rise of paramilitary groups in the United States. These secretive, paranoid, and obsessed groups, while not new to America, raise significant concerns for local, state, and federal regulatory agencies. They are highly trained, heavily armed, and have strong grievances, which, if not addressed, are likely to cause them to become very militant.

Jean Callahan, in her report "Forgiving the Unforgivable," argues that until victims can let go of their anger, frustration, anguish, and status as a victim, they remain captives of their abuser/criminal. To move on with their lives, they must cut their bonds and free themselves. But the only way this can occur is to forgive.

Nuclear weapons are a fact of life, they are with us to stay, and we must learn how to live with them. The fact that nuclear weapons exist is the single greatest deterrence against their use. Michael May, in "Fearsome Security: The Role of Nuclear Weapons," argues that the right time to maintain the deterrence and to formulate how to deal with nuclear weapons is during peacetime.

Looking Ahead: Challenge Questions

Is there any evidence to support the belief that the severity of punishment deters crime?

What effect does being a victim have on the individual? What are the most productive ways of dealing with being a victim?

Is it possible to eliminate violence? Explain.

How should the federal government respond to terrorism?

Is domestic terrorism a new phenomenon in America?

What seem to be the major factors giving rise to paramilitary groups in America?

How would a functionalist's approach to the problem of crime, terrorism, and violence differ from that of a conflict theorist?

Getting Serious About Crime

The system treats it like a game, and we're losing

George Lardner

George Lardner is a Washington Post reporter. This article is adapted from a speech delivered in October to the Kiplinger Midcareer Program in Public Affairs Reporting at Ohio State University.

"To wink at a fault causes trouble" is an old saying from the Book of Proverbs. It is also an apt description of what's gone wrong with our criminal justice system—especially when it comes to violent crime. Every day, in every courthouse across the country, we keep recycling the same criminals onto the streets to commit the same crimes again and again. The system keeps winking, as though the people who keep getting arrested, sentenced, convicted—and released—haven't learned how to play the game.

In fact, they know how to play it very well. They know they can count on being set free—on bond, on their own recognizance, for rehabilitation, for counseling, for supervision by probation and parole officers too busy to do any real supervising.

Consider, for example, a recent Washington Post report on the laxity accorded five of the seven men allegedly involved in a rash of fatal shootings and robberies in the Washington area. Two of them walked out of halfway houses, where one had been allowed to stay even after formal revocation of his parole. Another, who was the star of a jewelry store videotape that showed him pistol-whipping a woman and shooting a man, was free despite an outstanding charge of threatening to do bodily harm to two men, including a police officer. He had been released from custody on the strength of a promise to return for his trial in November. A fourth man was on parole from a Virginia prison—and also free on bond in a nearby county, on armed robbery charges. That robbery took place while he was still on parole for selling PCP and carrying a concealed weapon.

The fifth man was in a somewhat different category. He would have been better off if he had been required to serve more of his 1990 prison term for selling cocaine or if his parole had been revoked in light of a June 1993 arrest for trying to murder someone. Instead he was killed while watching a neighborhood football game. So was a 4-year-old girl standing nearby, leaving shock waves in the city that are still reverberating.

Something very much like this story could be written about the suspects in almost any rash of killings in any number of American cities. But it wasn't until my own daughter, Kristin, was murdered two years ago that I began paying closer attention to the supposedly routine violence that judges yawn at every day. It wasn't until then that I realized how hard it is to be put behind bars.

I've been covering courts and crimes for more than 30 years. But most of them were high-profile cases: Mafia figures in New York; contract killers in Cleveland; Teamsters in Chicago; Robert Kennedy's assassin in Los Angeles. These defendants were convicted and went to jail as they deserved. In the commonplace justice system, though, things work differently: Across the country, according to a recent Justice Department study, 62 percent of the 4.3 million people convicted of a crime and under active correctional supervision were on probation and another 12 percent were free on parole. Only 26 percent were in prisons or jails. In other words, three of every four people serving a criminal sentence on any given day in this country are rubbing shoulders with us.

This 75 percent is supposed to be under supervision of a probation or parole officer. But a 1990 study of three California programs found that the courts put many high-risk offenders on routine probation even though probation officers have caseloads of 150 or more. In Los Angeles County, the average caseload is reportedly as high as 600 per officer. Probationers in the three-county study saw their case officers an average of 15 minutes a month.

The results are about what you would expect. A Justice Department study of 79,000 felony probationers found that 43 percent of them were rearrested for another felony within their own state within three years of their sentencing, while still on probation. Half of the fresh arrests were for a violent crime or a drug offense.

Much is made of the costs of keeping a criminal behind bars. In fiscal 1990, the average annual cost was $15,603 per inmate—slightly less than that for federal prisoners and slightly more for state prisoners. But that's hardly bankrupting the system. As statistics compiled by the Justice Department show, state prisons cost only $41.91 per taxpayer, accounting for a measly 1 percent of all state and local spending. Federal prisons cost $3.46 for every U.S. resident, less than a tenth of 1 percent of federal spending. As a special committee of the American Bar Association found several years ago, "The entire criminal justice system is starved for resources."

Less than 4 percent of all U.S. government spending—that's federal, state and local—goes to support all justice activities, civil and criminal. That's less than 4 percent for everything— police, the courts, prosecutors, prisons, public defenders, the works. Barely more than 1 percent goes into the operation of our correctional system, including jails, prisons, probation and parole. In the year of the gulf war, U.S. taxpayers spent more on restoring Kuwait to its arguably corrupt rulers than they did on their federal justice system that year.

No doubt we'd much rather spend our money routing a villain like Saddam Hussein or building a new highway than we would on housing thugs. We need to overcome that reluctance.

◾

WE LIKE TO THINK THAT REHABILITATION WORKS, but there is no evidence, except in isolated instances, that it does. A landmark study in 1975 by the late Robert Martinson established that point. He reviewed the results of more than 200 separate efforts to measure the effects of programs designed to rehabilitate convicted offenders and concluded that rehabilitative efforts "have had no appreciable effect on recidivism." Harvard professor James Q. Wilson summed up the findings in his book "Thinking About Crime": "It did not seem to matter what form of treatment in the correctional system was attempted. Indeed, some forms of treatment (notably a few experiments with psychotherapy) actually produced an increase in the rate of recidivism."

By repeating these rather grim conclusions, I don't mean to suggest that I'm opposed to attacking the so-called "root causes" of crime. We need social programs to fight poverty and deprivation. Those conditions are unjust, whether they lead to crime or not. But social programs are not going to eradicate crime. As Wilson puts it, "If kindness, better housing, improved diets or lessened child abuse will reduce crime, I favor them. I only ask that the capacity of such measures to reduce crime be demonstrated and that their employment for crime-reduction purposes not be at the expense of society's desire to see justice done to those who have violated its moral imperatives."

And by that, Wilson means those who are guilty of predatory crime.

◾

VIOLENT CRIME MAY NOT BE AS FISCALLY COSTLY as, say, white-collar crime—and it may not produce such celebrity criminals as Michael Milken—but predatory crime is what worries most people and drives them apart from one another. It is—we have to face it—the biggest problem facing the country today.

The violence has not only grown in alarming quantity; it is also qualitatively more horrific. But what can we expect when movie and video heroes are glorified for electrocuting their foes, or tearing their hearts out? As President Clinton has said, "We have got to understand that we are raising a generation without the structure and order and predictability and support and reinforcement that most of us just took for granted."

Meanwhile, too many dangerous people are being set free. In Florida, a supposedly tough-on-crime state, the prisons have become so crowded that officials have been tossing more and more violent offenders into their "early release" program to meet federal court mandates.

In the District of Columbia, more than 1,500 individuals serving time for anything from murders to misdemeanors have strolled out of halfway houses since Jan. 1. About 500 of them are still at large. Weeks go by before the Corrections Department gets around to obtaining arrest warrants. The escapees often commit new crimes. An average of three to five defendants who are escapees appear in Superior Court each week, The Post disclosed in October.

Another important story certainly is the number of unserved warrants that pile up in every jurisdiction in the country. In Massachusetts, the commissioner of probation, Donald Cochran, told me that nobody knows how many outstanding warrants there are in his state. A probation officer who at one point supervised the man who stalked and killed my daughter told me of his frustrations in issuing warrants for probation violators. He said they just stack up at the police stations and are sometimes given lesser status because they didn't originate with the police.

Curiously, the press rarely seems to treat the failures of our justice system as real news. Rather, newspapers are too busy reporting what happened in Sarajevo or Mogadishu than domestic stories on violence, including family violence, battered women, spouse abuse, child abuse and assaults on the aged. The Washington Post, for example, printed 853 stories on Bosnia and Somalia from January through September, but only 38 stories in the categories of violence listed here. We've turned the news upside down. Events that we can do the least about command the biggest headlines. We forget that what our readers, or viewers, need is the news no one else can tell us about: the robbery at the grocery store, the mayhem on the playground, the shenanigans at City Hall.

◾

I AM NOT SUGGESTING THAT SERIOUS NEWSPAPERS put every grisly local crime on Page 1 as the tabloids do. I am suggesting that what we need on Page 1 are more stories that are as insightful about crime and the failures of our criminal justice system as the ones we run about foreign policy.

Those of us who cover the courts know that judges are a thin-skinned lot. When you scratch, they howl. But how many courthouse reporters, print or broadcast, tell their audience which judges are worth their salt, and which are not?

The same holds true for prosecutors and police. How many stories or newscasts challenge the plea-bargaining that goes on day after day? Is this justice? Or is it a cynical search for the least common denominator? The system is rarely questioned as U.S. involvement in Somalia may be questioned. But this is the system that released a Florida man who killed an 11-year-old boy after his early release for raping another. He should have gotten two life sentences, but they were plea-bargained down to an eight-year term, of which he served less than half.

Prosecutors argue that it already takes too long to bring cases to trial, that the system will collapse without pleas that won't be contested. That's an old lament, and I doubt the system would come anywhere near to collapse. But it certainly is a system that deserves to teeter a bit if that will expose its faults. Recent hearings in New York City have illustrated the corruption there. Police officers in some precincts take up to $8,000 a week for protecting drug dealers. They attack people with nightsticks, flashlights and lead-loaded gloves just "to show who's in charge." And they carry throwaway guns to explain away inconvenient homicides. Exceptions to the rule? Maybe. But how exceptional? And what have our news organizations done lately to find out?

"To wink at a fault causes trouble," the Proverbs say. The next line is, "A bold reproof makes peace."

ETHICS, NEUROCHEMISTRY, AND VIOLENCE CONTROL

Stephen G. Post

Stephen G. Post is assistant professor of medical humanities at the Center for Biomedical Ethics, Case Western Reserve University School of Medicine, Cleveland, Ohio.

The rapidly increasing human knowledge of neurochemistry is both medical miracle and moral muddle.

Today's so-called designer pharmacology involves the use of drugs to fine-tune mood, confidence, and anxiety levels even though no clinical condition exists. A useful analogy is to desired but unnecessary cosmetic surgery such as a slight modification of nose shape or perhaps yet another tummy tuck.

The question arises, then, will we gradually become a society of "happy" psychotropic hedonists? Or, on the other hand, should we be psychotropic Calvinists, striving hard to deal with the challenges of life by drawing on our inner resources and rejecting mind-and-mood-altering drugs? This is an old dilemma that can be raised at a new level, given the extent of recent scientific developments. How far shall we go in letting healthy people artificially fine-tune their sense of peacefulness and well-being?

Yet other questions surround new drugs that might eventually be proven useful in the control of socially undesirable and illicit behaviors. A debate, for example, has arisen over the possible use of serotonin to inhibit aggression.

Urgent questions mount over reliance on psychopharmacology to solve people's social and relational difficulties. They generally center around the concern that, although drugs are cheaper than psychotherapy, they absolve the individual of responsibility to sort out the underlying causes of his problem.

Anthony Burgess published his novella *A Clockwork Orange* in 1962, spawning the unforgettable Stanley Kubrick film in which Alex and his three "droogs" Pete, Georgie, and Dim engage in adolescent "ultraviolence" to strains of Beethoven's Ninth. Alex, prisoner 6655321, is eventually forced to undergo Dr. Brodsky's behavior-control process. Alex describes the doctor as "a malenky veck, very fat, with all curly hair curling all over his gulliver, and on his spuddy nose he had very thick otchkies" and as "all smiling as though to give me confidence."

For a fortnight, Alex is jabbed with syringes in his backside ("rooker") and made to view films of violence that, due to the injection, make him vomit repeatedly in anguished disgust. At the end of the process, Dr. Brodsky proclaims, Alex "will be your true Christian ready to turn the other cheek, ready to be crucified rather than crucify, sick to the very heart at the thought even of killing a fly."

Whatever one's interpretation of the novella's conclusions, it provides a fitting entry into the topic of this article, that is, the biologizing of human violence and the current debate over the possible role of psychiatry and neuroscience in eradicating the proclivity for wanton harm with new mind-altering drugs. I proceed by describing this acrimonious debate and providing some ethical analysis, although I am finally empirically skeptical of the genetic-biological interpretation of violence as well as suspicious of its political implications.

But before proceeding, clarity on the state of current biological science in relation to violence is essential. Thus far, *none* of the leads for a biological basis of violence have been scientifically verified.

One lead that has never panned out is the link between violence and low levels of serotonin, a brain chemical that affects behavior in some mental disorders. Based on some preliminary studies, biological psychiatrists loosely speculated that people in their early years might be treated with drugs to raise their serotonin levels. However, hundreds of recent studies indicate no consistent link between violence and serotonin levels. The leading researcher in this area, Dr. Klaus Miczek of Tufts University, has been widely quoted as denying that a serotonin-aggression link has yet been established.[1] Thus far, the attempt to biologize violence has failed. Even the studies carried out on criminals in the 1970s suggesting that high testosterone levels in males might be linked with violence and increased aggression proved inconclusive.

A phenomenon so multifactorial and complex as violence will probably never be reducible solely or even largely to genes and biochemistry. Yet there is a continuing tendency among some scientists and the media to overstate the biological hypothesis.[2]

This is probably because of the alluring simplicity of the notion of a possible link between genes and violence, such that violence-prone people would be found to have a distinctive neurochemistry that might be altered in the name of peace by physicians working for the state. Writing in the journal *Science*, Gary Taubes asks if scientists should be free to search for such a link and, if discovered, whether this knowledge would be misused: "Could it even lead to a sort of Holocaust—as nonviolent people who carry 'violence genes' were rounded up and dosed with drugs to ensure that they remain harmless to their law-abiding neighbors?"[3]

CURRENT DEBATE FOCUSES ON BLACK AMERICANS

The proposed "violence initiative" of the U.S. Department of Health and Human Services (HHS) was in large part the creation of then-HHS Secretary Dr. Louis Sullivan. In September 1992, the initiative was blasted by the Congressional Black Caucus, catching Sullivan, himself black, off guard. The Caucus feared that the research would focus on young inner-city blacks, who would be "discovered" to be biologically prone toward aggressive and violent acts, the solution for which could be the massive use of behavior-control drugs.

Sullivan accurately responded that in fact no race-specific studies of the genetic and biological basis of violence were contemplated, and that the HHS funds for such biological research were minuscule. Nevertheless, the initiative was halted for further review, which is still ongoing.

On January 15, 1993, HHS issued *The Report of the Secretary's Blue Ribbon Panel on Violence Prevention*, a project convened by Sullivan in December 1992. The panel was charged to advise him on the validity of allegations about inappropriate research, how to go about understanding violence, and how to assure that the HHS activities in violence research are open and supported by the wider community. Franklyn Jenifer, then-president of Howard University, served as chairman. The report found that HHS was neither attempting to establish any genetic correlation between race and violence nor

1. Richard Saltus, "Evidence That Genes Play a Role in Violence Is Weak," *Boston Globe*, 8 Feb. 1993.
2. Lisabeth DiLalla and Irving Gottesman, "Biological and Genetic Contributions to Violence—Wisdom's Untold Tale," *Psychological Bulletin* 109 (1991): 125–29.

3. Gary Taubes, "HHS 'Violence Initiative' Caught in a Crossfire," *Science* 258 (1992): 212–15.

Three neurosurgeons from Harvard, authors of a controversial letter to the Journal of the American Medical Association *in 1967, associated the urban riots of that period with the brain dysfunction of "slum dwellers."*

targeting black American males, ages five to nine years, for purposes of medication. Moreover, the study recommended that blacks and other minorities be invited to join in ethical review of all research on violence and aggression.

Yet the black community, rightly suspicious of biomedical research in light of the decades-long Tuskegee studies in which black males were made to die of syphilis long after penicillin became available, is not easily calmed. Suspicions are exacerbated by recollection that three neurosurgeons from Harvard, authors of an extremely controversial letter to the *Journal of the American Medical Association* in 1967, associated the urban riots of that period with the brain dysfunction of "slum dwellers." These neurosurgeons, in 1970, with funding from the Department of Justice, performed experimental surgery on thirteen men and women in which they implanted electrodes to destroy tissue in the amygdala area of the temporal lobe, intending to quell violence. Black civil rights leaders succeeded in having the funding halted. And the recent controversy over decades of radiation research by the Department of Energy has hardly mitigated minority suspicions of big science in collusion with government.

Clarification of the nonracist character of intended HHS studies might have been possible but for inflammatory remarks made in late 1992 by Dr. Frederick Goodwin, then director of the HHS Alcohol, Drug Abuse, and Mental Health Administration (ADAMH). A biologically oriented psychiatrist, Goodwin has long been a proponent of large-scale pharmacological interventions to control violence. In a speech that led to a national uproar, Goodwin stated that inner-city black youths are like jungle monkeys, capable of killing, sex, and reproduction. Sullivan removed Goodwin from his position.

The allegations that the "violence initiative" would try to link violence to race were firmly rooted in legitimate black suspicions of a history of government-sponsored racist research in the United States. Such allegations, although ultimately unfounded, were popularized by Dr. Peter Breggin, a well-known psychiatrist who categorically rejects the growing psychiatric emphasis on genetic-biological etiology of mental illness coupled with almost purely pharmacological treatment.

Breggin hit the talk-show circuit in 1992, charging that government-sponsored studies would lead to young black children being forced to take mind-numbing drugs to control their perceived proclivity for violence. He also brought this scenario to the attention of the Congressional Black Caucus, and, partly through his testimony to Congress, the "violence initiative" was shelved.

Recently, the influential *Journal of NIH Research* published a condemnation of HHS leadership for "caving in to political pressure," as no federal funds were ever approved for studies that link violence and race: "Over the course of a lifetime, one in 27 black males and one in 117 black females die from violent acts, compared with one in 205 white men and one in 496 white women. However, no studies supported by HHS even try to link violent or criminal behavior to race."[4]

---

4. Nancy Touchette, "Growing Inferno: Clearing the Smoke on Violence Research," *Journal of NIH Research* 4 (1994): 31–33.
5. Peter Breggin, *Psychiatric Drugs: Hazards to the Brain* (New York: Springer, 1983); *Toxic Psychiatry* (New York: St. Martin's Press, 1991).

"Increasingly, schools and parents accept the new approach that declares the youngster to be genetically defective and suitable for psychiatric treatment, including drugs and hospitalization."

CRITICISM OF BIOLOGICAL PSYCHIATRY

Biological psychiatrists are predictably critical of Breggin for what they consider to be his bias against the theory of brain-behavior interaction and for his allegedly antiscientific attacks on the use of pharmacologic medication. Breggin's two major books have the pointed titles *Psychiatric Drugs: Hazards to the Brain* and *Toxic Psychiatry*.[5] In these books, Breggin is critical of biological reductionism and treatment that impinges on individual rights.

Although Breggin has erroneously interpreted the HHS research initiative as racist and as gearing up for a totalitarian assault on antisocial behavior akin to that in George Orwell's *1984*, I nevertheless consider his critique of biological psychiatry as necessary, even if too one-sided. In a compelling article appearing in the *Wall Street Journal*, Breggin criticized the overuse of drugs and mental hospitalization to deal with emotional stress among the nation's children. This overuse is, he claims, financially driven. Hospitalization and pharmacological treatment based on diagnosis of mental illness are highly remunerative at a time when psychotherapy and family therapy are not well covered by health insurance. Breggin points to more than one million youngsters on Ritalin, a drug used to sedate unruly and rebellious schoolchildren, most of them boys.[6]

I hasten to add that there are some cases in which Ritalin is the only solution to hyperactivity and attention-deficit disorder, and it can work well. Yet it is overused, can have adverse side effects in some cases (although it is generally safe), and is a convenient technological substitute for the more time-consuming social, familial, and environmental interventions that often can mitigate such disorders.

Breggin argues that the etiology of such disorders lies principally in family trends: two working parents with a latchkey child, for whom drugs are more affordable than time. And Breggin points out that the single mother may find it impossible to handle the rambunctious boy, a task difficult for even the more sizable male mentor. A hasty diagnosis of hyperactivity and attention-deficit disorder comes in handy, as does Ritalin.

So Breggin concludes that by biologizing these so-called diagnoses we are

blaming the child for the problems of parents, families, schools, and society. Increasingly, schools and parents find it comforting to accept the new biological psychiatry approach that declares the youngster to be genetically and biologically defective, and suitable for psychiatric treatment, including drugs and hospitalization.

His remedy is for parents to "retake responsibility for our children." Although I would not take the case against biological psychiatry as far as Breggin does, I think that he is an important corrective voice.

There is absolutely no question that American psychiatry, once under the influence of Freud—and therefore psychoanalytic rather than biological-neurological in orientation—is now attempting

6. Peter Breggin, "The Scapegoating of American Children," *Wall Street Journal*, 7 Nov. 1989.

to regain scientific respectability and ensure research funding by focusing on the "hard" sciences of biochemistry, neuroanatomy, and pharmacology. Over the past decade, entire departments of psychiatry have been reshaped in accord with the hard-science model. Fortunately, the members of another school of psychiatry, the "ethnopsychiatrists," have been successful critics of the biological school, and we may see a partial swing back toward the psychosocial and analytic models.

LOCATING THE ROOTS OF VIOLENCE

It is not only legitimate but vitally important to question the psychiatric abuse of behavior-control drugs and the biological distraction from root social causes of violence. Biological psychiatry, in its attempt to gain scientific credibility in a time of tremendous growth in genetics, has looked to molecular biology to solve a problem that is located not so much within cells as within culture, injustice, and the history of human resentment. Any genetic predisposition toward violence, if discovered, would likely involve a number of genes in interaction with the environment and therefore would have little or no power to predict individual behavior.

Among the causes of violence are racism, poverty, poor schools, media inculcation, unemployment, cultural traditions that sanction forms of spouse and child abuse, religious fanaticism, and the brute "will to power" and domination characteristic of classes and nations. In addition, there are a host of other cofactors. The breakdown of the nuclear family, leaving young boys with no strong male role models, results in gang recruitment and immense wanton violence. The decline of the ethos of delayed gratification, coupled with greed, the striking visual contrast between the lives of the rich and the poor, the unfortunate sense among many adolescents that their value lies in the designer jackets and gold chains that some believe are worth killing for, the tremendous power of peer pressure, the sense of absolute power that comes with the taking of a life, the feeling that one's life is so hopeless that one may

as well kill with no concern for future punishment, and a general decline in the respect afforded human life explain why violence among adolescents is up. The images of *A Clockwork Orange* resonate with the fears that many experience in their neighborhoods.

There is no biomedical, technical fix for problems such as these. The only real solution is a familial, social, cultural, moral, religious, and economic transition that no syringe can supply. Despite technological progress, the close of the twentieth century leaves us with the antiprinciple "respect no life."

All criminal-justice professionals, like every first-year law student, know that violence cannot ultimately be controlled by law and the criminal-justice system. When the internal and characterological controls over violence are shattered, law is almost powerless. I say *almost* powerless because law in its most draconian form can succeed in controlling violence—though only by abrogating the human liberties of a free society. This is why freedom and virtue are inextricably linked, and why the annihilation of the latter inevitably entails the loss of the former.

ENVOI

Returning to *A Clockwork Orange*, just prior to Alex's undergoing of the Brodsky process, the prison warden states: "I shall have many sleepless nights about this. What does God want? Does God want goodness or the choice of goodness? Is a man who chooses the bad perhaps in some way better than the man who has the good imposed on him?" Would we want a state to achieve perfect peace, if it could, at the expense of human freedom?

The problem of violence should be solved in a manner that actively engages the entire person. To consider the wide-scale and routine use of mind-altering drugs makes a mockery of the human propensity for goodness and people's ability to recognize and condemn the evil in their own lives.

That our society has become so much more violent in recent decades has nothing to do with human biology but with the gradual inculcation of the spirit of violence, the rise of a "me-first" culture, growing economic pressures, and a crumbling of traditional family life. It would be a travesty to revictimize the young victims of all the social, economic, familial, and cultural factors that spawn violence by placing them on behavior-control drugs.

We all live in fear. A Hobbesian "war of all against all" prevails in our worst neighborhoods and floods into suburban enclaves. Some begin to speak of the cycle of civilizations and wonder if a nation with our degree of urban violence can long survive. As Lord Acton commented, social-political freedom is historically a thin veneer easily removed in times of social disintegration in favor of the absolute state. It is important that we preserve freedom and dignity in the struggle against violence, appealing to reason and shared values rather than to illusory biological solutions that intervene into the sacred neurological center of personal identity.

There is not one iota of evidence that race is relevant to the cause of violence. Nor is there any persuasive evidence of a consistent biochemical cause. But it is tempting to search for the "violence gene," although it will prove as nonexistent as the gene for schizophrenia that was announced with such media attention yet turned out to be utterly invalid. And if science ever discovers some genetic-biological link with violence, it will have varying expression and genetic penetrance, making it one vague cofactor among many others. Thus, it would be of little social value.

Yet the scientific desire to create the chemical imitation of human goodness through wide-scale medication is unlikely to diminish. As early as 1971, Kenneth Clark, in a presidential address to the American Psychological Association, proclaimed that society was on the verge of a new era in which biochemical intervention would stabilize human moral propensities. Dr. José Delgado had just dramatically tamed the aggression of bulls by implanting electrodes into the amygdala and caudate nucleus, the region of the brain presumed to be involved in their aggression. A wildly charging bull came to a sudden stop with minor electronic stimulation. This, as previously stated, was for some neurosurgeons the fitting response to urban violence.

In Michael Crichton's *Terminal Man*, Harry Benson learns to love the electrical charge he gets from forty electrodes implanted in his brain. An article appeared in the *Yale Alumni Magazine* titled "Psycho-civilization or Electroliarchy: Dr. Delgado's Amazing World of ESB." All this suggested that mass behavior control was imminent and necessary and good. But as it turned out, electrostimulation of the brain was shown to produce completely different emotional responses in the brains of human subjects and to have no power to fine-control affect or function.

The issue of behavior control clearly informed the beginnings of bioethics in the early 1970s, faded from prominence, and may now be ready to reassert itself. Fundamental questions seem to be surfacing of whether chemical shortcuts should be used to control human behavioral problems that appear too expensive to solve at their root. As biological psychiatry continues to seek etiologies of violence and many mental disorders, violence may be subsumed under the medical model. Then, instead of teaching the perennial moral law of "do no harm" through religion and reason, we will have arrived at a technocratic society that to those lacking wisdom will appear utopian but will in fact be as dystopian as Orwell and Burgess suggested. In this society, the pills of technocrats will substitute for freedom, discipline, tradition, wisdom, and virtue. In a manner more total than Hannah Arendt predicted, *Homo faber* will have displaced and replaced *Homo sapiens*.

In his classic 1969 book, *Behavior Control*,[7] the late Perry London wrote that we were moving beyond the inculcation of values through "primitive" persuasion by education or inspiration to a world in which we "take over" people's lives by technological means. I confess a preference for the "primitive" way.

7. Perry London, *Behavior Control* (New York: Perennial Books, 1969).

Terrorism

Let's Take Decisive Action

Orrin Hatch

Republican Sen. Orrin Hatch is the senior senator from Utah and chairman of the Senate Judiciary Committee.

The Dole-Hatch Comprehensive Terrorism Prevention Act of 1995 represents a landmark, bipartisan effort to address an issue of grave national importance—the prevention and punishment of acts of domestic and international terrorism. This legislation adds important tools to the government's fight against terrorism, and does so in a temperate manner that is protective of civil liberties. I believe this bill is the most comprehensive antiterrorism bill ever considered in the Senate.

This legislation increases the penalties for acts of foreign and domestic terrorism, including the use of weapons of mass destruction, attacks on officials and employees of the United States, and conspiracy to commit terrorist acts.

It gives the president enhanced tools to use his foreign policy powers to combat terrorism

overseas, and it gives those of our citizens harmed by the terrorist acts of outlaw states the right to sue their attackers in our courts.

Our bill provides a constitutional mechanism to the government to deport aliens suspected of engaging in terrorist activity without divulging our national security secrets.

It also includes a provision that constitutionally limits the ability of foreign terrorist organizations to raise funds in the United States.

Our bill also provides measured enhancements to the authority of federal law enforcement to investigate terrorist threats and acts. In addition to giving law enforcement the legal tools they need to do the job, our bill also authorizes increased resources for law enforcement to carry out its mission. The bill provides $1.6 billion over five years for an enhanced antiterrorism effort at the federal and state levels.

The bill also implements the convention on the marking of plastic explosives. It requires that the makers of plastic explosives make the explosives detectable.

Finally, the bill appropriately reforms habeas corpus. Habeas corpus allows those con-

victed of brutal crimes, including terrorism, to delay the imposition of just punishment for years.

Several points, however, should be addressed. I have long opposed the unchecked expansion of federal authority, and will continue to do so. Still, the federal government has a legitimate role to play in our national life and in law enforcement. In particular, the federal government has an obligation to protect all of our citizens from serious criminal threats emanating from abroad or that involve a national interest.

We must nevertheless remember that our response to terrorism carries with it the grave risk of impinging on the rights of free speech, assembly, petition for the redress of grievances, and the right to keep and bear arms. We cannot allow this to happen. It would be cruel irony if, in response to the acts of evil and misguided men hostile to our government, we stifled true debate on the proper role of that government.

The legislation enhances our safety without sacrificing the liberty of American citizens. Each of the provisions of this bill

(continued on page 60)

Excerpted from the speech given by Senator Hatch as he submitted the Dole-Hatch Counterterrorism bill on May 29, 1995.

in America

Let's Not Overreact

Doug Bandow

Doug Bandow is a senior fellow at the Cato Institute and a former special assistant to President Reagan. He is the author of The Politics of Envy: Statism as Theology *(Transaction).*

The reactions inside and outside of Washington to the Oklahoma City bombing were sadly predictable. Around the country was anger, desire for understanding, and hope for healing. In the halls of the White House and Congress was shock, followed by a race for political advantage and demand for more power. In short, everyone did what came most naturally—citizens worried about their country while politicians worried about their influence.

This reaction was evident in attempts to brand critics of government as contributing to a "climate of hate" in which violence might occur. Needless to say, it is in the interest of presidents, legislators, and bureaucrats alike to discourage criticism. And many were quick to use the tragedy in Oklahoma City in an attempt to place themselves beyond reproach.

Second, politicians of both parties began posturing with proposals for new "counterterrorism"

legislation. These bills would vest the federal government with vast new powers to wiretap, investigate, deport, use the military, and rely on secret evidence. If people don't already have reason to fear government, they certainly will if these measures become law.

Before Congress acts precipitously, legislators should answer four questions. Is terrorism so serious a threat that it requires an immediate, draconian response? Has government policy contributed to violence, like the bombing of the Alfred P. Murrah Building in Oklahoma City? Do federal agencies require more power to combat terrorism? Does the law enforcement interest outweigh the rights and liberties of citizens that would be sacrificed?

LET'S CONSIDER FOUR QUESTIONS

1. Is terrorism so serious a threat that it requires an immediate, draconian response? The Oklahoma City bombing was a hideous act, but, thankfully, it represents the exception rather than the rule. There were no terrorist incidents in 1994, either actual or prevented. Of 11 incidents in 1993, 9 were committed by animal rights activists in one night. Over the past 11 years

there has been only one incident of international origin, the World Trade Center bombing. The State Department reports that international terrorist attacks are at their lowest level in nearly a quarter century.

Of course, even one attack is too many. But the current level of terrorist activity provides no cause for Congress to act without due deliberation. Legislators need to recognize that law enforcement agencies today often abuse their power, thereby stoking violent passions. In any case, the police already possess expansive authority to combat terrorism; Congress should honestly assess whether increasing these powers would do anything to combat real crime. Finally, legislators need to remember that it is a free society that they are attempting to protect. Marginal gains in a campaign against minimal threats are not worth the sacrifice of fundamental liberties.

2. Has government policy contributed to violence, like the bombing of the Alfred P. Murrah Building in Oklahoma City? Nothing can justify terrorism. Nevertheless, public officials must recognize that distrust of government is not limited to

(continued on page 62)

(continued from page 58)

strikes a careful balance between necessary vigilance against the terrorist threat and preserving our cherished freedom. Several of the provisions deserve special mention.

WHAT ABOUT UNLAWFUL ALIENS?

First, I would like to discuss the Alien Terrorist Removal Act. I firmly believe that it is time to give our law enforcement and courts the tools they need to quickly remove alien terrorists from our midst without jeopardizing national security or the lives of law enforcement personnel.

This provision provides the Justice Department with a mechanism to do this. It allows for a special deportation hearing and *in camera, ex parte* review by a special panel of federal judges when the disclosure in open court of government evidence would pose a threat to national security.

Sound policy dictates that we take steps to ensure that we deport alien terrorists without disclosing to them and their partners our national security secrets. The success of our counterterrorist efforts depends on the effective use of classified information used to infiltrate foreign terrorist groups. We cannot afford to turn over these secrets in open court, jeopardizing both the future success of these programs and the lives of those who carry them out.

Some raise heart-felt concerns about the precedence of this provision. I believe their opposition is sincere, and I respect their views. Yet, these special proceedings are not criminal proceedings for which the alien will be incarcerated. Rather, the result will simply be the removal of these aliens from U.S. soil—that is all.

■

Congress has a responsibility to minimize the prospect that something like the Oklahoma City bombing can happen again.

■

Americans are a fair people. Our nation has always emphasized that its procedures be just and fair. And the procedures in this bill are in keeping with that tradition. The Special Court would have to determine that:

1. the alien in question was an alien terrorist;

2. an ordinary deportation hearing would pose a security risk; and

3. the threat by the alien's physical presence is grave and immediate.

The alien would be provided with counsel, given all information which would not pose a risk if disclosed, would be provided with a summary of the evidence, and would have the right of appeal. Still, in our effort to be fair, we must not provide to terrorists and to their supporters abroad the informational means to wreak more havoc on our society. This provision is an appropriate means to ensure that we do not.

Second, this bill includes provisions making it a crime to knowingly provide material support to the terrorist functions of foreign groups designated by a presidential finding to be engaged in terrorist activities.

Nothing in the Dole-Hatch version of this provision prohibits the free exercise of religion or speech, or impinges on the free-

dom of association. Moreover, nothing in the Constitution provides the right to engage in violence against fellow citizens. Aiding and financing terrorist bombings is not constitutionally protected activity. Additionally, I have to believe that honest donors to any organization would want to know if their contributions were being used for such scurrilous purposes.

PROTECTING HABEAS CORPUS

Finally, I would like to address an issue which has inappropriately overshadowed all of the other fine provisions of this legislation—the inclusion of the Specter-Hatch habeas corpus reform in this bill. Some have stated that the inclusion of habeas reform in this bill is political opportunism. Nothing could be further from the truth. The plain truth is, habeas corpus reform is entirely germane to this legislation. The president has asked for this reform. And the American people are demanding it.

Although most capital cases are state cases (and the state of Oklahoma could still prosecute this case), the habeas reform proposal in this bill would apply to federal death penalty cases as well. It would directly affect the government's prosecution of the Oklahoma bombing case:

1. It would place a one-year limit for the filing of a habeas petition on all death row inmates—state and federal inmates.

2. It would limit condemned killers convicted in state and federal court to one habeas corpus petition. In contrast, under current law, there is currently no limit to the number of petitions he may file.

3. It requires the federal courts, once a petition is filed, to complete judicial action within a specified time period.

Antiterrorism Bill Passes

- The Senate responded to the Oklahoma City bombing by passing major antiterrorism legislation June 7 that would expand law enforcement's powers and limit appeals by death-row inmates.

- The $2 billion measure, passed by a 91–8 vote, includes provisions sought by President Clinton to enlarge federal law enforcement agencies and the government's wiretapping authority and allow use of the military in emergencies involving chemical or biological weapons.

- A House version of the bill passed the Judiciary Committee on June 14 and is expected to reach the House floor after July 4.

- At the White House, Clinton praised the Senate's bipartisan vote—52 Republicans and 39 Democrats in favor—and expressed hope that the House could quickly pass the same bill so that any attack similar to the one that killed 168 people in Oklahoma City could be forestalled or prevented.

—The Editor

Therefore, if the federal government prosecutes this case and the death penalty is sought and imposed, the execution of sentence could take as little as one year if our proposal passes. This stands in stark contrast to the 8 to 10 years of delay we are so used to under the current system.

President Clinton vowed that justice in the wake of the Oklahoma tragedy would be "swift, certain, and severe." We must help him keep this promise to the families of those who were murdered in Oklahoma City by passing comprehensive habeas corpus reform.

The Comprehensive Terrorism Prevention Act of 1995 provides for numerous other needed improvements in the law to fight the scourge of terrorism, including the authorization of additional appropriations—nearly $1.6 billion—to law enforcement to beef up counterterrorism efforts and increasing the maximum rewards permitted for information concerning international terrorism.

CERTAIN, SWIFT, AND UNIFIED RESPONSE

The people of the United States and around the world must know that terrorism is an issue that transcends politics and political parties. Our resolve in this matter must be clear: Our response to the terrorist threat, and to acts of terrorism, will be certain, swift, and unified.

Ours is a free society. Our liberties, the openness of our institutions, and our freedom of movement are what make America a nation we are willing to defend. These freedoms are cherished by virtually every American.

We must now redouble our efforts to combat terrorism and to protect our citizens. A worthy first step is the enactment of these sound provisions to provide law enforcement with the tools to fight terrorism.

In closing, what is shocking to so many of us is the apparent fact that those responsible for the Oklahoma atrocity are U.S. citizens. To think that Americans could do this to one another! Yet, these killers are not true Americans—not in my book. Americans are the men, women, and children who died under a sea of concrete and steel. Americans are the rescue workers, the volunteers, the law enforcement officials, and investigators who are cleaning up the chaos in Oklahoma City. The genuine Americans are the overwhelming majority of us who will forever reel at the senselessness and horror of April 19, 1995.

It falls on all of us, as Americans in heart and spirit, to condemn this sort of political extremism and to take responsible steps to limit the prospect for its recurrence. Can Congress pass legislation that will guarantee an end to domestic and international terrorism? We cannot.

Nevertheless, Congress has a responsibility to minimize the prospect that something like this can happen again. We must resolve that anarchistic radicalism—be it from the left or the right—will not prevail in our freedom-loving democracy. The rule of law and popular government will prevail.

(continued from page 59)

fringe groups. A recent Gallup poll found that an astounding 52 percent of people believed "the federal government has become so large and powerful that it poses a threat to the rights and freedoms of ordinary citizens." Four out of 10 thought the danger was "immediate."

There is much to fear. Government misbehavior in Waco, Texas, against the Branch Davidians and in Ruby Ridge, Idaho, against Randy Weaver and his family was well-publicized and deadly. Yet rather than holding law enforcement officials accountable, the Clinton administration promoted one FBI agent, reprimanded for his role in both affairs, to deputy director. Congress has yet to hold hearings, despite abundant evidence of government agencies abusing their vast authority. [Waco hearings were slated to begin July 14.] These cases, along with numerous brutal and erroneous DEA, ATF, and local police raids, suggest that government power itself is a serious problem.

Placing even greater authority in agencies that have abused their trust would only exacerbate peoples' fears of Washington. Therefore, legislators should first concentrate on reforming the present system. Unnecessary powers need to be terminated; abuses need to be curbed; accountability needs to be reestablished. Only then, when people's liberties would be less at risk, should Congress consider expanding the authority of law enforcement.

3. Do federal agencies require more power to combat terrorism? Although Oklahoma City has become the justification for the pending antiterrorism bills, the alleged perpetrators of that bombing were quickly apprehended. So, too, were the bombers of the World Trade Center. Moreover, since 1989, law enforcement officials have prevented nearly as many terrorist attacks as have been committed, 23 compared to 31. There is no evidence that federal agencies need more power to respond to terrorist threats.

Federal law already bars financial support for foreign terrorist groups. Proposals to expand this prohibition, give the president unreviewable authority to designate groups as terrorist, and investigate people where no evidence of a legal violation exists are unjustified. Similarly, terrorist acts, like the Oklahoma City bombing, are already against the law. There is no need to expand the definition to include literally every crime—"any unlawful destruction of property"—for example, which may be best handled by local authorities (such as animal rights activists).

THE GOVERNMENT HAS ENOUGH AUTHORITY

The federal government already has wiretap authority for such crimes as arson and homicide; proposals to expand that power to almost any crime (including misdemeanors, in the Clinton administration legislation) have nothing to do with combating terrorism. After all, of 7,554 requests for wiretap authority submitted by the FBI since 1978, only one has been rejected by the special seven-member court that oversees the process. The many new powers being proposed by President Clinton, Majority Leader Robert Dole, and others are no more necessary to the prevention of terrorism.

4. Does the law enforcement interest outweigh the rights and liberties of citizens that would be sacrificed? Even if increased power might marginally improve gov-

A Hasty Response to Terrorism

■ The Senate is congratulating itself for passing the Comprehensive Terrorism Protection Act of 1995 just seven weeks after the Oklahoma City bombing. But the Senate's hasty and ill-considered action has come at a price. Steps designed to protect Americans' physical safety will in many cases erode their liberties.

■ The legislation, a grab-bag of bills proposed by the Clinton Administration and members of Congress, contains some sound provisions. It provides, for example, more FBI personnel and resources to combat terrorism, increased penalties for dealing in explosives used to commit crimes and measures to make bombs easier to trace.

■ But the temptation was too strong, both in the White House and the Senate, to load the bill with tougher-sounding, more crowd-pleasing provisions. These include wide-ranging surveillance power for law enforcement agencies, crackdowns on suspected aliens and more blurring of the line between military forces and domestic peacekeeping police.

—Editorial, excerpted from *New York Times*
June 9, 1995

ernment's ability to respond to terrorism, Congress must still weigh the benefits against the costs. For example, the FBI investigative guidelines were created for a reason: the agency's Counter-Intelligence Program (COINTELPRO) resulted in spying on literally millions of law-abiding Americans from the 1940s through the 1970s. Yet this orgy of surveillance did not make America more secure. Nearly 700 FBI operations yielded a grand total of four convictions.

Similarly, the wholesale federalization of crimes would make Americans less free without making them more secure. State law already covers violent crime; existing federal law reaches special offenses, such as threats against the president. Proposals to expand federal jurisdiction combined with a broadening of the much-abused RICO statute, enhanced restrictions on money laundering, loosening of restraints on wiretapping, and use of the military to enforce domestic law would provide numerous opportunities for government to abuse citizens' rights.

Expansion of wiretaps to almost any felony would also cost the American people more in lost liberty than any security they might gain. Today, the government is empowered to seek wiretaps in cases involving arson and homicide, typical ingredients of terrorist acts. Yet federal wiretaps rarely involve these issues. In fact, wiretapping is focused on, of all things, gambling, along with racketeering and drugs.

Other assaults on individual liberty that have been tied to terrorism include proposals to restrict habeas corpus, which requires the government to justify holding a citizen, and limit encryption software, which ensures the privacy of computer communication. Neither proposal is designed to combat terror-

■

Citizens worried about their country while politicians worried about their influence.

■

ism. After all, habeas corpus, such a jealously guarded right that the Constitution permits only Congress to suspend its application, and to do so only during "rebellion or invasion," applies to those already in government custody. And computers have played no role in any recent terrorist plot.

More closely tied to international terrorism is the proposal to allow special courts to use secret evidence, withheld from the defendant, in deportation proceedings of legal residents of the United States. Yet the right of "confrontation" is a critical procedural safeguard. Once Congress embarks upon the slippery slope of allowing the government to present arguments without giving the defendant a chance to directly respond, legislators could apply this principle against citizens in any case involving a serious crime: murder, arson, and the like. Either the courts would void such laws as unconstitutional, as they have done in similar cases in the past, or American citizens could end up appearing before a tribunal akin to that of Great Britain's hated "star chamber."

DON'T SUBVERT POSSE COMITATUS

The president and Senator Dole have proposed increasing the role of the military in terror-

ism cases—essentially, repealing the Posse Comitatus Act whenever the attorney general desires military assistance. At the same time, both proposals would eliminate jurisdictional restrictions on such agencies as the ATF, allowing them to act however they pleased against anything termed "terrorism."

But there are very good reasons for retaining a bright line between the military and domestic law enforcement. The Defense Department should not be diverted from its most important job of defending America from international foes. Soldiers are not trained in the niceties of civil liberties; involving the Pentagon will simultaneously militarize and centralize law enforcement, poor practices in a republic. In fact, abuses have been evident in the ongoing use of the National Guard in drug interdiction campaigns. Similarly, reducing restraints on specialized law enforcement agencies will encourage further malfeasance by bureaucracies that already exceed their rightful authority, without any concomitant improvement in domestic security.

Terrorism obviously poses a serious threat to a free society like our own. But legislators should tailor their response to meet the threat, not garner votes. Despite the hideous Oklahoma City bombing, America remains largely free of terrorism. Congress' first task, then, should be to investigate how renegade government agencies are abusing their power and creating grievances that some misguided people believe are properly addressed through violence. Only then should legislators consider expanding federal law enforcement authority, and then only if they can do so without undermining the basic freedoms that make this nation unique—and worth living in.

Enemies of The State

America's "patriots" have a tough list of demands: keep your hands off my land, my wallet—and my guns

Jill Smolowe

Annamarie Miller is a dedicated schoolteacher with an obvious love of history and ideas, who dresses fastidiously in neatly pressed shirts and slacks and is inclined to exclaim "Gosh!" when she gets excited. Though hardly a menacing presence, Miller, 27, is a determined renegade who refuses to take any authority figure's word at face value. It all began, she says, during her student days at California State University at Chico. "I became disillusioned by the revisionism of history," she says. "A lot of stuff they were teaching me twisted the truth." Inspired by campaign literature, she began to question the "truths" of authorities far more powerful than her college professors. The Federal Reserve Board, for instance. Why had it never been audited? Had it perhaps already bankrupted the country? Or the Social Security Administration. Was it going to collapse before Miller was old enough to collect? Through such questions, Miller gradually arrived at a hard "truth" of her own. The constitutional rights of all Americans, she believes, are threatened by an overgrasping, irresponsible government.

She doesn't keep it to herself. Each Tuesday at 7 p.m., Miller broadcasts that unflinching message via public-access TV to an audience of 50,000 viewers in Northern California. Along with her husband Scott, a retail clerk, and his brother Randall, a chef, she uses their half-hour show, *The Informed Citizen*, to warn of threats to the American way of life. Among them: a con-

Would you describe the members of militia groups as:

	Describes	Doesn't describe
DANGEROUS	80%	11%
A THREAT TO OUR WAY OF LIFE	63%	26%
CRAZY	55%	33%
WELL INTENTIONED	30%	58%
PATRIOTS	21%	55%

Do you think the Federal Government should spy on the militias in order to monitor their activities?

YES	68%
NO	26%

From a telephone poll of 600 adult Americans taken for TIME/CNN on April 27 by Yankelovich Partners Inc. Sampling error is ± 27%. "Not sures" omitted.

spiratorial U.S. government that is surrendering its sovereignty to the U.N.; efforts by police and gun-control advocates to disarm citizens; and a tax burden that is robbing Americans of their hard-earned income. Her aim, she insists, is simply to inform and motivate. "A lot of people," she says, "are willing to give up their rights and freedom out of fear."

Before the bombing in Oklahoma City, few Americans would have thought that either Miller or her show posed a serious threat to the civic order. Unlike many other citizens who identify themselves as "patriots"—an amorphous, far-right populist movement of both armed militias and un-

armed groups that harbor a deep distrust of government—Miller does not spend her weekends running around in camouflage, shooting at imagined enemies. Nor does she buy into every wild conspiracy theory that crackles along the patriot grapevine, like last week's alert that the Oklahoma catastrophe—which "patriots" suspect involved three bombs, not one—was a government plot to enable President Clinton to proclaim martial law and divert public attention from forthcoming Whitewater hearings. Indeed, Miller's attitude toward the Oklahoma City culprits—"I say hang 'em"—sounded much like the President's.

But as Americans try to understand the social currents that could wash a home-grown terrorist up to the front doors of the Alfred P. Murrah Federal Building, they are taking a second look at people like Miller. It's not because Miller shows any signs of violent tendencies herself, but because she is one of the disseminators of a virulent antigovernment philosophy that may have helped plant thoughts of insurrection in someone else's head. Miller's own first thought upon hearing of the bombing was, "Oh, my gosh, I hope some idiot calling himself a patriot didn't do this." She admits that her own unarmed group, the Sons of Liberty, had attracted a "loose cannon," a young man who tried to join last summer. "He was saying things like, 'We ought to blow up the federal building,'" she recalls. The Sons of Liberty promptly tossed him out.

But what ideas do these fringe characters decamp with? Where do they go? And

 From *Time*, May 8, 1995, pp. 58-64, 66, 68-69. © 1995 by Time Inc. Magazine Company. Reprinted by permission.

what, if anything, are they up to now? What is most perplexing is the vague intersection between those so-called patriots who merely spread the word Paul Revere–style, those who are arming themselves in anticipation of a fight to defend their rights, and those who are already taking aim at perceived enemies. In recent months there have been several incidents between armed, angry citizens and government agents that have prompted officials to take these groups more seriously.

Last September, for instance, three men driving a Saturn were stopped in Fowlerville, Michigan, by a police officer after their vehicle crossed the center line. According to the town's police chief, Gary Krause, an officer found the car packed with weapons, including a .357-cal. revolver, three assault rifles, three 9-mm semiautomatic pistols and 700 rounds of ammunition. The three men identified themselves as bodyguards of Mark Koernke, the self-promoting militia propagandist. "They said they had just completed maneuvers," Krause recalls. While those three men didn't show up for their arraignment six days later, dozens of militia members did, turning out in camouflage fatigues and taunting police officers.

How many people have reached that breaking point with their Federal Government—and are they acting alone or together? If you count just the people who are arming themselves against the day when U.N. tanks roll through the heartland to establish the one-world order, estimates range only as high as 100,000. But if you include all the people in as many as 40 states who respond to the patriot rhetoric about a sinister, out-of-control federal bureaucracy—all the ranchers fed up with land- and water-use policies, all the loggers who feel besieged by environmentalists, all the underemployed who blame their plight on NAFTA and GATT—then the count soars upwards of 12 million. "People are drawn in under this soft umbrella of anger at the government and soon taken into the more violent part of the movement if they continue to express interest," says Mary Ann Mauney of the Atlanta-based Center for Democratic Renewal, which monitors hate groups.

Unfortunately, newcomers to the movement will find few guideposts that signal, This way the true believers, that way the dangerous zealots. The ranks of the antifederalist insurgency include plenty of the former: tax protesters, home schoolers, Christian fundamentalists and well-versed Constitutionalists. But the groups also contain an insidious sprinkling of the latter, including neo-Nazis and white supremacists. What binds these diverse elements is a fervent paranoia. The most fearful patriots believe that Soviet fighter jets are on standby in Biloxi, Mis-

sissippi, that frequent flyovers by "black helicopters" signal an imminent occupation by the armies of a one-world government, and that stickers on some interstate highways are coded to direct the invading armies. They also regard such federal agencies as the FBI, the Bureau of Alcohol, Tobacco and Firearms and particularly the Federal Emergency Management Agency as the shock troops for an all-out war on personal liberties.

WHILE FEAR IS A COMMON DENOMINATOR, not everyone worries about the same things. Tom Metzger, who founded White Aryan Resistance in 1980 after breaking with the Ku Klux Klan, ridicules talk of a military invasion. "Ninety percent of that stuff is nonsense," he says. "We've got 10 million Mexicans flooding into this country, and the militias are worried about repainted helicopters." For their part, many militia groups aggressively weed out racists, and a few even have minority members. According to its leader, Fitzhugh MacCrae, New Hampshire's Hillsborough County Dragoons includes blacks, Latinos and Asians, and favors good works like shoveling snow for the elderly. "I'm pro-choice and I donate money to PBS," he says. "How subversive is that? But I also support the Second Amendment. It is the only amendment that empowers the rest of them."

Indeed, the right to bear arms seems to be the one altar where moderate Constitutionalists and armed zealots can worship comfortably side by side. "There's a real fear that once the Second Amendment is abridged, the First will be the next to go," says Scott Wheeler, a writer for the U.S. Patriot Network. Despite the reverence for guns, however, "the vast majority of people in the militias are not violent or dangerous," says James Aho, a sociologist at Idaho State University who has interviewed 368 members of the radical right.

They do, however, have an unusually vigorous commitment to self-defense. "Within two years, I expect to see the Constitution suspended. We will be prepared to defend it," says Norman Olson, an independent Baptist minister who together with real estate salesman Ray Southwell founded the Michigan Militia. Toward that end, Olson has led army-style maneuvers on an 80-acre tract of scrub pine and meadow dotted with obstacle courses and bunkers. Most of those who come for the training sessions are middle-aged, white, family men who must struggle to support their loved ones and struggle even harder to catch their breath during Olson's exercises, which require them to traverse rugged terrain shouldering semiautomatic rifles. Despite the popularity of these exercises, the militia stripped Olson of his com-

mand last Friday after he sent inflammatory faxes to the news media blaming the Oklahoma explosion on the Japanese government. When a TIME reporter knocked on Olson's door later that day, Olson appeared in a blue bathrobe. "Why are you bothering me?" he asked. "Can't you see I'm trying to stop World War III?" The next day, both Olson and Southwell, who had helped prepare the fax, resigned under pressure from the militia.

AS BEFITS THESE GO-IT-ALONERS, militia members favor decentralization in their own ranks. The movement has "no national structure, no central command and no central leadership, either recognized from within the movement or without," says Jonathan Mozzochi, executive director of the Coalition for Human Dignity in Oregon. Partly, he believes, this is because it is a "grass-roots upsurge," but the lack of clear structure is intentional as well.

In 1987, Robert Miles, a former Ku Klux Klan Grand Dragon who was convicted in 1971 of burning school buses in Pontiac, Michigan, articulated the idea of "leaderless cells," an organizational structure of small autonomous groups that effectively thwarts infiltration and defuses culpability. "Miles compared his new concept to a spider web," says Richard Lobenthal of the Anti-Defamation League of B'nai B'rith. "You can put your hand in it and it gives, and when you remove the hand, it is still there."

That web is further fortified by the information revolution, which enables people to disseminate their ideas widely, cheaply and often under the safe cloak of anonymity. Bomb recipes have been transmitted across computer bulletin boards. CB and shortwave radios enable militia members not only to communicate between themselves but also to monitor the communications of law-enforcement officials. In the gray split-level house that serves as the nerve center of the Michigan Militia there are 15 phone lines, four computer, multiple fax machines, a professional printing press and a full television-production facility.

Less well-funded patriots mount inexpensive programs on public-access or satellite TV. Or they can make and market their own videotapes—a propaganda tactic that insulated the patriot evangelists from any direct blame for the antigovernment acts they may inspire. The handful of celebrities on the patriot circuit—people like Koernke, attorney Linda Thompson and Militia of Montana founder John Trochmann—all have tapes in circulation that promote their theories about the plot to take over the world. In a two-hour video called *America in Peril: A Call to Arms,*

AMERICA'S MILITIAS: A PRIMER

CATALYSTS Of The MOVEMENT

Oct. 24, 1945: United Nations founded, beginnings of "one-world government"

1958: John Birch Society founded; advocates anticommunism, minimal Federal Government, abandonment of Federal Reserve System, U.S. withdrawal from the United Nations

June 3, 1983: Tax resister and Posse Comitatus member **Gordon Kahl,** wanted in the killings of two U.S. Marshals in North Dakota, is "martyred" in shoot-out with a county sheriff and federal agents in northwest Arkansas

Sept. 11, 1990: In an address to a joint session of Congress after Iraq invades Kuwait, President George Bush proclaims a new world order based on multinational action under U. N. aegis

Aug. 31, 1992: Idaho white separatist **Randy Weaver** surrenders after a standoff with federal agents in which his wife, his 14-year-old son and a U.S. Marshal are shot and killed. A jury later acquits Weaver and co-defendant Kevin Harris on charges of killing the Marshal. No one is indicted in the deaths of Weaver's wife and son. He now lives in Grand Junction, Iowa.

April 19, 1993: FBI launches an attack on the Branch Davidian compound in Waco, Texas, and more than 70 Davidians are killed as the settlement burns to the ground

Nov. 30, 1993: President Clinton signs the Brady bill into law; it requires a five-day waiting period for all handgun purchases

FAVORITE CONSPIRACY THEORIES

According to many militia members, the U. N. plans to conquer the U.S. using the National Guard and L.A. gangs to disarm the public.

Recent chemical spills are practice runs for a much larger series of disasters, faked by the government, to draw people out of their homes and enable U.N. forces to enter homes and seize guns.

Before the U.N. takes over, the Federal Emergency Management Agency (FEMA) will head up an interim government.

The Amtrak repair yards in Indianapolis will be used as a huge crematorium to dispose of political dissidents.

Black helicopters have been buzzing Western states on missions of surveillance for the invading U.N. troops.

Salt mines beneath Detroit hold a division of Russian troops waiting for the order to rise and take over the U.S.

Small colored bar-code stickers found on the back of road signs will help direct the invading troops.

The government has installed electronic devices in car ignitions to stall autos on the day the new world order takes over.

Paper currency has bar codes on it so government agents can drive by each house with secret scanners and count how much money each family has.

GEOGRAPHY OF ZEALOTRY

United States Militia Association Blackfoot, Idaho
Founder Samuel Sherwood identifies closely with the Weaver siege. He has said that "Civil War could be coming, and with it the need to shoot Idaho legislators."

Almost Heaven Kamiah, Idaho
This armed community created by **Bo Gritz** will be made up of about 30 families. It hopes to be self-sufficient and obey all laws "unless they go against the laws of God and common sense." Gritz has written, "The tyrants who ordered the assault on the Weavers and Waco should be tried and executed as traitors."

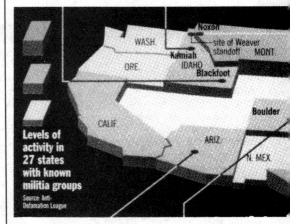

Levels of activity in 27 states with known militia groups
Source: Anti-Defamation League

Police Against the New World Order Arizona
Leader Jack McLamb, a former Phoenix police officer, puts out the monthly *Aid and Abet Police News-letter,* which discusses "constitutional issues for lawmen," and he broadcasts from his home outside Phoenix an hour-long call-in radio program.

Guardians of American Liberties Boulder, Colo.
Leader Stewart Webb, has a history of anti-Semitism and has appeared on right-wing radio shows discussing his conspiracy theories. The group describes itself as a network of American citizens, formed to ensure the government is free of corruption and to safeguard the U.S. Constitution.

ENEMIES LIST

Council on Foreign Relations:
New York City-based foreign policy group whose board includes the heads of Xerox and AT&T and former Federal Reserve chairman Paul Volcker; patriot activists see the council as an advocate of destroying U.S. sovereignty

United Nations:
The Trojan horse of one-world government

Bureau of Alcohol, Tobacco and Firearms:
Accused by militia members of oppressive enforcement of federal gun laws

Attorney General Janet Reno:
Ordered the attack on the Branch Davidian's Waco, Texas, compound

Trilateral Commission:
Long the bête noire of Pat Robertson and the John Birch Society, the commission is a conclave of American, European and Japanese business leaders and politicians that was established and partly funded by

banker David Rockefeller in 1973. Prominent Trilateralists: Jimmy Carter, George Bush, Bill Clinton, Henry Kissinger

Federal Emergency Management Agency:
Established during the Carter Administration to deal with hurricanes, earthquakes and other disasters but actually "the most powerful organization in the United States," according to anonymous patriot Internet postings; seen by patriots as a tool of the Trilateral Commission "to seize control of the reins of government through emergency fiat"

**Militia of Montana
Noxon, Mont.**
MOM is one of the most visible and extreme militias, created by **John Trochmann,** his brother David and nephew Randy to protest the Weaver siege. They feel citizens must form unorganized militias to protect themselves. They also advertise and distribute books, tapes and videos.

**Michigan Militia
Corps
Harbor Springs,
Mich.**
Started in April 1994 in response to gun-control legislation. **Norman Olson,** a Baptist minister and gun shop owner, was its commander until his ouster last week. It believes the U.N. plans to lead the U.S. into a socialist world government. The corps claims a membership of 12,000.

**Mark Koernke
"Mark from Michigan," Dexter, Mich.**
A leading propagandist of the militia movement. Until last week he had an hour-long shortwave radio show, *The Intelligence Report,* five nights a week over World Wide Christian Radio WWCR. He has ties to the Militia of Montana and John Trochmann.

**American Justice
Federation
Indianapolis, Ind.**
Chaired by attorney Linda Thompson after the federal assault on the Branch Davidians. It is "dedicated to stopping the New World Order and getting the truth out to the American public." She called for an armed march on Washington and treason trials for congressional traitors.

**Constitution Defense
Militia
N.H.**
A small, well-organized group led by Edward Brown. New Hampshire law provides for an unorganized militia. Brown is opposed to gun control, the U.N. and the Federal Government.

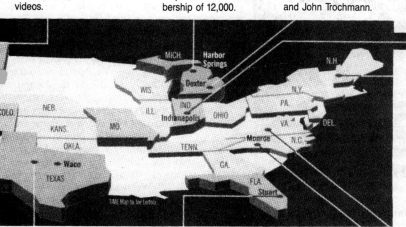

**Texas Constitutional
Militia**
Set up by Jon Roland, it began in early 1994 and held its first "muster" on April 19, 1994, Waco's first anniversary. Its coded E-mail network serves as an information highway for the underground. Roland claims to have penetrated the government's electronic intelligence.

**Florida State Militia
Stuart, Fla.**
Founded by Robert Pummer. Its handbook says, "We have had enough—enough drugs and crime, violence and bloodshed, enough Waco . . . and government attacks on Christian Americans." It warns, "Buy Ammo now! You will not be able to get it later!"

**Citizens for the Reinstatement of
Constitutional
Government
Monroe, N.C.**
Albert Esposito, its leader, urges his group to amass the four B's: Bibles, bullets, beans and bandages. The group aims to "make the Holy Bible and the U.S. Constitution the law of the land."

**Blue Ridge Hunt Club
Virginia**
Founder James Roy Mullins and other members were arrested in July and charged with possession and sale of a short-barreled rifle and unregistered silencers. Officials said Mullins formed the club to arm its members in preparation for war with the government.

TELLING THEM APART

Aryan Nations: White-supremacist group based near Hayden Lake, Idaho, headed by the Rev, Richard Butler

Survivalists: People who prepare for imminent breakdown of the economy and government by stockpiling food, water, guns and ammunition and moving to wilderness hideouts in Idaho, Northern California and Montana

Patriots: Network of antifederal activists; they stress the 10th Amendment to the Constitution, which says powers not delegated to the Federal Government are reserved to the states or to the people themselves

Militias: Groups that arm themselves to defend the Constitution, which they believe is in peril

Christian Identity: Movement that believes Northern Europeans are the chosen people of the Old Testament and Jews are the offspring of Satan; calls the Federal Government the "Zionist Occupational Government"

Posse Comitatus: Tax-resistance movement that included many Midwesterners who were hard pressed by farm crisis of the early- and mid-1980s; believed that IRS was a tool of Zionist international bankers

Wise Use: Movement based in the West and financed by mining and timber companies, seeks to lift restrictions on grazing, logging and mining on federal lands

Koernke, an Ann Arbor janitor who goes by the handle "Mark from Michigan," ominously reviews the "evidence" of one-world conspiracy. At FEMA, he asserts, fewer than 64 employees are engaged in disaster work; the other 3,600 are "there to manage the system after they take over." The incursion is inevitable, he argues, and the only choice is "to lock and load."

Koernke unequivocally denies any involvement in the Oklahoma blast, but he has capitalized on the atrocity to rally his followers around the idea of government complicity in the explosion. On his shortwave radio broadcast the day of the bombing, he exhorted true believers in Oklahoma to grab their video cameras and shoot footage of the site. "Document *what* agencies were coming in and out. As a matter of fact, [my wife] Nancy and the kids, watching the initial footage of this, saw what appeared to be United Nations observers' badges." The next day, patriot computer bulletin-board systems were rife with messages like this one on the Citizenship BBS in California's San Fernando Valley: "This was orchestrated by the shadow government (i.e., Trilateralists, ATF, FEMA, etc.) to whip the public into such a frenzy that Americans will BEG to surrender their privacy for some government-provided protection from terrorism." At week's end,

the shortwave station carrying Koernke's broadcast dropped his show.

Other patriots are worried that their own agendas will be confused with the as-yet-unexplained agenda of the Oklahoma bomber. "If you get one crazy out there who doesn't have a brain, then everybody gets lumped in," complains Dean Compton, 33, who heads an armed militia in California's Sierra Nevada foothills. In dread of just such an event, he announced the formation of a group in March called the National Alliance of Christian Militia. Compton, who claims 85% of the militia movement is Christian, says the new alliance is an attempt to distinguish their efforts from "the hate groups and the Klan."

SUCH DISTINCTIONS, HOWEVER, ARE not always apparent. Two days after the bombing, 550 patriot Christians gathered in Branson, Missouri, for the International Coalition of Covenant Congregations Conference. "I mingled with a lot of people there, and there was not a shred of sympathy for what happened in Oklahoma," an attendee told TIME. According to this source, some participants felt the carnage was understandable retaliation for the 1993 deaths of children during the government raid in Waco, Texas.

California's Compton asserts that "mainstream" militias are working round the clock to assist in the investigation of the bombing. "We want worse than anybody to make sure these guys come to justice." But, he warns, "if the government gets heavy-handed" in its search, "we'll have some problems." Easygoing and articulate, Compton, the father of three, discusses his apocalyptic convictions with patience and occasional humor. Yet he is girding for guerrilla-style warfare against his own government. He's got a 9-mm semiautomatic pistol strapped to his hip, a wad of emergency cash and enough ammunition to fight a small battle. In the back of his battered Chevy Silverado, he packs a green .223-cal. Sporter assault rifle, a $200 Kevlar helmet, a CB radio, walkie-talkies, camouflage uniforms and 15 days of provisions.

Compton, who quit his job as a real estate agent in the lumber community of Shingletown to run armed-militia training camps, says all these preparations are for the sake of his children. "I decided I'd do everything in my power to make sure that when my son grows up, he'll have the same freedoms I had," he explains. His children, who range in age from 3 to 11, are schooled at home by Compton and his wife. Compton fled the San Francisco Bay Area 10 years ago to settle on a 120-acre mountain ranch, and his rage against the government seems to have grown in this region where more jobs than trees have been felled in recent years. "Three local lumber mills have been closed in the past year because of spotted owls," he claims. Compton also complains that he can't dig up the manzanita bushes on his own land because of local ordinances. "But," he adds cynically, "you sure better pay taxes on it, or they'll take it all away from you."

That part of Compton's rant is familiar territory for those caught up in the modern Sagebrush Rebellion, a land-rights movement that is spreading rapidly in Western states. Over the past few years, offices of the Bureau of Land Management and the Forest Service have come under increasing attack by ranchers, farmers and loggers fed up with federal rules about land use, water rights and endangered habitats. In Nevada, where more than 80% of the state is public land, federal employees have been refused service in restaurants, taunted at public gatherings and harassed with vulgar gestures. In March a bomb exploded in the forest rangers' district headquarters in Carson City, shattering windows and damaging the office of the chief ranger.

Do you agree citizens have the right to arm themselves in order to oppose the power of the Federal Government?

	Yes
WHITE MALES	34%
ALL OTHERS	22%

Do you agree Americans have the constitutional right to buy and store large amounts of weapons?

	Yes
WHITE MALES	34%
ALL OTHERS	18%

Increasingly these local-control activists are finding common cause with the militias. "Both have an antifederal outlook," says Dan Barry of the Environmental Working Group in Washington. "They run into each other because they have similar priorities." Indeed, their complaints are often indistinguishable. "We've been pushed so far by rules and regulations, the feds are in our pockets so deep, people are outraged," says Ronny Rardin, a commissioner in New Mexico's Otero County. The land-reform rebels have also been developing an appetite for militia-style conspiracy theories. "The New World Order will be running our lives through the United Nations!" warns a fund-raising letter for the National Federal Lands Conference, one of the leading groups.

Meanwhile, the conspiracy theories grow wilder by the day. In one, Queen Elizabeth is working through British conglomerates to regain control of the colonies—witness the purchase of Burger King and Holiday Inn by British companies. There is also rumored to be a global conspiracy to implant newborn babies with microchips. Robert Brown, editor and publisher of *Soldier of Fortune*, a must-read for many gun advocates and survivalists, has tracked some of these wacky conspiracies and discounted them, including one much vaunted black helicopter sighting. But that hasn't quieted the patriot grapevine. "It's all bull. But they don't want reasonable explanations," he says, "because they don't fit their preconceived notions."

The movement's communications network is often more sophisticated than its judgment, which means that any mysterious incident gets blown into a conspiracy epic. Take, for instance, the "invasion" of Okanogan County in northwest Washington State. It began last Labor Day when a local cattle rancher stumbled across a backwoods military camp teeming with men in fatigues. Word quickly spread that the invasion of U.N. troops had finally begun. When concerned citizens showed up at Sheriff Jim Weed's office, Weed grabbed the telephone and soon learned that the men in cammies were actually border-patrol officials conducting a joint operation with Canadian authorities. By then, though, panic had spread throughout the state, prompting phone calls from state senators and representatives. To this day, there are some patriots who still don't believe Weed's explanation. "I was accused by one person of being seen getting off a U.N. helicopter at an airport wearing a blue helmet," Weed says.

In the wake of Oklahoma City, many U.S. agencies are stepping up their watch of militia activities, but they may only feed the patriots' paranoia about government. If investigators start knocking on the doors of militia members, warns Ron Cole, who is a lecturer on the patriot circuit, "it could conceivably turn into an armed struggle against the government."

Chip Berlet, who tracks right-wing populism for Political Research Associates, based in Cambridge, Massachusetts, is not alone in drawing parallels between America's patriot movement and Germany's Weimar Republic. "You see the rise of a large group of disaffected middle-class and working-class people with a strong sense of grievance," he says. "None of the major parties speak for them." If their grievances aren't resolved, he warns, they are likely to become more militant. The message from the militias is largely the same: whether it takes a whisper or a shout, we will be heard.

—Reported by Sam Allis/Boston, Edward Barnes/Petoskey, Michigan, Patrick Dawson/Billings, David S. Jackson/San Francisco, Scott Norvell/Atlanta and Richard Woodbury/Denver

Forgiving the
Unforgivable

Survivors of crime and abuse are learning an unlikely method of freeing themselves from their anguish: forgiveness. It's a skill, say therapists, that can benefit us all.

Jean Callahan

Former NEW AGE JOURNAL *articles editor Jean Callahan is a Boston-based freelance writer. Her article "Spiritual Adventures in the Borscht Belt" appeared in the May/June issue.*

Four years ago, Phyllis Hotchkiss woke up in the middle of the night with a terrible ache in her chest. Her nineteen-year-old son, Brian, who had gone out to a carnival earlier in the evening, still wasn't home, and she was worried. A few hours later, two policemen rang the doorbell and told her that Brian was dead. His head had been bashed in, probably with a tire iron, although the murder weapon was never located. For months the police had no suspect, either, but Hotchkiss knew—the way a mother knows—that his killer was the neighbor with whom Brian had spent his last hours. Eventually that neighbor would be arrested, tried, and convicted, but in the months after Brian's death, his freedom tortured Hotchkiss. With alarming cruelty, he would station himself across the street from her home, staring and laughing at family members as they came and went. When the truth about Brian's death finally came out, it made no more sense than did his murderer's persecution of the family: Brian had simply balked at pitching in money for gas; the two young men had argued, then fought; some time later, Brian was killed.

Today, taped to the wall above the computer in the Hotchkisses' suburban Massachusetts home office is a photograph of Brian's murderer. Push pins are stuck into his eyes, his cheeks, his neck. "On bad days," says this small, soft-spoken woman in her mid-forties, "I move them around, add more, or push them in further."

Phyllis Hotchkiss has lived through a parent's worst nightmare, and a day doesn't go by when she doesn't feel hatred for the remorseless young man who took her son's life. "I will never forgive him for Brian's death," she says. It was rage, in fact, that gave her the energy to form a local chapter of Parents of Murdered Children, a group that has supported dozens of other people who have faced similar tragedies.

But several months ago, something happened that seems to be softening Hotchkiss's anger. As part of her work with the parents' group, she initiated a series of weekly meetings with prisoners—mostly convicted murderers—at the Bay State Correctional Institute in nearby Norfolk, Massachusetts. She had proposed the meetings to the prison chaplain, she explains, so that she and other women whose children have been murdered could "tell our stories and make sure these men realize how much they've hurt people." She expected to see the prisoners as "human garbage," the way she sees Brian's murderer, but instead she was touched by the courage the men showed in facing the grieving mothers. She was especially moved by one man who broke down sobbing when he described himself as a victim as well as a criminal because his own son had been murdered.

As each series of meetings ends, Hotchkiss and the other women hold a simple ceremony in which the men are given a remembrance—a tiny gold angel lapel pin. "It's never too late to change a life," she says. "If I can touch one prisoner's heart, maybe he won't hurt anyone else."

Talking to Hotchkiss now, it's clear that a subtle shift has occurred as she has opened her own heart to these strangers. She is surprised herself at how the meetings with these prisoners have affected her. She seems to be on the verge of redefining herself, not only as the mother of a murder victim but also as someone who can integrate that terrible experience, who can remember Brian without constantly feeling the pain of his loss. Phyllis Hotchkiss is not ready to forgive her son's murderer yet, but she has nonetheless begun to experience what a number of psychotherapists describe as the healing power of forgiveness.

CONFRONTED WITH such a story, many of us will shudder—perhaps as much in response to the word *forgiveness* as to the callousness of the crime. In such a case, forgiveness, at least as the term is widely understood, would seem entirely inappropriate—even dangerous. Shouldn't people who commit crimes be condemned and held accountable for their wrongdoing? Wouldn't "forgiving" a brutal killer merely send a message that society will tolerate those who murder, steal, rape, or in some other way slash the social fabric? Isn't Phyllis Hotchkiss's sense of righteous wrath a natural human—and wholly justifiable—response to being so cruelly victimized?

Some things, we might argue, are just unforgivable. Drawing upon the same logic, we might similarly justify our own long-term anger and resentment about far less catastrophic tragedies—the boss who fired us precipitously, the alcoholic father who was never there for us emotionally, the girlfriend who unceremoniously dumped us just when we needed her most. Even those who are at peace with their personal histories can, in a heartbeat, label any number of social offenses absolutely "unforgivable": Rape. Torture. Child abuse. Drunk driving. Infidelity.

There may be compelling reasons to cling to our grudges and animosities, and significant satisfactions in doing so. But we hold on, say those who advocate forgiveness, at a very high price—emotionally, physically, even spiritually. "There are people who wake up in a rage every morning over something that happened thirty or forty years ago," notes Robin Casarjian, psychotherapist, author of the recently published *Forgiveness: A Bold Choice for a Peaceful Heart,* and a leading voice in the growing forgiveness movement. "If anger is running your life, who is it hurting?"

For more than a decade, Casarjian has been helping people let go of old anger and resentments through the practice of forgiveness. She's presented the idea to recovering addicts and alcoholics, to prisoners, to mothers living in homeless shelters with their children, to public school teachers, and to groups in the corporate, health-care, and military communities. At the beginning of each forgiveness workshop—no matter what type of audience she's addressing—Casarjian must confront her listeners' inevitable resistance to the concept.

"So often when people think about forgiveness they think about what it's going to do for someone else," she says. "They say, 'I'm not going to forgive them, after what they did,' as if forgiving them would be doing the other person a favor. What they don't realize is that forgiveness is really an act of self-interest. We're doing ourselves a favor, because we become free to have a more peaceful life—we free ourselves from being emotional victims of others."

Robert Enright, a University of Wisconsin professor who has documented connections between forgiving and mental health in groups of elderly women, college students, and middle-aged adults, would agree. Enright has found that people who forgive long-standing grievances decrease their levels of anxiety and depression and raise levels of self-esteem. Their blood

pressure tends to drop and the tension in their faces eases. The greatest emotional transformation occurs, Enright says, among those for whom the stakes are highest: someone, say, who has been deeply wounded in a very close relationship.

Mind-body research also suggests that holding onto anger and resentment can make you more than depressed and anxious; it can also make you physically sick. For years, psychoneuroimmunologists have shown how emotional stress changes the way the immune system functions. People under stress routinely develop more colds, flus, and infections, and stress may help trigger autoimmune diseases such as lupus and rheumatoid arthritis. Describing the cancer-prone personality in their book *Getting Well Again*, O. Carl Simonton, M.D., Stephanie Matthews-Simonton, and James Creighton cite "a tendency to hold resentment and a marked inability to forgive" as part of the process through which some people develop serious illnesses. And in his books *The Trusting Heart* and *Anger Kills*, Duke University medical school professor Redford Williams, M.D., makes a convincing case that of all the Type A traits, clinging to anger is the one most likely to trigger the development of heart disease. He also says that people who relax and learn to let go of their anger are likely to live longer even when they do get sick.

OK. So forgiveness may have its benefits. But what if you just can't bring yourself to do it? Not to worry, says Casarjian. "When people tell me that, I ask them not to say 'I *can't* do it,' but to say 'I haven't been able to.'" Forgiveness, Casarjian explains, seldom occurs spontaneously, like some mystical bolt of lightning that strikes if you're lucky. Rather, it's a skill that can be practiced and learned. But before it can be learned, it's important to understand what forgiveness does and does not mean.

MOST OF US LEARNED the word *forgiveness* in childhood religious training. In the Old Testament, God forgave the Israelites for worshiping false idols, but not until he'd sent them reeling through the desert as punishment. In the New Testament, Jesus forgives those who crucify him, a superhumanly hard act to follow. Our early efforts at forgiving are usually false starts, no deeper or more sincere than a five-year-old's mumbled "That's OK." But when advocates such as Casarjian use the term

forgiveness, they are not talking about patriarchal noblesse oblige, turning the other cheek, condoning offensive behavior, letting the bastards off the hook, pretending everything's fine when really it isn't, making nice, denying anger, or any of the other popular definitions. "Forgiveness does not in any way justify or condone harmful actions," explains noted Vipassana meditation teacher Jack Kornfield in his new book, *A Path with Heart.* "While you forgive, you may also say, 'Never again will I knowingly allow this to happen.'" Casarjian concurs: "You can even forgive someone and at the same time work very hard at getting them convicted for the crime they've committed."

Nor does forgiveness mean that you're inviting the person to commit the act all over again. "People often have an underlying fear that they're setting themselves up to be hurt again, because they aren't clear about their own boundaries," says Casarjian. "They don't realize they can forgive a person and at the same time confront them and really challenge them to be accountable for growing up." Nor does it mean you have to become best friends with the person who has harmed you. "Just because you forgive someone," says Casarjian, "it doesn't mean you have to have dinner with them or see them or even talk to them again."

In fact, forgiving someone doesn't require that you see or talk to the person at all, since forgiveness is basically an inner process. Writes Kornfield: "Forgiveness is simply an act of the heart, a movement to let go of the pain, the resentment, the outrage that you have carried as a burden for so long. It is an easing of your own heart." Gerald Jampolsky, M.D., a psychiatrist who works with children facing catastrophic illnesses at the Center for Attitudinal Healing in Tiburon, California, describes forgiveness as a matter of perception—"seeing the light instead of the lamp shade"—seeing through the dumb, thoughtless, crazy things people do to the soul shining within each person. Casarjian likes to amend Jampolsky's definition by saying that forgiveness really means seeing the light as well as the lamp shade. You can acknowledge somebody's faults and still keep your heart open to that other human being.

For Casarjian, this choice to see in a new way—to "see with spiritual eyes rather than physical eyes"—is the crux of forgiveness. "I don't just look at a person and say they're a jerk. I look at them and, yes, I see that, but I also see their behavior in the context of a much greater reality about them—I see a fundamental goodness that may be buried under the way they're acting." The side benefit of this practice, she says, is that when you start seeing the goodness in others, it reflects back on yourself. You begin to experience your own goodness as well.

FORGIVENESS, IT SHOULD be noted, remains a controversial subject, especially among survivors of child abuse and many therapists who work with them. Because the victims of childhood brutality find it so hard to believe that someone they love would hurt them, because they need parents' love and approval no matter how badly the parents have treated them, and because they want to stop hurting and be part of a family again, they are all too willing to forgive, these therapists say.

Having witnessed the emotional and physical costs of premature forgiveness, many therapists who work with survivors of child abuse and incest actually caution against forgiving. Judith Herman, M.D., author of *Trauma and Recovery*, maintains

that in cases of childhood incest, forgiveness is not possible until the perpetrator has made amends. Alice Miller, the renowned Swiss psychotherapist, actually calls forgiveness a form of collaboration with the perpetrator in cases of incest and other child abuse. Speaking from her own experience in *Breaking Down the Wall of Silence*, Miller writes that "it was precisely the opposite of forgiveness—namely, rebellion against mistreatment suffered . . . that ultimately freed me from the past."

The problem with Herman's thinking, say forgiveness advocates, is the fact that perpetrators seldom make amends. And, although they agree with Miller that rebellion may be the most healthy response to mistreatment in the short run, it limits development when it becomes a general response to life. "People who have been deeply and profoundly abused, especially as children, may well need to work on rage and grief for a long time," says Casarjian, emphasizing that no one can ever tell anyone else that it's time to forgive. Says Kornfield: "When you have been deeply wounded, the work of forgiveness can take years. It will go through many stages —grief, rage, sorrow, fear, and confusion

—and in the end, if you let yourself feel the pain you carry, it will come as a relief, as a release for your heart."

CASARJIAN SUGGESTS starting out the practice of forgiveness slow and easy. "When I first introduce the notion, I say, Don't even think about forgiving the people you have a real historical charge with—say, your mother or father." Instead, she suggests practicing on what she calls "neutral territory"—with people you feel you don't even know: "people in elevators, or strangers walking down the street." But, she warns, you'll soon find that there is little neutral territory: "What becomes particularly interesting is to observe that our 'ego' minds or personalities have judgments about so many people. I don't like the way that person looks or the way she dresses, or he looks like a nerd. We make character judgments about people based on their behavior or their dress."

One of the most enlightening, and certainly the most amusing, ways Casarjian has developed for helping people step out

---

How Compassion Caught a Kidnapper

In 1973, Marietta Jaeger and her husband took their five children on their dream vacation—a month camping in Montana. As she recounted recently before a gathering hosted by Murder Victim Families for Reconciliation, the dream turned tragic just three days into the trip, when the couple's youngest daughter, seven-year-old Susie, was found to be missing from her tent.

Search parties scoured the area, boats dragged the nearby river, police investigated the possibility of kidnapping. A week later a man called saying he had Susie and would exchange her for a ransom, but for various reasons the deal fell through. As the frustrations and uncertainty mounted, Jaeger was filled with hatred for the kidnapper and fantasies of revenge: "I would have killed him with my bare hands and a smile on my face."

As weeks gave way to months, Jaeger, a devout Christian, decided to try another approach. She surrendered to God. "I said, OK, I give God permission to change my heart." She began trying to see the

kidnapper as one of God's creations. "No matter how I felt about this man, in God's eyes he was just as precious as Susie." She began praying for him, wanting him to experience the love of God in his life. Months gave way to a year. To mark the anniversary of the kidnapping, a reporter from a Montana paper wrote a story about the Jaegers' ordeal, quoting Marietta that she would welcome a chance to talk to the kidnapper herself. Apparently, the kidnapper read the paper.

The phone rang in the middle of the night. "It was clear that he called to taunt," she recalls. " 'You wanted to talk to me, well, here I am. What are you going to do about it? I'm the one who calls the shots.'. . . But despite the fact that he was being smug and nasty, something incredible began to happen in me. As desperate as I was to get Susie back, I wanted to reach him with all my heart." The compassion caught the man by surprise, and he stayed on the phone for some time. When she asked what she could do to help him, he finally broke down

and wept.

All the while, Jaeger's tape recorder—hooked to the telephone—was running. Based on the recording, and one of a subsequent call, investigators were able to determine that the man was a suspect they had previously interrogated. He was soon apprehended. The penalty for kidnapping in Montana was death, but at Jaeger's request, the kidnapper was offered a chance to confess in exchange for life in prison. As it turned out, he had killed several other children and teenagers besides Susie, who, investigators discovered, had been murdered a week after she was taken.

"By the time he was arrested I had come to realize that God's idea of justice is not punishment," says Jaeger, "but restoration. I wanted him to receive the help he needed to become the man God created him to be."

Murder Victim Families for Reconciliation, 2093 Willow Creek Rd., Portage IN 46368; (219) 763-2170.

of this maze of judgment to experiment with the transformative powers of forgiveness is something she calls "the forgiveness walk." She asks you to simply walk through an ordinary half-hour of your life with an open heart, assuming that everyone you encounter is a fundamentally decent, good human being. As you meet each person or situation, assume the best and send out gentle thought-messages of love and respect. Try this exercise and you will probably be surprised to discover how quickly and how often the world gets the better of you. From ill-mannered drivers to incompetent sales clerks, from recalcitrant coworkers to your own dear children, the opportunities for irritation are infinite.

Who among us has never flown into a rage over some petty injustice? "Forgiving the big stuff is relatively easy," observes Marianne Williamson, author of the best sellers *Return to Love* and *A Woman's Worth* and a teacher of the forgiveness-heavy *Course in Miracles.* "What's really hard is forgiving the courier for not delivering the Federal Express package on time, or forgiving the telephone company because the line was supposed to be turned on at two o'clock and now it's five. In a crisis, something kicks in. You get a special grace. But on a daily basis, forgiving is harder."

With a little practice, says Casarjian, you'll soon begin to understand how remarkably the world changes if you just step back a bit and respond to minor aggravations intentionally and lovingly, keeping everyone's basic innocence in mind. Your mood will lighten, you'll have more fun, and you'll make much more profound connections with the people you meet.

Another first step toward forgiveness, says Casarjian, is to sit down and write a list of all the benefits you get from holding onto anger. Is it a way to prove you're "right"? Is it an effort to control a situation? Is it a way to be heard? Is it a way to avoid the risks of opening up to other feelings? Bodywork can help, too, she says. Practices such as therapeutic massage, bioenergetics, Alexander Technique, or Feldenkrais Method exercises can free up emotions held in the joints and muscles. Once you've dredged up all those hostile feelings, what do you do with them? Expressing anger can be a crucial prerequisite to forgiving. Communicate your hostile feelings in a positive way, whenever possible. When you can't communicate directly, write angry letters you have no intention of mailing. Devise a ritual to dispel the bad vibrations. Scream at the top of your lungs while you drive down the interstate

with the windows rolled up and the radio blaring. Run a marathon. No matter how you choose to do it, the point is to work through your rage instead of holding onto it.

Once anger has been explored and expressed, says Carsarjian, you can more readily move beyond it to forgiveness by adopting the following viewpoint: Almost all human behavior is driven by a primal need for love and respect. Although at first it may seem absurd to imagine this about, say, the creep who steals your car, just try to imagine that each mean or seemingly stupid thing you see somebody do is an expression of fear and a very limited, very warped way of looking for love. If you can succeed even occasionally at this reframing, Casarjian says, if—just once in a while—you can weigh vulnerabilities, weaknesses, new stresses, old traumas, you will begin to make fewer harsh judgments.

There are times when expressing your anger directly by talking it through with the other person isn't desirable—or even possible. Say, for example, you harbor old resentments toward an ex-lover you haven't seen for years or a family member who is now dead. In such situations, Casarjian recommends a meditation she calls the Love and Forgiveness visualization.

After getting in a quiet, meditative state, you picture in your imagination a safe and comfortable place, one in which you feel peaceful and strong. Then you mentally invite someone you'd like to forgive to join you in this place. Take some time to talk in your imagination to this person, sharing the truth of your experience, including how that person has hurt and disappointed you. Then listen to the truth of that person's experience, trying to let go of blame and judgment.

When someone is openhearted and willing to heal a rift, says Casarjian, such a visualization can lead to tremendous change in a relationship, without the other person taking any part in the process. Jack Kornfield discovered this several years ago through the remarkable experience of a child abuse survivor who had attended one of his meditation retreats. "She'd been angry, depressed, and grieving for many years," he writes in *A Path with Heart.* "She had worked in therapy and meditation through a long process to heal these wounds. Finally in this retreat she came to a place of forgiveness for the person who had abused her. She wept with deep forgiveness, not for the act, which can never be condoned, but because she no longer wished to carry the bitterness and hatred in her heart.

"She left the retreat and returned home and found a letter waiting in her mailbox. It had been written by the man who had abused her, with whom she had no contact for fifteen years. While in many cases abusers will deny their actions to the last, in spite of forgiveness, something had changed this man's mind. He wrote, 'For some reason I felt compelled to write to you. I've been thinking about you so much this week. I know I caused you great harm and suffering and brought great suffering on myself as well. But I simply want to ask your forgiveness. I don't know what else I can say.' Then she looked at the date at the top of the letter. It was written the same day she completed her inner work of forgiveness."

B Y FAR, THE MOST POWerful and mysterious act of forgiving is self-forgiveness. Without even knowing it, Robin Casarjian says, most of us severely limit the joy we experience because we hold ourselves accountable for "sins" committed in the past. By far the most extreme examples of this can be found among men in prison, with whom Casarjian has been working for the past several years. For many people, she acknowledges, the idea of convicted rapists and murderers forgiving themselves is "as unacceptable as the actual committing of the crime." But if the objection is that the guilty should suffer emotionally for their sins, in fact the hard work of self-forgiveness is far more wrenching for these men than is simply continuing a life of denial, Casarjian notes.

One of the techniques she asks the men to try is called mirror-work, an exercise that involves looking yourself in the eye in a mirror and asking, Who am I? "I sometimes do not even look at myself when I am shaving," one prisoner wrote when he first looked at the man in the mirror. "There is something in my own eyes I want to avoid. What I feel is confusion and what I see are the bones of a lifetime of regret."

When Casarjian asks prisoners to write letters to themselves about forgiveness, litanies of pain and anger pour out. One begins like this: "Dear Ron, I forgive you for hurting yourself both physically and mentally. I forgive you for fucking up two marriages, for being bulimic, and for taking so many drugs. I forgive you for being so mean to your stepchildren and to your own kids and for not letting them love you." Another ends this way: "I know you've felt guilty about your past and present situations, but it's OK now. It's OK to feel guilt but it shouldn't be 'held onto' and 'lingered in' throughout the rest of your life. You can forgive yourself for those times. You didn't forget them or repeat them. You've held onto them long enough to LEARN from them. Growth is the most important aspect of making a mistake. You've done that. "

Far from a superficial act of pardoning themselves, the process of self-forgiveness causes these men to suffer greatly, Casarjian says. In examining their lives and their actions, often for the first time, they are forced to acknowledge deep guilt and remorse.

IT IS NOT SURPRISING THAT ISSUES OF forgiveness often arise in the middle years. The process of self-evaluation and reflection that characterizes this period of life usually helps people develop more realistic self-images. And as we get in touch with our own weaknesses, something paradoxical happens. Other people's weaknesses are easier to understand: We develop empathy. And, when we become more aware of others' pain, our own pain seems easier to accept. "Everyone in this life encounters pain," says Enright. "A crucial part of carrying on is accepting it." Those who accept life's pain instead of blaming it on the actions of others are relieved of a greater pain—the pain of bitterness and hostility. And they also avoid a further risk, notes Enright: that the pain will be passed on. Miserable married couples toss their anger back and forth to each other and at the children. A major family feud that is never resolved is handed down from generation to generation, a secret, unintentional heirloom.

In the end, forgiveness proceeds a step at a time. No matter how earnestly you try, waves of anger will sweep you away from time to time. "It's not a matter of black and white," says Casarjian. "At first, there may be just a few moments in the day when you are more understanding, when you can live closer to love than to fear. Then maybe if you embrace that state of being, a year from now there may be an hour of greater compassion in your day. In another year, more. The work gradually gets integrated." Be gentle with yourself, she says, and, as you continue to work on forgiveness, you will become more peaceful, more insightful. When you resent someone you're bound to them. When you forgive, you're free.

How Forgiveness Saved My Job

I was ready to quit my job. It had gotten to the point where I would wake up in the morning already filled with anxiety about the day to come. The truth was, I loved my position in sales. It was my boss, the manager of my department, who drove me crazy.

Although I was the highest-earning salesperson in the division, still, my boss, Joanna, always found something wrong with my work. I'd be sitting at my desk processing paperwork when my line would buzz. I'd fill with fear and anger when I heard Joanna's cold voice ask to see me in her office.

As I walked down the hall I'd notice my jaw clenching and my hands curled in fists. Once inside her office, facing her angry face, I had to respond to a ritual check-off list of "Did you do_____? Did you take care of _____?" She would go on until I was ready to throttle her. She would often find some small omission to criticize me for.

By then I was so angry that I would go back to my desk and spend some time stabbing holes in my desk blotter with my pen while fantasizing scenarios of revenge.

When I went for my annual physical, my doctor warned me that my blood pressure and cholesterol were inching steadily upward. He inquired about my stress level at work and made a point of telling me that I'd better do something about it. The next week a friend invited me to a lecture on forgiveness. I didn't even think of Joanna when I went to the lecture—she was beyond forgiving as far as I was concerned. But I thought perhaps it was time to think about forgiving an old boyfriend—and besides, it was a night out with my friend.

The concepts that were presented were completely new to me, and to my surprise, I was inspired to actually start applying them to Joanna. The next day I promised myself that no matter what Joanna said or did, I would see it as a sign of her fear or insecurity—and once I thought about it, I knew this was accurate. When her call came, I took three or four deep breaths and walked as calmly as I could into her office. The routine went on as usual, only this time I remembered to breathe and tried to practice forgiveness. For the first time ever, I looked closely at her face and saw deep lines of what looked like pain and fear. This time I elaborated on my answers, trying to reassure her that I was taking care of business and would make sure everything was covered. Unexpectedly, Joanna's face softened a bit. The questioning was shorter than usual and she said good-bye with an uncharacteristic warmth.

Later that day I found out that her teen-age son was having some rare health problem (this came only a few months after her divorce). My perceptions of Joanna shifted from seeing her as a blaming, critical mother figure to seeing her as an overburdened, stressed-out, frightened woman. As I cultivated this new understanding, I began to see that beneath all that fear, blame, and judgment was just another struggling human being trying to get love, acknowledgement, and attention in the best way she knew. Her job had become for her the last bastion of control, so she desperately fought to ensure the success of her department. Now, instead of wanting to kill Joanna, I began wanting to help her. The more I did that, the less frightened she became. Amazingly, she began to confide in me and become a friend.

Fearsome Security

THE ROLE OF NUCLEAR WEAPONS

MICHAEL M. MAY

Michael M. May is professor of engineering-economic systems and co-director of the Center for International Security and Arms Control at Stanford University. He is director emeritus of Lawrence Livermore National Laboratory and has published widely on nuclear weapons and arms control, most recently in American Scientist, *November-December 1994.*

A Hiroshima-size nuclear bomb would be about a thousand times as destructive as the Oklahoma City truckload of explosives that destroyed a large modern building and killed nearly 200 people. It could destroy about one square mile of the city, an area roughly 20 by 20 blocks, and kill perhaps 200,000 people, the destruction depending on such things as building construction and weather. A typical thermonuclear weapon, of which there are many in the weapon states' arsenals today, could destroy several square miles of a large city and kill as many as a million people. Either kind could destroy a large air base and everything on it, a large tank attack, or an aircraft carrier.

What is the role of these things? What does the United States need them for? What does anybody need them for?

The official U.S. answer, given last fall by Clinton administration spokesmen, is somewhat informally translated, "We're not sure, but there are a lot of nuclear weapons in Russian and other hands, there is a lot of unrest in the world, so we'll reduce the numbers gradually, in tandem with the Russians, and try to contain proliferation, but still keep several thousand around just in case." This position has been criticized as lacking vision. Much more fashionable in intellectual and academic circles has been a debate between abolitionists, who want to do away with nuclear weapons as soon as possible, and "marginalizers," who want to keep a few around but at the edge of polite

From *The Brookings Review*, Summer 1995, pp. 24-27. © 1995 by the Brookings Institution. Reprinted by permission.

policy discussion, unseen and unheard from, except in connection with the occasional rogue and pariah state.

However out of fashion, the U.S. position is right, and the abolitionists and marginalizers are wrong. But defending the U.S. position requires more unpalatable arguments than administration spokesmen could use, especially a few months before the recently concluded nuclear Non-Proliferation Treaty extension conference took place this spring.

Peace—The Essential Security Interest

The most basic argument is that nuclear weapons (and only they) transform peace among the most powerful states in the world from something that is nice to have but secondary to essential security interests as seen by governments, into the essential security interest of governments and governed alike. It does this at some risk of potential catastrophe. If we were in a world of stable states with no rival territorial and other interests that could not be dealt with by empowered and respected international institutions, this risk would be the main matter, and marginalization of nuclear weapons would indeed be in order. But we are not.

Contrary to what many wish, the states of the world are not becoming law-abiding citizens of one world, at least not in essential security matters. In such matters, the United States, as do other states, relies ultimately on its own forces, for the good and sufficient reason that there is nothing else reliable around. As a result, traditional security-oriented behavior abounds today. What is going on in Central Europe, in East Asia, in the Middle East would be familiar to Metternich and Bismarck. This is not to deny that our world is in many respects different from theirs, in particular that it is interactive, reactive, and interdependent as never before. But it is insecure now in much the ways it was then. And now, as then, having the most powerful weapons and deterrent plays an essential role in attaining the number one security policy objective of the United States, which is to preserve our central interests abroad without involving us in war.

Nuclear weapons are not all that is needed to make war obsolete, but they have no real substitute. Modern weapons such as those used in the Gulf War promise victory to the side that has them and leave the other side eager to build or buy them. Students of international politics have long noted this security dilemma: in the measure that a states's search for security through conventional armaments and alliances is successful, it makes its neighbors and rivals insecure and leads to wars that may be disastrous for everyone. To make things worse, unscrupulous politicians maintain themselves in power by preying on and exacerbating these longstanding fears among neighbors, as we now see tragically around the globe. Gulf War weaponry offers nothing new in this regard.

Nuclear weapons do something different. They cheaply and predictably destroy whatever both sides are fighting for. It is just that ability to destroy the battlefield as well as the enemy, to leave war without winners, that makes them essential. Abolitionists and marginalizers have nothing realistic to offer to replace them in that role.

War Is Not Obsolete

But surely war is over among advanced industrialized nations, whose prosperity and very survival rests on the maintenance of peace among themselves? Unfortunately, there is no sign that the forces that led to the most disastrous wars in the past are spent.

The world balance of military power (a consequence, among other things, of the balance of economic power), is changing and will continue to change. Reasonably or not, that makes other powers insecure. World War I and World War II were the way the major and most civilized powers in the world handled the changing balance of power occasioned by the growth of Germany and Japan in relation to the others. It need not have happened that way. It shouldn't have happened that way. As early as 1913, thoughtful people pointed out that Europe was so interdependent economically that war would destroy it and that war was therefore obsolete. They were right about the first observation and wrong about the second. Why?

Most popular analyses of these wars, especially now, on the 50th anniversary of our victory in World War II, focus on who was right and who was wrong, on the fanatical or evil groups who were the more obvious sources of the catastrophes. But that is like focusing on the match and not on the tinder. It is good drama but poor analysis. Why did a few such leaders have the power to send tens of millions to their death? Why was the system, staffed for the most part, then as now, with ordinary, not particularly incompetent or evil men, unable to handle their challenge?

The answers are the stuff of international relations libraries, but at the very heart is the security dilemma noted above: so long as security depends ultimately on rival goods, goods that have to be competed for, such as territory, alliances, access to scarce resources, then more security for one state will mean ultimately less for the other. Maintaining a peaceful balance would be to everyone's advantage, at least for advanced nations no longer bent on acquiring virgin lands for plunder. But that makes peace a public good. Like all public goods, it requires an agreed-on authority able to coerce rebels and free-riders into supporting it if it is to be provided. Reason alone has never been enough: to be the last state to defect is just too dangerous.

There was no such authority earlier this century. Is there one today? The United Nations Security Council? The International Court of Justice? Maybe someday, but not this century or perhaps the next. When have we or any other major nation submitted to these institutions when our central, or sometimes even our peripheral, interests were involved?

What we are seeing instead is the major powers of the world, the United States, Russia, China, Japan, the European Union, mixing universalist global or regional initiatives with the carving out of

Winston Churchill warned at the beginning of the atomic age that safety could be the sturdy child of terror, and that we should not give up atomic weapons until we were sure and doubly sure that we had something better to take the place of terror in that respect.

spheres of influence in much the same way their predecessors on the world stage did. Spheres of influence no longer involve gunboats and marching armies most of the time— though sometimes they still do. Usually they involve such things as supplier-client relationships in arms and nuclear fuel, alliances and stationing of troops abroad, rule-writing in international agreements, and support in negotiations with rival powers.

The major security questions of the day are all handled with considerable attention to this traditional concern: the expansion of NATO; the tip-toeing around Serb aggression; Russia's policy in its "near-abroad," a balance of power term if ever there was one; China's policy in the South China Sea; continuing U.S. willingness to pay with blood and money to keep its suzerainty over Latin America and the Gulf States; China's blocking of UN sanctions in North Korea, sanctions that would have increased U.S. influence on the peninsula and decreased the value of Chinese security guarantees; Russia's and China's offer of nuclear help to Iran.

Even nuclear nonproliferation policies, which contain an element of universalist values, reflect this attempt to acquire or augment spheres of influence. How explain otherwise China's relative unconcern about a nuclear North Korea or Russia's about a nuclear Iran? Nuclear weapons in the hands of these countries would mainly limit U.S. power projections in the area, which necessarily depend on such concentrated and therefore vulnerable military assets as air bases, ports, and aircraft carriers. They would do relatively little to limit the influence of the big near-neighbors.

A Perilous Balancing Act

None of this makes the states involved evil. All of it is understandable. But it is dangerous. It is fraught with risks of escalation, whether owing to the accession to power of leaders who stake their political future on extremist or irredentist positions, or owing to perfectly well-meaning and ordinary leaders finding themselves in a corner none of them predicted or can deal with.

It also has the consequence that a number of states are less secure now than they were during the Cold War. The Cold War carried with it oppression and suffering, but it provided a stable security framework for many states located in traditionally troubled areas—traditionally troubled because in between, or of interest to, multiple larger states. These states are now having to look to new arrangements for their security. Some will find it in reliable alliances with larger powers, some will not. The latter are good candidates to look to nuclear weapons for their security, especially if, as is the case for Iran and North Korea, they are isolated from much of the world community.

We are told by abolitionists and marginalizers that the main threat to the United States are these isolated states, that nuclear weapons are not otherwise relevant to our security situation, and that therefore now is a good time to give them up or marginalize them. If marginalizing carries the somewhat trivial meaning of not talking about the nuclear balance constantly, of not measuring our security solely by that balance, that is a good idea and would have been a good idea during the Cold War. It might have allowed us to see something other than a monolithic threat in the Soviet Union. But if marginalizing means not paying careful attention to the influence of nuclear weapons on the security situation of various states, including us, it is a bad idea.

Nuclear weapons do not of themselves create the authority to provide and maintain peace, but they impose a penalty, obvious to all, not least to volatile democratic electorates, for overlooking this truth. Thereby, they have and will continue to have a profound influence on our security. They will do so in at least two ways: they will continue to put a considerable premium on caution when one nuclear state deals with another in matters either or both consider central, and, partly as a result, they will continue to tend to freeze lines of demarcations between spheres of influence where these lines matter to either or both of the contending major states.

Thus, in Central Europe, in East Asia, in the Middle East, not only do local powers have a strong incentive not to get caught in some euphemistically-called "buffer zone," but also the major powers are equally strongly impelled to make sure there is no misunderstanding about who gets to do what where. As a result, for the next several years, possibly decades, we are going to witness again a definition and consolidation of spheres of influence that will remain irreversible until some cataclysmic change, such as recently rocked the former Soviet Union, takes place in one of the major powers. Reversing it by force otherwise would be too dangerous to attempt.

The Czechs, Hungarians, and Poles are thus perfectly right to press for early incorporation into NATO and the EU. They have only a limited time window, while Russia cannot press its demands too forcibly. The United States may think it is pressuring the present Iranian regime to behave somewhat more acceptably. Instead, it may be giving up Iran to Russian influence for a long time to come. And the *New York Times* is wrong to press for recognition of Taiwanese independence on ideological grounds: China has said it would go to war to prevent Taiwanese independence, and we will not go to war to bring it about. Taiwan is on the Chinese side of the divide, as Ukraine is on the Russian side. These sides exist, however we may dislike it.

Millennial Hopes Deferred

All this makes unpleasant reading. It is not the brave new world of international commerce and cooperative endeavors for solving global problems. That new world is indeed here, and, on most days, occupies and will continue to occupy the attention of governments and political commentators and analysts. But that world will also continue to bring out conflicting interests, and these interests will continue to be pursued by independent states with the full political backing of

their populations. The ultimate limit on this pursuit will be the fear of nuclear escalation, not some supranational law.

Nuclear deterrence is thus a fact of modern life. It is inherent in the technology. The only question is how it will be handled. My guess is that it will not be handled better if the United States backs out of the job of deterrence. And it will not be handled better if, by some unlikely chance, everyone were to back out of the job of deterrence, and the task of implementing it were left to some future government in an emergency situation scurrying to resurrect the caution-inducing deterrent it once had. Peacetime is the right time to maintain the deterrent and to formulate how we will deal with it.

Thus, not only is abolition impossible under present circumstances, it would be a mistake even if it were possible. And marginalization is meaningless: nuclear weapons do not and should not enter daily calculations but do and should enter calculations of ultimate security. Deterrence was far stronger and more stable in the last 50 years than most lay commentators thought. Perversely, perhaps because it worked so well, many are now willing to give it up. But people should not give up fire insurance because fires have been rare, although it is reasonable to look for lower premiums and to work on less risky means of fire containment.

We don't, however, have these less risky means. Winston Churchill is not particularly in favor these days. But Churchill, whatever his failings, understood what led to war. He warned at the beginning of the atomic age that safety could be the sturdy child of terror, and that we should not give up atomic weapons until we were sure and doubly sure that we had something better to take the place of terror in that respect. Look around: we have nothing better to take its place.

Health and Health Care Issues

According to the Clinton administration, access to quality health care should be the right of every American citizen, which is not the case at this time. Thirty-five million individuals have no health insurance and many more are underinsured; therefore, access to quality health care is problematic. Those trying to do something about it are confronted with the harsh realities of limited resources. The pressure to cut the deficit, balance the budget, clean up the environment, fight crime, stop the decline of our cities, and maintain the deteriorating infrastructure of America has placed severe constraints on the amount of federal monies available to fund an ever-expanding number of individuals requiring and demanding health care. This demand is further expanded by the consequences of pandemics such as AIDS, a growing proportion of the aged with noncurable chronic disorders, and an ever-advancing technology that can save the lives of very premature infants and extend the lives of terminal individuals. This unit looks at some of the problems facing individuals and society as we agonize over the hard choices that must be made.

Sharman Stein's report, "The Cruelest Choice," looks at the consequences associated with medicine's ability to "save" severely premature babies. Babies as young as 23 weeks, weighing only 12 ounces, have been preserved, but at horrendous financial costs to society (over $5.6 billion a year). In addition, a significant proportion of severely premature infants suffer brain abnormalities, are disabled, and exhibit a wide range of learning disabilities.

"A New Look at Health Care Reform" suggests that if any meaningful changes in health care are to occur, we must seriously confront the attitude that medical care is "free," or at least very low in cost. If health care is free, then the attitude that nothing is too good for me and mine drives consumer actions. Murray Weidenbaum suggests that competition needs to be introduced into medicine, that people pay for the medical coverage they desire, that advertising be permitted and encouraged, and that consumers be informed of available options.

"A Doctor's Dilemma," by James Dillard, is a short article by a physician expressing his frustration at the potential threat to his career if he were to stop to help an accident victim. Doctors take an oath to serve their fellow humans, but if they do, they could be sued, charged with malpractice, and lose their licenses.

"The Pension Time Bomb" is set to explode, according to Gareth Cook. The only question is when and how much devastation it will cause. Cook is troubled by the policy of many federal, state, and local governments to underfund pension plans for their employees. Public officials make promises to their retirees that are increasingly hard to keep and may become impossible.

The next article, "Breathing Fire on Tobacco," reviews the largest product liability suit ever filed in the United States. Representing over 90 million smokers, the class-action suit against American Tobacco could win damages of over $40 billion. How and if this suit can be settled is problematic and will affect many corporations and a large part of the population.

"Confronting the AIDS Pandemic" looks at the toll in lives, resources, and economic costs that AIDS will take by the year 2000. Entire societies are likely to be deci-mated, causing significant repercussions around the world. The problem of AIDS necessitates a coordinated worldwide effort that is not occurring because many industrialized nations are electing to tackle "their" problem independently.

The author of "Mental Illness Is Still a Myth" is a most vocal critic of psychiatry and its treatment of those displaying unusual and dysfunctional behaviors. Thomas Szasz cogently argues that psychiatry, and the activities of most psychiatrists, could be best understood if viewed as a branch of law or as a type of secular religion, but not as a "science."

Looking Ahead: Challenge Questions

Is adequate health care in the United States a right or a privilege? In your estimation, which should it be? Why?

What reforms, if any, should the government of the United States be making in health care?

What criteria must we consider in attempting to save severely premature infants?

What should be done to protect doctors who function as "good Samaritans"?

What should be done to bring governmental pension funding into line with those of private organizations?

How might AIDS impact on the world's economy?

What threat does the AIDS pandemic pose for the rights and freedoms of those with AIDS or the HIV virus?

What can each individual do to contribute to the solution or control of AIDS?

What are the implications of thinking of psychiatry as a branch of law or as a type of secular religion rather than as a branch of scientific medicine?

In what significant ways would the approaches of the three major types of sociological theories differ in relation to the study of health issues?

What conflicts in values, rights, obligations, and harms seem to underlie the issues and problems covered in this unit?

The Cruelest Choice

Medicine is forcing some parents to decide the fate of their severely premature babies

Sharman Stein
Sharman Stein is a Tribune staff writer.

In her sunny, North Side Chicago apartment, Ellen Baren Skowronski feeds raisins one by one to her son.

"Chew, Leon, chew," she tells the 4-year-old. Lying on a pillow at the center of a living room crowded with toys, Leon smiles hugely at his mother and his 2-year-old sister, Phoebe.

Leon, who weighed 677 grams at his birth—about a pound and a half—was born at Evanston Hospital 24 weeks into his mother's pregnancy. He was nearly four months early. Due Nov. 16, 1990, he was born July 27.

The doctor held him in one hand. It would be nearly 5½ weeks before he would be strong enough to be held in his mother's arms. Wide-eyed and sweet-tempered, fair-haired Leon now weighs just 27 pounds, the weight of an average 2-year-old. He cannot walk, talk, sit up or stand. He can hardly hear. He has cerebral palsy—moderate in his arms, severe in his legs. He is brain-damaged. It takes him nearly 45 minutes to chew his food at each meal.

"He can't hug me, even though I know in his mind he would like to," says Baren Skowronski, 36, a dark-haired, outspoken woman who studied photography at The School of the Art Institute and now waitresses nights at Second City Comedy Club. "He can't even kiss me. He has never said 'Mom.' When he's hungry, he can't tell me what he wants to eat. Sometimes when I'm not giving him what he wants, he just starts to cry. At 4 years old, he should be able to say, 'Mom, I want a peanut butter sandwich.' "

Born at the very threshold of viability, Leon would have died at birth if he had been born just a few years ago. Medical technology has advanced to the point of saving babies as premature as he was; doctors can save 90 percent of infants born as early as 28 weeks.

What the doctors cannot do is to predict with certainty which of these premature children will turn into so-called "miracle babies" without lingering disabilities and which will live severely handicapped lives. It is akin to a surgeon who might capably remove your appendix but could not give you any reliable projection of how you would fare after the operation or whether you would survive.

The younger and smaller the babies are, the greater the possibility of severe disability and death. Leon was born in the so-called "gray zone" between 23 and 27 weeks, the size and weight of five or six sticks of butter, his eyes still closed, his skin covered with lanugo, the fine, soft hair that covers the infant inside the mother's womb.

With the ability to save ever-tinier babies—a Ft. Worth girl weighing just 12 ounces at birth went home from the hospital a few months ago—parents and doctors confront a Solomon-size dilemma.

Under the stark fluorescent lights of the hospital and the glare of attention from doctors and nurses and strangers, parents who had anticipated the joyful delivery of a healthy baby now end up facing the spectre of death or long-term disability for their child.

Baren Skowronski says she now wishes the doctors had told her how grim the future could be while Leon, the baby she had very much wanted, lay there in the neonatal intensive care unit. "He was just born too early," she says, her tone alternating between sadness and anger. "They didn't have any business saving Leon. They were experimenting with a fetus, keeping it alive outside his mother's womb. The doctors say they care for humanity, but they're not here taking care of him now."

Helen Harrison, author of "The Premature Baby Book," whose severely disabled 19-year-old son was born prematurely, hears frequently from parents around the country who claim their physicians did not give them the opportunity to have a say about their baby's future. "So many of these babies are saveable [but] for lives of incredible handicap and impairment," Harrison says. "They're not going to be healthy, functioning citizens. They're in incredible pain for months, sometimes years.

"Some doctors say babies weighing 800 grams or less shouldn't be treated because their outcome is so bad; some say they have to treat every baby with a heartbeat," she says. "In some hospitals, lots of babies are not resuscitated to begin with because of their gestational age. There is no standard procedure."

Nor is there any case law codifying what the procedures are or should be. Much of what happens—how much the parents' wishes are honored and what doctors do after the birth of a severely disabled child—depends largely on the policies of the individual doctors and hospitals.

A Michigan case due to go to trial in January has called the question of parental-infant rights into sharp focus. Gregory Messenger, a dermatologist on staff at the East Lansing hospital where his wife, Traci, had a premature delivery, requested that doctors take no actions to save the infant after birth. At the hospital, in the hours before the 1-pound-11-ounce boy was born, a neonatologist had informed the couple that the baby's prospects were very doubtful.

But after the delivery, a physician's assistant placed the infant boy on a respirator anyway. As doctors and nurses watched but did nothing to stop him, Messenger disconnected the machine, and his wife held the infant until he died.

Messenger will go on trial for involuntary manslaughter in mid-January. The case is being closely watched by parents, neonatologists and ethicists, even though, because of its dramatic and unusual nature, it may not set a precedent.

Society's devotion to the sanctity of life demands that separate attention be paid to the interests of the child—a person, even when handicapped, with the right to life.

The so-called Baby Doe laws passed in the 1980s required doctors to try their utmost to save children with Down's syndrome and spina bifida. No laws have been passed to address the issue of premature infants, of whom more than 29,000 are born severely premature—more than three months before term—each year. Nearly 40 percent of those infants born at less than 28 weeks gestation die.

Neonatology advances can now save preterm babies as early as 22 weeks gestation (normal gestation is 39 to 40 weeks). At 28 weeks, the infant is considered to have an excellent chance of survival, and many doctors believe they should give these babies their best chance at survival, all the more so as technology is making it more and more possible to do so.

It is the parents, however, who have to live with the consequences of medical intervention at such a stage, and on this basis, Frank Reynolds, Gregory Messenger's attorney, argues: "The real important issue here is parental rights. These parents made a medical decision that was within their rights as parents to make. They did not want to prolong their child's death. Their concern was to provide care and comfort and to bond with the baby until he died."

Michigan law indicates that parents do have the right to make decisions affecting their children. But Ingham County, Mich., prosecutor Donald Martin says Messenger made his decision without waiting for standard medical tests on the baby, which determine, among other things, how well oxygen is being processed through the blood and the development of the baby's lungs.

"What information did the good doctor-father have to justify his actions that whatever he was doing was in the best interest of his child?" Martin asks. "He made a unilateral decision to end his infant son's life. And we believe that in so doing, he did not act in the child's best interest. It was a reckless act that brought about the child's death."

Dr. Mark Siegler, a professor of internal medicine and director of the University of Chicago's MacLean Center for Clinical Medical Ethics, calls Messenger's actions "outside the bounds of a civilized response to a tragic situation." A great ethical divide occurs once the baby leaves the woman's womb, and "comes under the protection of our society," Siegler says. Neonatologists eventually would have backed the parents' decision to remove the baby from life support if he were truly beyond help, he adds. "What the father did sets a terrible precedent."

I n Baren Skowronski's case, she has had plenty of time to think about the freakish turn her life took with Leon's birth. That she and her husband, Mike Skowronski, love him de-

votedly, there is no doubt. But they also agonize over their ability to care for Leon as he gets bigger. In a year or two, they will have to move from their second-floor apartment to something more wheelchair-accessible.

Mike, a tall, burly man, insists that Ellen immediately fell in love with the baby and could not bear to think of letting him go, and he says his impulse at the time was to support her. But he is frank about how difficult life has become. Other men he has met through support groups also complain, he says, and many men end up walking out, overwhelmed by this kind of fatherhood. "The big thing with these guys is that that their wives are never the same; the fun is no longer there. They're always going, going, going with the child. They don't get back to themselves."

The Skowronskis are sadly acquainted with some of the perils in Leon's future. The Johnsons, of Oak Brook, are at the beginning of their journey with an extremely premature infant.

Karen Johnson gave birth to a daughter three months early in September at University of Chicago Hospitals. She and her husband, Dwain, named the baby Faith. "We're rather religious, we have a strong belief in God, and we believe it's a miracle so far," says Karen Johnson, 32, an accountant.

Born weighing 1 pound 6 ounces, Faith appeared to be doing well from the start, and the couple never considered letting her die, despite her extreme prematurity and the risks ahead. "We don't want her to suffer for the rest of her life. If she can be healthy and normal, we want her to live. If she had to suffer, God would do the best thing."

Each day, sometimes twice a day, she and Dwain visit Faith at the hospital. They were hoping she would be well enough to come home at Christmas, but an infection and a couple of other setbacks may delay that homecoming.

A ctually, many infants with a poor chance of remotely healthy survival are being allowed to die quietly in hospitals throughout the country, including the University of Chicago, Northwestern, Evanston and other local hospitals that care for severely premature infants.

But such situations are handled quite differently in each hospital, depending on the doctor, the prognosis for the infant and the hospital's general policies.

One physician who strongly favors saving any baby with a chance of survival is Dr. Sheldon Korones, professor of pediatrics at the University of Tennessee College of Medicine in Memphis. "When I look at a baby, he's the whole world," Korones says. "I don't know where that baby is going to fall in the statistics of outcomes.

Preterm babies can now be saved as early as 22 weeks gestation out of the normal 39 to 40 weeks.

I can't predict. So I opt for support. I can't go by parents' fears of outcome. If they ask me to let the baby die and the baby is responding to treatment, I tell them this is murder, that's what it is."

Many of the highly premature infants being saved by Dr. Korones and others like him face a highly risky future. In the hospital, many suffer brain bleeds, seizures, difficulty in breathing and swallowing and require painful operations. Afterward, they often suffer cerebral palsy, mental retardation, respiratory problems, deafness, blindness and a host of other disabilities.

The seriousness of some disabilities sometimes are not readily apparent, says author Harrison, who lives in Berkeley, Calif. "Our son, who tests as mildly retarded, can't leave the house by himself. He can read and count, but he can't understand what he's reading or counting. He can never live independently."

The financial costs of prematurity are enormous. The Center for Risk Management and Insurance Research at Georgia State University in 1992 estimated that cost at $5.6 billion a year nationally. The average amount that the Illinois Department of Public Aid spends for its clients for a normal vaginal delivery and a hospital stay of about two days is $2,814. For extremely premature deliveries, which involves an average hospital stay of 46 days, its average bill is nearly $60,000.

Blue Cross/Blue Shield of Illinois estimates that doctor and hospital costs for a premature infant are nine times as expensive as a normal delivery. Doctors' fees start at $1,250 the first day, compared to $200 a day for normal births.

The costs of caring for a very premature baby who has been in the hospital for many months can easily total hundreds of thousands of dollars.

Each additional week of gestation makes an enormous difference in the ability of a premature infant to survive intact. In the gray area, between 22 and 26 weeks of gestation, the chances are greater for an infant to survive, but with serious disabilities.

A recent study by the Johns Hopkins University School of Medicine showed that 39 percent of 142 infants born between 22 and 25 weeks of gestation survived six months; nearly 100 percent of the babies at the lowest gestational age, 22 or 23 weeks, either died or had severe brain damage. Among those born at 25 weeks gestation, or about four months early, 26 percent had severe brain abnormalities.

Joanne Bregman, a developmental psychologist at Evanston Hospital, says most studies at neonatology wards in hospitals across the country show that between 15 and 20 percent of infants born between 24 and 26 weeks gestation are severely disabled, and about half of them exhibit a wide range of learning disabilities.

"The best interests of the child may not always mean saving the child, if the child is going to suffer a lifetime of pain and hospitalization," Harrison says. Treating every newborn, no matter how severely premature, is a step back to Baby Doe laws, she says, which required every newborn to be treated until death is unavoidable. "I hear from parents every day who are being put through the mill on this," Harrison says.

Some 800 to 1,000 very premature babies weighing less than a pound and a half are born at the University of Chicago Hospitals every year. About twice a week, parents and doctors decide to stop treatment and let the baby die.

Dr. William Meadow, associate professor of pediatrics at the U. of C., says some of these infants, especially as they get closer to weighing about 2 pounds, are "obviously viable," and in those cases, there is less of an issue about whether or not the babies should be given every chance of surviving.

But when babies are considered "previable," Meadow says, "the most compassionate thing to do is to put it in the arms of its loving parents rather than on a ventilator and prolonging the dying."

Most very small newborns, depressed by the rigors of labor, are fairly inactive at delivery. They are scrawny, and their eyes are sometimes still fused shut. What usually happens, Meadow says, is that the child is stabilized initially as more information is gathered. "Many options are perfectly reasonable," he says. "I never really *know* what to do next."

Many of the smallest and sickest babies die very quickly—70 to 80 percent of them within the first 48 hours. "No matter what the doctors do, nature takes its course," says Dr. John Lantos, a pediatrician and ethicist at the U. of C.

For most of the remaining 20 percent, doctors and parents reach an agreement without much trouble, Lantos adds. And contrary to the impression left by the most controversial cases, like that of the Messengers, most decisions to stop treatment are initiated by doctors, not parents, he says.

When parents resist stopping treatment and ask for more time, a meeting is held with additional family members and hospital staff present. Usually there is a consensus after that second meeting. Sometimes a third meeting is needed,

but eventually treatment is stopped, Lantos says.

"It's a well-kept secret among neonatologists that the problem is not with parents begging us to stop treatment," Lantos says. "In the majority of problem cases, it's the parents who are hoping for a miracle. They don't trust the doctors; they feel that stopping treatment is killing the baby."

Indeed, a Georgia doctor has been charged with murder after she allowed a 39-day-old newborn to die because the baby had lung disease and failing kidneys and, in the doctor's judgment, its vital signs had irreversibly dropped. But the parents said the doctor did not ask for their consent before stopping treatment.

In a minority of cases, the roles are reversed, with parents opting to stop intervention and doctors wanting to continue it, Lantos says. "The neonatologists get pressure from the parents not to be so aggressive, to think about quality of life, to give parents the right to participate."

In the thorniest situations, the choices—even when the ethics committee and a host of professionals are consulted—can be difficult, Meadow says.

In a recent case at the U. of C., a tiny preemie had had a very bad episode of bleeding in his brain, the most common neurological abnormality in premature infants and which often leads to significant degrees of mental retardation. Eight neonatologists who considered the case could not agree on whether or not to treat the baby. Meadow, the attending neonatologist, explained the options to the parents. They elected to discontinue treatment.

"I believe the families should be empowered to make these decisions," Meadow says. "Many times, I would recommend one thing, and the parent chooses another. If a parent asks what I think they should do, I try to give them the sense of how strongly *I* feel one way or another, but I also say that there are many options that are perfectly reasonable."

Dr. Elaine Farrell, a neonatologist at Evanston Hospital, says there is usually enough time after the expectant mother is admitted to the hospital to fully inform the family about the baby's chances, the risks and potential problems.

"If the families say, 'Don't do this, don't try to save them,' I support that," Farrell says. "I feel that, for them, it is the right decision. You have to have a committed family to take that on. If they think that the risks are too high, that they have three other kids at home, and if they consider the emotional, the physical and the financial costs, all of which are prohibitive, they could conclude that nature did not intend this child to be there."

In that case, Farrell says, the nurses help to make the baby comfortable. They wrap the infant in a blanket, put a hat on it and let the parents hold it. "We encourage them to take pictures, and when the baby dies, we give them the baby's wrist band. These mementos are the only ones these parents are going to have. They grieve, they say goodbye. They made the best decision they could. They made a decision in the child's best interests."

The most difficult cases for her, Farrell says, are the full-term infants who suddenly run into problems, whether it's something congenital, an infection or some other unexpected trauma. "Our complacency and our sense of entitlement in the United States is that if you get to full term, you will go home with a [healthy] baby. That doesn't always happen. With preterm babies, everyone knows we're doing the best we can, pushing the frontiers forward, doing amazing things, and everybody knows what's on the line. With full-term babies, parents' expectations are so high, that when the baby is hurt, or dies, that's the hardest."

The parents' grief at their babies' deaths is so strong, Farrell says, it would be classified as "psychotic" if it were occurring in any other instance. "The bond is so deep, and the parents are so bound up in the sense of responsibility and expectations . . . they have bonded with the baby since the time they first thought they might be having a baby."

The first group of very tiny premature children born in the mid-1980s are just now reaching school age. And the news is not good.

A new study published Sept. 22 in the New England Journal of Medicine tracked 68 children born five to nine years ago weighing less than 1 pound 10 ounces. Researchers found that the children had a greatly increased chance of mental retardation, cerebral palsy and severe vision problems and were below average in cognitive ability, psychomotor skills and academic achievement.

About half of the children in the study had borderline-to-normal IQs or lower; many of the rest were having a lot of trouble in school trying to pay attention, follow directions and learn some subjects, especially mathematics. "These children are at serious disadvantage in every skill required for adequate performance in school," the study said.

"I talk about three categories of treatment," says Dr. Robert Nelson, associate professor of pediatrics and bioethics at the Medical College of Wisconsin in Milwaukee. "The first category is what's clearly beneficial to the child; the next is the clearly useless, where continuing it could be seen as medical abuse; and the third is a midrange category, where it's not clear if treatment is beneficial; and usually under those circumstances, people err on the side of continuing therapy until the uncertainty is resolved."

Dr. William Silverman, a retired California obstetrician who is credited with helping to create modern neonatal intensive care, calls the outcome of infants weighing below 750 grams (a little over a pound) a "no man's land, with no set guidelines," and where treatment is still largely experimental.

Silverman recalls realizing that "the timid notion of a 'natural limit of viability' vanished" in the mid-1950s, shortly after the Apgar score was introduced to systematically appraise the health of newborns. Requiring that Apgar scores be taken for every newborn eliminated the previous practice of allowing marginally viable infants to die quietly and labeling them stillborns.

"We don't know enough to guarantee results," Silverman says. "We don't know how much oxygen to give them, what kind of feeding; every aspect of their care is controversial. Every aspect convinces me that the parental view has to be taken into account. The professional view is so weak, so iffy, so difficult to defend."

Others disagree. Dr. Korones of Memphis says he is not an extremist; he regularly stops treatment for babies when it is clear that they are going to die soon anyway. But he admits that he is one of those physicians decried by parents because he does not believe that parents should have the ultimate decision over the baby's life. He insists on trying to save every infant with even the slightest chance of living, whatever the problems they may have to face later on. "Can I ask parents, 'Do you want this baby or not?' I can't do that," he says.

Korones, 70, says he frequently sees the severely disabled children he has saved and is aware of the pain they and their families are bearing. "I know I'm causing misery, but I don't know if I'm causing any more misery than they are," Korones says, referring to other physicians who may be more willing to give up on babies when the prognosis is poor and the parents want to let them die. "I don't know how many otherwise normal, gratifying human beings are being killed in that process. The basic difficulty is, my mistakes you see; the other guy's mistakes you bury."

The United States is considerably more aggressive in its efforts to save very small premature infants than most other countries, except perhaps Canada.

In Denmark, doctors generally would not try to save infants below 25 or 26 weeks gestation. In Australia, they would not treat infants smaller than 650 grams, or about 25 weeks. In Sweden, doctors withhold artificial ventilation from the most premature babies, those weighing less than 750 grams.

In Japan and other countries, doctors consider it cruel to let the parents make final decisions about the baby's fate.

Many states have laws that permit parents and other surrogates to act on behalf of their sick children. A 1991 Illinois law gives parents the right to make life-or-death decisions when children suffer from a terminal, incurable or irreversible condition. The law does not specifically address prematurity.

"Parents are supposed to obtain medical care for their children, to protect their children from harm, to relieve suffering, and failure to do so is neglect," says Dr. Norman Fost, professor of pediatrics and director of the program in medical ethics at the University of Wisconsin. "Our society is based on a pro-life assumption; we assume life is better than death, even handicapped life, but undertreatment has been replaced with overtreatment."

Neonatologists say that parents with more formal education choose to stop treatment more frequently than those with less education, probably because they are better informed about possible problems.

At Evanston Hospital, where 86 percent of those who come to its maternity ward are from the middle and upper-middle class, Farrell says parents have very high expectations for their children, and when the child's outcome is very risky, "they generally say we should stop treatment. But I have had families who look me right in the eye and say, 'We've been trying for 15 years [to have a child], and we can't stop now.' And then we go on. And usually those children turn out to be what we say they are.' "

Doctors say, however, that there are many good reasons not to allow parents to make unilateral decisions and instead lead doctors to consider themselves the representative of the child. Farrell recalls a father—a doctor but with no professional experience with newborns—who requested that attending doctors stop feeding and treating his daughter, born at 28 weeks. He was concerned about the effects of prematurity on the child's brain development. With doctors convinced that the child would thrive, the hospital went to court for authority to treat the child against the parents' wishes. And the girl did very well, Farrell says.

Between 15 and 20 percent of infants born between 24 and 26 weeks gestation are severely disabled.

A 1992 Georgia State University study estimated the financial cost of prematurity at $5.6 billion a year nationally.

Farrell could not comment on Leon Skowronski's case, but she says Evanston Hospital physicians provide parents with abundant information about the possible handicaps children could suffer. "There are a lot of angry parents, what with all their sorrow and loss and pain and work, who don't remember what they were told," Farrell says. "They only know what they're dealing with now."

"These are agonizing decisions," says Dr. Arthur Kohrman, president of LaRabida Children's Hospital in Chicago. "These are issues about the nature of futility, the likelihood the child will live and the question of if they do survive, as what? You can't standardize this. We're all mucking around in the unknown together."

Ellen Baren Skowronski well remembers the feeling of euphoria she felt after giving birth to Leon. "I remembered thinking of all the things a son represents. I had all those feelings."

She has thought about it a lot. She has heard the well-meaning "but condescending" comment that "God does not give you more than you can handle." As she considers the hardships Leon and her family have already been through—the heart surgery, the seizures, the spasms, the frustrations—and her fears for a future of many more miseries and difficulties, Baren Skowronski says she believes her son was not intended to live.

"But he has helped me put my life into perspective," she says. "He renewed my faith in humanity." She's particularly touched by the committed professionals who have dedicated their lives to helping handicapped children such as Leon.

"If I had another child born prematurely, I wouldn't go to the hospital. There's no need. I would just stay at home. When Leon was born, I needed somebody to say there's a really good chance this baby will be severely disabled and that we'll have to take care of him for the rest of his life."

Even then her words belie the uncertainty that must always be there. "If I had known what was ahead, if they had told me, I probably would have decided to let him go."

Probably.

A New Look at Health Care Reform

COMPETITIVE MARKET FORCES

Delivered as the Keynote Address to the Annual Health Policy Conference of the Quincy Foundation for Medical Research, San Francisco, California, February 9, 1995

MURRAY WEIDENBAUM

MURRAY WEIDENBAUM, *Mallinckrodt Distinguished University Professor and Director of the Center for the Study of American Business, Washington University*

THE time is ripe for taking a new look at health-care reform. Conventional approaches have bogged down in the legislative process. A fresh start is necessary. Truly reforming the health-care delivery system of the United States requires developing a sensible and sensitive mechanism to balance the demand for health care with its supply. That is the only effective way of dealing simultaneously with the powerful demand for medical services, the limited resources available, and the pressures of rising costs and prices.

I put aside the question of lack of universal health-insurance coverage. My justification for doing so is that most public discussions equate lack of insurance with lack of medical care. That is erroneous. A large array of health-care providers do give medical services — at low or no cost — to those without insurance. To be sure, often the result is inefficient, such as the excessive use of emergency rooms. But, that is just a special case of a problem that I will be dealing with — people demanding expensive health care without paying the full cost.

One complication is curable. At present, employees — or employers acting in their behalf — cannot buy a modest health-care plan. State insurance commissions dictate the composition of these plans and they are very amenable to lobbying by special interests. In many states, the plans must include hair transplants, acupuncture, and other optional items. The purchaser of health insurance cannot buy a Ford. It must be a Lincoln — or nothing. As Voltaire said it, the best is the enemy of the good. Of course, this is not a federal case. Each state insurance commission should shift its focus from serving the special interests among health-care providers to meeting the needs of the patients.

The Two Basic Alternatives

Let us begin with the fundamentals. There is a spectrum of possible responses to the health-care dilemma, each with its own set of advantages and disadvantages.

At the free market end of the policy spectrum is an approach based on each family or unattached individual making their own choices on what type of medical outlays they will request — and pay for. This means a general elimination of third-party payments and a restoration of the traditional producer-consumer relationship which is found in most other product and service markets.

The primary reliance on third-party payments is a relatively recent phenomenon — which reminds us that the present pattern can be changed. Third-party payments have become important only in the last several decades. Back in 1960, people paid 49 percent of their health-care costs, while government agencies paid 24 percent and insurance companies paid 22 percent. A complete reversal has occurred in the intervening years. By 1993, people paid less than 18 percent of their medical costs. The lion's share was borne by government (44 percent) and insurance (34 percent). For hospital service, the patient now pays only 3 percent. For doctor bills, the average patient payment is 15 percent of the total.

The implication of the shift to "third-party" financing of health care cannot be overestimated. Important evidence comes from an experiment by the non-profit Rand Corporation. Thousands of families were given one of four health insurance plans. The difference between the plans was the co-payment rate, the portion of health expenses paid by the family. The co-payment rate varied from 0 to 95 percent. Under all the plans, if a family's out-of-pocket expenses reached $1,000, the insurance paid for all additional expenses.

The main finding was that the higher a family's co-payment rate, the less often members of that family went to a doctor and the less often they incurred medical expenses generally. In the words of my colleague David R. Henderson,

> "People do consume more health care when they are spending other people's money."

Rand found no substantial improvement in health outcomes for the higher spending by the families with low co-payment rates.

Relying on the marketplace is the self-policing way to control medical costs. When patients pay the bills directly, they become cost conscious — and so do the people and organizations serving them. The market approach differs fundamentally from the typical "third-party" payments so widely used in the United States. Under this latter method, patients usually do not know the prices and costs of their medical care before hand, if ever.

Third parties that pay the bills have effectively removed the patient from the traditional consumer role of watchdog.

From *Vital Speeches of the Day,* April 1, 1995, pp. 381-384. © 1995 by Murray Weidenbaum. Reprinted by permission of the author.

Rarely are prices of physician and hospital services or goods such as prescription drugs advertised to consumers.

Of course, there always were exceptions to the operation of the free market in health care. Modern society has never been willing to accept the full consequences of allocating medical care solely on the desire and ability to pay. However, in this approach, market forces are supplemented, not supplanted. Poor people receive free or low-cost medical treatment, although sometimes of a lower quality than the rest of the society and usually at greater inconvenience.

Primary reliance on the market means that the price system rations the amount of health care produced and consumed. That amount is likely to be less than the results of current policy. A sensible step toward the free-market approach is to reduce the governmental subsidies which increase people's demand for the "best" health-care service. A good place to begin is to eliminate the tax advantage now given to health care over other consumer expenditures. Employer-financed health insurance should be included in taxable employee compensation along with direct payments of wages and salaries. Employer-financed insurance plans became popular during World War II as a loophole to get around wage controls. The special tax treatment is not justified by any canon of efficiency or fairness and should be eliminated.

Much of the formal effort to "economize" on health-care costs by departing from marketplace competition is illusory. A major example is the cost shifting under Medicaid and Medicare. That does little to reduce the nation's total medical outlays. That procedure forces other patients to pay for a portion of health care for the poor and the elderly.

To some significant extent, private health plans — goaded by employers who are unhappy at the steady stream of premium increases — can try to weed out high-cost providers, to limit the use of expensive specialists, to monitor closely the performance of health-care providers, and to emphasize preventative care. Such pressures can be reinforced by giving employees a similar stake in controlling health-insurance premiums.

At the other end of the policy spectrum is the notion that the society should finance whatever level of health care is required by each citizen. This general notion is embodied in the "single payer" plan, whereby government simply pays everyone's health bills. Practical problems abound. When health care becomes a free good, the individual response quickly becomes "Nothing's too good for me if I don't have to pay for it."

Because human wants are insatiable, the notion that each of us is entitled to all the medical care that we ask for exhausts the ability of even the most generous source of financing. Therefore, in practice, each single payer plan adopts some form of rationing. One of the most widely used means of limiting care is indirect. It is the bureaucratic technique of delay and inconvenience — forcing people to wait longer than they now do before they receive medical services, including having to go through a variety of reviews or "gatekeeper" approvals. It has been said of some high-risk surgical procedures under the Canadian system that the patient is more likely to die while waiting his or her turn than on the operating table.

Rationing by delay appeals to the bureaucratic instinct. It does not require making many difficult decisions. It is easy to administer. The queue even sounds fair: first come, first served. But, rationing by delay distributes the benefits of limited care arbitrarily.

A safety valve often accompanies the queue approach. It favors upper income individuals or at least people who value health care highly enough to pay for it. Wealthy Canadians, for example, come to the United States for serious surgery when they are not content with the quality or the time availability of the health care provided in Canada.

One of the claimed benefits of the single payer approach could be achieved without resorting to a massive expansion of the government's role. A standard medical card for each person with the vital personal and insurance information would avoid the repetitious collection of the same data by each health-care provider. The transcription errors which occur so frequently would be avoided, as well as the delays bedeviling patients and medical offices alike.

Surely, in this electronic age, the paperwork burden could be reduced substantially. Voluntary cooperation on the part of key private associations — the American Medical Association, the American Hospital Association, the American Pharmaceutical Association, etc. — should be able to accomplish this useful change.

Along these lines, the Quincy Foundation for Medical Research has proposed the establishment of a network of computer terminals located at care delivery sites. Each participant in the program would receive a code card containing his or her social security number and basic personal and medical data. We can endorse this proposal without embracing the notion of using the card to administer eligibility for a variety of governmentally imposed benefits.

All in all, it seems unlikely that public policy will adopt either of the two extremes. Yet, it is useful to view the various individual proposals in terms of whether they move the health-care system toward the governmental pole or toward the individual choice pole.

An Upbeat Outlook

It is pertinent to acknowledge a separate and noteworthy development. While the Congress and the Clinton Administration have been debating inconclusively how to provide and finance better health care, the institutions that actually provide medical care have been undergoing an unprecedented but voluntary restructuring. The health-care delivery system is being reformed. The marketplace is transforming itself and is delivering health care at reduced costs or at a slower rate of price increase.

The voluntary changes being made in health care are taking many forms. By the end of 1994, a majority of privately insured Americans were enrolled in managed-care plans that limit choice of doctors and treatments. In California, three-fourths of all privately insured patients are now in Health Maintenance Organizations. Three-fourths of all physicians had signed contracts, covering at least some of their patients, to reduce their fees and to accept oversight of their medical decisions. About nine out of every ten doctors who work in group practices have agreed to managed-care arrangements.

Large insurance companies are setting up "community care" networks. They are acquiring hospitals and clinics, so that they can offer a full spectrum of treatment for a fixed price. In suburban Atlanta, Aetna has opened six primary care centers. In the same area, another large insurance company, Cigna, has acquired medical practices and is recruiting doctors for its own clinics.

The Michigan health care network is a good example of the voluntary changes taking place. The network is vertically integrating the Henry Ford Health System, Mercy Health Services, and Michigan Blue Cross/Blue Shield. The network of 13 hospitals offers health care to groups of 100 employees or more. It requires a fixed monthly payment for an individual or a family. New York Hospital has established a regional alliance with seven other non-profit hospitals, two nursing homes, and four walk-in clinics.

Three large hospital alliances, created in the last two years, now care for three-fourths of the hospital patients in the St. Louis area. Each alliance is actively buying up the practices of primary-care physicians.

In many communities, hospitals have been hiring or buying out the practices of primary care doctors — family practitioners, general internists, and pediatricians — to assure a stream of patient referrals and to increase their bargaining power with insurance companies. The South Carolina Medical Association has been developing an alternative approach. It is forming a statewide network of doctors to negotiate contracts with employers and take responsibility for controlling their health costs.

Health-care networks already dominate Southern California. Hospitals, physicians, and insurance companies all have established health-care networks. Mullikin Medical Enterprises, which is owned by 200 physicians in Southern California, is acquiring the practices of other medical groups around the state. Solo practitioners are becoming rare.

On a national scale, an unprecedented wave of mergers and acquisitions is occurring among major health-care providers. Columbia/HCA Healthcare, the country's largest for-profit hospital chain, has bought out Medical Care America, the largest chain of surgery centers. In contrast, Surgical Care Affiliates, which operates a chain of outpatient surgery centers, is luring patients away from hospitals. These centers provide a lower-cost setting for many of the less critical operations, such as removal of cataracts, tonsillectomies, and laparoscopic gallbladder removals.

The large pharmaceutical companies — squeezed by national policy and regional health-care providers — have been actively diversifying within the health-care sector. Merck acquired Medco, the managed-care drug distributor. SmithKline Beecham merged with Diversified Pharmaceutical, another managed-care drug marketer. Eli Lilly bought PCS Health Systems, the largest processor of payments for prescription drugs. Zeneca Group, a manufacturer of cancer drugs, acquired 50 percent of Salick Healthcare, an operator of cancer care centers. Thrifty Drug Stores bought the Payless drugstores of Kmart. Revco acquired Hook-Supe Rx and Rite Aid purchased Perry Drug Stores.

Meanwhile, many individually owned pharmacies are finding that they lack the resources to compete for managed-care business and are becoming members of chains, franchises, and other group efforts. In the future, perhaps insurance companies and hospitals will get together. Between them, they have the large organizational skills and recordkeeping that are necessary. Hospitals have the patients and insurance companies have the market — the willingness of employers to pay for the health care of the employees.

Ultimately, these conglomerates may include, in addition to insurance companies and hospitals, some of the following — outpatient clinics, doctors' offices, nursing homes, hospices, home health-care services, pharmacies, drug treatment centers, and medical equipment suppliers.

Conclusions and Recommendations

The operation of market forces often proceeds more rapidly and more effectively in responding to serious problems than do the more ponderous decisionmaking mechanisms of the public sector. Often the reduction of governmental impediments to competition represents the most efficient and least costly solution. Medical care is no exception to that basic proposition.

The most effective driving force to slow the rapid rise in health-care costs is now the business firms who find that this special expense reduces their competitiveness in an increasingly global marketplace. The pressure they exert on their health-insurance carriers, in turn, is transmitted to health-care providers. As we have seen, hospitals, physicians, and pharmaceutical firms have been engaged in an unprecedented effort to restructure, streamline, diversify, and otherwise reduce their costs — while they maintain or expand their share of a rapidly and radically changing marketplace for health care.

There is an important role for public policy in this important adjustment process, but it is not the role usually envisioned. To continue the movement to greater efficiency while meeting the needs of the patient, it is necessary to further reduce the impediments to the fuller operation of competitive market forces.

The most fundamental change needed is to reduce the dependence on third-party reimbursements. To the extent that patients view medical care as a "free" or low-cost good to them, the ability to contain costs will be greatly limited.

For the typical middle class patient/consumer, it makes no sense to go through an insurance/reimbursement system for routine office and out-patient hospital visits and procedures. What is required is to stop looking at health insurance as a benefit or, worse yet, as an entitlement. Rather, each of us must consider health insurance as a form of insurance protecting us from chance but potentially devastating circumstances. The implication of that seemingly simplistic change is profound.

Take automobile insurance as a basis for comparison. Each vehicle owner chooses a form of deductible. This means that many fender benders or paint scratches (the equivalent of the routine office visit) are not covered by insurance. There is no massive outcry that this approach is "unfair" to poor people. Motorists generally understand that a deductible is necessary to avoid swamping the insurance system with the paperwork that would push up premiums very sharply. As a result, of course, many paint scratches and dented fenders go unfixed — but that is considered choice of the owners who would rather spend their money on something else.

Indeed, one company in Virginia has moved in this direction. It treats its health program like true insurance, reimbursing for insurable events rather than for routine medical expenditures. The plan is structured so that employees are reimbursed for a small number of large claims rather than a large number of small claims. Savings from shifting away from traditional health-care coverage are shared equally between the employer and the employees.

Under the present array of public policies, primary reliance on third-party reimbursement strikes most taxpayers as highly desirable. Not many citizens are sophisticated enough to understand that such fringe benefits as employer-paid health insurance are a substitute for wages in the employee's compensation package. But even among the growing minority that comprehend the process, the status quo is still considered to be a good deal because wages and salaries are taxable income, while fringe benefits are not.

The answer is to make the entire compensation package taxable, including employer-paid health-insurance premiums. That will not eliminate the demand for such fringes, even among the most sophisticated, for a variety of reasons. Some of these are eminently sensible, such as the desire to obtain the economies of scale that result in lower group rates. A level playing field in the taxation of compensation would not constitute a panacea but it surely will help.

Increasing the knowledge available to consumers will enable them to make more informed choices. In the purchase of pharmaceutical products, government policy now restricts or prevents the patient from acquiring information concerning the prices charged by different providers for the same or similar products. Many states prohibit advertising the price of prescription drugs. Such restrictions make it difficult for consumers to shop for the best price. Every state which has enacted such anti-consumer legislation should promptly repeal it.

At the federal level, the Food and Drug Administration should reduce the barriers it has set up that inhibit advertising prescription medicines. Because consumers must obtain a prescription from a physician in order to acquire prescription drugs, there is little reason to fear deception in advertising in this market. Experience shows that direct advertising can reduce the prices that consumers pay. Such evidence was cited by the Supreme Court in the decision overturning state bans on advertising of eyeglasses.

The current FDA rules on advertising are needlessly bureaucratic. The agency should reconsider the requirement for the misnamed "brief summary" which must accompany any ad that both mentions a health condition and the name of a drug which can be used for the condition. The "brief summary" is actually a lengthy statement in small print listing side effects and contraindications associated with a prescription drug. Such information is essential for physicians, for whom the brief summaries were originally designed. But, for the average patient, the technical language is incomprehensible.

The FDA also discourages prescription drug ads from being shown on television, a major source of information for many consumers. The high cost of ads in the print media — resulting from the FDA requirements — also reduces their use. Like so much government regulation, the result is the opposite of what the FDA says it wants. Due to the restraint on advertising, consumers may not be aware that a treatment exists for a certain condition and so they will not consult a physician. In other circumstances, consumers may suffer some symptoms (e.g., thirst) without realizing that these are symptoms of a treatable disease (e.g., diabetes). Alternatively, a new remedy with reduced side effects may become available, but patients are not aware of it and do not visit their physicians to obtain a prescription.

If there is any single conclusion that emerges from this presentation, it is that no single solution — no silver bullet — is available to cure all the ailments besetting the American health-care system. What will help in a fundamental way is to acknowledge that difficult choices have to be made among imperfect alternatives. I trust that the package of alternatives I propose, based primarily on the free market, is less imperfect than the others.

A Doctor's Dilemma

Helping an accident victim on the road could land you in court

James N. Dillard

Dillard, affiliated with Columbia-Presbyterian Medical Center, practices rehabilitation medicine in New York City.

It was a bright, clear February afternoon in Gettysburg. A strong sun and layers of down did little to ease the biting cold. Our climb to the crest of Little Roundtop wound past somber monuments, barren trees and polished cannon. From the top, we peered down on the wheat field where men had fallen so close together that one could not see the ground. Rifle balls had whined as thick as bee swarms through the trees, and cannon shots had torn limbs from the young men fighting there. A frozen wind whipped tears from our eyes. My friend Amy huddled close, using me as a wind breaker. Despite the cold, it was hard to leave this place.

Driving east out of Gettysburg on a country blacktop, the gray Bronco ahead of us passed through a rural crossroad just as a small pickup truck tried to take a left turn. The Bronco swerved, but slammed into the pickup on the passenger side. We immediately slowed to a crawl as we passed the scene. The Bronco's driver looked fine, but we couldn't see the driver of the pickup. I pulled over on the shoulder and got out to investigate.

The right side of the truck was smashed in, and the side window was shattered. The driver was partly out of the truck. His head hung forward over the edge of the passenger-side window, the front of his neck crushed on the shattered windowsill. He was unconscious and starting to turn a dusky blue. His chest slowly heaved against a blocked windpipe.

A young man ran out of a house at the crossroad. "Get an ambulance out here," I shouted against the wind. "Tell them a man is dying."

I know now that despite my oath of serving the injured, I'd drive on

---

I looked down again at the driver hanging from the windowsill. There were six empty beer bottles on the floor of the truck. I could smell the beer through the window. I knew I had to move him, to open his airway. I had no idea what neck injuries he had sustained. He would easily end up a quadriplegic. But I thought: he'll be dead by the time the ambulance gets here if I don't move him and try to do something to help him.

An image flashed before my mind. I could see the courtroom and the driver of the truck sitting in a wheelchair. I could see his attorney pointing at me and thundering at the jury: "This young doctor, with still a year left in his residency training, took it upon himself to play God. He took it upon himself to move this gravely injured man, condemning him forever to this wheelchair . . ." I imagined the millions of dollars in award money. And all the years of hard work lost. I'd be paying him off for the rest of my life. Amy touched my shoulder. "What are you going to do?"

The automatic response from long hours in the emergency room kicked in. I pulled off my overcoat and rolled up my sleeves. The trick would be to keep enough traction straight up on his head while I moved his torso, so that his probable broken neck and spinal-cord injury wouldn't be made worse. Amy came around the driver's side, climbed half in and grabbed his belt and shirt collar. Together we lifted him off the windowsill.

He was still out cold, limp as a rag doll. His throat was crushed and blood from the jugular vein was running down my arms. He still couldn't breathe. He was deep blue-magenta now, his pulse was rapid and thready. The stench of alcohol turned my stomach, but I positioned his jaw and tried to blow air down into his lungs. It wouldn't go.

Amy had brought some supplies from my car. I opened an oversize intravenous needle and groped on the man's neck. My hands were numb, covered with freezing blood and bits of broken glass. Hyoid bone—God, I can't even feel the thyroid cartilage, it's gone . . . OK, the thyroid gland is about there, cricoid rings are here . . . we'll go in right here. . . .

It was a lucky first shot. Pink air sprayed through the IV needle. I placed a second needle next to the first. The air began whistling though it. Almost immediately, the driver's face turned bright red. After a minute, his pulse slowed down and his eyes moved slightly. I stood up, took a step back and looked down. He was going to make it. He was going to live. A siren wailed in the distance. I turned and saw Amy holding my overcoat. I was shivering and my arms were turning white with cold.

The ambulance captain looked around and bellowed, "What the hell . . . who did this?", as his team scurried over to the man lying in the truck.

"I did," I replied. He took down my name and address for his reports. I had just destroyed my career. I would never be able to finish my residency with a massive lawsuit pending. My life was over.

The truckdriver was strapped onto a backboard, his neck in a stiff collar. The ambulance crew had controlled the bleeding and started intravenous fluid. He was slowly waking up. As they loaded him into the ambulance, I saw him move his feet. Maybe my future wasn't lost.

A police sergeant called me from Pennsylvania three weeks later. Six days after successful throat-reconstruction surgery, the driver had signed out, against medical advice, from the hospital because he couldn't get a drink on the ward. He was being arraigned on drunk-driving charges.

A few days later, I went into the office of one of my senior professors, to tell the story. He peered over his half glasses and his eyes narrowed. "Well, you did the right thing medically of course. But, James, do you know what you put at risk by doing that?" he said sternly. "What was I supposed to do?" I asked.

"Drive on," he replied. "There is an army of lawyers out there who would stand in line to get a case like that. If that driver had turned out to be a quadriplegic, you might never have practiced medicine again. You were a very lucky young man."

The day I graduated from medical school, I took an oath to serve the sick and the injured. I remember truly believing I would be able to do just that. But I have found out it isn't so simple. I understand now what a foolish thing I did that day. Despite my oath, I know what I would do on that cold roadside near Gettysburg today. I would drive on.

The Pension Time Bomb

The $1.7 trillion—that's right, trillion—*government employee pension scandal could make us all nostalgic for the days of the S&L crisis. Here's how to fix it*

Gareth G. Cook

Gareth G. Cook is a reporter for U.S. News & World Report

To judge by the last election, most Americans can only smile at the thought of an unemployed congressman pounding the pavement in search of work. Others might feel a slight twinge of empathy for the suddenly jobless. But few suspect what every congressman knows: Thanks to an extremely generous pension program, many retiring members can live very well, at taxpayer expense, without lifting a finger.

Consider fallen House Speaker Tom Foley. According to the National Taxpayers Union Foundation, his lifetime pension will start this year at $123,804. Multimillionaire Dennis DeConcini, retiring under the cloud of the Keating Five S&L scandal, will take in $55,669 this year. And Dan Rostenkowski, long-time chairman of the powerful House Ways and Means Committee, can expect his checks to start at $96,468 per year—and they will continue uninterrupted even if he is convicted of all the corruption charges on which he was indicted last year.

But the real surprise is that these are not examples of congressional perks gone mad. Many federal employees—and some state and local workers—are treated to pensions far more lavish than those of their counterparts in the private sector. So generous are government pensions, in fact, and so poorly are they financed for the future, that, absent serious reforms, the eventual price tag could trigger a financial crash that will make the S&L crisis look like a Big Wheels pile-up at the local playground.

Already, ballooning retirement payments are squeezing the very programs for which the government was established in the first place. Last year, for instance, pension checks for retired federal workers and military personnel ate up $65 billion. That's enough to fund the entire 1994 budget for welfare, education, and the National Endowment for the Humanities. Add to that the total cost, over five years, of the crime bill. And then add everything we spend on foreign aid and highways. You'd still have a ways to go.

It is the future, though, that is truly worrisome. In the good old days, a pension plan meant solemn accountants carefully putting aside and investing money so there will be enough when all the retirement checks start coming due. Put in the language of the green-eyeshade set: Without prudent investments, made with every pay period, public and private plans accumulate substantial "unfunded liabilities." And the government does not come close to investing each year what it needs to, and its unfunded liability—the bill that future taxpayers will get for today's public servants—is frighteningly large.

For federal employees, according to the Employee Benefit Research Institute (EBRI), unfunded liabilities have already hit $870 billion dollars. If you also include military retirees, total unfunded liabilities of the federal retirement system—money that has been promised but is not there—are now $1,497,000,000,000. If the federal government used the same accounting conventions as private businesses, the entire federal debt would jump, overnight, by a full third.

Though it is by far the worst offender, the federal government, unfortunately, does not have a monopoly on pension problems. According to a 1993 study by Wilshire Associates Inc., 28 states suffer from underfunding. More than 10 states are in serious trouble with less than 80 percent funding of their liabilities. Massachusetts has a $6.3 billion shortfall. West Virginia holds top unfunded honors with only 33 percent funding. According to a comprehensive survey conducted by Paul Zorn of the Government Financial Officers Association, states and localities have quietly put together unfunded liabilities of $164 billion.

Taken together, then, politicians have already indebted the next generation of taxpayers to today's government workers for nearly *$1.7 trillion.* But you would be hard-pressed to find a voter outside a few elite consulting firms who has any idea. "The public is ignorant," agrees Sylvester Sheiber, a former deputy director at the Social Security Administration and now research director of Wyatt, Co., a Washington, D.C. consulting firm. "And there's a reason for that: The people who've made these promises don't want the public to know."

The public will figure it out, though, as poorly run pension plans start to threaten critical services. In the Lilliputian District of Columbia, for example, the last few decades of generous pension promises have pushed unfunded liabilities to a giant-sized $5.5 billion, even as its operating budget has plunged deeper into the red. Along the streets, uncollected trash is a feast for rats and squirrels, but for the District's denizens, sad to say, it is a sign of things to come. As taxes have gone up, people have fled, leaving the pension burden on those who stay. Paying off D.C.'s pension liabilities would now require more than $9,000 from everyone still living in its borders.

With the government's own pension programs careening toward disaster, it is ironic how much energy is spent blaming private plans. Every fall, the federal government's Pension Benefit Guaranty Corporation releases a list of the 50 worst corporate offenders, outlining the billions for which they have not provided. Total private-sector underfunding, the PGBC reported last month, has now hit $71 billion. That is certainly a problem. Taxpayers should not be asked to bail out pension programs that have failed to plan for the future. But the potential bill from the federal government alone is 20 times *larger*.

A Pension for Trouble

Everyone agrees that public servants deserve fair and decent pensions. The thanks for a lifetime of public toil should not be dinners from an economy-sized can of tuna fish. And of course, back when civil servants were underpaid during their working lives, it made sense to send them off into the sunset with generous benefits. But over the last four decades, the salaries of federal workers have climbed a full 25 percent faster than private sector employees'. This makes the 24-karat federal retirement plans harder to justify.

To get an idea of how generous their pensions are, consider this. According to figures from the Bureau of Labor Statistics, an average worker "at a medium or large-size firm" making $35,000 and retiring at age 65 with 30 years service can expect about $10,800 a year in pension payments from his employer. That same worker, after 30 years with a state or local government, can expect a post-retirement take of $18,200. And, according to the Office of Personnel Management, a federal worker on the Civil Service Retirement System with the same profile gets $19,700.

To be sure, state and local government employees (but not the feds) often contribute more to their plans than private workers. And more private employees can participate in "defined contribution plans" like the 401K, where their retirement investments are matched by their employer. (Though, in fact, a recent federal plan, called the Federal Employee Retirement System, does allow for matched investment contributions.)

On the whole, however, governments end up paying a lot more for pensions than private employers do. According to EBRI's analysis, private companies need to set aside about 15 percent of payroll. For state and local plans, that figure is in the thirties. And for federal employees the same figure to cover the inordinately generous benefits is as high as 47 percent.

There's more: Federal workers enjoy luxuries not found in the marketplace. One of the best is early retirement. With 30 years of service, most civil servants can retire to the golf course at age 55 without penalty. For 93 percent of federal retirees in FY1993, the average age was 58. In the private sector, the typical person retires at age 63, five years later. If private employees want to retire at 55, their monthly checks are substantially docked.

But it is military retirees who truly enjoy the high ground. They can start collecting checks after only 20 years of service. Since many of them start out in the services while still in their teens, this means that taxpayers are writing substantial retirement checks to codgers in their late thirties. The *average* military man or woman retires at age 44. When he does, his father could well still be working—unless, of course, he works for the government, too. The unfunded liability of the Military Retirement System is now $627 billion.

Employees of local and state governments can also "spike"—vastly increase—their pensions. Almost all private pensions are calculated from a five-year salary average. But most public employee plans use a three-year average or less, and many also consider other forms of compensation, like overtime and, in some cases, even unused vacation time and the department car. This makes it easier for clever workers to spike their *lifetime* pensions by saving vacation days and jacking up their overtime as they approach retirement.

Although by no means a problem everywhere, there are still striking—and for local taxpayers, infuriating—examples of this across the country. In December 1993, for instance, Los Angeles County's Thomas Tidemanson was able to retire from his $158,000 a year job as director of public works with an annual pension of $190,000.

Of all the public sector perks, though, the most enviable is known by a modest sounding acronym: the yearly COLA, or Cost of Living Adjustment. COLAs are extra payments, added on to match inflation. One hundred percent of federal retirees and roughly 50 percent of state and local retirees get them every year, automatically, while only about 1 percent of private retirees do. Over time, the small boosts compound to substantial sums. EBRI's Salisbury likes to give the example of a retiring Secret Service officer with an average background. Without COLAs, the pension would be worth $389,000. With COLAs, though, its value jumps to $697,000.

Just ask former Congressman Hastings Keith. Although he paid only $50,000 toward his congressional pension, his monthly check is now $9,410, and, since he retired in 1973, he has collected more than $1.2 million—all because of COLAs and a rule that allows him to "double dip," counting his military service for both his civil service and military pensions. But Keith is begging to be cut off. "I should not be getting all this money," he declares. He directs the rag-tag "National Committee on Public Employee Pension Systems," which is fighting to turn off the COLA spigots. He estimates that of the $65 billion the government paid in retirement benefits last year, half is due to COLAs.

Of course, not every federal retiree is drawing in the big bucks. Ruth Hall retired in 1970 at age 55, after 28 years as a government clerk. Despite her long years, her modest salary means that her yearly pension—$10,543—is also quite modest. Inflation has boosted the 78-year-old Hall's rent from $117.50 a month when she retired to $605 now. "I've been so grateful for the COLAs," she says.

Retirees like Hall deserve protection, but the federal retirement plan gives COLAs to everyone—former clerks and millionaires alike. That is very expensive. Indeed, according to a recent estimate by *Money* magazine, if all government pensions were cut back to private sector standards, the average person's tax bill, including federal, state, and local taxes, would drop by about 8 percent. The more important point is not our current bills but the prospect of what our taxes will be like if all of these pensions are paid out. That's the real danger.

A number of states have, in fact, been trying to reform. In Illinois, long among the worst funded state retirement systems, the legislature passed a law last August which will make state contributions a continuing appropriation, remov-

ing the yearly temptation to avoid paying for pension promises.

But the federal government suffers from a serious case of denial, aided and abetted by powerful lobbies. One of the strongest is the 500,000-member National Association of Retired Federal Employees (NARFE). In the first 18 months of 1993-94, reports the Center for Responsive Politics, NARFE gave more than $350,000 to candidates for national office, placing this obscure-sounding PAC 54th on the list of 3,000 that the Center tracks. The main power of retirees, however, is their voting strength—both their own and that of civil servants who are looking forward to their own pensions. That's why when a vote on benefits comes up, the employees' unions know to remind members of Congress how many feds live in their districts. *Retirement Life*, NARFE's monthly magazine, for instance, recently listed the number of retirees by state and their combined retirement income. Bob Dole, for example, could go down the list and see that 39,903 retirees live, and presumably vote, in Kansas. He could run his finger across the chart and see that they brought $47,060,786 in government retirement payments to his state just last year. In case the point wasn't clear, the magazine dryly notes that "The numbers of retirees are useful to illustrate potential political impact, or clout."

Despite the feds' genetic resistance to change, there has been some reform. Starting in 1986, new federal employees are entered into the Federal Employee Retirement System, which requires more employee contributions and cuts back on the guaranteed pension. Around the same time, the military retirement system made 20-year retirements a little less lucrative.

One of the most obvious reforms for both civil servants and for the military—and one that has not been seriously addressed—is later retirement ages. When the current standards were set, people did not live as long. With modern medicine, we can no longer afford to let civil servants go at 55. The same is true for the military. In earlier eras, officers and enlisted men were justified in being let go at 44 after a dangerous and physically demanding career. Today, there are plenty of jobs in the services that don't require you to be in top physical shape (and in fact, virtually all of the 40-year-olds in the military now are in assignments that they could easily perform at age 55). It is time to raise the civil service retirement age to 65, the military's to 55, and, while we are at it, the Social Security age to 70, as the Bipartisan Commission on Entitlement and Tax Reform recommended in December.

The government can also not afford to keep paying out across-the-board COLAs regardless of the recipient's financial status. $50,000-a-year pensions do not need the same protection that $10,000-a-year pensions do. Right now, the bill for federal COLAs falls on the shoulders of a middle class that, broadly speaking, will have to make ends meet without inflation bonuses.

Above all, whatever the details of reform, the principle must be full financing. The bill for all governmental pension promises—local, state, and federal—must be paid as they are made, just as prudent private companies do. Otherwise, the average citizen does not have a say in deciding where the line between fair and luxurious is crossed. The work is done and then the younger generation is left to pay for the contract.

Now the budget shortfall stands at about $1 billion for every word in this article. Either re-

tirement payments have to be docked, or, notes EBRI's Salisbury, "we'll have to raise $1.5 trillion in taxes, borrow the money, or cut back federal benefits to other sectors of society." In December, President Clinton foolishly appeared to rule out reform of federal pension benefits, including the establishment of a later retirement age for civil servants. (This despite the fact that, in 1993, raising the civil service age to 65 came within six votes of passing the House.) But it is still possible for the Republicans now running Congress–and their Democratic colleagues–to demonstrate seriousness about pension reform. As a start, they could vow not to accept any COLAs on the already generous pensions that they will collect from Uncle Sam. Now *that* would be leadership.

WHERE THERE'S SMOKE . . .

Breathing Fire On Tobacco

DAN ZEGART

Dan Zegart, a freelance writer and reporter, is at work on a book about the tobacco industry.

Peter Castano couldn't quit smoking. It was humiliating. He first lit up at 16, and swore to stop when his fiancée insisted on it as a condition of their marriage. But he just couldn't do it. On their honeymoon, Dianne Castano caught him sneaking one and threw a drink at him. She never relented, and Castano spent ten years of marriage trying—with a spectacular lack of success—to hide his habit from his wife.

In 1993, Castano died of lung cancer at age 47, and an angry Dianne Castano approached the couple's best friend, Wendell Gauthier, a product liability lawyer in New Orleans, about suing the tobacco companies. Gauthier looked into it, but decided it was almost impossible to win a traditional wrongful death claim against the industry. Indeed, in more than 800 suits since 1954, the cigarette companies have gone to trial only twenty-three times, lost twice, and spent not a dime in damage payments.

But in February, a world-class group of lawyers led by Gauthier received certification from a federal court in New Orleans to bring a class-action suit on behalf of Peter Castano and three living, allegedly addicted smokers, thus launching *Castano v. American Tobacco*, the largest product liability suit in American history. If the case goes before a jury, it will be the first national class action for product liability ever to do so, one that could represent 90 million current and former smokers, who could win damages of $40 billion or more. To pull it off, more than sixty of the most prominent personal-injury law firms in the country have banded together to attack the tobacco industry in one mega-suit. As Gary Black, a tobacco specialist for New York financial analysts Sanford Bernstein and Co., characterizes it, "This case on a scale of one to ten is a nine-and-a-half."

Castano immediately stole the spotlight in a year that seems to be building toward an all-out assault against cigarette makers: Four states—Florida, West Virginia, Mississippi and Minnesota—are suing to recover billions in public health care costs for cigarette-related disease. Congress is considering additional restrictions on youth-oriented cigarette marketing, as is the Clinton Administration, which just accepted a recommendation by the Food and Drug Administration that nicotine face regulation as a drug. And a federal grand jury is investigating alleged tobacco company misrepresentations about the content and effects of cigarettes. Another may probe whether cigarette executives lied to Congress.

What frightens the financial community almost as much as a plaintiff's verdict in *Castano*—which Black says could drain the combined assets of Philip Morris and R.J. Reynolds, depending on the size of the class and the amount awarded per plaintiff—is the notification campaign. A good portion of *Castano*'s $6 million war chest will be spent on this pretrial media bombardment notifying 45 million current smokers and the same number of former smokers of their right to sue. To join would mean simply clipping a coupon from a full-page newspaper ad or responding to one on TV or the Internet.

By certifying an enormous class that includes all nicotine-dependent people, as well as the survivors of deceased smokers, U.S. District Judge Okla Jones II acknowledges he has embarked "on a road certainly less traveled, if ever taken at all." And although he allowed a classwide trial on key issues such as whether the companies conspired to hide information from smokers, he didn't permit that trial to determine how much to compensate victims. That means a way has to be found to determine damages based on the facts of individual cases or groups of cases. "That's a hell of a problem with 30 million or more plaintiffs," said Ronald Motley, one of the *Castano* lawyers.

The story of *Castano* is also the story of the 800 other suits defeated by the corporate world's most ferocious litigator, an opponent that never settles and spends whatever it takes to exhaust the usually small plaintiffs' firms. (The manpower of tobacco's three biggest defense practices outnumbers all the attorneys from the sixty-odd *Castano* firms combined.) The industry put up $50 million to defeat the *Cipollone* case in New Jersey, dragged it out for ten years and finally took it to the Supreme Court. It buried the other side in paper, filing 100 motions. One witness was questioned for nine days. The exhausted plaintiff's firm, having spent $5 million in a losing cause, finally quit.

Cipollone points up why the future of legal attacks on the industry is very much in doubt in the current political climate. Tobacco has poured money into national and state tort reform efforts, knowing that bills making it more difficult to bring product liability suits, like those awaiting approval in Congress, would be the death knell for the individual tobacco plaintiff. The effect of such bills on class-action suits like *Castano* is less obvious. But tinkering with the contingent fee system or limiting awards for pain and suffering or punitive damages will have a severe impact on the ability of the plaintiff's bar to go after any large, well-funded corporate adversary, particularly tobacco.

C*astano seeks to prove a conspiracy to bring off the deadliest, longest-running fraud in business history.*

At the state level, the $47 billion industry quietly gutted dozens of suits in California and New Jersey in 1987 (one was

Reprinted with permission from *The Nation* magazine, August 28/September 4, 1995, pp. 193-196. © 1995 by The Nation Company, L.P.

Cipollone) by having more restrictive tort laws passed. California's statute retroactively abolished suits that target "inherently unsafe" products, and listed butter, sugar, castor oil, alcohol and tobacco.

If ever a substance deserved the designation "inherently unsafe," it is nicotine, the psychoactive ingredient in tobacco, and the *casus belli* for *Castano*. This poisonous alkaloid has been studied since the late nineteenth century, when biologists used it to help define the modern concept of drug tolerance, a key criterion for judging addictiveness. Contemporary researchers have found that after just two hours without cigarettes, the brain wave activity of a heavy smoker is so badly disrupted that the brain's ability to process information virtually shuts down. Such disruption is associated with extremely addictive drugs.

The cigarette companies learned early that nicotine was addictive and left an extensive trail of internal memos that prove they knew. The American Tobacco Company did more than ninety studies on the pharmacological and other effects of nicotine, beginning in 1940. By the sixties and seventies, tobacco industry scientists were "way ahead of the outside" in their understanding of nicotine, according to Jack Henningfield, a researcher at the National Institute on Drug Abuse. In 1977, Philip Morris wanted its researchers to explore such questions as, "Given a fixed quantity of nicotine in the tobacco, what factors in cigarette design determine its availability . . . to the smoker?" "Does the smoker seek spike effects or bloodstream constancy?" and "What are the fundamental differences between the habit of tobacco smoking and heroin injection?" *The New York Times* has published excerpts from Brown & Williamson Tobacco Corporation internal documents describing decades of clandestine research that concluded cigarette smoking is a disease-causing "habit of addiction," and outlined a coordinated cover-up of this explosive knowledge.

Despite all this, few attorneys will take on the cigarette companies, which have a reputation for doing virtually anything to win. The defense kept Rose Cipollone for four depositions—a total of almost twenty-four hours—as she withered in the final months of an agonizing death from lung cancer. Burl Butler, a Mississippi barber and the plaintiff in a second-hand smoke suit, was lying on his bed the day before he died when a helicopter began hovering over the house. The tobacco lawyers were apparently waiting for Butler to die so they could immediately make a motion to autopsy the body.

But the single biggest reason for the plaintiffs' losing record is the fact that juries in most tobacco lawsuits have blamed the smoker for not having the willpower to quit what everyone believed was no more than a dangerous habit. The smoker had "assumed the risk" and the consequences were his or her responsibility. By March 1994, a year after the death of Peter Castano, the emerging evidence of tobacco industry nicotine manipulation had convinced Wendell Gauthier that he could beat the cigarette makers with a suit based solely on the addictiveness of cigarettes, because addiction cancels out the assumption-of-risk argument. If the industry lied about nic-

otine, the smoker was suckered. He couldn't have assumed a risk he didn't know existed.

"I think the attitude now is, We were deceived. The American public was deceived, because those rascals *knew* it was addicting and they *been* knowing it was addicting," said the 52-year-old Gauthier. The addiction claim has another major advantage. The suit doesn't ask for damages for lung cancer or heart disease or emphysema, so no link to them has to be proven. Anyone diagnosed as nicotine-dependent or who couldn't stop after being advised by a doctor to do so could sign on to *Castano*.

Gauthier's class action will try to make a jury believe a corporate crime story: that for at least thirty years the tobacco companies knew nicotine was addictive, learned precisely how to control the dose and hid what they knew from the American people. Making the charge stick means proving a conspiracy to bring off the deadliest, longest-running fraud in business history.

Most of the lawyers on Gauthier's team were seasoned in successful struggles with manufacturers of asbestos, breast implants, the Dalkon shield and other hazardous products. Gauthier himself chaired the plaintiffs' committee in the DuPont Plaza Hotel fire case in San Juan in the late eighties— a $250 million award—and the MGM Grand Hotel blaze in Las Vegas. A global suit on breast implants netted $4.3 billion. But as the jackpots got bigger, so did the plaintiffs' committees, which led to vicious infighting. Determined not to let this happen in *Castano*, Gauthier handpicked the attorneys. After decades of futility, the top rank of the country's personal-injury lawyers would be taking on the cigarette manufacturers for the first time.

One *Castano* lawyer calls Gauthier "Ike" for marshaling this unprecedented invasion force, whose member firms are involved in almost every important tobacco lawsuit. If Gauthier is Eisenhower, then Ronald Motley is Patton, a charismatic, acid-tongued, cowboy boot–wearing legal warrior. He is the man some say the industry should fear most in a courtroom and the leading candidate to try *Castano*. The son of a South Carolina gas station owner, the 50-year-old Motley is arguably the best plaintiff's trial lawyer in the country—certainly one of the richest, having won billions of dollars in asbestos awards since the mid-seventies. But friends say money has little to do with his interest in tobacco litigation.

"My mother died of emphysema from smoking, and after that I swore I'd get 'em," said Motley. "Now you asked why I'm in this? That's why. And I'll tell you something else," he said, a vein in his neck bulging as he warmed up in his New Orleans hotel room. "You can't find a family in this country they haven't touched. That's why we're going to win this thing."

He smiled. "Eventually."

While Gauthier unleashed the class-action approach on tobacco suits, Motley put his energy into finding a more sympathetic plaintiff than a smoker who'd puffed himself to death. His search led him to Burl Butler, who never smoked a cigarette but apparently died from inhaling the smoke of his customers. Motley reasons that a jury may find it easier to bring a verdict against the industry if all the victim did was breathe the air. He thinks another way around the blame-the-smoker tactic is a Mississippi state suit he helped design that would force the tobacco companies to reimburse the state for the health care costs of indigent smokers. Three other states filed similar actions, and Motley is trial counsel for two of them.

To understand what the anti-smoking movement is up against in court, you have to see a cigarette lawsuit in action. At a *Castano* hearing a year ago, no fewer than thirty industry lawyers were dispatched to New Orleans to press for immediate dismissal. In the legal trade it's called the "wall of flesh."

Despite the fact that four months earlier the heads of the tobacco companies swore to Congress that they believe nicotine is not addictive, one of the lawyers began arguing that the case should be thrown out because the plaintiffs knew for years they were nicotine addicts and should have sued earlier. "The Surgeon General told the nation in 1988 that nicotine was the substance in tobacco that caused addiction and that tobacco addiction was similar to hard drugs such as cocaine and heroin," boomed the lawyer. "It was on the cover of *Time*," he said. "Couldn't be clearer than that, Judge."

The key to any tobacco suit is documents, the DNA evidence of product liability cases. The critical turning points in asbestos litigation came when corporate reports were unearthed that unequivocally demonstrated the industry knew the hazards of its product. In another cigarette case in New Jersey, Motley is trying to unlock 1,500 explosive documents now under court seal in the hope that they may show the tobacco companies concealed potentially unfavorable health studies by bypassing the Council for Tobacco Research, their supposedly independent scientific funding organ. Instead, dangerous research was supervised directly as "special projects" by the companies and their law firms to cloak the work in attorney-client privilege and prevent its discovery in a lawsuit.

The manipulation of science is a key issue in *Castano* and other suits because schemes like "special projects" are powerful evidence of fraud, and fraud can trigger a crushing series of punitive damage awards. For that reason, the cigarette companies have fought tenaciously to keep the special projects documents sealed. Motley is now challenging the privilege under a crime/fraud exception.

The fear of product liability suits evidently led Brown & Williamson, makers of Kool, Viceroy and other brands, to create a comprehensive coding system to organize sensitive documents. A fifty-four-page master summary of the system prepared in 1989 offers an intriguing glimpse into how the company rated its own vulnerabilities, with the most delicate material being marked with a "1." The summary includes subject headings such as "Manipulation of Research/Data" and "Document Retention/Destruction." Another was titled "Significance—Target Markets" and read: "Unless there is a slur or an otherwise significant issue contained in a document or discussing a minority target market, apply normal significance to these documents. . . . If the document targets persons who are 18 to 21, i.e., 18 through 20, assign a significance of '2.' Assign a significance of '1' if the document targets persons under 18." Documents dealing with "lawyer involvement with scientists" also got a rating of 1.

In the end, many things were hauled under the mantle of attorney-client privilege, including industry lists of cigarette additives. One company list of more than 200 ingredients, stamped "Attorney Work Product" on every page, shows flavorings and their code names. Coca flavor was BINNET; pulverized deer tongue was CARPAS; propylene glycol was GRELANTER. All three were marked with an asterisk for "potentially hazardous."

It was tobacco's manipulation of science that brought the *Castano* lawyers to Washington, D.C., last year. In order to maintain its position that nicotine is not addictive and that no "causal link" has been shown between cigarette smoke and disease, the industry has funded a stable of scientists who cite one another, gain credence through publication in scholarly journals and attend tobacco-sponsored symposiums. When the Occupational Safety and Health Administration began hearings this past fall on a proposed rule that would ban smoking in about 6 million workplaces, the well-oiled industry machine simply buried the agency under testimony—R.J. Reynolds alone was responsible for more than 15,000 pages of submissions.

Working pro bono, the *Castano* attorneys represented health and labor groups and cross-examined tobacco-funded witnesses, which gave them a sneak preview of experts who might later testify for the cigarette makers. One target was Duke University economist W. Kip Viscusi, who expounded on his theory that cigarette smokers who die prematurely save society money in pension and nursing-home costs. Another witness conceded his testimony had been edited by cigarette company lawyers. R.J. Reynolds toxicologist Chris Coggins had to explain why his company spent millions of dollars developing the smokeless Premier cigarette if the industry is confident tobacco smoke is innocuous. Unhappy with the way things were going, Philip Morris withdrew in November.

Given a choice, the tobacco lawyers would rather talk about nicotine and addictiveness than what everyone calls "the youth issue," the most emotionally charged segment of struggle over tobacco. Some lawyers believe that *Castano* is most likely to win if it can convince a jury that the industry targets children to replace the over 400,000 smokers who die of cigarette-related disease each year and the thousands of others who quit. There's plenty of anecdotal evidence to support the charge. Ad campaigns like that featuring Joe Camel have dramatically boosted the size of the illicit youth market, to the point where a study released last month found that almost one of every five eighth graders smokes, up 30 percent in three years. Another survey showed that 25 percent of the high school seniors who tried cigarettes had done so by the sixth grade. In 1977, a Canadian cigarette maker studied why children begin smoking: "Ads for teenagers must be denoted by lack of artificiality, and a sense of honesty. Attempts at the use of celebrities like Farrah Fawcett or O.J. Simpson do not really click. If freedom from pressure and authority can be communicated, so much the better."

All four of *Castano*'s class representatives started smoking as teens, as did Gauthier's three daughters, a defiance by otherwise obedient children that puzzled and infuriated him. "We're going to show the American people they went after children *knowing* that it's going to addict them, knowing full well it's going to cause cancer, emphysema and cardiovascu-

lar disease," said Gauthier. "They choose to kill our kids. I think that's a strong argument."

With tort reform brewing, the tobacco industry may yet dodge even these harpoons. However, disgust at the world's most profitable and peculiar product is growing. As two armies of lawyers gird for battle in New Orleans, the issue of youth targeting is a mystery weapon that could decide the outcome. The difference between a sinister ad campaign and making the youth charge stick in court is considerable. But somewhere in the dark world of cigarette company memos, there just could be a folder of proof.

ANALYSIS

Confronting the AIDS Pandemic

Daniel J. M. Tarantola and Jonathan M. Mann

Daniel J. M. Tarantola, M.D., is a lecturer in international health at the Harvard School of Public Health. Jonathan M. Mann, M.D., is director of the International AIDS Center of the Harvard AIDS Institute.

In 1986, the world undertook to mobilize against the AIDS pandemic in an effort that continued to grow until the beginning of this decade, when it began to stall. Today, the global HIV/AIDS pandemic is spinning out of control—its broad course has yet to be influenced in any substantial way by policies and programs mounted against it.

In 1991–1992, the Harvard-based Global AIDS Policy Coalition undertook a review of the state of the AIDS pandemic. The findings of this review, which appear in our new book *AIDS in the World* (Harvard University Press, December 1992), raise the alarm and call for an urgent revival of the response to AIDS.

The magnitude of the pandemic has increased over 100-fold since AIDS was discovered in 1981. From an estimated 100,000 people infected with HIV world-wide in 1981, it is estimated that by early 1992, at least 12.9 million people around the world (7.1 million men, 4.7 million women, and 1.1 million children) had been infected with HIV. Of these, about one in five (2.6 million) have thus far developed AIDS, and nearly 2.5 million have died.

The spread of HIV has not been stopped in any community or country. In the United States, at least 40,000 to 80,000 new HIV infections were anticipated during 1992; in 1991, more than 75,000 new HIV infections occurred in Europe. In just five years, the cumulative number of HIV-infected Africans has tripled, from 2.5 million to over 7.5 million today. HIV is spreading to new communities and countries around the world—in some areas with great rapidity. An explosion of HIV has recently occurred in Southeast Asia, particularly in Thailand, Burma, and India, where, within only a few years, over one million people may have already been infected with HIV. HIV/AIDS is now reported from areas that, so far, had been left relatively untouched, such as Paraguay, Greenland, and the Pacific island nations of Fiji, Papua New Guinea, and Samoa. The global implications are clear: During the next decade, HIV will likely reach most communities around the world; geographic boundaries cannot protect against HIV. The question today is not *if* HIV will come, but only *when*.

INCREASED COMPLEXITY

The pandemic becomes more complex as it matures. Globally it is composed of thousands of separate and linked community epidemics. Every large metropolitan area affected—Miami, New York, Bangkok, London, Amsterdam, Sydney, Rio de Janeiro—contains several subepidemics of HIV going on at the same time. The impact on women is increasing dramatically, as heterosexual transmission accounts for almost 71 percent of HIV infections. Worldwide, the proportion of HIV infected who are women is rising rapidly, from 25 percent in 1990 to 40 percent by early 1992. The epidemic also evolves over time: In Brazil, the proportion of HIV infections linked with injection

This article originally appeared in *The World & I*, January 1993, pp. 80-87. Reprinted by permission of *The World & I*, a publication of The Washington Times Corporation. © 1993.

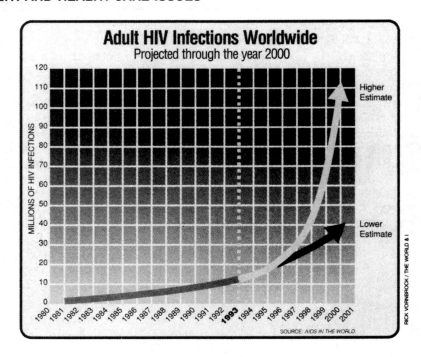

Adult HIV Infections Worldwide
Projected through the year 2000

MILLIONS OF HIV INFECTIONS

Higher Estimate

Lower Estimate

RICK VORNBROCK / THE WORLD & I

SOURCE: AIDS IN THE WORLD.

drug use has increased over tenfold since the early 1980s; in the Caribbean, heterosexual transmission has now replaced homosexual transmission as the major mode of HIV spread.

The pandemic's major impacts are yet to come. During the period 1992–95 alone, the number of people developing AIDS—3.8 million—will exceed the total number who developed the disease during the pandemic's history prior to 1992. The number of children orphaned by AIDS will more than double in the next three years: from approximately 1.8 million today to 3.7 million by 1995. The pandemic has not peaked in any country—no community or country can claim "victory" against HIV/AIDS. By 1995, an *additional* 5.7 million adults will become infected with HIV. Thus, from 1992 to 1995, the total number of HIV-infected adults will increase by 50 percent. During the same period, the number of children infected with HIV will more than double, from 1.1 million to an estimated 2.3 million.

By the year 2000, the Global AIDS Policy Coalition has projected that between 38 million and 110 million adults—and over 10 million children—will become HIV infected. The largest proportion of HIV infections will be in Asia (42 percent), surpassing sub-Saharan Africa (31 percent), Latin America (8 percent), and the Caribbean (6 percent). By the end of this decade, 24 million adults and several million children may have developed AIDS—

or up to 10 times as many as today.

Only a few years ago, tuberculosis was considered a stable problem that was endemic mostly in the developing world. If it was also prevalent in certain socioeconomic groups in industrialized countries, there was a common belief that the situation

was largely under control. This general sense of complacency, denounced by many who had been fighting the disease, led to a decline in resources allocated to surveillance, prevention, and treatment services. When HIV came on the scene, it found a vulnerable population.

There is a dangerous synergy between HIV and tuberculosis that makes the combined effects of both worse than their separate effects added together. HIV makes individuals and communities more vulnerable to tuberculosis; it increases the rate of reactivation of tuberculosis infection, shortens the delay between TB infection and disease, and reduces the accuracy of diagnostic methods. Recent outbreaks of multiple-drug resistant tuberculosis have occurred in New York City and in Miami, especially in hospitals and prisons. Combining its projections with estimates made by the World Health Organization, *AIDS in the World* estimates that, by early 1992, there were more than 4.6 million people with both TB and HIV infection

Geographic boundaries cannot protect against HIV. The question today is not *if* HIV will come, but only *when*.

worldwide, 81 percent of them in Africa.

TAKING STOCK

Confronting the growing pandemic are national AIDS programs. These actions may involve governmental institutions and agencies, nongovernmental organizations, and the private sector.

Almost invariably overseen by ministries of health, they are generally implemented through government agencies and health services.

The success of a national AIDS program involves the extent to which it helps curb the course of the HIV epidemic and provides quality care to those already affected. On this basis, no program in the world can yet claim success.

Of the 38 countries surveyed by the Global AIDS Policy Coalition, 24 reported having conducted an evaluation since the inception of their national program. In general, the evaluation findings can be summarized as follows:

• Once created, programs become operational rapidly.

• They were successful in raising public awareness on AIDS issues although they did not always prevent (and at times they even generated) misperceptions among certain communities.

• They raised appropriate human rights issues and in some instances managed to prevent violations of these rights.

• They exchanged information—and in some cases made funds and skills available—at the international level.

Industrialized countries were generally able to secure the financial, human, and technological resources required to increase drastically the safety of blood and blood products, and establish diagnostic and treatment schemes reaching most (but not all) people in need. The same could not be said, however, about developing countries, which are constrained by lack of resources, weak infrastructures, and multiple developmental or even survival issues.

Common criticisms of these programs are their lack of focus and priority setting, their weak management, their lack of inte-

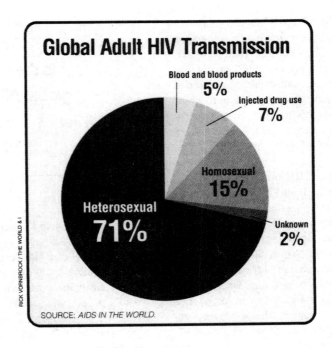

Global Adult HIV Transmission

Blood and blood products 5%
Injected drug use 7%
Homosexual 15%
Unknown 2%
Heterosexual 71%

RICK VORNBROCK / THE WORLD & I

SOURCE: *AIDS IN THE WORLD.*

gration with existing disease prevention and control services, and their inability to actively involve other health programs, sectors, and nongovernmental organizations. Denial persists about the pandemic's impact upon women; prevention and research efforts worldwide still inadequately involve them.

In its report, the Global AIDS Policy Coalition suggests indexes that can be applied at the national or regional levels. Similar indexes are being developed for the assessment of community vulnerability.

THE COST OF AIDS

AIDS policies and programs used to be guided by two motives misperceived by many as antagonistic: a human rights/humanitarian approach and a public health perspective. The economic argument was seldom raised because it was not politically advantageous to make the cost of AIDS a major public issue. It did not conform to the humanitarian agenda (cost is secondary to human rights) nor to the public health perspective (the population must be protected). But with

the rising number of people and communities affected by the pandemic, the cost of prevention and care and the general economic impact of AIDS have become critical issues.

The economic perspective considers the impact of AIDS in a decade that began in a worldwide recession. It can be argued that the impact of HIV/AIDS on young, productive adults and their children will jeopardize the national development of many countries. In July 1992, a study conducted by an American team estimated the economic impact of the pandemic by feeding epidemiological projection data into a computer model of the global marketplace. It concluded that by the year 2000, the pandemic could drain between $356 billion and $514 billion from the world's economy, and developing countries are expected to be the hardest hit.

The Global AIDS Policy Coalition estimated that money spent on AIDS in a one-year period during 1990–91 was in the range of $1.4–$1.5 billion for prevention, approximately $3.5 billion for adult AIDS care alone, and $1.6 billion for research, for an adjusted total of $7.1 to $7.6 billion (including costs for treating those persons with HIV before AIDS occurs). Interestingly, about 95 percent was spent in industrialized countries that have less than 25 percent of the world's population, 18 percent of the people with AIDS, and 15 percent of HIV infections worldwide.

For HIV prevention activities in 1991, about $2.70 was spent *per person* in North America and $1.18 in Europe. In the developing world, spending on prevention amounted to only $0.07 per person in sub-Saharan Africa and $0.03 per person in Latin America. Of the $5.6 billion spent on AIDS research since the discovery of AIDS in 1981, $5.45 billion, or 97 percent, has been spent in industrialized countries. The United States is the biggest contributor to global AIDS research spending, with $4.8 billion, or 86 percent of the world total. Domestic and international research have led to a considerable advancement of knowledge. Research funds benefited from annual increases in the late 1980s, but resources support-

The United States is the biggest contributor to global AIDS research spending, with 86 percent of the world total.

ing this research are reaching a plateau.

For AIDS care, 89 percent of world spending in 1990 was used to help less than 30 percent of the world's people with AIDS—those living in North America and Europe. And yet, the cost of medical care for each person with AIDS—roughly equivalent to annual per capita income in developing countries—is overwhelming individuals and households everywhere. Inequities in treatment and prevention are growing. The cost of one year's treatment with AZT is about $2,500, while per capita income in all developing countries averages $700—in sub-Saharan Africa the

figure is $470—or less than one-fifth the cost of AZT for one year. Individual studies have indicated that the annual cost of care for an adult with AIDS varied in 1990–91 from $32,000 in the United States to $22,000 in western Europe, $2,000 in Latin America, and a mere $393 in sub-Saharan Africa.

These figures translate into the harsh reality of length of survival and quality of life of people with AIDS. The need for AIDS care and the inequity in access to quality services will continue to grow: The number of AIDS treatment years for adults alone will increase from an estimated 433,000 in 1992 to 619,000 in

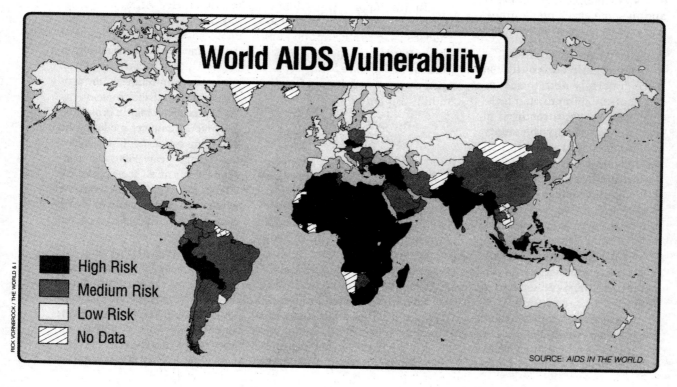

World AIDS Vulnerability

High Risk
Medium Risk
Low Risk
No Data

RICK VORNBROCK / THE WORLD & I

SOURCE: *AIDS IN THE WORLD*

1995; almost 60 percent of these will be in Africa and 26 percent in the industrialized world. Built into these estimates, however, is the average duration of survival of an adult with AIDS, which in Africa is estimated at about one year after diagnosis, less than half of the survival duration of an adult with AIDS in the industrialized world.

Despite the introduction of HIV diagnostic tests over seven years ago, unscreened blood is currently responsible for at least 5 percent of global HIV infections. Most sub-Saharan African countries still cannot afford a safe blood supply. And even if an AIDS vaccine became available today, its impact on the world would be limited by inequities in access to it.

NEED FOR A GLOBAL VISION

Where efforts have been made to provide a coordinated response to the growing crisis, there are clear signs of positive individual responses. But where programs are confronted with weak national commitment, declining resources, and a growing sense of complacency, national AIDS programs are in jeopardy and, together with them, the people they are intended to serve. Many governments, constrained by their lack of resources, continue to avoid the reality of the pandemic: More people become infected because they do not have sufficient access to information and services; more individuals require care that they cannot afford; more families and communities are affected by the impact of a pandemic that has only begun.

Industrialized nations are turning away from coordinated efforts, showing a growing preference to work independently, on a bilateral basis, with chosen developing countries. Fragmentation of efforts by industrialized countries has led to competition among donors in some countries. It is clear that as the pandemic continues to worsen, AIDS programs will be forced to struggle with insufficient funds.

Global efforts have failed to motivate low-prevalence countries to act before the epidemic reaches them in force. India, Burma, and the Sudan are examples of a delayed response and a failure to learn from the experience of heavily affected countries.

Overall, the world has become more vulnerable to HIV and AIDS. On the basis of the societal factors that create vulnerability to spread of HIV, *AIDS in the World* has identified 57 countries as *high risk* for HIV spread—including countries that have thus far escaped the brunt of the pandemic, such as Indonesia, Egypt, Bangladesh, and Nigeria. An additional 39 countries are considered to be at *substantial* risk of a major HIV epidemic, including 11 Latin American countries, 8 in the southeast Mediterranean, 7 in Asia (including China), 4 in the Caribbean, and 9 in other regions.

We *are* at a critical juncture in the confrontation with AIDS, but we are not helpless. By revitalizing leadership, by addressing prevention and the needs of the affected, by formulating clear, international strategies, by accelerating effective, safe, and affordable treatments and vaccines, it *is* possible to stall the future spread of the pandemic.

At a time when many countries are undergoing major geopolitical transitions and are facing severe economic recessions, HIV/AIDS is not simply fading away. The world will continue to experience a rapid increase in the number of people developing AIDS until there is a cure. In the meantime, a troubled world population can unite together to fairly and equitably make available prevention and treatment programs until that day comes.

Mental Illness Is Still a Myth

Thomas Szasz

Thomas Szasz is professor emeritus of psychiatry at the State University of New York in Syracuse, New York. He is author of The Myth of Mental Illness; Our Right to Drugs: The Case for a Free Market; *and* A Lexicon of Lunacy: Metaphoric Malady, Moral Responsibility, and Psychiatry (*the latter published by Transaction Publishers*). *His most recent book is* Cruel Compassion: Psychiatric Control of Society's Unwanted.

In a memorable statement C. S. Lewis once remarked, "Of all the tyrannies a tyranny sincerely exercised for the good of its victims may be the most oppressive. . . . To be 'cured' against one's will and cured of states which we may not regard as disease is to be put on a level with those who have not yet reached the age of reason or those who never will; to be classed with infants, imbeciles, and domestic animals." These words still apply to psychiatry today.

Anyone with an ear for language will recognize that the boundary that separates the serious vocabulary of psychiatry from the ludicrous lexicon of psychobabble, and both from playful slang, is thin and permeable to fashion. This is precisely wherein lies the richness and power of language that is inexorably metaphoric. Should a person want to say something sensitive tactfully, he can, as the adage suggests, say it in jest, but mean it in earnest. Bureaucrats, lawyers, politicians, quacks, and the assorted mountebanks of the "hindering professions" are in the habit of saying everything in earnest. If we want to protect ourselves from them, we had better hear what they tell us in jest, lest the joke be on us.

As far back as I can remember thinking about such things, I have been struck by the analogic-metaphoric character of the vocabulary of psychiatry, which is nevertheless accepted as a legitimate medical idiom. When I decided to discontinue my residency training in internal medicine and switch to psychiatry, I did so with the aim of exploring the nature and function of psychiatry's metaphors and to expose them to public scrutiny as figures of speech.

During the 1950s, I published a score of articles in professional journals, challenging the epistemological foundations of the concept of the mental illness and the moral basis of involuntary mental hospitalization. In 1958, as my book *The Myth of Mental Illness* was nearing completion, I wrote a short paper of the same title and submitted it to every major American psychiatric journal. Not one of them would accept it for publication. As fate would have it—and because the competition between psychologists and psychiatrists for a slice of the mental health pie was then even more intense than now—*The American Psychologist* published the essay in 1960. The following year, the book appeared. I think it is fair to say that psychiatry has not been the same since.

Responses to my work have varied from lavish praise to bitter denunciation. American psychiatrists quickly closed ranks against me. Official psychiatry simply dismissed my contention that (mis)behaviors are not diseases and asserted that I "deny the reality that mental diseases are like other diseases," and distorted my critique of psychiatric slavery as my "denying life-saving treatment to mental patients." Actually, I have sought to deprive psychiatrists of their power to involuntarily hospitalize or treat competent adults called "mental patients." My critics have chosen to interpret this proposal as my trying to deprive competent adults of their right or opportunity to seek or receive psychiatric help. By 1970, I had become a non-person in American psychiatry. The pages of American psychiatric journals were shut to my work. Soon, the very mention of my name became taboo and was omitted from new editions of texts that had previously featured my views. In short, I became the object of that most effective of all criticisms, the silent treatment—or, as the Germans so aptly call it, *Totschweigetaktik*.

In Great Britain, my views elicited a more favorable reception. Some English psychiatrists conceded that not all psychiatric diagnoses designate *bona fide* diseases. Others were sympathetic to the plight of persons in psychiatric custody. Regrettably, that posture rested heavily on the misguided patriotic belief that the practice of psychiatric slavery was less common in England than in the United States.

Not surprisingly, my work was received more favorably by philosophers, psychologists, sociologists, and civil libertarians, who recognized the merit of my cognitive challenge to the concept of mental illness, and the legitimacy of my questioning the morality of involuntary psychiatric interventions. I thus managed to set in motion a controversy about mental illness that is still raging.

When people now hear the term "mental illness," virtually everyone acts as if he were unaware of the distinction between literal and metaphoric uses of the word "illness." That is why people believe that finding brain lesions in some mental patients (for example, schizophrenics) would prove, or has already proven, that mental illnesses exist and are "like other illnesses." This is an error. If mental illnesses are diseases of the central nervous system (for example, paresis), then they are diseases of the brain, not the mind; and if they are the names of (mis)behaviors (for example, using illegal drugs), then they are not diseases. A screwdriver may be a drink or an implement. No amount of research on orange juice and vodka can establish that it is a hitherto unrecognized form of a carpenter's tool.

Such linguistic clarification is useful for persons who want to think clearly, regardless of consequences. However, it is not useful for persons who want to respect social institutions that rest on the literal uses of a master metaphor. In short, psychiatric metaphors play the same role in therapeutic societies as religious metaphors play in theological societies. Consider the similarities. Mohammedans believe that God wants them to worship on Friday, Jews that He wants them to worship on Saturday, and Christians that He wants them to worship on Sunday. The various versions of the American Psychiatric Association's (APA) *Diagnostic and Statistical Manual* rest on the same sort of consensus. How does behavior become illness? By the membership of the American Psychiatric Association reaching a consensus that, say, gambling is an illness and then issuing a declaration to that effect. Thereafter "pathological gambling" is a disease.

Obviously, belief in the reality of a psychiatric fiction, such as mental illness, cannot be dispelled by logical argument any more than belief in the reality of a religious fiction, such as life after death, can be. That is because, *inter alia*, religion is the denial of the human foundations of meaning and of the finitude of life; this authenticated denial lets those who yearn for a theo-mythological foundation of meaning and who reject the reality of death to theologize life and entrust its management to clerical professionals. Similarly, psychiatry is the denial of the reality of free will and of the tragic nature of life; this authenticated denial lets those who seek a neuro-mythological explanation of human wickedness and who reject the inevitability of personal responsibility to medicalize life and entrust its management to health professionals. Marx was close to the mark when he asserted that religion was "the opiate of the people." But religion is not the opiate of the people. The human mind is. For both religion and psychiatry are the products of our own minds. Hence, the mind is its own opiate; and its ultimate drug is the word.

Freud himself flirted with such a formulation. But he shied away from its implications, choosing instead to believe that "neuroses" are literal diseases, and that "psychoanalysis" is a literal treatment. As he wrote in his essay "Psychical (or Mental) Treatment":

> Foremost among such measures [which operate upon the human mind] is the use of words; and words are the essential tool of mental treatment. A layman will no doubt find it hard to understand how pathological disorders of the body and mind can be eliminated by 'mere' words. He will feel that he is being asked to believe in magic. And he will not be so very wrong. . . . But we shall have to follow a roundabout path in order to explain how science sets about restoring to words a part at least of their former magical power.

I took up the profession of psychiatry in part to combat the contention that abnormal behaviors are the products of abnormal brains. Ironically, it was easier to do this fifty years ago than today. In the 1940s, the idea that every phenomenon named a "mental illness" will prove to be a bona fide brain disease was considered to be only a hypothesis, the validity of which one could doubt and still be regarded as reasonable. Since the 1960s, however, the view that mental diseases are diseases of the brain has become scientific fact. This contention is the bedrock claim of the National Alliance for the Mentally Ill (NAMI), an organization of and for the relatives of mental patients, with a membership in excess of one hundred thousand. Its "public service" slogan, intoned like a mantra, is: "Learn to recognize the symptoms of Mental Illness. Schizophrenia, Manic Depression, and Severe Depression are Brain Diseases."

Diagnoses are social constructs which vary from time to time and from culture to culture.

Psychiatrists and their powerful allies have thus succeeded in persuading the scientific community, the courts, the media, and the general public that the conditions they call "mental disorders" are diseases—that is, phenomena independent of human motivation or will. This development is at once curious and sinister. Until recently, only psychiatrists—who know little about medicine and less about science—embraced such blind physical reductionism.

Most scientists knew better. For example, Michael Polanyi, who made important contributions to both physical chemistry and social philosophy, observed: "The recognition of certain basic impossibilities has laid the foundations of some major principles of physics and chemistry; similarly, recognition of the impossibility of understanding living things in terms of physics and chemistry, far from setting limits to our understanding of life, will guide it in the right direction." It is no accident that the more firmly psychiatrically inspired ideas take hold of the collective American mind, the more foolishness and injustice they generate. The specifications of the Americans With Disabilities Act (AWDA), a federal law enacted in 1990, is a case in point.

Long ago, American lawmakers allowed psychiatrists to literalize the metaphor of mental illness. Having accepted fictitious mental diseases as facts, politicians could not avoid specifying which of these manufactured maladies were covered, and which

were not covered, under the AWDA. They had no trouble doing so, creating a veritable "DSM-Congress," that is, a list of mental diseases accredited by a congressional, rather than a psychiatric, consensus group. Thus, the AWDA covers "claustrophobia, personality problems, and mental retardation, [but does not cover] kleptomania, pyromania, compulsive gambling, and. . .transvestism." It is reassuring to know that the Congress of the United States agrees with me that stealing, setting fires, gambling, and cross-dressing are not diseases.

Thus, the various versions of the APA's *Diagnostic and Statistical Manual of Mental Disorders* are not classifications of mental disorders that "patients have," but are rosters of officially accredited psychiatric diagnoses. This is why in psychiatry, unlike in the rest of medicine, members of "consensus groups" and "task forces," appointed by officers of the APA, make and unmake diagnoses, the membership sometimes voting on whether a controversial diagnosis is or is not a disease. For more than a century, psychiatrists constructed diagnoses, pretended that they are diseases, and no one in authority challenged their deceptions. The result is that few people now realize that diagnoses are not diseases.

Diseases are demonstrable anatomical or physiological lesions, that may occur naturally or be caused by human agents. Although diseases may not be recognized or understood, they "exist." People have hypertension and malaria, regardless of whether or not they know it or physicians diagnose it.

Diagnoses are disease names. Because diagnoses are social constructs, they vary from time to time, and from culture to culture. Focal infections, masturbatory insanity, and homosexuality were diagnoses in the past; now they are considered to be diagnostic errors or normal behaviors. In France, physicians diagnose "liver crises"; in Germany, "low blood pressure"; in the United States, "nicotine dependence."

These considerations raise the question: Why do we make diagnoses? There are several reasons: 1) Scientific—to identify the organs or tissues affected and perhaps the cause of the illness; 2) Professional—to enlarge the scope, and thus the power and prestige, of a state-protected medical monopoly and the income of its practitioners; 3) Legal—to justify state-sanctioned coercive interventions outside of the criminal justice system; 4) Political-economic—to justify enacting and enforcing measures aimed at promoting public health and providing funds for research and treatment on projects classified as medical; 5) Personal—to enlist the support of public opinion, the media, and the legal system for bestowing special privileges (and impose special hardships) on persons diagnosed as (mentally) ill.

It is no coincidence that most psychiatric diagnoses are twentieth-century inventions. The aim of the classic, nineteenth-century model of diagnosis was to identify bodily lesions (diseases) and their material causes (etiology). The term "pneumococcal pneumonia," for example, identifies the organ affected, the lungs, and the cause of the illness, infection with the pneumococcus. Pneumococcal pneumonia is an example of a pathology-driven diagnosis.

Diagnoses driven by other motives—such as the desire to coerce the patient or to secure government funding for the treatment of the illness—generate different diagnostic constructions and lead to different conceptions of disease. Today, even diagnoses of (what used to be) strictly medical diseases are no longer principally pathology-driven. Because of third-party funding of hospital costs and physicians' fees, even the diagnoses of persons suffering from *bona fide* illnesses—for example, asthma or arthritis—are distorted by economic considerations. Final diagnoses on the discharge summaries of hospitalized patients are often no longer made by physicians, but by bureaucrats skilled in the ways of Medicare, Medicaid, and private health insurance reimbursement—based partly on what ails the patient, and partly on which medical terms for his ailment and treatment ensure the most generous reimbursement for the services rendered.

As for psychiatry, it ought to be clear that, except for the diagnoses of neurological diseases (treated by neurologists), no psychiatric diagnosis is, or can be, pathology-driven. Instead, all such diagnoses are driven by non-medical, that is, economic, personal, legal, political, or social considerations and incentives. Hence, psychiatric diagnoses point neither to anatomical or physiological lesions, nor to disease-causative agents, but allude to human behaviors and human problems. These problems include not only the plight of the denominated patient, but also the dilemmas with which the patient, relatives, and the psychiatrist must cope and which each tries to exploit.

My critique of psychiatry is two-pronged, partly conceptual, partly moral and political. At the core of my conceptual critique lies the distinction between the literal and metaphorical use of language—with mental illness as a metaphor. At the core of my moral-political critique lies the distinction between relating to grown persons as responsible adults and as irresponsible insane persons (quasi-infants or idiots)—

the former possessing free will, the latter lacking this moral attribute because of being "possessed" by mental illness. Instead of addressing these issues, my critics have concentrated on analyzing my motives and defending psychiatric slavery as benefiting the "slaves" and society alike. The reason for this impasse is that psychiatrists regard their own claims as the truths of medical science, and the claims of mental patients as the manifestations of mental diseases; whereas I regard both sets of claims as unwarranted justifications for imposing the claimants' beliefs and behavior on others. Because the secret to unraveling many of the mysteries of psychiatry lies in distinguishing claims from assertions, descriptions, suggestions, or hypotheses, let us briefly examine this concept.

Psychiatrists have the power to accredit their claims as scientific facts and rational treatments.

Advancing a claim means seeking, by virtue of authority or right, the recognition of a demand—say, the validity of an assertion (in religion), or entitlement to money damages (in tort litigation). To use my previous example, Muslims, Jews, and Christians all claim that God created the world in six days and on the seventh He rested. However, each faith names a different day of the week as the day of rest. Similarly, (some so-called) psychotics assert that they hear voices that command them to kill their wives or children; psychiatrists assert that such persons suffer from a brain disease called "schizophrenia," which can be effectively treated with certain chemicals; and I claim that the assertions of psychotics and psychiatrists alike are claims unsubstantiated by evidence. The point, however, is that psychiatrists have the power to accredit their own claims as scientific facts and rational treatments, discredit the claims of mental patients and psychiatric critics as delusions and denials, and enlist the coercive power of the state to impose their views on involuntary "patients."

The difference between a description and a claim is sometimes a matter of context rather than vocabulary. For example, the adjective "schizophrenic" may describe a man who asserts that his wife is trying to poison him (assuming that she is not); but it functions as a claim when, after shooting his wife, the killer's court-appointed lawyer, desperate to "defend" him (perhaps against his nominal client's wishes), claims that the illegal act was caused by schizophrenia and that the killer should therefore be "acquitted" and treated in a mental hospital, rather than punished by imprisonment. Because psychiatrists view mental diseases and their treatments as facts rather than as claims, they reject the possibility that the words "illness" and "treatment" may, as all words, have a literal or metaphorical usage. Although some psychiatrists now concede that hysteria is not a genuine disease, they are loath to acknowledge that it is a metaphorical disease, that is, not a disease at all. Similarly, many psychiatrists acknowledge that psychotherapy—that is, two or more persons listening and talking to one another—is radically unlike surgical and medical treatment. But, again, they do not acknowledge that it is a metaphorical treatment—that is, not a treatment at all.

Psychiatry is a branch of the law and a secular religion rather than a science or a therapy.

Finally, psychiatrists, who potentially always deal with involuntary patients, delight in the doubly self-serving claim that their patients suffer from brain diseases and that these (psychiatric) brain diseases (unlike others, such as Parkinsonism) render their sufferers incompetent. This claim lets psychiatrists pretend that coercion is a necessary, yet insignificant, element in contemporary psychiatric practice, a claim daily contradicted by reports in the newspapers. Understandably, psychiatrists prefer to occupy themselves with the putative brain diseases of persons called "mental patients" than with the proven social functions of psychiatric diagnoses, hospitals, and treatments.

Lawmakers do not discover prohibited rules of conduct, called crimes, they create them. Killing is not a crime; only unlawful killing is—for example, murder. Similarly, psychiatrists do not discover (mis)behaviors, called mental diseases, they create them. Killing is not a mental disease; only killing defined as due to mental illness is; schizophrenia thus "causes" hetero-homicide (not called "murder") and bipolar illness "causes" auto-homicide (called "suicide").

My point is that psychiatrists, who create diagnoses of mental diseases by giving disease names to personal (mis)conduct, function as legislators, not as scientists. It was this sort of diagnosis making alienists engaged in when they created masturbatory insanity; that Paul Eugen Bleuler engaged in when he created schizophrenia; and that the task force committees of the American Psychiatric Association engage in when they construct new psychiatric diagnoses, such as body dysmorphic disorder, and deconstruct old ones, such as homosexuality.

I am not arguing that rule making, such as politicians engage in, is not important. I am merely insisting on the differences between phenomena and rules, science and law, cure and control. Treating the sick and punishing criminals are both necessary for maintaining the social order. Indeed, breakdown in the just enforcement of just laws is far more destructive to the social order than the absence of equitable access to effective medical treatment. The medical profession's traditional social mandate is healing the sick; the criminal justice system's, punishing the lawbreaker; and the psychiatric profession's, confining and controlling the "deviant" (ostensibly as diseased, supposedly for the purpose of treatment). This is why I regard psychiatry as a branch of the law and a secular religion, rather than a science or therapy.

I want to add a brief remark here on the so-called anti-psychiatry movement with which my name is often associated. As detailed elsewhere, I consider the term anti-psychiatry imprudent and the movement it names irresponsible. As a classical liberal, I support the rights of physicians to engage in mutually consenting psychiatric acts with other adults. By the same token, I object to involuntary psychiatric interventions, regardless of how they are justified. Psychiatrists *qua* physicians should never deprive individuals of their lives, liberties, and properties, even if the security of society requires that they engage in such acts. In adopting this view, I follow the example of the great Hungarian physician Ignaz Semmelweis who believed that obstetricians, *qua* physicians, should never infect their patients, even if the advancement of medical education requires that they do so.

I do not deny that involuntary psychiatric interventions might be justified vis-à-vis individuals declared to be legally incompetent, just as involuntary financial or medical interventions are justified under such circumstances. Individuals who are disabled by a stroke or are in a coma cannot discharge their duties or represent their desires. Accordingly, there are procedures for relieving them—with due process of law—of their rights and responsibilities as full-fledged adults. Although the persons entrusted with the task of reclassifying citizens from moral agents to wards of the state might make use of medical information, they should be lay persons (jurors) and judges, not physicians or mental health specialists. Their determination should be viewed as a legal and political procedure, not as a medical or therapeutic intervention.

I have sought to alert the professions as well as the public to the tendency in modern societies—whether capitalist or communist, democratic, or totalitarian—to reclassify deviant conduct as (mental) disease, deviant actor as (psychiatric) patient, and activities aimed at controlling deviants as therapeutic interventions. And I have warned against the dangers of the destruction of self-discipline and criminal sanctions which these practices create—specifically the replacing of penal sanctions with psychiatric coercions rationalized as "hospitalization" and "treatment." To describe the confusion arising from the use of the metaphorical term "mental disease," I have suggested the phrase "the myth of mental illness." For a political order that uses physicians and hospitals in place of policemen and prisons to coerce and confine miscreants and which justifies constraint and compulsion as therapy rather than punishment, I have proposed the name "therapeutic state."

The personal freedom of which the English and American people are justly proud rests on the assumption of a fundamental right to life, liberty, and property. This is why deprivations of life, liberty, and property have traditionally been regarded as punishments (execution, imprisonment, and the imposition of a fine), that is, legal and political acts whose lawful performance is delegated to specific agents of the state and is regulated by due process of law. No physician *qua* medical healer has the right to deprive another of life, liberty, or property. Formerly, when the clergy was allied with the state, a priest had the right to deprive a person of life and liberty. In the seventeenth century, the state began to transfer this role to psychiatrists (alienists or mad-doctors), who eagerly accepted the assignment and have served as state agents authorized to deprive persons of liberty under medical auspices. Now, we are witnessing a clamor for granting physicians the right to kill persons—an ostensibly medical intervention euphemized as "physician-assisted suicide."

It is a truism that the interests of the individual, the family, and the state often conflict. Medicalizing interpersonal conflicts, that is, disagreements among family members, the members of society, and between citizens and the state, threatens to destroy not only respect for persons as responsible moral agents, but also for the state as an arbiter and dispenser of justice. Let us never forget that the state is an organ of coercion with a monopoly on force—for good or ill. The more the state empowers doctors, the more physicians will strengthen the state (by authenticating political preferences as health values), and the more the resulting union of medicine and the state will enfeeble the individual (by depriving him of the right to reject interventions classified as therapeutic). If that is the kind of society we want, that is the kind we shall get—and deserve.

Poverty and Inequality

It is not clear whether poverty is the result or the cause of inequality, but where one is found, so is the other. Most individuals, regardless of how little or how much they have, would agree that poverty is bad, but they do not necessarily agree that inequality is bad. To those raised in capitalistic societies, inequality is seen as the driving force behind the American success story. The ability to improve one's economic position, the chance to move up through corporate hierarchies, and the opportunity to have access to the best that life offers is what has made America great. Conversely, the lack of any real upward mobility is the direct cause of the fall of communism. It is not inequality that is bad, but the degree of inequality. It is when the gap between the top and bottom becomes extreme, when the number of individuals at the bottom greatly exceeds that of those at the top, and when the opportunity of improving one's self is removed, that questions of inequality emerge as a social problem.

President Clinton has vowed to end welfare as we know it, a declaration that appeals to many Americans. But his ability to achieve his vow is highly problematic. "Old Traps, New Twists" identifies six traps that have frustrated all prior attempts at welfare reform and assesses the probability that President Clinton (or anyone) will ever be able to accomplish meaningful reform.

"Gap in Wealth in U.S. Called Widest in West," by Keith Bradsher, shows a remarkable disparity in U.S. wealth and income compared to other countries.

"Does Welfare Bring More Babies?" Many critics of the existing welfare system argue that it does. But empirical evidence does not indicate this. Charles Murray discovered, after conducting detailed statistical analysis of data collected on African Americans, that moderate differences in welfare benefits produce only small difference in childbearing behaviors.

The Republican-controlled Congress believes that the states' "Taking Over" the administration of welfare through block grants could solve the welfare mess. But are all the states prepared to take on this responsibility? Eliza Carney argues that they are not and attempts to show why. She is firmly convinced that block grants not only will not work but will make the "welfare mess" even worse.

In "It's Not Working: Why Many Single Mothers Can't Work Their Way Out of Poverty," the authors show how difficult it is for many single mothers to work themselves out of poverty. Most of these mothers work less than full-time, experience job discrimination, and lack adequate child and health care.

Chuck Collins, in his essay "Aid to Dependent Corporations: Exposing Federal Handouts to the Wealthy," claims that many major corporations receive substantial handouts from the federal government, which he labels "wealthfare." These handouts include major tax benefits, accelerated depreciation, subsidies, and funded research (which allows the benefits to be reaped by private firms).

"Inequality: For Richer, for Poorer" compares income inequalities in America and Britain and discovers that they are greater than in any time in the past 50 years. This report speculates as to why this has occurred, its implications for the United States, and why it has not occurred to the same degree in other nations.

Looking Ahead: Challenge Questions

How is the distribution of poverty changing?

What are the major problems facing a president who wants to eliminate or reduce poverty significantly?

What societal-level problems are ensuring that the poor stay poor?

Does welfare bring more babies? Defend your answer.

Will turning money over to the states resolve the welfare mess?

Will forcing welfare mothers to go to work within two years of going on welfare, work? Why or why not?

Why are the income inequalities in the United States greater today than any other time in the last 50 years?

What is "wealthfare" and does it hurt the middle class taxpayer?

How would sociologists differ in the ways they go about studying problems of inequality and poverty?

What are the conflicts in rights, values, obligations, and harms that seem to be underlying each of the issues covered in this section?

OLD TRAPS NEW TWISTS

Kent Weaver

Kent Weaver, a senior fellow in the Brookings Governmental Studies program, is the author of Automatic Government: The Politics of Indexation. *This article is adapted from his Brookings book,* Welfare Reform.

One of President Clinton's boldest and most popular electoral pledges was to "end welfare as we know it." He promised to place time limits on receipt of benefits in the Aid to Families with Dependent Children program and to require recipients to undergo training and move into public- and private-sector jobs within two years. His objectives are clear: to give a new set of incentives to welfare recipients, lessen long-term dependence on welfare, move poor families into America's economic mainstream, and reduce poverty among American children.

The president's call for welfare reform should not come as a surprise. Rising AFDC costs and caseloads and increasing percentages of out-of-wedlock births have widened the perception that current policies have failed and have increased public and policymaker interest in reform.

Welfare reform is an unusually knotty policymaking task, however. Critics of AFDC have long lamented the "welfare traps" that bedevil efforts to help poor families. David Ellwood, co-chair of the administration's task force on welfare reform, has pointed out three "helping conundrums"—problems with no satisfactory solutions. First, providing support to poor families is likely to reduce the rewards to work, as well as work effort—in some cases, increased work actually makes them worse off. Second, focusing support on families most likely to need help, single-parent families, can encourage out-of-wedlock births and divorce or separation. Finally, targeting aid to those who need it most tends to isolate recipients politically, while diminishing the relative status of those who are doing a bit better—notably working, two-parent families.

That these traps in policy design are a serious obstacle to welfare reform is widely acknowledged. Less often recognized is that reform poses a set of *political* traps, outlined below, that are equally serious and hard to avoid. All these traps have contributed mightily to the repeated failure or watering down of past efforts to reform AFDC. And all loom large in the current round of reform, often with new and more perilous twists. Thus while the public may be ready for a big change, it is far from certain that policymakers will be able to deliver it. And if welfare reform does get through Congress, it is far from clear that it will take a form that will aid poor children.

The Clinton Proposal and Its Rivals

Although details of the administration's plan remain to be worked out, its outlines are clear. Efforts to establish paternity and enforce child support payments will be stepped up. Teenage mothers will be required, in most circumstances, to live with their parents rather than set up new households. AFDC recipients will sign contracts that specify reciprocal obligations: the state will provide education and job training; the recipient will participate in these programs and take a job when it becomes available. After two years, recipients who have not found private-sector jobs will take community service jobs. These new obligations will be phased in gradually, beginning with younger AFDC mothers, in a bow to the budgetary reality that it is cheaper to pay benefits than provide jobs and support services, notably child care and transportation. Finally, state welfare offices will be reoriented—away from checking on eligibility and toward helping recipients gain job skills and find work.

The administration does not have the field to itself. The House Republican Welfare Reform Task Force has proposed a more expensive package with a greater emphasis on work requirements. They would pay for

From *The Brookings Review*, Summer 1994, pp. 18-21. © 1994 by the Brookings Institution. Reprinted by permission.

it primarily by cutting off most means-tested benefits to legal residents of the United States who are not citizens. Another Republican proposal, backed by the conservative group Empower America, would cut off all AFDC, food stamp, and housing benefits to unmarried mothers under age 21 and encourage states to establish "orphanages" for children and group homes for unwed mothers. Both Republican plans would cap most spending programs for low-income Americans.

The shape—indeed the existence—of any final legislation depends on how these proposals thread their way through the political traps in store for welfare reformers.

The Dual-Clientele Trap

Perhaps the central political problem for American family support policy is the dual-clientele trap: policymakers can't help poor children (which is popular) without also aiding their parents (which is unpopular); they can't dramatically increase disincentives for out-of-wedlock childbearing without also risking making poor children worse off. Recent welfare reform debates have featured a continuing clash between concerns about ensuring the welfare of children and concerns about the behavior (and how to alter it) of parents and prospective parents. That the AFDC caseload, like the poverty population generally, is made up heavily of racial and ethnic minorities has made the debate even more contentious and inflammatory.

Many of those focusing on parental behavior are convinced that stiff punitive reforms in AFDC's incentives structure are necessary to force recipients to change their behavior. Punitive incentives, however, would seriously harm those unable or unwilling to make the necessary changes. More important, they would hurt their children. This prospect has, until recently, kept discussions of the most draconian welfare reforms—for example, Charles Murray's proposal to end AFDC—on the fringes of the welfare debate. But as illegitimacy rates continue to rise and other solutions elude reformers, proponents of punitive policies have begun to dominate the public debate and to deride those who voice concern for children as "paleo-liberals." The administration has not bought into this rhetoric, but its talk of "ending welfare as we know it" has allowed concern over children to be nearly forgotten in the focus on parents' behavior. By soft-pedaling children's welfare, it has facilitated the weakening of the political dual-clientele trap without changing the social reality that precipitous, poorly thought out welfare reforms could lead to a social disaster for many poor children.

The Perverse Incentives Trap

The perverse incentives trap flows from the helping conundrums noted earlier. Giving cash to unmarried mothers lowers their incentives to marry or forgo childbearing. Providing them with Medicaid health insurance or child care makes it harder for them to leave AFDC and accept low-paying private-sector jobs that offer no such benefits: if they do, they may suffer real income declines.

Perverse incentives also feed on themselves: efforts to eliminate or reduce one set can lead to a new set. For example, providing temporary access to Medicaid or child care benefits to families who leave welfare helps them make the transition—but it also encourages people who lose their jobs to go on welfare to take advantage of these benefits before returning to work. The fact is that no plausible reform of the existing system can avoid creating some new perverse incentives or worsening some existing ones.

The political trap posed by perverse incentives is this: if policymakers ignore those incentives in their reform proposals, public confidence is likely to falter when critics of reform point them out—as they surely will. But actually coming to grips with perverse incentives may be very expensive and may make reform harder to pass, as scarce resources are diverted from core reform initiatives.

The Clinton plan encounters the perverse incentives trap in several ways. First, it relies on health care reform to extend health insurance to the working poor,

WHY

WELFARE

IS SO

HARD TO

REFORM

IN 1994

thus easing the way for AFDC recipients to leave welfare for low-paying jobs. But this seems to argue for delaying action on AFDC, because the projected costs and caseload estimates for welfare reform are likely to be higher (and thus harder to sell politically and harder to get through the budget scorekeeping process) now than they would be after a comprehensive health care reform package is in place—if that ever happens. Second, recent drafts of the Clinton plan propose substantial spending on child care for the working poor to lessen AFDC's attractions for this group. But spending more on the working poor will not please lawmakers who want to concentrate resources on current recipients. Nor will it suit those fearful of making more people dependent on government aid or those who simply don't want to spend more money.

The Money Trap

The AFDC money trap is simple: any reform likely to improve the prospects for poor children means spending more money than the public thinks is necessary or Congress wants to spend. Most people already think that too many people receive AFDC and that it is too costly. They think welfare reform should save money immediately. But few reform proposals would do that. Almost inevitably, they require at least short-term spending increases for education, job training, or other services. But to increase spending, government must increase taxes, increase the deficit, or cut other programs—all anathema to legislators. So even when Congress adopts welfare reform initiatives, they are underfunded—and therefore hobbled from the start in achieving their goals. The JOBS program of the Family Support Act of 1988, for example, was supposed to have a dramatic impact on the AFDC clientele while increasing spending only $3 billion over five years for education, training, and employment.

The money trap is made even worse this year by the financing proposals already on the table. The proposal by the Republican Welfare Reform Task Force would pay for its work program by stopping almost all means-tested transfers and social services to noncitizens, both legal and illegal. The Clinton plan is likely to call for a more targeted restriction on Supplemental Security Income benefits for "sponsored aliens"—family members who join earlier immigrants and are eligible, after five years, to apply for the SSI program. But both proposals raise serious political problems. States fear that they will inherit the job of caring for the immigrants. And the Hispanic Caucus in the House opposes the proposals because many affected immigrants are from Latin America.

The Overselling Trap

With AFDC so unpopular, its clientele so politically weak, and the record of derailed reform so long, legislators are reluctant to undertake reform for only modest policy gains. Thus to get welfare reform on the agenda, much less pass it, advocates must promise far more than they can deliver.

But overselling has serious costs. Not only does it threaten the credibility of specific reform proposals, it also increases public cynicism about *any* reform. If reform didn't live up to expectations last time, why will it do so this time? Thus politicians grow even more reluctant to wade into the welfare reform swamp, necessitating yet more overpromising—and so the cycle goes.

The overselling trap this time began with the president's promise to end welfare as we know it and to limit recipients to two years of benefits before being expected to work. The image conveyed to the public was that of an income transfer program being transformed into a work program. But the reality is different. Many welfare mothers will not be expected to work, either because they are caring for infants or because they are seriously disabled or care for children who are. But the biggest hurdle is money. Providing jobs, even low-skilled jobs, takes lots of it—upwards of $20 billion a year for administration, transportation, and child care for all AFDC families. Thus recent drafts of the Clinton plan call for a slow phase-in and many exemptions. By 1999 fewer than 170,000 parents—out of almost 5 million AFDC families—are expected to be at work in government-provided or -subsidized jobs. Such phase-ins may be fiscally and administratively prudent, but they will not end welfare as we know it. Pressure will no doubt be felt in Congress to increase work requirements while simultaneously lowering funding levels.

The Fragile-Coalitions Trap

Too weak to make its own way, AFDC is also too unpopular to be quietly tucked into a legislative package featuring more popular programs. Its precarious political situation, together with the money trap and the perverse incentives trap, dooms reformers to face the fragile-coalitions trap: no legislative majority can be built for reform without including lawmakers who disagree with some part of the package and who would probably defect if a separate vote were held on that part. The risk of a collapsing coalition can be minimized if reform sponsors can limit amendments, but they usually cannot, especially in the Senate.

Clinton's coalition is particularly prone to collapse. Child advocacy groups may oppose the plan if they think it will deprive many families of cash benefits without guaranteeing a job or if it fails to provide adequate child care. Conservative Democrats may not approve its slow phase-in of work requirements. The Hispanic Caucus may oppose its financing provisions. Public-sector unions worry that a large public jobs program would displace their workers. Others fear that it could turn into another CETA public service employment program, which was so unpopular that it, almost alone among social programs, was killed outright by the Reagan administration in 1981. Limiting payments to women who have children while on AFDC is likely to be opposed by right-to-life groups, who fear it would encourage abortions, *and* by pro-choice groups in states that do not allow Medicaid funding of abortions.

How these conflicting pressures would affect lawmakers' votes is hard to predict, but they could certainly provide ample reason for wavering legislators to oppose welfare reform. Neither a generous nor a highly punitive version of reform is likely to command a congressional majority, and it is far from clear that there is adequate middle ground for significant reform. Pressure for more punitive, less expensive reform is likely to grow if Congress waits until after the fall congressional elections, when Republicans are likely to gain seats, at least in the House.

The Federalism Trap

States have great leeway both in the AFDC benefits they pay and in the obligations they impose. They can also apply for waivers to deviate from existing national standards. That freedom allows states to be responsive to local conditions, such as differences in the cost of living, and to experiment to find out how changes in incentives affect recipients' behavior. Wisconsin, for example, is testing two-year limits on benefits. New Jersey denies AFDC mothers additional payments for children conceived while the mothers are on the program.

But allowing state flexibility also poses a trap: it can subject individuals to extremely unequal treatment based on where they live, and it can start a "race to the bottom," as states scale back benefits and impose ever more onerous obligations to avoid becoming welfare magnets.

The extent to which this federalism trap leads to reforms that hurt the poor depends in part on the other traps. If state budgets are tight—as many are because of exploding Medicaid spending—state innovations are more likely to emphasize punitive measures. And Washington's leeway in rejecting punitive state reforms will be affected by commitments it has made. Having promised to "end welfare as we know it," will the administration be able to reject state efforts to impose time limits without providing jobs to those that hit the limits?

Prognosis and Recommendations

What then is the prognosis for this round of welfare reform? And what *should* welfare reform include and exclude? By their very nature, the political traps in welfare policymaking cannot be avoided. Choices must be made. And there is no such thing as welfare reform that does not pose risks for the welfare of children. But by choosing carefully, the administration and Congress can both improve the prospects for maneuvering through the traps to secure significant reform legislation *and* improve the prospect that reform will genuinely improve the life chances for poor children.

While Congress must make choices on hundreds of specific issues, four broad possibilities seem most plausible as outcomes in this round of reform. The first, and most likely, is stalemate. Second is a phased work and time limits plan, similar to the Clinton plan and perhaps allowing more flexibility to the states. Third is a stronger set of work requirements and time limits, along the lines of the House Republican task force plan. Fourth is legislation heavy on sanctions and time limits and light on funding to finance work.

Among these options the last comes closest to ending welfare as we know it, but it poses the greatest risk of leaving many poor children destitute and homeless. Nor do conservative prescriptions to rely on residential facilities (orphanages for non-orphans) for children taken away from indigent mothers make this option more palatable, even if the process of becoming homeless were an efficient way to sort unfit mothers from fit ones. Running group facilities on a large scale is difficult, and financially strapped states lack the resources to make them work well. The American experience in running programs ranging from mental hospitals to reform schools to foster care

suggests that such "orphanages" would more closely resemble Bleak House than Boys Town.

The first option, stalemate, is little better than the last, if for no other reason than that it is likely to end up in the same place. By reinforcing the perception that nothing is being done about welfare, stalemate may eventually lead to radical, heavily punitive reform.

That leaves options two and three. Option three has much to recommend it—but also a powerful argument against it. We don't know much about how time limits are likely to work. Imposing them on a nationwide scale is "Thelma and Louise" policymaking: shoot without considering the consequences, then drive off a cliff. Experiments on time limits are under way, but the results are not yet in. What combinations of time limits and sanctions for noncompliance work best, for example? Which segments of the welfare population should be targeted first? How much is homelessness likely to increase? At present, decisions about these issues are likely to be the product of guesswork informed by varying combinations of theory and prejudice, rather than by solid data. To minimize the risk that this giant policy leap into the unknown will result in social disaster, we should be cautious in both policy design and implementation.

The second possibility, cautious and phased reform, is thus the best option—but not necessarily the most likely one. What can the administration do to improve the prospects for its plan?

First, it can change its rhetoric. With its promise to end welfare as we know it, the administration has fallen into the overselling trap in a big way. At this point, the best thing it can do is emphasize the need to make solid progress on a problem that cannot be ended overnight. It can also reemphasize the importance of children's welfare.

The administration can do much to avoid the fragile-coalitions trap. It can state, as it did with health care, a set of bottom-line conditions—in particular, adequate funding for child care and training to accompany any broad-scale time limits—that, if not met, will provoke a veto. The risk is that the minimum will become the maximum that Congress will pass. But at least such a move would ensure that welfare reform does not become a political cover for abandoning poor children.

The administration should also recognize that the lack of money to undertake a nationwide time-limits-plus-jobs program presents an opportunity as well as a problem. In the absence of good data on time limits, the administration should continue to encourage experimentation by states. It should make sure the results are carefully evaluated so that the lessons learned can be applied more broadly. But it should also clearly signal the sorts of state plans that it cannot accept—in particular, statewide time limits on benefits without an adequate jobs program at the end.

The problem of welfare dependency has, in short, no magic solutions. The key to making progress, as conservatives are fond of saying, is sustained work—and not just by welfare recipients, but by those who design and implement policy.

Gap in Wealth In U.S. Called Widest in West

Keith Bradsher

Washington, April 12—New studies on the growing concentration of American wealth and income challenge a cherished part of the country's self-image: They show that rather than being an egalitarian society, the United States has become the most economically stratified of industrial nations.

Even traditional class societies like Britain, which have inherited large differences in income and wealth over centuries, going back to feudal times, now have greater economic equality than the United States, according to the latest economic and statistical research, much of which is to be published soon.

Economic inequality has been rising in the United States since the 1970's. Since 1992, when Bill Clinton charged that Republican tax cuts in the 1980's had broadened the gap between the rich and the middle class, it has become more sharply focused as a political issue.

Many of the new studies are based on the data available then, but provide new analyses that coincide with a vigorous debate in Congress over provisions in the Republican Contract With America.

Indeed, the drive by Republicans to reduce Federal welfare programs and cut taxes is expected, at least in the short term, to widen disparities between rich and poor.

Federal Reserve figures from 1989, the most recent available, show that the richest 1 percent of American households—with net worth of at least $2.3 million each—have nearly 40 percent of the nation's wealth. By contrast, the richest 1 percent of British population has about 18 percent of the wealth there—down from 59 percent in the early 1920's.

Further down the scale, the top 20 percent of Americans—households worth $180,000 or more—have more than 80 percent of the country's wealth, a figure higher than in other industrial nations.

Income statistics are similarly skewed. At the bottom end of the scale, the lowest-earning 20 percent of Americans earn only 5.7 percent of all the after-tax income paid to individuals in the United States each year. In Finland, a nation with an exceptionally even distribution of income, the lowest-earning 20 percent receive 10.8 percent of such income.

The top 20 percent of American households in terms of annual income—$55,000 or more—have 55 percent of all after-tax income.

"We are the most unequal industrialized country in terms of income and wealth," said Edward N. Wolff, an economics professor at New York University, "and we're growing more unequal faster than the other industrialized countries." In coming months, he will publish two papers that compare patterns of wealth in Western countries.

Liberal social scientists worry about poor people's shrinking share of the nation's resources, and the consequences in terms of economic performance and social tension.

Margaret Weir, a senior fellow in government studies at the Brookings Institution, called the higher concentration of incomes and wealth "quite divisive," especially in a country where the political system requires so much campaign money.

"It tilts the political system toward those who have more resources," she said, adding that financial extremes also undermined the "sense of community and commonality of purpose."

Robert Greenstein, executive director of the Center on Budget and Policy Priorities, a Washington research group, observed, "When you have a child poverty rate that is four times the average of Western European countries that are our principal industrial competitors, and when those children are a significant part of our future work force, you have to worry about the competitive effects as well as the social-fabric effects."

Conservatives have tended to pay less attention to rising inequality, and some express skepticism about the statistics or their significance. Marvin H. Kosters, an economist at the American Enterprise Institute here, said he thought the gap, as measured, was being used as a false villain. "I think we have important sociological problems," he said, "but I don't think this gets at it all that well."

Murray L. Weidenbaum, professor of economics at Washington University in St. Louis and chairman of the Council of Economic Advisers under President Ronald Reagan in 1981–82, said he thought the measures tended to overstate the gap by overlooking Government programs like food stamps or Medicaid.

Still, he said he was uncomfortable with greater concentration of wealth "unless there's a rapid turnover" in which "this year's losers will be next year's winners."

He noted that many wealthy people have bad years and that a lot of middle-class people, like graduate students, briefly look statistically as if they are starving. The United States, he said, has "very substantial mobility."

Mr. Weidenbaum said he doubted that the Republican agenda, if it became law, would have any substantial effect on the disparity in wealth. He added that the static effect might be somewhat more concentration, but that the dynamic effect would produce a bigger economic pool for all to share.

There is little agreement as to why inequality is rising faster in the United States than elsewhere. Explanations include falling wages for unskilled workers as automation spreads, low tax rates on the rich during the 1980's, relatively low minimum wages, the decline of trade unions and the rapid rise in the 1980's of the stock and bond markets, in which rich people are heavily invested.

The most common view seems to be that Americans have witnessed the more extreme effects of several international trends toward greater economic inequality. "While many of the countries experienced many pieces of inequality, the United States is the one country that seems to have experienced all the pieces," said Peter T. Gottschalk, an economics professor at Boston College.

Mr. Wolff's papers are based on data that run through 1989. But Census Bureau figures show that the trend toward greater income inequality continued during the first year of the Clinton Administration. While incomes rose for the most affluent two-fifths of the nation's households as the economy expanded in 1993, the rest of the country suffered from falling incomes, after adjustments for inflation.

"U.S. wage distribution is more unequal than other countries and we do less in terms of tax and transfer policy" to cushion the disparities, said Timothy M. Smeeding, an American who is director of the Luxembourg Income Study Project. Mr. Smeeding is preparing two papers drawing international comparisons of income.

The project, based in Walferdange, Luxembourg, is supported by the national science foundations of nearly two dozen countries including the United States, and has gathered Government data from the member nations showing that the United States has the greatest inequalities in income distribution.

Most economists believe that wealth and income are more concentrated in the United States than in Japan. But while data show that wealth is more equitably distributed in Japan, the Government there has not released enough detailed information to make statistical comparisons possible.

Anecdotal information strongly suggests that Japan has a more equal distribution of income. The chief executives of Japanese manufacturing companies, for example, make an average of 10 times the pay of their workers. American chief executives in manufacturing are paid 25 times as much, according to a 1994 study by Towers Perrin, a management-consulting company.

Professor Gottschalk said Canada and the Netherlands seemed to have minimized disparities involving higher wages for highly skilled workers, because the number of college graduates over all had sharply increased in those countries. But other trends toward inequality, like a widening wage gap between experienced and inexperienced workers, had affected them, as well.

When American inequality began to increase is also debated, with various economists putting it anywhere from the mid-1970's to the early 1980's.

The double-digit inflation and stock market slumps that followed the quadrupling of oil prices in 1973 temporarily produced greater equality, as the stocks and bonds of the rich lost value. But that effect gradually disappeared, with Mr. Wolff's data showing that the concentration of wealth among the richest had consistently exceeded Britain's level since 1978. British records are especially complete, making such comparisons easier.

The comparison with Britain is all the more striking because President Reagan and former Prime Minister Margaret Thatcher pursued broadly similar economic policies in the 1980's.

Rising housing prices have increased the holdings of the British middle class and limited the growth in inequality there. But Mr. Gottschalk said most evidence indicated that income inequality had risen much faster in the United States and Britain than elsewhere.

Richard V. Burkhauser, an economics professor at Syracuse University, said that in studying thousands of people in Germany and the United States over seven-year periods in the 1980's, he found that the two countries had roughly the same level of social mobility.

As part of the Contract With America's tax provisions, the House on April 5 approved an increase in individuals' exemptions from the estate tax. By the Treasury's estimate, this would cut in half the number of people subject to the tax—to one-half of 1 percent of the estates of those dying each year.

Republicans have argued that the overall tax-cut provisions would reduce annual tax bills by roughly equal percentages for rich and poor. Democrats say that because the annual tax bills of rich Americans are much larger, reducing them by about the same percentage means that most of the money would go to the rich rather than the poor or the middle class, further concentrating wealth and income.

DOES WELFARE BRING MORE BABIES?

CHARLES MURRAY

Charles Murray is Bradley fellow at the American Enterprise Institute.

Last October, I published a long piece on the op-ed page of the *Wall Street Journal* entitled "The Coming White Underclass." Its thesis was that white illegitimacy—22 percent of all live births as of the latest (1991) figures—is now moving into the same dangerous range that prompted the young Daniel Patrick Moynihan to write about the breakdown of the black family in 1964, and that the ensuing social deterioration in lower-class communities may be as devastating for whites in the 1990s as it was for blacks in the 1960s. The centerpiece of my solution was to abolish all federal support for single women with children.

The response was, for me, unique. It is not just that the piece aroused more intense reaction than anything I have written since *Losing Ground,* but that so many people agreed with me. This is not normal. After I publish something, my mail and phone calls are usually split about 50/50 pro and con. This time, almost everyone agreed that the problem of illegitimacy was just as bad as I described, and a surprising number of people, including some ordinarily prudent people in the public eye, endorsed my radical notion of ending welfare altogether.

All this leads me to believe that illegitimacy is about to replace abortion as the next great national social debate. It should; not because the nation spends too much on welfare but because, as Moynihan said first and best, a community that allows a large number of young men to grow up without fathers "asks for and gets chaos." I believe it is not hyperbole but sober fact that the current levels of illegitimacy already threaten the institutions necessary to sustain a free society.

And so I want to end welfare. But this raises an obvious question: do we have any reason to believe that ending welfare will in fact cause a large-scale reduction in illegitimacy? Does welfare cause illegitimacy?

The answer has seemed self-evident to people ranging from the man in the street to Nobel laureate economists. The answer has not been nearly so clear, however, to social scientists who have studied the problem, nor has the search for an answer been conducted with stately scholarly detachment. It has instead been a hard-fought battle stretching back many years. Almost everyone has brought convictions about what the answer ought to be, for few issues have been so politically charged. But with a few lapses, the combatants have played by the technical rules in making their points, and, after all this time, we have learned at least a few things on which we can agree.

Two detailed reviews summarize the academic evidence. One, by Brown University economist Robert Moffitt, is called "Incentive Effects of the U.S. Welfare System: A Review," and it appeared in the *Journal of Economic Literature* in March 1992. I wrote the other one, called "Welfare and the Family: The U.S. Experience," as part of a special issue of the *Journal of Labor Economics* in January 1993, devoted to a set of articles comparing the American and Canadian social policy sponsored by the William H. Donner Foundation.

What follows summarizes the major area of agreement that has developed over the last 10 years—necessarily simplifying many findings and ignoring nuances. Then I turn to the major remaining area of disagreement. It brings to the attention of a general audience—for the first time, to my knowledge—a major technical error in the understanding of black illegitimacy that has large consequences for the subsequent debate. Bluntly: an important and commonly used argument of those who say that welfare does not cause illegitimacy is 180 degrees wrong.

Where Analysts Agree: Studies of Differences Among States

If the agreement could be summed up in a single sentence, it is that moderate differences in welfare benefits produce some differences in childbearing behavior, but only small ones. The main research strategy for reaching this conclusion has been to explore the effects of variations in AFDC (Aid to Families with Dependent Children) benefits across states. The hypothesis has been that since benefits vary widely, there should be differences in childbearing behavior as well, if indeed welfare is a culprit in producing illegitimacy.

Back in 1983, David Ellwood and Mary Jo Bane—both now senior officials in Clinton's Department of Health and Human Services—wrote the early version of a paper (still being circulated in typescript) during the debate over *Losing Ground* that everyone interpreted as proving that welfare doesn't cause increases in illegitimacy. That's not exactly what the analysis found—their approach to the issue was indirect and used a methodology so complex that evaluating the results is difficult even for specialists—but "Ellwood and Bane" is nevertheless still cited in the media as the definitive study that welfare does not affect illegitimacy.

Since then, several studies have explored the issue more directly, and the consensus has shifted to a tentative conclusion that welfare is implicated, but not dramatically. The results from the recent studies have many differences, and it would be unrealistic to try to draw a consensus from them about the magnitude of the effect of welfare. One study found a fairly large effect on childbearing behavior (for example, a predicted increase of 16 percent in the probability of teen births if welfare benefits rose 20 percent), but the effect was statistically insignificant. (This can happen when samples are small or the variation in results is very large.) Another found an effect that was in the same ballpark (a 6 percent increase in childbearing by unmarried women in response to a 10 percent increase in welfare benefits) and was also statistically significant. Other studies have found statistically significant effects without reporting the magnitude.

Until recently, studies of this issue have concluded that the effects of welfare are much easier to find among whites than among blacks. In two of the studies mentioned above, all of the apparent effect of differing welfare benefits on childbearing behavior was accounted for by the behavior of whites. An additional study that was limited to black teenagers found only a small, statistically insignificant effect.

But the situation is changing. A recent detailed study by Mark Fossett and Jill Kiecolt in *Journal of Marriage and the Family* using 1980 census data found a substantial and consistent relationship between the size of public assistance payments and illegitimacy among black women ages 20–24, even after controlling for a wide variety of economic, social, and demographic factors. Why did this study find a relationship where others had not? Partly because the analysis was more tightly focused than the others, using metropolitan areas rather than states; partly because the study focused on a particular

IF THE AREA OF AGREEMENT [IN THE WELFARE/ILLEGITIMACY DEBATE] COULD BE SUMMED UP IN A SINGLE SENTENCE, IT IS THAT MODERATE DIFFERENCES IN WELFARE BENEFITS PRODUCE SOME DIFFERENCES IN CHILDBEARING BEHAVIOR, BUT ONLY SMALL ONES.

age group (women ages 20–24) instead of lumping all women together. Much more work remains to be done regarding black illegitimacy and welfare, but the best bet at this time is that the results for blacks and whites will converge. Using what the social scientists call "cross-sectional data"—comparing different places at the same historical moment—it seems likely that welfare will be found to cause some portion of illegitimacy, but not a lot.

The area of agreement, limited though it may sound, has important policy implications. Even taking the studies showing the largest statistically significant effect of welfare on childbearing, there is no reason to suppose that reducing welfare benefits by 10 percent will produce more than about a 6 percent drop in

childbearing among single women. This is not enough to make much difference in anything. More generally, if you were to ask scholars of various political viewpoints in the welfare/illegitimacy debate about the prospective effects of other welfare proposals that have been in the news recently—stopping the increase in benefits that kicks in when a second child is born, toughening workfare requirements, linking welfare to school attendance, and so forth—almost all of us would be pessimistic. We have different reasons for thinking that such changes would be good or bad, but the available data do not give much cause to think that such small changes will produce more than small effects.

Where Analysts Disagree: Variation Across Time

The favored way of examining the effects of welfare, taking advantage of the natural variation in AFDC payments across states, has a number of defects.

One problem with drawing comparisons across states is that state-by-state differences in welfare benefits are not so great as they seem. When you are first told that Louisiana has an average monthly AFDC payment of $169 and California has a monthly payment of $640 (the 1990 figures), the difference looks huge. But some federal benefits (such as food stamps) are more generous in low AFDC states, and Medicaid is available everywhere. Adding in everything, the proportional differences in the welfare packages available in different states shrink. And when you then put those differences in terms of the local economy, the difference nearly disappears. When the General Accounting Office compared the value of welfare packages in 13 locations across the country in the late 1970s, when state-by-state AFDC differences were near their peak, the agency found that the San Francisco package turned out to provide an income equivalent to 66 percent of the median household income in San Francisco, while the New Orleans package provided an income equivalent to 65 percent of the median household income in New Orleans. Should we be surprised to find that welfare differences between Louisiana and San Francisco do not produce much difference in out-of-wedlock childbearing?

4. POVERTY AND INEQUALITY

Another problem is that a powerful factor masks the effects of welfare on blacks when scholars base the analysis on states. The black-white difference in illegitimacy goes back to the earliest post-Civil War data. No scholar has ever succeeded in explaining away this racial difference with any combination of economic, social, or educational control variables. The residual difference is astonishingly large. In a large national database (the National Longitudinal Study of Youth), the probability that a baby will be born to a single woman is more than twice as high for blacks as whites *after* controlling for age, education, socioeconomic background, and poverty. For reasons that are still not understood, something in black culture tolerates or encourages birth out of wedlock at higher rates than apply to white culture in any given year, and this has been true before and after welfare was introduced. The problem is that "black culture" (a term I am using because no one knows how to describe it more specifically) is not spread evenly across the United States. The states in which blacks have the very lowest illegimacy ratios are places like Idaho, Montana, North and South Dakota, Alaska, Hawaii, New Hampshire, and Maine, where AFDC payments are often well

above the national average, but a very small black population lives in the midst of a dominating white culture (with its much lower illegitimacy ratios). Most of the states with the very lowest AFDC payments are in the Deep South, where blacks not only constitute a major portion of the population, but are densely concentrated in given areas—also, in other words, where whatever-it-is about black culture that produces high illegitimacy is likely to permeate the world in which black youngsters grow up. In statistical terms, this means that a great deal of noise is introduced when one analyzes the effect of varying AFDC payments. The same data that show no relationship between welfare and illegitimacy among blacks across states suddenly show such a relationship when one controls for the size and density of the black population.

The main problem with comparisons across states is that they ignore the overriding historical reality that welfare went up everywhere in the United States in a concentrated period of time, producing an overall national change that dwarfs the importance of between-state differences. Focusing on differences between states ignores the main effect.

Even when one takes a historical perspective, the story is a complex one. Here,

pictorially, is the main battleground in the debate over whether welfare causes illegitimacy (see Figure 1).

There are many things to argue about in this figure. Probably the one you have heard most often involves the size of the welfare package. I have shown it as a combination of AFDC, food stamps, Medicaid, and public housing subsidies, using conservative methods for valuing these components. Those who argue for an expansion of welfare benefits would have shown a much different figure, showing just the AFDC benefit, which in real terms has retreated to 1950s levels.

But to focus on just the AFDC cash payment is an example of the bogus part of the welfare/illegitimacy debate that most parties to the debate are now beyond, at least when they talk among themselves. Statements such as "welfare benefits are now back to 1950s levels" often show up in congressional testimony and the network news shows, but no serious student will deny that food stamps, Medicaid, and housing benefits are part of the relevant package available to a young woman with a baby and that those have expanded dramatically, along with a hodge podge of other benefits both federal (the Women, Infants, and Children's Supplemental Feeding Program, for example) and state or municipal (heating fuel subsidies, eviction protection, for example). Arguments about the specific value of Medicaid and public housing subsidies could result in minor shifts in the trend line shown in the figure, but the overall shape must remain the same by any method of computation: a very large increase in the last half of the 1960s, a smaller drop in real value in the last half of the 1970s (because of inflation—the nominal value of benefits continued to rise), and only small changes since the early 1980s, when inflation subsided. This basic shape of the trend in welfare benefits sparks the authentic part of the debate, which may be summarized as follows.

Looking at the figure, we see that the real value of the AFDC benefit first available in 1936 begins to rise in the mid-1940s. By the end of the 1940s, the illegitimacy ratio begins a modest rise too. The increase in AFDC steepens somewhat in the mid-1950s, and within a few years the slope of the illegitimacy ratio steepens as well. Then in the mid-

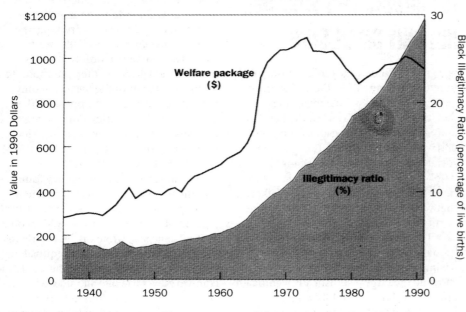

FIGURE 1
WELFARE BENEFITS AND ILLEGITIMACY
A SIMPLE COMPARISON

Source: Illegitimacy data since 1960: National Center for Health Statistics, "Advance Report of Final Natality Statistics," *Monthly Vital Statistics Report*, vol. 42, no. 3(S) (Sept. 9, 1993), table 16, and comparable tables in earlier volumes. Data prior to 1960: National Center for Health Statistics. *Vital Statistics*. Computation of the welfare package uses budget data from U.S. Bureau of the Census on AFDC, food stamps, public housing, and Medicaid, *Statistical Abstract of the United States*. The method of computation is described in Charles Murray, "Welfare and the Family: The American Experience," *Journal of Labor Economics*, vol. 11, no. 1, part 2, (Jan. 1993).

1960s the trend lines for both the value of the welfare package and illegitimacy shoot sharply upward. All of this is consistent with an argument that welfare is an important cause of illegitimacy.

But there is another side to this story, as shown in the graph after the early 1970s. After 1973, the value of the welfare package begins to drop, while illegitimacy continues to increase. This is inconsistent with a simple relationship of welfare to illegitimacy. Why didn't illegitimacy decrease a few years after the value of welfare began to decline?

At this point, the published research literature is little help. The "research," if it may be called that, has consisted mostly of pointing to the part of the graph that is consistent with one's position. But the contending parties in the debate must hold certain underlying assumptions about how causation is going to work in such a situation. Let's suppose you want to argue that the trend in illegitimacy should have flattened and reversed when the real value of welfare benefits stopped climbing. It seems to me that this implies two assumptions: (1) fertility behavior is highly sensitive to incremental changes in welfare benefits, independent of existing fertility trends among single women, and (2) young women accurately and quickly discount nominal increases in welfare according to changes in the Consumer Price Index.

I do not find either of those assumptions plausible. In the late 1970s, social

I WAS PERSUADED BY THE EVIDENCE THAT A CASE COULD NOT BE MADE THAT WELFARE CAUSED MORE ILLEGITIMATE BIRTHS, ONLY THAT WELFARE RAISED THE PROBABILITY THAT A GIVEN BIRTH WOULD BE ILLEGITIMATE. I WAS WRONG.

scientists knew that the real value of the welfare benefit was declining, but the young woman in the street probably did not. She was, after all, seeing her friends on welfare get checks that were larger every year, and health care and housing benefits that were more important every year as prices went up.

People like me also have to meet a burden, however. The main one, as I see it, is to spell out how a complex causal sequence is working, for, clearly, a simple causal link (fertility behavior among single women goes up and down with the value of the welfare check) doesn't work. One of the key features of my explanation is the assumption that many of the social restraints on illegitimacy erode as out-of-wedlock births become more common. Thus we may argue that the very large increase in benefits in the 1960s was indeed a major culprit in jacking up the illegitimacy ratio, but that the increased prevalence took on a life of its own in the 1970s. I find this plausible but, obviously, many who use the 1970s as evidence that welfare does not cause illegitimacy must not find it plausible. Here, the prescription to improve the quality of the debate is for both sides to spell out the assumptions that go into their causal arguments and test them against the data.

The Great Black Fertility Illusion

This brings us to the issue I mentioned earlier, that on one argument crucial to the debate, the accepted wisdom is 180 degrees wrong. It involves black illegitimacy, which has always been at the center of public concern about illegitimacy, and at the center of debate about causes. Many of you who have followed the welfare debate will recognize it, for the argument is made frequently and volubly. It goes like this:

Yes, the *proportion* of black children born to single women started to shoot up rapidly during the 1960s. But during that same period, the *incidence* of births among single black women was actually going down. If the increases in welfare during the 1960s had such terrible effects, why were fewer single black women having babies? Here are the trend lines for the proportion (represented by the line labeled *proportion*) and incidence (represented by the line labeled *incidence*) (see Figure 2).

As one writer put it: "Unmarried black women were having babies at a considerably lower rate in 1980 than they were in 1960. Further, the birth rate among black single women had fallen almost without a break since its high in 1961." The author? Me, writing in *Losing Ground.* At that time, like everyone else involved in the welfare/illegitimacy debate, I took for granted that the production of black illegitimate babies was falling, even though the proportion of black children born to single women was rising, and that this was something that those who would blame welfare for illegitimacy would have to explain away.

Such explanations are available because fertility rates were falling for married women as well. One may acknowledge that broad social forces can have an overriding influence on the propensity of women to have children and still argue that welfare has an independent role in shaping the marital circumstances surrounding the children who are born. But, given the figure shown here, it becomes implausible to make the more ambitious argument that welfare bribes women to have children, no matter how often social workers tell you that they know of many such cases. That is why, in the example of Harold and Phyllis, which became one of the best-known sections of *Losing Ground,* I was careful to begin the scenario with Phyllis already pregnant. I was persuaded by the evidence summarized in the paragraph above that a case could not be made that welfare caused more illegitimate births, only that welfare raised the probability that a given birth would be illegitimate.

I was wrong. Figure 2 reflects a statistical illusion. Here is the appropriate way to view the production of black babies out of wedlock from 1960 to 1990 (see Figure 3).

The line for the proportion remains unchanged, but what a dramatic difference in the measure of incidence. The incidence of black illegitimacy did not peak in 1960; on the contrary, it remained roughly steady until 1967, when suddenly it shot up and continued increasing with only short breaks through the end of the 1980s.

What statistical game has been played? If you take a careful look at the labels in the figures, you may be able to figure it out for yourself—notice the slight

TWO WAYS OF LOOKING AT BLACK ILLEGITIMACY

Illegitimacy can be represented by two measures: the *proportion* and the *incidence* of babies born out of wedlock. Figures 2 and 3 show identical upward lines for the *proportion* (the illegitimacy ratio). Figure 2, however, shows that the *incidence* of out-of-wedlock births has trended downward unevenly until the mid-1980s, while Figure 3 shows an upward trajectory. Both figures measure the *incidence* of births to single black women, but they do so in different ways. Which is the more useful measure to understand the rate at which illegitimate babies are being born?

In Figure 2, the number of illegitimate births to black women is expressed in terms of the population of single black women. That measure would be appropriate if the proportion of single women in the black population held constant. But it didn't; it soared over the period shown here. To get an accurate measure of the changing "production of illegitimate babies," we need to compare illegitimate births to the black female population. The slope of the line in Figure 2 reverses.

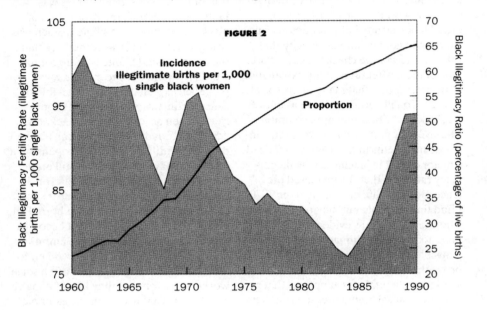

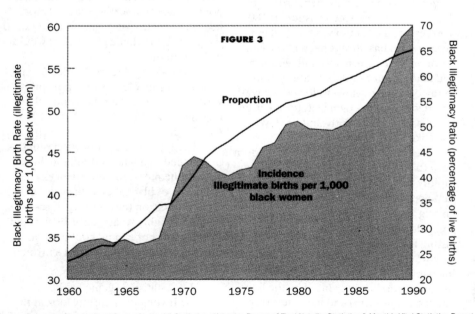

difference in wording between "illegitimate births per 1,000 single black women" in the first graph and "illegitimate births per 1,000 black women."

Statistics don't lie, as long as everyone is clear on precisely what question is being asked and precisely what the statistic measures. Here, we are interested in two separate phenomena: proportion and incidence. Proportion can be measured only one way (divide the number of illegitimate babies by the total number of live births). But in Figures 2 and 3, we used two different ways of measuring incidence, and they showed utterly different results. They cannot both be right. Which one is?

The underlying sense of "incidence" is "frequency relative to a consistent base." If the size of a population were constant, then we could simply use the raw number of illegitimate births as our measure of incidence. But populations do not remain constant. Therefore we need to divide the number of births by some denominator that will hold the population factor constant. The usual way to do this is by using the number of single women as the denominator. This makes intuitive sense, since we are talking about illegitimate births. But it is an inferior measure of incidence because the real issue we are interested in is the production of illegitimate babies per unit of population. What few people, including me, thought about for many years is that it is possible for the production of illegitimate babies per unit of population to go up even while the probability that single women have babies goes down.

This seeming paradox can occur if the number of single women suddenly changes far out of proportion to the increase in the overall population, and that's what happened to blacks during the 1960s. In a mere five-year period from 1965 to 1970, the proportion of black women ages 15–44 who were married plummeted by 10 percentage points, from 64.4 to 54.6 percent—an incredible change in such a basic social behavior during such a short period of time. (During the same period, the comparable figure for whites fell from 69 to 66 percent.) Black marriage continued to fall throughout the 1970s and 1980s, hitting a low of 34 percent in 1989—barely more than half the proportion that prevailed in 1960.

Source: Computed from National Center for Health Statistics, "Advance Report of Final Natality Statistics," *Monthly Vital Statistics Report*, vol. 42, no. 3(S) (Sept. 9, 1993), Figure 2: tables 1 and 17, and comparable tables in earlier volumes. Figure 3: tables 1 and 16, and comparable tables in earlier volumes.

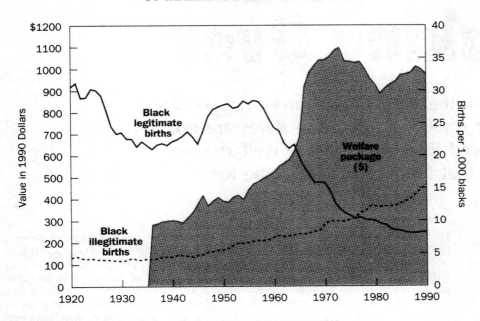

FIGURE 4
BLACK BIRTHS INSIDE AND OUTSIDE OF MARRIAGE AND WELFARE

Note: Incidence is based on the entire black population to provide a consistent base since 1920.
Source: Same sources used in Figure 1, plus population data from *Historical Statistics of the United States, Colonial Times to 1970*, vol. 1 (Washington, DC: U.S. Bureau of the Census, 1975), Table A23–28, and U.S. Bureau of the Census, *Statistical Abstract of the United States*.

behavior toward both marriage and out-of-wedlock childbearing during the period in which welfare benefits rose so swiftly behaved exactly as one would predict if one expected welfare to discourage women from getting married and induce single women to have babies.

When we then take the same measure and look at it over the 70-year sweep from 1920 to 1990, comparing black incidence of birth within marriage and outside marriage, all against the backdrop of the value of the welfare package, this is how the picture looks (see Figure 4).

The figure is not in any way "proof" of a causal relationship. But it is equally important to confront the plain message of these data. At the same time that powerful social and economic forces were pushing down the incidence of black children born to married couples, the incidence of black children born to unmarried women increased, eventually surpassing the rate for married couples. Something was making that particular behavior swim against a very strong tide, and, to say the least, the growth of welfare is a suspect with the means and opportunity.

This new look at black illegitimacy, then, knocks the legs out from under one of the main arguments that has been used to exculpate welfare's role in promoting illegitimacy 20 years from now. This will not stop the debate. The map linking welfare and illegitimacy still has big gaps. Optimistically, the progress we have been making in the last decade will continue. Pessimistically, it had better. For if illegitimacy is as serious a problem as I think, we cannot afford to waste much more time in deciding what needs to be done.

To see what this does to the interpretation of fertility rates, think of the familiar problem of interpreting Scholastic Aptitude Test (SAT) scores. Whenever the scores go down, you read news stories pointing out that maybe education isn't getting worse but that more disadvantaged students (who always would have scored low, but had not been taking the SAT) have entered the SAT pool, therefore causing the scores to fall. It is a similar scenario with the pool of black single women: By 1970, a large number of black women who would have been married in the world of 1960 were not married. The pool was being flooded. Did these new additions to the pool of single women have the same propensity to have babies out of wedlock as the old pool of single women? The contrast between the two figures suggests that the plausible answer, no, is correct.

The crucial point is that the number of illegitimate babies in the black population—not just the proportion, but the number—produced in any given year among a given number of blacks nearly doubled between 1967 and 1990, even though the fertility rate among single black women fell. It increased most radically from 1967 to 1971, tracking (with a two-year time lag) the most rapid rise in welfare benefits. Or in other words, black

Taking Over

Critics of the Republican's proposed welfare block grant argue that the states are not prepared financially to take welfare over and that the needy will be the losers.

ELIZA NEWLIN CARNEY

Don't even ask Wisconsin Gov. Tommy G. Thompson whether states have the resources to fix the nation's broken welfare system. For him, it goes without saying.

It's the "arrogance of the monolithic power structure in Washington, D.C.," that boggles his mind, Thompson said in a telephone interview. "These people in Washington who have screwed up the system so badly now think that they are the only ones that can fix it—that they are the only ones that have the ability to take care of the sick and the elderly and the infirm."

Thompson, along with a handful of other Republican governors, has made his case forcefully in recent months—so forcefully, in fact, that Congress is poised to hand the responsibility for welfare over to the governors with few strings attached.

The heart of the Republican welfare reform plan is an unprecedented power shift to the states. Legislation that the House has approved and that the Senate Finance Committee has signed off on would replace hundreds of entitlement programs for low-income families with billions of dollars in federal block grants that would be capped at 1994 spending levels for five years. Senate leaders are also considering block grants for food stamps and medicaid.

Republican lawmakers' enthusiasm for block grants is testimony to the influence of Thompson and Republican Govs. John M. Engler of Michigan and William Weld of Massachusetts, who have dominated the welfare debate. The enthusiasm for block grants also reflects Republicans' distrust of big government and of Washington-based solutions. States are closer to social problems than Washington bureaucrats are and will be thriftier, more efficient and more effective in addressing them, Republican leaders say.

Block grants will "unleash 51 state experiments," House Speaker Newt Gingrich of Georgia has declared. Finance Committee chairman Bob Packwood, R-Ore., concedes that some states won't be successful but argues that it's worth the risk because the federal government has failed so badly. Nothing could be worse than the current system, Republicans insist.

Or could it?

Even as the Republican plan marches toward final approval, alarm and controversy over block grants are growing. Advocates for the needy protest that block grants would encourage states to slash their welfare spending and leave frightening holes in the social safety net. State and local legislators warn that block grants might force them to raise taxes and would overwhelm community social services.

Some governors complain that block grants would distribute welfare dollars unevenly among the states and could leave them ill-equipped to handle rising caseloads during a recession. Recently, 30 Senators from the South and Southwest echoed that concern, warning that the proposed spending would put states with rapid population growth in a severe financial bind.

Even some conservative policy analysts have faulted the Republican plan for placing too much faith in often bloated and inefficient state bureaucracies. By handing the problem off to the states, which may not enact meaningful reforms, the Republicans would be missing a critical opportunity, they say, to root out problems in the welfare system.

At bottom, the block grant approach strikes some critics as passing the buck. "Block granting is not a solution to any problem," said Sen. John B. Breaux of Louisiana, who sits on the Finance Committee and has crafted a Democratic alternative with Minority Leader Thomas A. Daschle of South Dakota. "It just shifts the problem to somebody else to solve. Instead of having one bureaucracy to work on [welfare] in Washington, [Republicans] are saying they're going to give it to 50 different bureaucracies and make them solve it."

DEVOLUTION FEVER

The infatuation with block grants is not new—nor is it restricted to the GOP. The federal government has long given grants-in-aid to the states, and block grants mushroomed during the 1970s and 1980s. (*See box, p. 125.*)

But welfare is different. It is an open-ended entitlement program that expands as the number of eligibles and the price of subsistence increase. The Republican plan would not only turn welfare over to the states but would also provide finite funds. If the caseload or the costs rise, neither Washington nor the states would have any obligation to spend more.

By capping spending at last year's levels, both the House-passed bill and the Finance Committee measure would reduce after-inflation spending. The bottom line, many welfare policy analysts agree, would be deep reductions in public assistance.

Turning responsibility over to the states, Republican leaders say, would encourage state creativity and improve efficiency by pooling funds from a variety of welfare programs, including aid to families with dependent children (AFDC), child care and perhaps food stamps. A principal problem with the current system is that eligibility criteria differ for cash, food and other aid programs, causing administrative headaches and piles of redundant paperwork.

But critics say that the Republican leaders' real agenda is to cut welfare spending. If you want to give states more flexibility, the critics point out, it's not necessary to eliminate welfare's entitlement status.

According to the Health and Human Services Department (HHS), welfare spending would plunge by $68.6 billion under the House plan and $31.5 billion under the Senate bill over the next five years—an estimate that Packwood disputes. The Congressional Budget Office (CBO) estimates that the House bill would save $64.5 billion and the Senate bill $26 billion over five years.

"Some [lawmakers] genuinely promote state flexibility; some are genuinely deferring to the governors," said Ed Kilgore, a senior fellow at the Progressive Policy Institute, the Democratic Leadership Council's think tank. "But the lowest common denominator of Republican intent on block grants is funding. One thing that it guarantees is you spend less federal money. And that seems to be the real motive."

Packwood denies that budget cutting is the hidden agenda. His bill, he said during a briefing for reporters, "is driven more by the desire to experiment, to innovate, and the frustration that what we're doing isn't working. I find that a much greater drive here than the budget."

A RACE TO THE BOTTOM?

But capping block grants may actually stifle innovation by putting states in a fiscal vise, critics say, particularly if there's a recession. Though Republican leaders predict that local control will reduce states' administrative costs, savings are likely to be minimal.

Administrative costs account for only 12 per cent of AFDC spending, according to the Center for Law and Social Policy. So even if states reduced AFDC administrative costs by as much as a fifth, the overall saving would be only 2.4 per cent.

Moreover, states could face new administrative costs as they try to meet the strict work requirements in the Republican legislation. Under the Finance Committee's bill, states would have to put 45 per cent of welfare recipients in work or training programs by 2000. The House bill calls for half of the unmarried adult welfare recipients to be working by 2002. But putting recipients to work almost invariably requires up-front investments in job training and child care.

In fact, meeting the Senate work requirement would cost states a whopping $10 billion a year by 2000, according to CBO welfare analyst John W. Tapogna. That's more than half the $16.7 billion that the Senate bill would set aside annually for welfare block grants. Tapogna predicted that a significant share of states would simply opt out of

A SPOTTY TRACK RECORD

This year's welfare reform debate echoes with the promises of block grants past. Two decades ago, block grants were the Republican Party's government reform tool of choice, a cure for mismanagement and waste at the federal level.

President Nixon launched three block grant initiatives, and President Reagan instituted nine. Then as now, the goal was to move federal programs closer to the local level and to free the states to manage them creatively. But the results suggest that the sweeping block grants proposed in the Republican welfare reform plan could be a headache for governors and federal officials alike.

The states' track record is spotty and inconclusive, partly because the federal government has done a poor job of evaluating performance. Governors didn't win the hoped-for relief from cumbersome federal regulations because Congress couldn't resist attaching additional strings to the block grants. The grants also proved easy targets for federal budget cutting, leaving states with less flexibility than they started with.

Nevertheless, block grants have not been a disaster. Just as they have with this year's welfare bill, advocates for low-income families greeted the block grant proposals of the 1970s and 1980s with dire warnings that states would slash social services. But these fears went largely unrealized, according to a recent study by the Finance Project, a Washington group that tracks public financing for education and other children's programs.

"While most states made minimal adjustments in the first year after the block grants were implemented, in later years they began to provide greater contributions," the Finance Project study found. "Social services spending, which had seemed especially vulnerable, received surprisingly strong support."

But the subsequent spending cuts and additional federal restrictions altered the nature of the the block grants. In the case of the nine Reagan block grants, for example, Congress imposed new spending ceilings and earmarked spending 58 times from 1983-91, according to the General Accounting Office (GAO).

A recent GAO report also found that Congress didn't consistently gather and evaluate data on the state programs financed by the block grants. Republican leaders this year have predicted an increase in state experiments that will light the way on welfare reform. But experience suggests that state programs may yield little new information without rigorous federal evaluation—requirements for which are largely missing from this year's welfare bill.

Block grants have also taken a drubbing from critics who say that corrupt or inefficient state bureaucracies have run amok with federal dollars. At a minimum, states tend to be less innovative with block grants than many federal officials would like them to be. "Despite greater flexibility, many states did not rush to radically gut or overhaul their programs, management systems or service delivery systems," the Finance Project concludes.

If the Republican welfare legislation becomes law, states suddenly required to administer huge blocks of programs would need all the help they can get in implementing reforms, said Michael E. Laracy, a senior program associate at the Annie E. Casey Foundation in Baltimore, which helps disadvantaged children. For all the hype about state experiments, he said, many states have little to show for their welfare reform efforts.

"The record of block grants is uneven," he added, "and I think the states' track record in welfare reform is uneven. For as many states that claim success, there are at least as many states where the results were minimal or absolutely abysmal or they never even implemented it."

The foundation hopes to set up the National Center for State and Community Based Welfare Reform, which would provide technical and planning aid to states. The center, which would get its money from a consortium of foundations, would act as a broker and fiscal intermediary between state governments and organizations that offer welfare expertise.

The states "are not going to have a lot of money to spend on planning and design, and they are going to have to move quickly," Laracy said, "because the governors have promised a virtual panacea once they are given control."

Given states' past experience with block grants, it's a promise that may be hard to keep.

Photos by Shepard Sherbell/SABA

Local officials worry that families and children who fall through the cracks will land on local agencies' doorsteps.

the work requirement and accept whatever penalty HHS chooses to impose.

Republican leaders argue that the legislation would make up for lost welfare dollars through state and federal "rainy day funds." The states could set aside some of the block grant to cover unexpected welfare demands down the road. They could also borrow from a federal rainy day fund—set at $1 billion in the House bill and $1.7 billion in the Finance Committee version—to be repaid with interest within three years.

But if the federal fund had been around during the most recent recession, it would have covered only a fraction of the extra cost. From 1990-92, federal AFDC spending rose almost $6 billion during the three years, said Robert Greenstein, executive director of the Center on Budget and Policy Priorities, a Washington advocacy group. That's about six times the House bill's rainy day fund and almost three and a half times the Senate's.

Even a larger fund would do little to refill depleted state coffers, groups representing state and local legislators say,

because the money would have to be paid back with interest.

"Our view is that a loan is not sufficient, that the federal government needs to share in the costs of those increases," said Sheri E. Steisel, director of the Human Services Committee of the National Conference of State Legislatures. "Our concern is that states will be left holding the bag for changes in the economy and changes in the population. And that's not the way that a federal-state partnership is supposed to work."

Cash shortages would discourage states from engaging in dramatic new welfare experiments, critics of the block grant formula contend.

"They will be under tremendous pressure to reduce benefits," Paul Offner, a top aide to Daniel Patrick Moynihan of New York, the Finance Committee's senior Democrat, said of state legislators. "The first thing that will happen is [that], faced with a shortage of funds, they will squeeze the money that is spent on education and training and job search and all the activities that help get people off welfare."

At worst, advocates for the needy warn, states may be forced to slash welfare benefits, either by reducing the level of aid available to families or by tightening eligibility criteria to force people off the rolls. Some predict that governors will join a "race to the bottom," driven by the fear that generous welfare benefits would attract poor families from other states and send some businesses to low-welfare, low-tax states.

"The legislation . . . would place upon the states the full cost of any additional welfare recipient," said Paul E. Peterson, professor of government and director of the Center for American Political Studies at Harvard University. "So this means that every state is going to try very hard to keep poor people [from] moving into their state. And the best way to do that is to reduce the cash benefits to recipients."

Peterson's studies of interstate migration conclude that poor people take benefit levels into account when deciding where to live. Other studies play down the welfare magnet effect, concluding that families tend to move in search of jobs and economic opportunities. But even if welfare plays only a small role in migration, welfare policy experts say, governors believe that there's a magnet effect and will act accordingly.

That view strikes some reform advocates as highly cynical. Governors will be under considerable political pressure to enact substantial welfare reforms, Republican block grant advocates say, and will have to answer to the voters if the system fails.

"This is an argument—and I find it unfathomable—that legislatures and governors just don't care, that they want to drive all their welfare people out of the state," Packwood said. "And that was not my experience when I was in the legislature 30 years ago."

But some block grant critics maintain that the race to the bottom—what a welfare analyst termed a scramble of "spiraling parsimony"—is already under way. They point to New England, where tough new welfare legislation in Massachusetts has prompted similar bills in New Hampshire and Connecticut.

The Massachusetts law, set to take effect on July 1, will cut basic AFDC benefits by 2.75 per cent, require able-bodied recipients with school-age children to go to work after 60 days and cut off cash benefits after two years. The bill passed the Democratic legislature on Feb. 10; within a week, New Hampshire's Republican Gov. Steve Merrill proposed legislation that would require welfare recipients to go to work within 26 weeks.

"I do not propose to reform welfare," Merrill told *The Boston Globe.* "I propose to eliminate it."

Also in mid-February, Gov. John G. Rowland, R-Conn., unveiled a plan that, effective in July, would cut monthly AFDC benefits for a family of three from $581 to $514. Recipients would be limited to 21 months on welfare. Rowland has repeatedly talked about the problem of welfare-driven migration because of lower benefit levels in states that border Connecticut.

In New York City, Mayor Rudolph W. Giuliani came under fire in April after telling a talk radio host that proposed city and state welfare cuts could prompt many recipients to move out of New York and adding that the move "would be a good thing" for them. Giuliani later backed away from the statement as well as from an early estimate that the city's plan would make 30 per cent of applicants ineligible for welfare.

The prospect of substantial state reductions either in benefits or in the number of people eligible for assistance terrifies many local legislators. Groups representing cities, counties, mayors and local educators are among the loudest critics of welfare block grants. Many fear that if

Even if local control cuts administrative costs, the savings may well be minimal.

shortages of funds drive up hunger or homelessness, they'll be left to pick up the pieces.

"While a lot of us don't manage the welfare system, we do deal with the problems [when] people don't get assistance—homelessness, health considerations, the kinds of things that are the result of poverty without assistance," said Seattle Mayor Norman B. Rice, the incoming president of the U.S. Conference of Mayors. Rice estimates that Washington state would lose $1.2 billion in federal welfare funds over five years under the House legislation.

The mayors' group recently held a news conference with six other associations representing local governments and school administrators to warn that the Republican plan could foist poverty problems onto ill-prepared local agencies.

Local officials "will see the fallout if this doesn't work," said Randall Franke, president of the National Association of Counties (NACo). Families and children who fall through the cracks as a result of welfare block grants will land on local agencies' doorsteps, Franke and other local officials predicted, possibly forcing up local property taxes.

"They're our citizens," Franke said, "and we can't hide from them."

Together with the National League of Cities and the Conference of Mayors, NACo has formed the Local Government Welfare Reform Coalition, which is lobbying for amendments to the Republican welfare legislation that would protect local governments.

The coalition is pushing requirements that state legislators work with local offi-

cials in designing welfare reforms. The group also seeks guarantees that federal financing would increase if welfare caseloads rise and opposes work requirements unless they're accompanied by affordable child care. Welfare reform should be a federal-state-local partnership, not a handoff to the states, the coalition maintains.

UNEQUAL SHARES

Some governors also worry that the GOP's block grant formula would leave states with vastly differing slices of the federal welfare pie. Welfare benefits already vary considerably from state to state—a family of three in Alaska received $923 a month in AFDC payments in 1993, for example, but only $120 in Mississippi.

The differences would be far more pronounced under the proposed formula, block grant skeptics say. Freezing financing at 1994 levels, for example, fails to account for population increases in high-growth states.

Some governors argue that the Republican plan would lock existing inequities in place. Federal welfare grants are based in part on how much of the money each state matches. Under the plan, not only would the grants stay at 1994 levels for five years, but also the states would no longer be obligated to match them.

That means that a state that has not invested heavily in welfare would end up with far less federal money than a state that's been more generous—even if both states decided to zero out their matching funds.

Low-income states that have skimped on matching funds would fare the worst, and yet their welfare needs are the greatest, Democrats critical of the Republican plan say. Under the Senate bill, for example, lost federal dollars would vary from $8.5 billion for California to $26 million for North Dakota over five years, according to a recent HHS analysis.

"The current block plan does not work for all America," Gov. Lawton Chiles, D-Fla., said in a National Press Club speech last month attacking the proposal. "It favors some states over others."

It's no wonder that governors such as Engler and Weld support block grants, Chiles complained, because "their states are either held harmless or delivered a jackpot . . . at the expense of growth states like Florida." The plan would be "a disaster" for Florida and other states with growing populations, he predicted, and would lead to "a not-so-civil war of dollars among the states."

Such complaints are parochial, congressional Republicans counter. The Florida governor's criticism "establishes him in the forefront of provincial politicians," Sen. Hank Brown, R-Colo., a leading welfare reform advocate, said in an interview. "If you're looking for a champion of 'Let's make sure I get mine,' why, he's a real leader."

If governors want to run welfare programs without federal interference, some conservatives argue, they should be willing to raise taxes to pay for them.

During the past 15 years, however, many states have imposed constitutional limits on tax increases. In 11 states, a two-thirds vote is needed to pass some or all tax increases; in Florida and Nevada, the constitutions bar legislators from enacting a personal income tax. In many cases, property taxes are all that are left to state and local legislators, who hesitate to levy them for fear of driving out middle-income residents.

The specter of state tax increases has fed recent anxiety in the statehouses about block grants. Thompson, Engler and Weld seized the initiative in promoting the block grant concept, and for the most part, Republican congressional leaders have negotiated exclusively with the three governors.

But some Republican governors are getting nervous about what block grants would mean for their states. In March, Gov. George V. Voinovich of Ohio wrote to Republican congressional leaders to warn that the House bill "does not include sufficient protections for states in the event of an economic downturn," and that "states are placed in an extremely vulnerable position should the welfare-eligible population increase significantly."

And in April, Gov. J. Fife Symington III of Arizona expressed similar concerns in a letter to Senate Majority Leader Robert Dole of Kansas. Block grants based on states' current levels of matching funds "would be patently unfair to the taxpayers of many states," Symington wrote, and would "result in a bitter political conflict between the states."

Thirty Senators from high-growth states, including Texas Republicans Phil Gramm and Kay Bailey Hutchison, also raised the alarm about financing inequities in a letter last month to Packwood and Moynihan. By freezing welfare financing without regard to state population growth, they warned, the Republican bill "would produce devastating results over a five-year period."

Even the architects of the welfare bills admit that there's no guarantee that block grants will spark significant state reforms. Some state programs will be very successful, Sen. Brown predicted. But, he added, "some states are going to drop the ball. Some states are not going to do much better than what the federal government does right now."

That's the big risk in the Republican proposal, block grant critics in both parties say: that a substantial number of governors will simply choose to perpetuate the status quo. Though some states, including Michigan and Wisconsin, have been hailed as trailblazers, others have had little or no success with welfare reform schemes. The missing link in the Republican legislation, some welfare reform advocates say, is any assurance that the states will be held accountable for their performance.

An alternative to no-strings-attached block grants are performance-based grants that would reward states for meeting measurable targets—a reduction in the teen pregnancy rate, for example, or an increase in the number of welfare recipients who are working. The Clinton Administration is testing the concept on several fronts, including three that have been proposed at the Housing and Urban Development Department.

An objective of performance-based grants is to give local officials and agencies an even greater role in administering public programs—a sort of super-devolution.

The idea of improving local control over government programs enjoys bipartisan support both on and off Capitol Hill. Sens. Breaux and Brown have teamed up on legislation that would allow states to provide education and training to welfare recipients through vouchers that could be redeemed at local job placement centers, either public or private. The voucher concept may be applicable to other types of welfare services, Brown said.

If anything, lawmakers from both political parties say, block grants should not signal a return to general revenue sharing, under which about $6 billion a year in federal money was shipped to state and local governments from 1972-86 with virtually no restrictions.

Federal lawmakers have a responsibility, reform advocates argue, to make sure that welfare tax dollars are well spent and that a critical chance to reinvent the system isn't lost.

"If this is the time for a change, then let's look at real changes," said Michael S. Joyce, president of the conservative Milwaukee-based Bradley Foundation. "I'm not sure that simple block grants, and simple application of federalist principles, is going to get us there."

It's Not Working

Why Many Single Mothers Can't Work Their Way Out of Poverty

Chris Tilly and Randy Albelda

Most current welfare reform proposals assume that all single mothers can simply work their way out of poverty—that it's a matter of will. President Clinton's "two years and out" time limit on benefits before mandatory work, along with the renewed emphasis on job search and short-term training programs, arises from an increasingly common determination to have poor women lift themselves up by their bootstraps.

For many single mothers, this strategy cannot work. In the absence of universal child care, health care, and an abundance of good jobs, welfare plays a crucial role as a safety net. And even if the government were to offset the daunting demands of caring for children, provide health care, and brighten the limited opportunities at the bottom of the labor market, large numbers of single mothers would continue to require public assistance.

It's not for want of trying that single mothers have not been able to make ends meet. They work for pay about as many hours per year, on average, as other mothers: about 1,000 hours a year (a year-round, full-time job logs 2,000 hours). But less than full-time work for most women in this country just doesn't pay enough to feed mouths, make rent payments, and provide care for children while at work.

Not all single mothers are poor—but half of them are (compared to a 5% poverty rate for married couples). For poor single mothers, the labor market usually doesn't pro-

Chris Tilly teaches public policy at UMass-Lowell. Randy Albelda teaches economics at UMass-Boston. Both are members of the D&S Collective.

vide a ticket off of welfare or out of poverty. That's why AFDC (Aid to Families with Dependent Children, the program known as welfare) works like a revolving door for so many of them.

Heidi Hartmann and Roberta Spalter-Roth of the Institute for Women's Policy Research (IWPR) report that half of single mothers who spend any time on welfare during a two-year period also work for pay. But that work only generates about one-third of their families' incomes. In short, work is not enough; like other mothers, they "package" their income from three sources: work in the labor market, support from men or other family members, and government aid. "Mothers typically need at least two of those sources to survive," says Spalter-Roth.

THE TRIPLE WHAMMY

While all women, especially mothers, face barriers to employment with good wages and benefits, single mothers face a "triple whammy" that sharply limits what they can earn. Three factors—job discrimination against women, the time and money it takes to care for children, and the presence of only one adult—combine to make it nearly impossible for women to move off of welfare through work alone, without sufficient and stable supplemental income supports.

First, the average woman earns about two-thirds as much per hour as her male counterpart. Women who need to rely on AFDC earn even less, since they often have lower skills, less work experience and more physical disabilities than other women. Between 1984 and 1988, IWPR researchers found, welfare mothers who worked for pay averaged a disastrous $4.18 per hour. Welfare mothers with

Reprinted with permission from *Dollars and Sense*, November/December 1994, pp. 8-10. © 1994 by *Dollars & Sense*, a progressive economics magazine published six times a year. First-year subscriptions cost $18.95 and may be ordered by writing to *Dollars and Sense*, One Summer Street, Somerville, MA 02143.

jobs received employer-provided health benefits only one-quarter of the time. AFDC mothers are three times as likely as other women to work as maids, cashiers, nursing aides, child care workers, and waitresses — the lowest of the low-paid women's jobs.

Second, these families include kids. Like all mothers, single mothers have to deal with both greater demands on their time and larger financial demands — more "mouths to feed." A 1987 time-budget study found that the average time spent in household work for employed women with two or more children was 51 hours a week. Child care demands limit the time women can put into their jobs, and interrupt them with periodic crises, ranging from a sick child to a school's summer break. This takes its toll on both the amount and the quality of work many mothers can obtain. "There's a sad match between women's needs for a little flexibility and time, and the growth in contingent jobs, part-time jobs, jobs that don't last all year," comments Spalter-Roth. "That's the kind of jobs they're getting."

Finally, and unlike other mothers, single mothers have only one adult in the family to juggle child care and a job. Fewer adults means fewer opportunities for paid work. And while a single mother may receive child support from an absent father, she certainly cannot count on the consistent assistance—be it financial support or help with child care—that a resident father can provide.

No Room at the Bottom?

Suppose Clinton and company make good on their promise to give welfare mothers a quick shove into the labor market. What kind of prospects will they face there? Two-thirds of AFDC recipients hold no more than a high school diploma. The best way to tell how work requirements will work is to look at the women who already have the jobs that welfare recipients would be compelled to seek.

The news is not good. An unforgiving labor market, in recession and recovery alike, has hammered young, less-educated women, according to economists Jared Bernstein and Lawrence Mishel of the Economic Policy Institute, a Washington, D.C. think tank. Between 1979 and 1989, hourly wages plummeted for these women, falling most rapidly for African American women who didn't finish high school. This group's hourly wages, adjusted for inflation, fell 20% in that ten year period. Most young high-school-or-less women continued to lose during 1989-93. At the end of this losing streak, average hourly wages ranged from $5 an hour for younger high school dropouts to $8 an hour for older women with high school diplomas.

Unemployment rates in 1993 for most of these young women are stunning: 42% for black female high school dropouts aged 16-25, and 26% for their Latina counterparts.

But young women don't have a monopoly on labor market distress: workforce-wide hourly wages fell 14% between 1973 and 1993, after controlling for inflation. Given the collapse of wage rates, work simply is not enough to lift many families out of poverty. Two-thirds of all people living in poor families with children — 15 million Americans — lived in families *with a worker* in 1991, report Isaac Shapiro and Robert Greenstein of the Center on Budget and Policy Priorities. And 5.5 million of these people in poverty had a family member who worked *year-round, full-time.*

Reforms That Would Work

The problems of insufficient pay and time to raise children that face single-mother families — and indeed many families — go far beyond the welfare system. So the solution must be much more comprehensive than simply reforming that system. What we need is a set of thorough changes in the relations among work, family, and income. Some of the Clinton administration's proposals actually fit into this larger package, but these positive elements are for the most part buried in get-tough posturing and wishful thinking. Here's what's needed:

•*Provide supports for low-wage workers.* The two most important supports are universal health coverage — going down in flames in Congress at the time of this writing — and a universal child care plan. Two-thirds of welfare recipients leave the rolls within two years, but lack of health insurance and child care drive many of them back: over half of women who leave welfare to work come back to AFDC. A society that expects all able-bodied adults to work — regardless of the age of their children — should also be a society that socializes the costs of going to work, by offering programs to care for children of all ages.

•*Create jobs.* This item seems to have dropped off the national policy agenda. Deficit-phobia has hogtied any attempt at fiscal stimulus, and the Federal Reserve seems bent on stamping out growth in the name of preventing inflation. And yet Clinton and Congress could call for reform at the Fed, use government spending to boost job growth, and even invest in creating public service jobs.

•*Make work pay by changing taxes and government assistance.* Make it pay not only for women working their way off welfare, but for everybody at the low end of the labor market. Clinton's preferred tool for this has been the Earned Income Tax Credit (EITC) — which gives tax credits to low-wage workers with children (this tax provision now outspends AFDC). Although they get the EITC, women on welfare who work suffer a penalty that takes away nearly a dollar of the AFDC grant for every dollar earned. Making work pay would mean reducing or eliminating this penalty.

•*Make work pay by shoring up wages and benefits.* To ensure that the private sector does its part, raise the minimum wage. A full-time, year-round minimum wage job pays less than the poverty income threshold for a family of one. Conservatives and the small business lobby will trot out the bogeyman of job destruction, but studies on the last minimum wage increase showed a zero or even positive effect on employment. Hiking the minimum wage does eliminate lousy jobs, but the greater purchasing power created by a higher wage floor generates roughly the same number of *better* jobs. In addition, mandate benefit parity for part-time, temporary, and subcontracted workers. This would close a loophole that a growing number of employers use to dodge fringe benefits.

•*Make a serious commitment to life-long education and training.* Education and training do help welfare recipients and other disadvantaged workers. But significant impacts depend on longer-term, intensive — and expensive — programs. We also need to expand training to a broader constituency, since training targeted only to the worst-off workers helps neither these workers, who get stigmatized in the eyes of employers, nor the remainder of the workforce, who get excluded. In Sweden, half the workforce takes some time off work for education in any given year.

•*Build flexibility into work.* "Increasingly," says Spalter-Roth, "all men and all women are workers *and* nurturers." Some unions have begun to bargain for the ability to move between full-time and part-time work, but in most workplaces changing hours means quitting a job and finding a new one. And though employees now have the right to unpaid family or medical leave, many can't afford to take time off. *Paid* leave would, of course, solve this problem. Failing that, temporary disability insurance (TDI) that is extended beyond disability situations to those facing a wide range of family needs could help. Five states (California, New York, New Jersey, Rhode Island, and Hawaii) currently run TDI systems funded by payroll taxes.

•*Mend the safety net, for times when earnings aren't enough.* Unemployment insurance has important gaps: low-wage earners receive even lower unemployment benefits, the long-term unemployed get cut off, new labor market entrants and re-entrants have no access to benefits, and in many states people seeking part-time work cannot collect. Closing these gaps would help welfare "packagers," as well as others at the low end of the labor market, to make ends meet. But even with all of these policies in place, there will be times when single mothers will either choose or be compelled to set aside paid work, sometimes for extended periods, to care for their families. For the foreseeable future, we still need Aid to Families with Dependent Children as a backstop. But at its current level, AFDC rarely acts as a safety net: Hartmann and Spalter-Roth found that AFDC recipients without significant earnings received incomes worth only two-thirds of the poverty line on average.

So welcome to reality. Most single mothers *cannot* work their way out of poverty — definitely not without supplemental support. There are many possible policy steps that could be taken to help them and other low-wage workers get the most out of an inhospitable labor market. But ultimately, old-fashioned welfare must remain part of the formula.

Resources: Heidi Hartmann and Roberta Spalter-Roth, "The real employment opportunities of women participating in AFDC: What the market can provide" (1993) and "Welfare that works: An assessment of the administration's welfare reform proposal" (1994), Institute for Women's Policy Research; Jared Bernstein and Lawrence Mishel, "Trends in the low-wage labor market and welfare reform: The constraints on making work pay," Economic Policy Institute 1994; Isaac Shapiro and Robert Greenstein, *Making Work Pay: The Unfinished Agenda*, Center on Budget and Policy Priorities 1993; Randy Albelda and Chris Tilly, *Glass Ceilings and Bottomless Pits: Women, Income, and Poverty in Massachusetts*, Women's Statewide Legislative Network (Massachusetts) 1994.

AID TO DEPENDENT CORPORATIONS

EXPOSING FEDERAL HANDOUTS TO THE WEALTHY

CHUCK COLLINS

In 1992 rancher J.R. Simplot of Grandview, Idaho paid the U.S. government $87,000 for grazing rights on federal lands, about one-quarter the rate charged by private land-owners. Simplot's implicit subsidy from U.S. taxpayers, $261,000, would have covered the welfare costs of about 60 poor families. With a net worth exceeding $500 million, it's hard to argue that Simplot needed the money.

Since 1987, American Barrick Resources Corporation has pocketed $8.75 billion by extracting gold from a Nevada mine owned by the U.S. government. But Barrick has paid only minimal rent to the Department of the Interior. In 1992 Barrick's founder was rewarded for his business acumen with a $32 million annual salary.

Such discounts are only one form of corporate welfare, dubbed "wealthfare" by some activists, that U.S.

Chuck Collins is the Co-Coordinator of the Share the Wealth Project, and works with the Tax Equity Alliance of Massachusetts.

taxpayers fund. At a time when Congress is attempting to slash or eliminate the meager benefits received by the poor, we are spending far more to subsidize wealthy corporations and individuals. Wealthfare comes in five main varieties: discounted user fees for public resources; direct grants; corporate tax reductions and loopholes; giveaways of publicly funded research and development (R&D) to private profit-making companies; and tax breaks for wealthy individuals.

Within the Clinton administration Secretary of Labor Robert Reich and Budget Director Alice Rivlin have attacked "welfare for the rich." Armed with a study from the Progressive Policy Institute, the Democratic Leadership Council's think tank, Reich floated the notion that over $200 billion in corporate welfare could be trimmed over the next five years. In a sign of the problems with our two-party system, Clinton discouraged Reich from taking this campaign further, for fear of alienating big Democratic Party funders.

TAX AVOIDANCE

The largest, yet most invisible, part of wealthfare is tax breaks for corporations and wealthy individuals. The federal Office of Management and Budget (OMB) estimates that these credits, deductions, and exemptions, called "tax expenditures," will cost $440 billion in fiscal 1996. This compares, for example, to the $16 billion annual federal cost of child support programs.

Due both to lower basic tax rates and to myriad loopholes, corporate taxes fell from one-third of total federal revenues in 1953 to less than 10% today (see "Disappearing Corporate Taxes," *Dollars & Sense*, July 1994). Were corporations paying as much tax now as they did in the 1950s, the government would take in another $250 billion a year — more than the entire budget deficit.

The tax code is riddled with tax breaks for the natural resource, construction, corporate agri-business, and financial industries. Some serve legitimate purposes, or did at one time. Others have been distorted to create tax shelters and perpetuate bad business practices. During the 1993 budget battle, New Jersey Senator Bill Bradley attacked the "loophole writing" industry in Washington, where inserting a single sentence into the tax laws can save millions, even billions, in taxes for a corporate client.

Depreciation on equipment and buildings, for example, is a legitimate business expense. But the "accelerated depreciation" rule allows corporations to take this deduction far faster than their assets are wearing out. This simply lets businesses make billions of dollars in untaxed profits. One estimate is that this loophole will cost $164 billion over the next five years.

One particularly generous tax break is the foreign tax credit, which allows U.S.-based multinational corporations to deduct from their U.S. taxes the income taxes they pay to other nations. Donald Barlett and James Steele, authors of *America: Who Really Pays the Taxes*, say that by 1990 this writeoff was worth $25 billion a year.

While in many cases this credit is a valid method of preventing double taxation on profits earned overseas, the oil companies have used it to avoid most of their U.S. tax obligations. Until 1950, Saudi Arabia had no income tax, but charged royalties on all oil taken from their wells. Such royalties are a payment for use of a natural resource. They are a standard business expense, payable *before* a corporation calculates the profits on which it will pay taxes.

These royalties were a major cost to ARAMCO, the oil consortium operating there (consisting of Exxon, Mobil, Chevron, and Texaco). But since royalties are not income taxes, they could not be used to reduce Exxon and friends' tax bills back home.

When King Saud decided to increase the royalty payments, ARAMCO convinced him to institute a corporate income tax and to substitute this for the royalties. The tax was a sham, since it applied only to ARAMCO, not to any other business in Saudi Arabia's relatively primitive economy. The result was that the oil companies avoided hundreds of millions of dollars in their American taxes. Eventually the other oil-producing nations, including Kuwait, Iraq, and Nigeria, followed suit, at huge cost to the U.S. Treasury.

In contrast to the ARAMCO problem, many corporate executive salaries should not be counted as deductible expenses. These salaries and bonuses are often so large today that they constitute disguised profits. Twenty years ago the average top executive made 34 times the wages of the firm's lowest paid workers. Today the ratio is 140 to one. The Hospital Corporation of America, for example, paid its chairman $127 million in 1992—$61,000 on hour! In 1993 the Clinton administration capped the deductibility of salaries at $1 million, but the law has several loopholes that allow for easy evasion.

CHICKEN McNUGGETS AND OTHER VITAL MATTERS

Taxes are but one form of wealthfare. Subsidized use of public resources, as with J. R. Simplot's grazing and American Barrick's mining, is also widespread. Barrick's profit-making was allowed by the General Mining Law of 1872. Just last year the government finally put a one-year moratorium on this resource-raiding.

In a manner similar to the mining situation, the U.S. Forest Service under-charges timber companies for the logs they take from publicly-owned land. The Forest Service also builds roads and other infrastructure needed by the timber industry, investing $140 million last year.

Many corporations also receive direct payments from the federal government. The libertarian Cato Institute argues that every cabinet department "has become a conduit for government funding of private industry. Within some cabinet agencies, such as the U.S. Department of Agriculture and the Department of Commerce, almost every spending program underwrites private business."

Agriculture subsidies typically flow in greater quantities the larger is the recipient firm. Of the $1.4 billion in annual sugar price supports, for example, 40% of the money goes to the largest 1% of firms, with the largest ones receiving more than $1 million each.

The Agriculture Department also spends $110 million a year to help U.S. companies advertise abroad. In 1992 Sunkist Growers got $10 million, Gallo Wines $4.5 million, M&M/Mars $1.1 million, McDonalds $466,000 to promote Chicken McNuggets, and American Legend Fur Coats $1.2 million.

The Progressive Policy Institute estimates that taxpayers could save $114 billion over five years by eliminating or restricting such direct subsidies. Farm subsidies, for example, could be limited to only small farmers.

The government also pays for scientific research and development, then allows the benefits to be reaped by private firms. This occurs commonly in medical research. One product, the anti-cancer drug Taxol, cost the U.S. government $32 million to develop as part of a joint venture with private industry. But in the end the government gave its share to Bristol-Myers Squibb, which now charges cancer patients almost $1,000 for a three-week supply of the drug.

WHO IS ENTITLED?

Beyond corporate subsidies, the government also spends far more than necessary to help support the lifestyles of wealthy individuals. This largess pertains to several of the most expensive and popular "entitlements" in the federal budget, such as Social Security, Medicare, and the deductibility of interest on home mortgages. As the current budget-cutting moves in Congress demonstrate, such universal programs have much greater political strength than do programs targetted solely at low-income households.

While this broad appeal is essential to maintain, billions of dollars could be saved by restricting the degree to which the wealthy benefit from universal programs. If Social Security and Medicare payments were denied to just the richest 3% of households this would reduce federal spending by $30 to $40 billion a year—more than the total federal cost of food stamps.

Similarly, mortgage interest is currently deductible up to $1 million per home, justifying the term "mansion subsidy" for its use by the rich. The government could continue allowing everyone to use this deduction, but limit it to $250,000 per home. This would affect only the wealthiest 5% of Americans, but would save taxpayers $10 billion a year.

Progressive organizations have mounted a renewed focus on the myriad handouts to the corporate and individual rich. One effort is the Green Scissors coalition, an unusual alliance of environmental groups such as Friends of the Earth, and conservative taxcutters, such as the National Taxpayers Union. Last January Green Scissors proposed cutting $33 billion over the next ten years in subsidies that they contend are wasteful and environmentally damaging. These include boondoggle water projects, public land subsidies, highways, foreign aid projects, and agricultural programs.

Another new organization, Share the Wealth, is a coalition of labor, religious, and economic justice organizations. It recently launched the "Campaign for Wealth-Fare Reform," whose initial proposal targets over $35 billion in annual subsidies that benefit the wealthiest 3% of the population. The campaign rejects the term "corporate welfare" because it reinforces punitive anti-welfare sentiments. Welfare is something a humane society guarantees to people facing poverty, unemployment, low wages, and racism. "Wealthfare," in contrast, is the fees and subsidies extracted from the public by the wealthy and powerful—those who are least in need.

Today's Congress is not sympathetic to such arguments. But the blatant anti-poor, pro-corporate bias of the Republicans has already begun to awaken a dormant public consciousness. This will leave more openings, not less, for progressives to engage in public education around the true nature of government waste.

Resources: Green Scissors Report: Cutting Wasteful and Environmentally Harmful Spending and Subsidies, Friends of the Earth, 1995; *Killing the Sacred Cows,* Anne Crittendon, Penguin Books, 1993; *Aid to Dependent Corporations,* Janice C. Shields, Essential Information, 1994; *Cut-and-Invest to Compete and Win: A Budget Strategy for American Growth,* Robert Shapiro, Progressive Policy Institute, 1994; *America: Who Really Pays the Taxes,* Donald Barlett and James Steele, Simon and Schuster, 1994.

LET US COUNT THE WAYS

A few of the many subsidies received by the wealthy are:

• *The Mansion Subsidy.* Home mortgage interest is deductible up to $1 million per year. Reducing the limit to $250,000 would save the government $10 billion a year.

• *The Accelerated Depreciation Subsidy.* Companies get to depreciate their equipment much faster than it wears out. The cost: $32 billion a year.

• *The Advertising Subsidy.* Corporations fully deduct the cost of their advertising. If only one-fifth of advertising expenses were considered a capital cost of building brand name recognition, and so deductible gradually over time, taxpayers would save $3.5 billion a year.

• *McSubsidies.* $110 million a year goes directly to companies that advertise their products abroad. Beneficiaries include Sunkist, McDonalds, and M&M/Mars.

• *Wealthfare for Mining Companies.* The U.S. lets big mining companies pay peanuts for the use of federally-owned lands — our lands. An 8% royalty would earn $200 million a year.

• *Corporate Agri-Business Subsidy.* The federal government gives $200 million a year to corporate farms that each have incomes over $5 million a year.

INEQUALITY

For richer, for poorer

Income inequalities in America and Britain are greater than at any time in the past 50 years. The social consequences of this change worry many. Why has it happened?

PLATO told his pupil Aristotle that, within any organisation, nobody should earn more than five times as much as the lowliest worker. But things change: the chief executive of a big American firm can now expect to earn more than $1m a year—at least 40 times as much as an ordinary production worker. Even Ben & Jerry's Homemade, an engagingly informal Vermont ice-cream company, abandoned a cherished principle that its highest-paid executive could not be paid more than seven times the wage of its lowest-paid worker when head-hunting for a new chief executive this year.

In other industrial countries too, the gap between rich and poor has widened over the past decade or two. In Britain, the Commission for Social Justice, set up with encouragement from the opposition Labour Party, painted a grim picture of poverty amid wealth. If Marx's prediction of a proletariat plunged into abject misery under capitalism has so far been unfulfilled, the widening gap between haves and have-nots is causing some to think that Marx might yet be proved right on this point after all.

It is no coincidence that the biggest increases in income inequalities have occurred in economies such as those of America, Britain and New Zealand, where free-market economic policies have been pursued most zealously. The collapse of communism may have proved Adam Smith's invisible hand to be a superior economic engine, but it is one that is still morally suspect to many who worry that economic rewards are not being shared adequately. For the market economy has no moral sensibility: income inequalities arise from the independent actions of individuals with different skills and assets who are rewarded according to what consumers and producers are prepared to pay.

Concerns about widening income inequalities played a big role in Bill Clinton's election victory in 1992, and are likely to loom large in Britain's next general election. The recent publication of "The Bell Curve", a book by Charles Murray, a sociologist, and the late Richard Herrnstein, a psychologist, has added to America's debate on inequality by renewing a claim that intelligence as measured by IQ testing plays a main role in deciding society's winners and losers, and that genetic inheritance may be a main determinant of IQ. But even if that thesis were proved correct, it would not explain fully why inequalities of income were widening.

Figuring it out

To measure inequality, statisticians favour two common methods. The first is to use a ratio called the Gini coefficient, which is expressed as a scale running from 0 to 1 on which 0 signifies perfect equality (everybody has the same income) and 1 signifies extreme inequality (one person gets the lot). The second method is to look at the share of total income earned by different percentile groups in society—the share earned by the poorest 20% and that by the richest 20%, for example. Both methods include all forms of income in the calculation—welfare payments and investment income, for example—not wages alone.

On both measures, inequality in America narrowed from 1929 until 1969, but then started to widen. In 1992 the top 20% of American households received 11 times as much income as the bottom 20%, up from a multiple of 7.5 in 1969. The effect was to give the richest 20% of households a 45% share of the country's total net income in 1992, a post-war high, and the poorest 20% of households a mere 4% share. The Gini coefficient rose from 0.35 to 0.40 over the same period (see chart 1, next page).

In Britain too, the gap between rich and poor has been widening since 1977—two years before the political watershed associated with the arrival of Margaret Thatcher as prime minister. A recent study by the Institute for Fiscal Studies, an independent think-tank, estimated that, for Britain, the Gini coefficient rose from 0.23 in 1977 to 0.34 in 1991, a bigger jump than in any other country. In 1977 the income of the richest 20% of Britons was four times as big as the income of the poorest 20%; by 1991 that multiple had increased to seven. An even more striking result could be obtained by looking only at wage income: the gap between the highest- and lowest-paid male workers in Britain is at its widest since the 1880s when such figures were first compiled.

In both America and Britain, income inequalities are now larger than at any time since the 1930s. But there is one big difference between the two countries: in Britain average real incomes have risen fairly briskly over the past two decades; in America they have risen only slightly. Combined with greater inequality, this means that America's poor, unlike Britain's, have grown poorer absolutely in the past two decades. The poorest 10% of American families suffered an 11% drop in real income between 1973 and 1992; the richest 10% enjoyed an 18% increase in real income. In Britain, by contrast, the real income of the bottom 10% continued to increase, albeit by only 10% in 1973-91, compared with the 55% gain enjoyed by the top 10% (see chart 2).

Income inequality in America is not only high historically, but high also in relation to other rich countries (see chart 3). After America in the inequality league-table come Australia, New Zealand, and Switzerland. In all four countries the ratio of the income of the richest 20% to the poorest 20% is between 8.5 and 11. Japan and Germany are among the most equal societies, with ratios of 4 to 5.5. Britain, Canada and France fall somewhere in between.

It depends what you mean by poor

There is an overlap between the question of income inequality and the question of poverty; but there is also an essential difference. If poverty is defined as the condition of families with, say, less than half median income, then countries with wider inequalities will tend to have more poverty. By this last definition 18% of Americans are "poor", compared with only 6-9% in Britain, France, Germany and Sweden.

But America is also the world's richest country; so comparisons with Europe tend to exaggerate the extent of its absolute poverty. In a paper published last year by the Luxembourg Income Study, an international project to monitor inequality and poverty, Michael Förster, an OECD economist, took the figure for half median income in America and converted it into other countries' currencies at purchasing-power parity (to take account of differences in the cost of living). America's poverty rate then

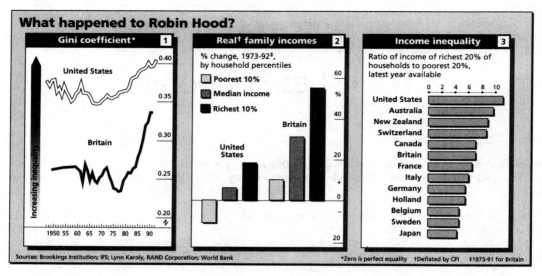

What happened to Robin Hood?

Gini coefficient* **1**

United States

Britain

0.40
0.35
0.30
0.25
0.20

Increasing inequality

1950 55 60 65 70 75 80 85 90

Real† family incomes **2**

% change, 1973-92‡,
by household percentiles

☐ Poorest 10%
▨ Median income
■ Richest 10%

United States

Britain

60
%
40
20
+
0
–
20

Income inequality **3**

Ratio of income of richest 20% of
households to poorest 20%,
latest year available

0 2 4 6 8 10

United States
Australia
New Zealand
Switzerland
Canada
Britain
France
Italy
Germany
Holland
Belgium
Sweden
Japan

Sources: Brookings Institution; IFS; Lynn Karoly, RAND Corporation; World Bank   *Zero is perfect equality †Deflated by CPI ‡1973-91 for Britain

ranked below those of all other West European countries including Sweden (24%) and Germany (19%).

As to the causes of increasing inequality, government policies to cut tax rates and welfare benefits are most commonly blamed in America and Britain. There, as in several other countries in the 1980s, governments lost their enthusiasm for redistributive policies and instead made changes in taxes and transfers that favoured the rich. Britain's top rate of marginal income tax was cut from 98% to 40%. Some countries did their best to curb welfare spending by linking unemployment benefits and pensions to prices rather than to wages, and by restricting benefits.

Most studies suggest, however, that although the richest 1-2% of earners gained handsomely from such tax cuts, the direct effects of changes in taxes and benefits on overall income inequalities in the 1980s were relatively modest; and despite the changes, tax and benefit systems remained strongly progressive. According to Britain's Central Statistical Office, in 1992 the richest 20% of Britons had 25 times as much income as the poorest 20% before taxes and transfers. Only after taxes and transfers did the multiple fall to seven.

Rather, it is a combination of lightly regulated labour markets and global economic forces that has done much more than particular fiscal policies to favour the rich over the poor. In America and Britain, except at the very bottom of the income distribution, wider wage differentials have been the most important force behind increasing income inequality in recent years. New technology and increased competition from low-wage developing countries have caused demand for unskilled workers in industrial economies to fall relative to demand for highly skilled and educated workers. Over the past decade or so the wage premium earned by 25-34-year-old American male college graduates relative to those who complete high school alone has risen by 30%.

All countries have been buffeted by the forces of changing technology and stronger global competition, however. So why should wage differentials in most of continental Europe have changed by much less? The answer is that deregulation in America and Britain has allowed market forces to do their work, whereas in continental Europe powerful trade unions, centralised wage bargaining and high minimum wages have propped up the wages of the low-paid.

Indeed, pay differentials narrowed through the 1980s in western Germany, where trade-union membership has held steady at around 40% of workers over the past 20 years; in America, membership has fallen from 30% to 12% since 1970. A study by Richard Freeman of Harvard University confirms that, in general, wage inequalities are smallest in highly unionised countries.

In America, the second most important cause of increased income inequality—accounting for some 35% of the increase versus 40% attributable to widening wage differentials—has been a change in household structure. In the 1950s most households consisted of two parents, only one of whom was a wage-earner. Now society is more polarised between two-earner households and jobless single-parent families. It is hard for single mothers to earn good incomes. The proportion of families headed by women among the poorest fifth of households has doubled over the past 40 years to around 35%. In contrast, the richest fifth of households is increasingly dominated by high-income two-earner couples: well-paid women tend to marry rich men.

In Britain, it is investment income that has been the second most important factor, after wages, in explaining widening income disparities. Wealth is even more unevenly distributed than income: the wealthiest 10% of Britons own 53% of total wealth. Investment income rose faster than wages as stockmarkets boomed in the 1980s.

Beggar my neighbour

Americans have long been willing to tolerate greater inequality. According to a poll published in *American Enterprise* magazine in 1990, only 29% of Americans thought it was the government's job to reduce income differentials (the view taken by 60-70% of Britons and Germans and by more than 80% of Italians and Austrians). Few Americans seem to begrudge the rich their wealth so long as they perceive the money to have been earned fairly and squarely: entrepreneurs are generally admired, and financial speculators resented.

Thus, in America, worries about inequality usually boil down to worries about poverty. If average wages were rising rapidly such that even the low-paid were enjoying increasing incomes, people might be less bothered about widening income differentials. It is the fact that many of the poor have become unambiguously poorer over the past two decades that is the focus of concern.

Europeans, in contrast, have tended to care more about relativities. The British Social Attitudes Survey asked workers in eight countries whether they agreed that large differences in income were necessary for economic prosperity. Some 37% of working-class Americans said Yes, compared with 25% of Britons, 23% of Germans and only 9% of Dutch. Survey evidence in Britain has also shown a rise over the past decade in the proportion of workers who believe that the gap between the highest- and lowest-paid is too large in their workplace.

The amount of mobility between income groups may play an important part in shaping attitudes to inequality. Mobility has been higher in America than in Europe: a study in the mid-1980s found that 18% of families in the bottom income quintile moved out of it in a single year; and that a third of families from the bottom quintile moved up into the top half within a generation. The snag, argues Frank Levy, an economist at MIT, lies with evidence that mobility is diminishing. There may still be plenty of movement in the middle of the scale, but it has become harder to climb out of poverty.

Societies in America and elsewhere are clearly less equal than they were; but are they less equal than they should be? Economic theory has little to say about this. But if income inequalities are taken to reflect a system of rewards intended to encourage maximum economic efficiency, then any government intervention to redistribute income will have economic costs: hence the popular notion of a trade-off between economic efficiency and equality.

The sharp increase in inequality in Britain and America over the past decade or so has given ammunition, nonetheless, to opponents of the free market. In some countries, voters who feel uncomfortable about homeless people on the streets may choose to sacrifice some growth to reduce income inequalities. That is a valid political choice. More striking is the emergence of a small but growing number of economists who are finding reasons to reject altogether the presumption of a trade-off between equality and economic efficiency.

Torsten Persson and Guido Tabellini, in the June 1994 issue of the *American Economic Review,* argue that inequality may even be harmful to growth. Their study of 56 countries finds a strong negative relationship between income inequality and growth in GDP per head. In less equal societies, they suggest, concerns about social and political conflict are more likely to lead to government policies that cramp growth.

In a similar vein, "Paying for Inequality", a recent book from the Institute for Public Policy Research, a left-of-centre British think-tank under whose auspices the Commission for Social Justice convened, also produces data linking income inequality with sluggish growth: America and Switzerland, countries with high income inequalities, had much slower productivity growth in the 1980s than did the more egalitarian Japan, Germany and Sweden (see chart 4). The authors find that societies with wider inequalities have more ill health, social stress and crime—which, they say, all hinder economic success.

Some are more equal than others

That Japan and Germany not only enjoy faster productivity growth, but also safer cities, than do less equal societies such as America and Britain, is an attractive argument. But statistical correlations do not by themselves prove causation; and nobody is suggesting that, directly or indirectly, redistributive policies such as penal tax rates, more generous unemployment benefits and higher trade barriers would serve to boost growth.

Perhaps the best lesson from these new studies is that, although some redistributive policies—such as high tax rates—hinder growth, there may be other policies, such as better access to good education for all, which can improve both equity and growth. Although these latter policies cannot guarantee greater equality of outcome, they can help ensure more equality of opportunity. Likewise, income supplements for the low-paid (such as the earned-income tax credit in America) are a much better way to help the poor than is a minimum wage.

Whatever the merits of the debate, the political fact is that in most countries there is no great appetite among the majority of voters for a return to income-tax rates of 80% or more, or for a massive increase in welfare spending. Optimistic free-marketeers argue that the increase in pay differentials will, in fact, be partly self-correcting as the rise in the college wage premium increases the incentive to get a better education and so boosts the supply of skilled workers. (Indeed, in America, the proportion of high-school leavers enrolling in college has risen from 49% in 1980 to 60% in the 1990s.)

Even so, to the extent that greater inequality is linked to fundamental changes in technology and global competition, the gap between skilled workers and unskilled workers is likely to continue to increase, all other things being equal. A widening of income differentials seems inevitable in continental Europe too over the next decade as high unemployment and rising public expenditure force governments to accept some degree of labour-market deregulation and to reduce welfare benefits.

Some commentators fear that wider income disparities in America and Britain will lead to social unrest. Short of that, there is a danger that unless some way is found to compensate the losers, an effective coalition will form against the liberal economic policies likely to incur popular blame for the widening gap. Support for protectionism, for increased government spending on benefits and subsidies and for higher tax rates to soak the rich could all form part of the backlash; trade unionism could revive. Many of the past decade's gains in efficiency would then be lost.

Such concerns make the 1980s seem with hindsight a time of comforting economic simplicity: the job was to cut taxes, trim the role of government, boost incentives and allow markets to work better. The task of the coming decade—discovering how to spread the benefits of economic efficiency more widely—will be far harder.

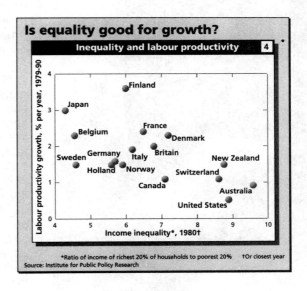

Is equality good for growth?

Inequality and labour productivity [4]

*Ratio of income of richest 20% of households to poorest 20%   †Or closest year
Source: Institute for Public Policy Research

Cultural Pluralism and Affirmative Action

America has been referred to as the melting pot of the world because individuals from radically different cultural and ethnic backgrounds have been melded into "Americans." This means they have largely abandoned their histories, unique cultural heritage, and languages as they have acquired a common identity. Thus we have Irish Americans, Italian Americans, African Americans, and so on, with the focus being on their common identity as Americans, which helped minimize cultural pluralism.

Some argue that this lack of cultural pluralism promoted unity and is what made America strong. As a result, their argument goes, people were not restricted to specific geographic localities by race or ethnicity. Even the American Civil War was not fought over cultural factors, but over economic ones. The consequences of true cultural pluralism can be clearly seen in such locations as the former Soviet Union, South Africa, and the Balkans.

Other individuals bemoan the fact that Americans expect new migrants to become both assimilated and acculturated. Newly arrived immigrants, they argue, should be able to retain most of their ethnic differences without becoming second-class citizens. Diversity, they claim, is the spice of life and ethnic tolerance the sign of social maturity.

But not all Americans have been able to realize the "American dream" equally. To level the playing field—so to speak—specific programs were instituted to reverse the consequences of blatant discrimination. These programs, to clarify their real intent, were called "affirmative action" and applied to those areas that were seen as major avenues to social equality—specifically education, employment, and government service. These programs were very effective in opening doors, keeping them open, and assuring that blatant discrimination was stopped. The major problem now is determining if the effects of historical discrimination have not only been addressed but corrected. If they have been, then these programs should be terminated. If they have not, where and how long should they continue to be employed?

"Reclaiming the Vision: What Should We Do after Affirmative Action?" argues that "examining the source of discontent with affirmative action policies and practices will help not only to design sound replacement policies, but also to create and sustain an expectation of good faith in the deliberations about what to do next."

Richard Lamm, author of "Enough" believes that the United States immigration policy is, in fact, a non-policy. It has no definable objective and not only fails to express a national interest, but is increasingly working against the interests of America and its current citizens.

In "What to Do about Affirmative Action," Arch Puddington asserts that current programs were based on legislation designed to stop blatant discrimination, not to create quotas. Thousands of presidential directives, court decisions, enforcement-agency guidelines, and regulatory rules have resulted in body counts to assure compliance. Puddington believes that current affirmative action practices do not reflect why they were created in the first place.

"A Twofer's Lament" reports on what it is like to be an unintended beneficiary of affirmative action. Yolanda Cruz thought that she had been admitted to graduate school because of her academic credentials, only to be shocked to discover she was a "twofer," which means that she had been admitted because she fulfilled two affirmative action criteria—she was a woman in a male-dominated field, and she was also not white.

The "Crisis of Community: Make America Work for Americans" has emerged because of the preoccupation of various groups with correcting wrongs and/or gaining advantage. Communities are being ripped apart because competing groups fail to distinguish between "enemies" (other competing groups) and the "problem." Thus we engage in a divisive struggle for advantage rather than jointly attacking problems.

Looking Ahead: Challenge Questions

Just what is meant by the concept "cultural pluralism"?

Should America continue to admit millions of foreign-born people fleeing poverty, racism, and war? Why or why not?

What implications do the existing U.S. immigration policies have for the current citizens of the United States?

Is cultural pluralism a potentially divisive philosophy, a unifying situation, or an enriching phenomena?

Are affirmative action programs still needed today? Under what conditions should affirmative action programs be eliminated?

What unexpected effects can being the recipient of affirmative action have on the recipient?

What are the conflicts in rights, values, obligations, and harms that seem to be underlying each of the issues covered in this section?

Reclaiming the Vision

What should we do after affirmative action?

Constance Horner

Constance Horner is a guest scholar in the Brookings Governmental Studies program. A former head of the U.S. Office of Personnel Management, she is a member of the U.S. Civil Rights Commission.

The powerful moral vision that generated America's civil rights movement is on the brink of disintegration. Unless that vision—of a racially integrated society aspiring to equal justice and equal opportunity for black Americans—is reclaimed, the United States will, on the cusp of a new millennium, fail at a crucial political task it has assigned itself since the Civil War. It will also diminish its signal historical standing as creator of exemplary solutions to the deepest dilemmas of civic life.

That is why the current debate over affirmative action matters greatly. How America deals with the challenges posed by this issue and how we explain what we are doing will define our strongest commitments and ideals for our time, just as our words and deeds over the 45 years of the Cold War defined our commitment to political and economic liberty in that time. For there can be no mistaking that civic harmony among racial and ethnic groups is among the most salient global challenges of the next half-century.

With the irony that colors so much of human affairs, the 30-year series of public policy and judicial decisions we know as affirmative action has come to threaten the vision of a just and integrated society that gave birth to it. Yet in the minds of many black Americans, affirmative action is identified with a national commitment to their advancement.

There is little question that affirmative action will be modified, phased out, or even, under a cascade of Supreme Court decisions, state initiatives, and federal legislative action, abruptly terminated. Therefore it is vital to understand the full range of reasons for its rejection. Black Americans should not come to believe that the decision against it constitutes a rejection of the vision that brought it into being, and the country needs an understanding of the elements that would comprise an effective replacement for it.

What Next?

A democratic polity can change the means by which it achieves its ends, provided that it operates in good faith and gives those most vulnerable to democratic decisions, the minority, reason to believe in the majority's good faith. Examining the sources of discontent with affirmative action policies and practices will help not only to design sound replacement policies, but also to create and sustain an expectation of good faith in the deliberations about what to do next.

One of the dilemmas confronting people in public life critical of affirmative action has been the concern that calling it into question would be viewed by black Americans as, at best, indifference to their historic plight or, at worst, a contributor to resurgent racism. Some proponents of affirmative action have, over several decades, taken advantage of this concern to enforce a politically correct silence that has precluded the incremental correction of a public policy gone awry that is preservative of peaceful democratic change. Indeed, some of the explosive force of the current critique results from the unleashed resentment over this intimidation.

Supporters of affirmative action have put forth various economic, political, and psychological explanations for the burgeoning opposition to it. Opposition results, they say, from a generalized hostility ("white male rage") stemming from low wage growth and job loss, exacerbated by partisan Republicans inflaming a "wedge" issue for the next election, or from the flaring up of a permanent or "institutional" racism that can never be fully suppressed, only contained through political *force majeure*.

At root these arguments are premised on an expectation of bad faith and a presumption of economic determinism. As such they deny the strength and persistence in American culture of the premises on which the civil rights movement was based and flourished—a sense of fairness, a belief in racial integration, and a presumption that a civically activist polity will voluntarily (if slowly) make positive social change. Therefore, whatever their truth, these explanations are questionable and limited guides to constructing a sustainable next generation of efforts to increase equality of opportunity.

From *The Brookings Review*, Summer 1995, pp. 6-11. © 1995 by the Brookings Institution. Reprinted by permission.

Moreover, they fail as full explanations for why the broad national revulsion toward the practices of affirmative action (including that felt by women and, to a lesser extent, blacks, its intended beneficiaries) is being expressed at this time and with such force.

Polls defining affirmative action as racial preferences show overwhelming white rejection (in the neighborhood of 75 percent) and an almost equal split for and against among blacks (46 percent for, 52 percent against in an April *Washington Post*–ABC national poll). An entirely separate set of polls taken in the same time frame suggests that an additional or different—and far more benign and hopeful—interpretation of the antipathy to affirmative action is available than the angry class- and race-based explanations advanced to date.

Antipathy toward "Big Government"

Almost 70 percent responding to one national poll indicated a belief that "the federal government controls too much of our daily lives." Another poll had two-thirds of Americans choosing "big government" as the country's gravest peril. In the light of these data and much more confirming their findings, it is hard to escape the observation that antipathy to big government and to affirmative action have emerged together as two of the most powerful political sentiments achieving national expression at this time. Although simultaneity does not demonstrate connection, it is at least suggestive of it.

The 30-year growth of affirmative action's regime of federal statute, regulation, judicial decision, and administrative practice, burgeoning well beyond its straightforward original purposes of nondiscrimination and equality of opportunity, not outcomes, has not occurred in a vacuum. It has developed simultaneously with and as part of the federal government's regulatory curtailment of private, discretionary, and voluntary action in many areas of American life—a curtailment compounded by federal support for social programs embodying and projecting values most Americans reject. The huge Republican victory in November likely reflected a rejection on both counts—a rejection of the degree of regulatory intrusion and a rejection of some of the values embodied in social welfare programs. It is very likely that rejection of affirmative action has been greatly intensified by its association with both, as well as by its provenance in the Democratic party—the "mommy party" for the "nanny state." If this is so, Americans may be viewing affirmative action as a regulatory structure to be dismantled more than a moral vision to be fulfilled. The moral vision was of a nondiscriminatory, integrated society; the regulatory structure, intending to integrate, now separates. The moral vision was democratically and openly implemented through legislation to affirm a commitment to equal opportunity and equal justice before the law; the regulatory structures are developed by fiat-oriented bureaucracies and by judges disdainful of the context of competing values and of the enormous vitality and variety of a culture bursting the bonds of regulatory structures and reverting to earlier, more clearly defined values in many areas.

> *Examining the sources of discontent with affirmative action policies and practices will help not only to design sound replacement policies, but also to create and sustain an expectation of good faith in the deliberations about what to do next.*

OMB Directive 15

To see these conflicts in play, one need only look at what is happening to a little-known but powerful directive governing the federal government's collection of racial statistics. Promulgated in 1977, Office of Management and Budget Directive 15, "Race and Ethnic Standards for Federal Statistics and Administrative Reporting," governs the categories the Bureau of the Census may use in assessing the country's racial composition. The racial statistics developed through its categories serve as the basis for enforcement of voting and other civil rights by the Department of Justice, the Equal Employment Opportunity Commission, and the civil rights offices of other federal agencies. Billions of dollars of federal spending are targeted for women and racial and ethnic minorities on the basis of these statistics. (Even Small Business Administration set-aside programs directed to "socially and economically disadvantaged" individuals and institutions are *de facto* allocated largely by race and ethnicity because administrative practice and law "presume" that certain racial and ethnic groups are "disadvantaged.") Allocation of not inconsiderable political power, through the drawing of congressional district lines, is based on their collection. Determinations of "adverse impact" in private-sector hiring practices rest on a racial count of an area's labor pool, and lawsuits may follow.

Virtually every arena of activity is affected by these categories. According to a Congressional Research Service report, "targeted funding, in various forms, and minority or disadvantaged set-asides or preferences have been included in major authorization or appropriation measures for agriculture, communications, defense, education, public works, transportation, foreign relations, energy and water development, banking, scientific research and space exploration, and other purposes." The distribution of a great deal of public and private money and a considerable amount of political power relies on the racial and ethnic numbers produced under Directive 15.

Currently, people being counted by the census under the categories of OMB Directive 15 are asked to identify themselves racially as white, black, Asian-Pacific Islander, American Indian–Alaskan native, or "other." If "other" is selected, the census taker is expected to "reclassify" that person into one of the four groups on the basis of appearance. (People are also asked an "ethnic" question as to whether they are Hispanic.) These tidy boxes constructed by the federal government bear, as is obvious, very little relationship to the racial and ethnic variety of the country. The OMB, as a result, is agonizing over whether to add a new category, "multiracial." So far it has been unable to do so (except in limited testing). Ironically, and much to the point of the country's discontent with government's affirmative action structures, the use of racial categorization is imposing a powerful set of incentives for those receiving benefits to remain distinctly within their categories.

Thus a governmental structure whose original intent was to overturn a regime of segregation has been transformed into an apparatus supporting its return. Policies growing out of a national commitment to

---

The static regulatory vision of racial America is empirically outmoded. It is also antithetical to the long-term interests of black Americans.

---

racial integration and designed to facilitate integration instead entitle and empower on the basis of separation. To do so, moreover, these policies must deny the reality of an increasingly racially mixed society. Indeed, the government's difficulty in changing OMB Directive 15 must call into question the degree of confidence the public may repose in its commitment to the ideal of racial integration. It surely must at least raise a suspicion that a tolerance (if not a preference) for separatism has infiltrated and is delegitimizing a significant underpinning of affirmative action.

Counterproductive Racial Pigeonholes

Meanwhile, American social vitality defies and discredits the official racial demarcations. In spite of the stresses and strains of historic antagonisms, racial and ethnic groups continue to integrate, even in the most intimate realms of marriage and family. Although the last state anti-miscegenation laws were struck down as recently as 1967, according to the latest census data more than 4 percent of blacks, and 6 percent of black men, are married to nonblacks. Ten percent of black men aged 25–34 have entered interracial marriages, mostly with white women. Thirty percent of Hispanics are married to non-Hispanics. Transracial adoption, strongly discouraged by most state and municipal governments, has nonetheless continued to grow. A provision in the Republican "Contract with America" denies federal funds to agencies that discriminate on the basis of race in child placement. The U.S. Department of Health and Human Services, long an opponent of transracial adoption, has recently, and grudgingly, yielded to public anger over adoptable black children languishing in foster care and issued guidelines that no longer actively discourage such adoptions.

Rita Simon, an academic sociologist who studied transracial adoption for several decades, was quoted in *USA Today* as believing that "Where we come down on transracial adoption should tell us what we really think about integration and separation." She reports polling data indicating that 70 percent of blacks and whites support such adoption. Syndicated columnist Ellen Goodman writes of children like multiracial golf star Tiger Woods, who is of black, Thai, Chinese, and American Indian origins, as affording America a racial "demilitarized zone" and a bridge among the races.

But interracial marriage and transracial adoption are small indicators of the extent to which government's racial and ethnic categories fail to comport with reality, compared with the consequences of the great wave of immigration since those categories were devised. Immigration now accounts for 37 percent of national population growth. More than one million legal and illegal immigrants enter the United States every year—in absolute numbers an historic peak—with the number of countries sending immigrants rising from 21 in 1970 to 27 in 1980 to 41 in 1990. More than 150 languages are spoken in the United States, and Americans claim almost 300 racial and ethnic groups. There is even an intellectual attack on the existence of race as a scientifically reliable concept among geneticists and physical anthropologists. Stanford genetics professor Luigi Cavalli-Sforza believes that classifying by race is a "futile exercise." In a February 13 *Newsweek* poll, one-third of American blacks said that blacks should not be considered a single race.

It would be naive to view these trends as suggesting that the country has, only 30 years after the end of legally sanctioned racial segregation, reached the point where there is no further need for the interventions of government to forestall or punish continuing acts of racial discrimination and to help expand opportunity for advancement. But it is also naive to ignore the belief of opponents of affirmative action that the federal government has far exceeded the bounds of common sense in the structures it has devised to ensure equal opportunity and that indeed many of those structures, like OMB Directive 15, now impede racial integration and advancement by their overreach and by their disconnection from a changing social reality.

Betraying the Vision of an Integrated Society

The static regulatory vision of racial America is empirically outmoded. It is also antithetical to the long-term interests of blacks. Drawing voting district lines on the basis of race and other mechanisms such as those proposed by Lani Guinier, for example, furthers separation by race on so crucial an act of citizenship as voting; it trades a short-term electoral reward for the creation of the idea of permanent, irreducible, separate interests based on race, hardly a vision of an integrated society. Maintaining important permanent structures based on race posits permanent separation and therefore economically, politically, and intellectually counterproductive isolation.

It is simply not possible to reduce the salience of race by enhancing its salience. The widespread application of lower standards for academic admissions, for example, has drawn ill-prepared students in over their heads and created, by this artificially contrived mismatch of student and school, the impression of black intellectual inferiority, a reactivation of the racial stereotype most dangerous to black advancement. These admission policies have allowed white-governed institutions to "feel better about themselves" at the expense of the full development of black intellectual potential. They have produced a college dropout rate for blacks of almost two-thirds. They have led to the spectacle of a university president, however unintentionally, questioning the "genetic, hereditary" capacities of black students. They have led to speculation by the chair of the U.S. Commission on Civil Rights in congressional testimony that if tests determined college admissions and entry-level jobs, "Asians and Jewish Americans would hold the best jobs everywhere and populate almost entirely the best colleges and universities." Similar policies have led municipal police and fire departments to hire, in the 1980s, underqualified recruits who were not able to achieve promotion in the '90s, thereby creating for blacks the appearance of racist promotion policies and for whites the appearance of black incapacity. When public and private institutions have denied or obscured the practices of these admissions and hiring policies, from a concern that the beneficiaries would be embarrassed or a fear that the policies would fail of public support in the sunshine, they have created a cynical distrust about their fairness or good sense that has contributed mightily to the strength of the opposition to affirmative action.

A New Beginning

Now, uphill, good faith must be reclaimed. It would be a tragic failure of American civic genius, and a great cruelty, not to take this opportunity to think the issue of equality of opportunity anew. Along with other 30- to 50-year-old structures of government, affirmative action is crumbling under the pressure of change. But if the regulatory structure on which affirmative action relies is, at best, counterproductive to the accomplishment of the purposes informing the civil rights movement and the antidiscrimination legislation that grew out of it, what then is to be done?

New approaches should align minority interests with ascendant and longstanding American values, so they will be both powerful and sustainable. What might such approaches look like?

First, public policy should promote racial integration, not only at work and at school, but also in the home. Anything weaker will allow separatists and racists, white and black, the wedge they need to indulge the fantasy of a more "comfortable" life, which is socially, if not legally, separate. The moral vision that galvanized national support for the civil rights movement was not "separate but equal."

Second, intentional racial discrimination of the sort the Civil Rights Act of 1964 had in mind should be powerfully stigmatized and punished. The law is a teaching instrument. The moral fuzziness of affirmative action has confused this teaching and undercut it.

Third, where intellectual attainment is properly the basis for decisions, as in some but not all entry-level hiring, promotions, and academic admissions, standards should be applied nonracially with no *de facto* "race norming." That implies the probability of some near-term decline in numbers of blacks in exchange for strengthened confidence in those who, in time, achieve in equal numbers. At the same time, there must be a revitalized commitment to dramatic improvement in the quality of education. Since, for the foreseeable future, almost all students will be in the public education system, its reform must be the focus of attention. There is general agreement on much of what needs to be done. Schools should run year-round. Teachers should be hired competitively and paid accordingly. Black mayors and city councils should stop using schools as jobs programs and be willing to hire the best teachers nationally, regardless of race. Curricula should be basic, tough, challenging, and fad-free. Parents with vouchers might accomplish these and other goals.

For 20 years, public agencies have devoted extraordinary resources to assembling racially representative workforces. The next generation of policies should be clearly non-racial and announced as such. Practical ways to bring race-based hiring to an end should be developed and implemented in ways that assure continuing public confidence in public processes.

Fourth, federal regulation—fiat—to assure outcomes should generally be replaced by greater room for discretion to offer opportunity. That will transform resentful but minimal "compliance" that is taken out of the hides of "beneficiaries" in other ways, into voluntary moral acts of good citizenship and common sense. It's not naive—it's human nature. People resent losing the opportunity to do the right thing freely.

Fifth, tortured attempts to substitute additional economic for racial entitlements should be dropped; as thinly disguised generic redistributionist policies, they are entirely contrary to the thinking of the times, administratively nightmarish, and therefore not at all likely to work.

Sixth, the bourgeois practices that help poor people improve their circumstances—study, work, saving, marriage, child-bearing, in that order—should be preached, not dismissed or ridiculed as they have been since the 1960s, and rewarded in the design of public policies.

However Long It Takes

Finally, American leaders in every sector and of all races should make the same kind of commitment to racial integration they made after World War II to fighting and winning the Cold War. Affirmative action arose from an impatience that the consequences of several hundred years of slavery and discrimination could not be overcome quickly. For many, those consequences have been largely overcome. For many others, they have not. How long the effort takes is less important than that it be headed in the right direction.

New directions, embodied in values and practices that have worked for America before, may help solve the problems of race in ways that can be sustained. If sustained, they will provide a model for other societies facing worse divisions and internal conflict.

Enough

We have an immigration policy that has no definable objective and fails to express a national interest.

Richard D. Lamm

RICHARD D. LAMM, former governor of Colorado, is director of the Center for Public Policy and Contemporary Issues at the University of Denver. This article was adapted from a speech to the Harris Bank Family Conference.

Illustration by Wojciech Wolynski

Joseph Stalin once said: "A single death is a tragedy, a million deaths is a statistic." Used in the health-care context, the quote intrigues me. In American health care, we have the rule of rescue and will go to unfathomable expense to save an individual, yet we have more than 30 million people without basic health insurance.

Society's focus on the individual often conflicts with what should be the ends of social policy. Does the right of a homeless person to loiter in a public library supersede the right of the rest of society to use the library in safety and in comfort? Does the right of a welfare mother to have additional children take precedence over the taxpayers' interest in her not having more kids?

It is a dilemma that we find when we try to formulate our immigration policies as well. Should we give greater weight to the interest of the individual immigrant, who simply wants to improve his or her life by settling in the United States, than to the interest society has in limiting immigration?

To govern is to choose. Yet choosing does not come easy to Americans: Our whole cultural heritage is that we can do everything for everybody. The idea of any limit is abhorrent.

But by not having the maturity to ask hard questions about our limited resources, we are not only doing many people injustice—we are doing the future injustice. We are stealing from our children's heritage.

This kind of lack of forethought or consideration of consequences has been the hallmark of our immigration policy for decades. Factoring in legal immigration, admission of refugees, political-asylum seekers, and illegal immigrants who settle permanently, the United States now admits between 1.2 million and 1.4 million people a year.

These are abstract numbers, so let me put them into context. I live in Denver, a city of approximately half a million people. In other words, our immigration policies are responsible for the equivalent of a new Denver every five months, with no end in sight.

What's even more astounding is that nobody really seems to know why. It is perhaps the only important public policy that has no definable objective. We cannot even articulate a national interest here. Ask the people who make the immigration laws why we have large-scale immigration and your response is likely to be a platitude: "We're a nation of immigrants," or someone will recite Emma Lazarus' poem.

Thus, as far as anyone can discern, we are adding a new Denver every five months out of habit, or because a 17-year-old wrote a nice poem in 1883. We have an immigration policy that is doomed to fail because nobody knows what we're aiming for, because we have never even defined what a successful immigration policy might be. And, like so many of our other failures, it will be our children and grandchildren who will live with the consequences of our unwillingness to even think about what we're doing.

When you see an immigrant on television, our whole heritage says we must be doing the right thing. But I increasingly question whether we are. Of the 160 countries that belong to the United Nations, only three take any appreciable number of legal immigrants. The United States takes about 1 million a year, Canada takes about 150,000 a year, and Australia takes about 125,000. So, perhaps 1.25 million people in a total pool of 5 billion are lucky enough to come to one of the immigrant-receiving countries. Yet that pool increases about 90 million people a year, almost all of the increase in underdeveloped countries.

The maximum amount of "good" that the immigrant-receiving countries can do—to alleviate the pressures on those countries to where people want to migrate—is infinitesimally small—less than .05 percent. We may be able to save a few highly identified individuals who appear on the evening news. But in terms of alleviating the pressures of world population, economic disruption, revolts, and revolutions, it is ridiculously small. Most people will have to solve their problems within their countries of origin. In an increasingly crowded world, we have to take great care not to engender unrealistic expectations.

The United States accepted more than 9 million immigrants during the 1980s. In contrast to its European and Asian trading partners, the United States is the only major nation accepting large numbers of newcomers. We backed into this role as the major destination of immigrants without planning for the current wave of newcomers who are crowding our metropolitan areas and posing massive problems for our health and educational institutions. Yet today, many voices from the right and left are heard arguing for more and more immigration. One commentator said it well: "The conservatives love their cheap labor; the liberals love their cheap cause."

Unfortunately, advocates of more immigration often confuse "pro-immigrant" and "pro-immigration." I am strongly "pro-immigrant" and favor assisting those already here to join our mainstream as soon as possible. I also believe that it is necessary to reduce the number of future immigrants if we are to adequately assist those already here.

Why do I, along with a significant majority of the American people (according to recent polls), favor a reduction in immigration levels? First, the presence of newcomers in such large numbers makes it impossible to deal with America's poor (whether native-born or immigrants) com-

> **Personal liberty, the ability to "do our own thing," is very much dependent on the size of our population. The more people we have, the more rules and regulations we require.**

passionately and effectively. The United States has a large and growing number of people—especially in the inner cities—with weak ties to the labor market but strong links to welfare programs, crime, and drugs. Many immigrants in these cities gain a foothold in the labor market and then preserve the status quo because they do not complain about inferior wages or working conditions.

As long as eager immigrants are available, private employers are not going to make the difficult and costly adjustments needed to employ the American underclass. Instead, they continue to operate their sweatshops and complain about the unwillingness of Americans with welfare and other options to be enthusiastic seamstresses or hotel maids alongside the

immigrants. If we are to end "welfare as we now know it," we must end "immigration as we now know it."

Armies of Marginal People

At a time when American minorities, Latino as well as black, suffer from double-digit unemployment, I believe it is immoral to continue accepting so many newcomers to compete with Americans for the jobs that are available. A tight labor market is a great friend to the poor.

Hannah Arendt once observed that there is nothing more dangerous to a society than to have large numbers of human beings who are not economically vital. With or without immigration, changing technology and an increasingly global economy are marginalizing large segments of people in our society.

We see evidence of it every day, in the once self-sufficient blue-collar worker struggling to hang on and doing menial labor for menial wages, and in the proliferation of homeless, who have ceased to have even marginal value to our economy. These people already pose a monumental challenge to our society: Armies of people who have no personal stake in the current order, and a society that has no real use for such people, constitute a formula for disaster, as Arendt warned.

The jobs that used to give the less educated in our country a stake in our society—the ability to contribute, to own a home, a college education for their children—are being lost to global competition. At a time when we should be engaging in a national effort to retrain such workers, to make them economically vital, we are doing something far different. We are forcing them to compete with a constantly growing pool of immigrant labor that further drives down wages and working conditions for those jobs that remain.

The second reason for reducing immigration is that the availability of such workers steers some of the economy in a losing direction. American products have to compete in international markets. The United States' competitive edge can be technological sophistication, quality and reliability, or price. Although large numbers of unskilled immigrants may help American businesses hold down wages and thus prices in order to remain competitive, a low-wage and low-price strategy simply cannot succeed in the global economy. Developing countries are becoming more adept at producing goods, such as garments and agricultural products, that are currently made in the United States by immigrant workers. Consequently, even wages low by U.S. standards are not low enough to compete with Malaysian seamstresses or Mexican farm workers.

Industries that rely on immigrant workers are often slow to innovate, and when developing countries ship similar products produced at even lower wages to the United States, these American businesses often turn protectionist. The result is familiar. The American industry that "needed" immigrant workers to survive and to ensure, for example, that grapes do not cost $2 a pound soon complains that cheaper foreign grapes threaten the survival of the American grape industry. The industry asks for restrictions on imports, which drives up consumer prices.

The third reason for limiting immigration is to ease the adaptation of newcomers into American society and facilitate their acceptance by the resident population. Earlier immigration waves contributed to positive changes in

American culture; many of us here today are second- and third-generation Americans justly proud of our heritage and our ancestors' contributions to American society. However, the immigration wave at the turn of the 20th century ended after 25 years, partly due to war and depression and also because of the 1920s' restrictive legislation. As a result, immigration dropped from more than 1 million annually in 1908-09 to fewer than 100,000 in the 1930s. No such abrupt end to current immigration is in sight.

The immigration laws of the 1920s were racist and are an embarrassing blot on the American conscience. Yet, by limiting the admission of newcomers, the new immigrants were encouraged to adapt to American society. And within two generations, they adapted with a vengeance—and, in the process, improved society. Tsongas is now as American as Clinton. Valdez is as common as Smith.

Today, with immigration increasing year after year, it is difficult for new Americans to adapt to the United States as did previous immigrants. Rather, the old norms and languages are reinforced in ever-growing ethnic enclaves; in Miami, according to the 1990 census, more than half of the population speaks English poorly or not at all.

Could We Become Another India?

The fourth reason to reduce immigration is to slow down rapid population growth. We are the world's fastest-growing industrial nation, adding about 3 million people annually. If current demographic trends continue, with fertility once again above 2.0 and immigration levels surpassing 1 million annually, thanks to the 1990 legislation, our population could approach half a billion by 2050, or 145 million more people than today. Demographers Dennis Ahlburg and J.W. Vaupel foresee a population of 811 million by 2080—bigger than India today!

Recently National Public Radio aired a piece about politics in India, featuring an Indian professor's comment that ought to serve as a warning to those of us in America. The professor began by saying: "We are the world's largest democracy. But because India is so overpopulated, Indians have very few personal freedoms."

Personal liberty, the ability to "do our own thing," is very much dependent on the size of our population. The more people we have, the more rules and regulations we require to govern what we do, when we do it, how we do it, and where it can be done. When everyone is living cheek to jowl, it becomes impossible for you to do your own thing without it impinging on me.

As we grow not just in numbers but in terms of people of different cultures living side by side, the tensions of overpopulation become even greater. A difficult situation is made all the more difficult because we begin to lose consensus about how members of a crowded society should co-exist.

Our infrastructure is already deteriorating; rapid population growth exacerbates this deterioration by increasing the burden on roads and water systems and creating demands for schools and other types of public investment. Americans are concerned about environmental issues, about air and water quality, and while population growth is not necessar-ily the major cause of environmental problems, more people are certainly an accomplice. Quality of life can improve faster with reduced population growth.

We must place our emphasis on helping those in need—where they are. In 1990, 58 percent of the $400 million that the United States committed to assisting refugees was spent to resettle 125,000 refugees in this country. By contrast, what we spent to help the 99 percent of world refugees we did *not* resettle amounted to a paltry four cents a day per capita. Resettling a few while neglecting the many is at best stupid and at worst immoral.

In addition to what we spent resettling a handful of refugees, the federal government spent (according to the Center for Immigration Studies) in excess of $2 billion in 1990 to take care of the needs of recent immigrants. By all indications, those costs are rising rapidly. California reports that it spent $700 million last year on health care to illegal aliens. That's not the cost for all immigrants in the state—that's just the health-care bill for people in the country illegally to begin with.

From the viewpoint of the recently resettled refugee or immigrant, these have been resources well spent. For the countless millions barely surviving in Third World shanty-towns, it was a gross miscalculation of resources.

What Controversy?

The underclass, the economic trajectory, cultural adaptation, and population growth are four reasons why the United States should reevaluate its immigration policy. Legal immigration should be limited to no more than 300,000 people a year—a level that the majority of Americans feel comfortable with.

We have an opportunity now for comprehensive immigration reform—and that is what is needed, a top-to-bottom overhaul of our immigration policies.

During the last session of Congress, we saw the first encouraging moves in that direction. For the first time in nearly 30 years, legislation was introduced to reform a policy that most Americans agree does not serve the interests of our nation. Even more encouraging, these first attempts at serious immigration reform had bipartisan support.

Limiting legal immigration and halting illegal immigration are often perceived as controversial issues. Quite the contrary: On practically no other public-policy matter is there greater political consensus among the American people. With a new Congress, with a clear message from the voters of California, and with the start of the 1996 presidential campaign, we have an opportunity to make some real reforms in the next two years.

One way or the other, our immigration dilemma will be resolved.

As George Kennan has suggested, it will be resolved either by rational decisions at this end—or by the achievement of some sort of a balance of misery between this country and the vast pools of poverty that confront it. The choice is ours to make, and the longer we put it off, the more difficult it will be to make those rational decisions—and the more certain it will be that the balance of misery will be achieved.

What To Do About Affirmative Action

Arch Puddington

ARCH PUDDINGTON is senior scholar at Freedom House. He writes frequently on American race relations. The present article is the eleventh in a series by diverse authors which was inaugurated in September 1994.

THE thinking behind the policy of racial preference which has been followed in America over the past quarter-century under the name of "affirmative action"* is best summed up by former Supreme Court Justice Harry Blackmun's famous dictum that, "In order to get beyond racism, we must first take race into account."

The Orwellian quality of Blackmun's admonition is obvious. Seldom has a democratic government's policy so completely contradicted the core values of its citizenry as racial preference does in violating the universally held American ideals of fairness and individual rights, including the right to be free from discrimination. Not surprisingly, then, where Americans regarded the original civil-rights legislation as representing a long-overdue fulfillment of the country's democratic promise, they overwhelmingly see racial preference as an undemocratic and alien concept, a policy implemented by stealth and subterfuge and defended by duplicity and legalistic tricks.

Americans do not believe that past discrimination against blacks in the workplace justifies

present discrimination against whites. Nor do they accept the thesis that tests and standards are tainted, *en masse*, by cultural bias against minorities. Having been taught in high-school civics classes that gerrymandering to ensure party domination represents a defect in democracy, Americans are bewildered by the argument that gerrymandering is necessary to ensure the political representation of blacks and Hispanics. They are unimpressed by the contention that a university's excellence is enhanced by the mere fact of racial and ethnic diversity in its student body, especially when entrance requirements must be lowered substantially to achieve that goal.

Americans, in short, oppose racial preference in all its embodiments, and have signified their opposition in opinion poll after opinion poll, usually by margins of three to one or more, with women as strongly opposed as men, and with an impressive proportion of blacks indicating opposition as well. The contention, repeatedly advanced by advocates of preferential policies, that a national consensus exists in support of such policies has been true only at the level of political elites. Americans do support what might be called soft affirmative action, entailing special recruitment, training, and outreach efforts, and are willing to accept some short-term compensatory measures to rectify obvious cases of proven discrimination. But attitudes have, if anything, hardened against the kind of aggressive, numbers-driven preference schemes increasingly encountered in university admissions and civil-service hiring.

NONETHELESS, up until this year, racial preference in its various manifestations has been impressively resistant to calls for reform, much less elimination. In fact, race consciousness has begun to insinuate itself into areas which, common sense alone would suggest,

---

* Affirmative action has, of course, been extended to women and certain other groups, but I will confine the discussion here to race. Affirmative action was devised primarily to promote the economic status of blacks, and the racial implications of the debate over this policy are far more significant than questions arising from preferences for women or other ethnic minorities. I should add that if preference for black Americans is unjustified, there is even less to be said for it when applied to women or to such immigrant groups as Hispanics and Asians.

should be immune to intrusive government social engineering. To cite but one example of this disturbing trend: Congress has mandated that guidelines be established guaranteeing the involvement of minorities (and women) in clinical research—a form of scientific experimentation by quota.

There is, furthermore, reason to question whether the advocates of race-conscious social policy continue to take seriously the objective of getting "beyond race," a condition which presumably would warrant the elimination of all preferential programs. The late Thurgood Marshall, an outspoken champion of preference while on the Supreme Court, is reported to have blurted out during an in-chambers discussion that blacks would need affirmative action for a hundred years. A similar opinion has been expressed by Benjamin Hooks, the former director of the National Association for the Advancement of Colored People (NAACP). Hooks contends that affirmative action in some form should be accepted as one of those permanent, irritating features of American life—he cited as examples speeding laws and the April 15 income-tax deadline— which citizens tolerate as essential to the efficient and just functioning of society.

Neither Marshall nor Hooks is regarded as an extremist on race matters; their advocacy of a permanent regime of affirmative action falls within the mainstream of present-day liberal thought. The promotion of "diversity"—the latest euphemism for preferential representation—is as fundamental to liberal governance as was the protection of labor unions in an earlier era. And until very recently, liberal proponents of preference clearly believed that history was on their side.

Thus, where enforcement agencies were formerly cautious in pressing affirmative action on the medical profession, the Clinton administration was formulating plans for a quota system throughout the health-care workforce. The goal, according to one memo of Hillary Clinton's task force, was nothing less than to ensure that this workforce achieve "sufficient racial, ethnic, gender, geographic, and cultural diversity to be representative of the people it serves." The task force also had plans to guide minority doctors into specialties while tracking other doctors into general practice. To realize this medical-care diversity blueprint, the task force proposed the creation of a bureaucracy with coercive powers to regulate the "geographic" and "cultural" distribution of physicians and other medical practitioners.

How did America drift from the ideal of a color-blind society to the current environment of quotas, goals, timetables, race-norming, set-asides, diversity-training, and the like?

Those troubled by this question often refer wistfully to Martin Luther King, Jr.'s declaration that he hoped to see the day when his children would be judged by the content of their character and not by the color of their skin. Yet it must be recognized that even when King uttered those inspirational words at the 1963 March on Washington, they no longer reflected the thinking of crucial segments of the civil-rights movement. Already, increasingly influential black activists and their white supporters were advancing demands for hiring plans based on racial quotas. In pressing for such plans (then called compensatory treatment), the civil-rights movement was being joined by officials from the Kennedy administration, as well as by white intellectuals who, going further, announced that black economic equality could never be attained without a wholesale adjustment of standards and the merit principle.

These ruminations were not lost on the Dixiecrat opponents of desegregation, and the charge was soon made that Title VII of the pending civil-rights bill—the section dealing with discrimination in the workplace—would lead to the widespread practice of reverse discrimination. This in turn provoked a series of statements and speeches by stalwart liberals like Senators Hubert Humphrey, Joseph Clark, and Clifford Case, adamantly and unequivocally denying that the bill could be interpreted to permit racial preference.

In order to dispel lingering doubts, Humphrey and other supporters inserted an amendment to the bill declaring flatly that the law's purpose was to rectify cases of intentional discrimination and that it was not intended to impose sanctions simply because a workplace contained few blacks or because few blacks passed an employment test. Armed with this and similar clauses prohibiting reverse discrimination, Humphrey promised to "start eating the pages [of the civil-rights bill] one after another" if anyone could discover language in it "which provides that an employer will have to hire on the basis of percentage or quota."

Under normal circumstances, the insertion of unambiguous anti-preference language, combined with the condemnations of reverse discrimination by the bill's sponsors, would have been sufficient to prevent the subsequent distortion of the law's intent. But these protections turned out to be useless against the determination of the country's elites (in the political system, in the media, in the universities, and in the courts) to override them. Having concluded (especially after the urban riots of the late 60's) that social peace demanded racial preference, political leaders from both parties, along with a growing number of intellectuals and activists, both white and black, began looking upon the anti-preference clauses in Title VII as obstacles to be circumvented rather than guides to be followed. The anti-preference language which had been added to ensure passage of the Civil Rights Act of

1964 was now not only ignored but treated as though it did not even exist.

Hence there was no serious effort by either Congress or the courts or anyone else to rein in the civil-rights bureaucracy, which dismissed the anti-preference provisions with contempt from the very outset. A "big zero, a nothing, a nullity," is how these provisions were characterized by an official of the Equal Employment Opportunity Commission (EEOC) at the time. Federal enforcement officials in general, most of whom were white, were more aggressive in pursuing preferences, and less inclined to reflect on the broader implications of affirmative action, than were many mainstream black leaders of that day, some of whom—Roy Wilkins, Bayard Rustin, and Clarence Mitchell, for example—opposed reverse discrimination on moral and political grounds.

The part played by the EEOC in putting together the structure of racial preference cannot be overstated. In blithe and conscious disregard of the anti-preference sections of Title VII, EEOC officials broadened the definition of discrimination to encompass anything which contributed to unequal outcomes. In its most far-reaching move, the EEOC launched an all-out assault on employment testing. The agency's mindset was reflected in comments about "irrelevant and unreasonable standards," "the cult of credentialism," and "artificial barriers."

Yet despite the ingenuity of its lawyers in devising intricate arguments to circumvent the strictures against reverse discrimination—and despite the willingness of activist judges to accept these arguments—the EEOC could never have achieved its aims had it not been for a transformation of elite attitudes toward the problem of race in America.

In 1964, the year the Civil Rights Act was passed, an optimistic and morally confident America believed that the challenge posed by the "Negro revolution" could be met through a combination of anti-discrimination laws, economic growth, and the voluntary good will of corporations, universities, and other institutions. But by the decade's end, a crucial segment of elite opinion had concluded that America was deeply flawed, even sick, and that racism, conscious or otherwise, permeated every institution and government policy. Where individual prejudice had previously been identified as the chief obstacle to black progress, now a new target, "institutional racism," was seen as the principal villain. And where it was once thought that democratic guarantees against discrimination, plus the inherent fairness of the American people, were sufficient to overcome injustice, the idea now took hold that since racism was built into the social order, coercive measures were required to root it out.

In this view, moreover, the gradualist Great Society approach launched by Lyndon Johnson, which stressed education, training, and the strengthening of black institutions, could not alleviate the misery of the inner-city poor, at least not as effectively as forcing employers to hire them. Even Johnson himself began calling for affirmative action and issued an executive order directing that federal contractors adopt hiring policies which did not discriminate on the basis of race (or gender); in a process that would soon become all too familiar, court decisions and the guidelines of regulators subsequently interpeted the directive as mandating racial balance in the workforce, thus paving the way for demands that companies doing business with the government institute what often amounted to quotas in order to qualify for contracts.

Little noticed at the time—or, for that matter, later—was that black America was in the midst of a period of unprecedented economic progress, during which black poverty declined, the racial income gap substantially narrowed, black college enrollment mushroomed, and black advancement into the professions took a substantial leap forward. All this, it should be stressed, occurred *prior* to the introduction of government-mandated racial preference.

Once affirmative action got going, there was no holding it back. The civil-rights movement and those responsible for implementing civil-rights policy simply refused to accept an approach under which preference would be limited to cases of overt discrimination, or applied to a narrow group of crucial institutions, such as urban police departments, where racial integration served a pressing public need. Instead, every precedent was exploited to further the permanent entrenchment of race consciousness.

For example, the Philadelphia Plan, the first preferential policy to enjoy presidential backing (the President being Richard Nixon), was a relatively limited effort calling for racial quotas in the Philadelphia building trades, an industry with a notorious record of racial exclusion. Yet this limited program was seized upon by the EEOC and other agencies as a basis for demanding hiring-by-the-numbers schemes throughout the economy, whether or not prior discrimination could be proved.

Similarly, once a race-conscious doctrine was applied to one institution, it inevitably expanded its reach into other arenas. The Supreme Court's decision in *Griggs* v. *Duke Power, Inc.*—that employment tests could be found to constitute illegal discrimination if blacks failed at a higher rate than whites—was ostensibly confined to hiring and promotion. But *Griggs* was used to legitimize the burgeoning movement against testing and standards in the educational world as well. Tracking by intellectual ability, special classes for high achievers, selective high schools requiring admissions tests, standardized examinations for university admissions—all were accused of perpetuating historic patterns of bias.

The campaign against testing and merit in turn gave rise to a series of myths about the economy, the schools, the workplace, about America itself. Thus, lowering job standards as a means of hiring enough blacks to fill a quota was justified on the grounds that merit had never figured prominently in the American workplace, that the dominant principles had always been nepotism, back-scratching, and conformism. To explain the racial gap in Scholastic Aptitude Test scores, the concept of cultural bias was advanced, according to which disparities in results derived from the tests' emphasis on events and ideas alien to urban black children. Another theory claimed that poor black children were not accustomed to speaking standard English and were therefore placed at a disadvantage in a normal classroom environment. It was duly proposed that black children be taught much like immigrant children, with bilingual classes in which both standard English and black English would be utilized. A related theory stated that black children retained a distinct learning style which differed in significant respects from the learning styles of other children. As one educator expressed the theory, any test which stressed "logical, analytical methods of problem-solving" would *ipso facto* be biased against blacks.

UNTIL quite recently, the very idea of abolishing racial preference was unthinkable; the most realistic ambitions for the critics of race-based social policy went no further than trying to limit—limit, not stop—the apparently relentless spread of racial preferences throughout the economy, the schools and universities, and the political system. Yet it now appears not only that the momentum of racial preference has been halted, but that, at a minimum, a part of the imposing affirmative-action edifice will be dismantled. Furthermore, a process has already been set in motion which could conceivably lead to the virtual elimination of race-based programs.

Racial preferences have become vulnerable mainly because of the sudden collapse of the elite consensus which always sustained affirmative action in the face of popular opposition. Where in the past many Republicans could be counted on to support, or at least tolerate, racial preferences, the new congressional majority seems much more inclined to take a sharply critical look at existing racial policies. Equally important is the erosion of support for preference within the Democratic party. While some newly skeptical Democrats are clearly motivated by worries about reelection, others have welcomed the opportunity to express long-suppressed reservations about policies which

they see as having corrupted, divided, and weakened their party.

The revolt against affirmative action has also been heavily influenced by the fact that, as preferential policies have extended throughout the economy, a critical mass of real or perceived victims of reverse discrimination has been reached—white males who have been denied jobs, rejected for promotion, or prevented from attending the college or professional school of their choice because slots were reserved for blacks (or other minorities or women).

There is, no doubt, an inclination on the part of white men to blame affirmative action when they are passed over for jobs or promotions, a tendency which is reinforced by the atmosphere of secrecy surrounding most preference programs. But enough is known about affirmative action in the public sector through information which has come out in the course of litigation to conclude that thousands of whites have indeed been passed over for civil-service jobs and university admissions because of outright quotas for racial minorities. It is also clear that a considerable number of private businesses have been denied government contracts because of minority set-asides.

Another major factor in the change of attitude toward affirmative action is the California Civil Rights Initiative (CCRI), which has already had an incalculable impact. The CCRI was organized by two white, male, and politically moderate professors in the California state-university system. The measure would amend the California constitution to prohibit the state government or any state agency (including the university system) from granting preference on the basis of race, ethnicity, or gender in employment, college admissions, or the awarding of contracts. It would, in other words, effectively ban affirmative-action programs mandated by the state.

Though limited to California, the CCRI is at heart a response to the logical destination of affirmative action everywhere in America: quota systems sustained by the support of elites from both political parties. To be sure, policy by racial classification has grown more pervasive in California than elsewhere in America. White males have been told not to bother applying for positions with the Los Angeles fire department due to the need to fill minority quotas. In San Francisco, Chinese students are denied admission to a selective public high school because of an ethnic cap; for similar reasons, whites, mainly Jews and East European immigrants, are often denied admission to magnet schools in Los Angeles. A de facto quota system effectively denies white males the opportunity to compete for faculty positions at certain state colleges. And, incredibly enough, the state legislature passed a bill calling for ethnic "guidelines" not only for admission to the state-university system but for graduation as well.

The bill was vetoed by Governor Pete Wilson; had a Democrat been governor, it would almost certainly have become law.

The true impact of the CCRI can be gauged by the degree of fear it has generated among supporters of affirmative action. So long as the debate could be limited to the courts, the agencies of race regulation, and, when unavoidable, the legislative arena, affirmative action was secure. The mere threat of taking the issue directly to the voters, as the CCRI's sponsors propose to do through the referendum process, has elicited a downright panicky response—itself a clear indication that the advocates of racial preference understand how unpopular their case is, and how weak.

BUT a note of caution must be sounded to those who believe that current developments will lead inexorably to the reinstitution of color-blindness as the reigning principle in racial matters. The resilience of affirmative action in the face of widespread popular hostility suggests that even a modest change of course could prove a difficult and highly divisive affair.

There is, to begin with, the fact that affirmative action has been introduced largely by skirting the normal democratic process of debate and legislative action. Affirmative action is by now rooted in literally thousands of presidential directives, court decisions, enforcement-agency guidelines, and regulatory rules. These will not easily be overturned.

There is also the complicating factor of the federal judiciary's central role in overseeing racial policy. Given the emotionally charged character of the racial debate, the critics of racial preference will be tempted to postpone legislative action in the hope that the Supreme Court will resolve the issue once and for all. But while the Court today is less prone to judicial activism than during the Warren and Burger years, and while it may decide to limit the conditions under which a preferential program can be applied, it is unlikely to do away with affirmative action altogether.

The Republicans will face another temptation: to exploit white hostility to racial preference but avoid serious political action to eliminate it. A powerful political logic lies behind this temptation, since getting rid of affirmative action would also deprive the Republicans of a potent wedge issue. Yet one can hardly imagine a less desirable outcome than a prolonged and angry political confrontation over race. Moreover, if responsible politicians who share a principled opposition to preference decline to take the initiative, the door will be opened to racists and unscrupulous demagogues.

An additional obstacle to change is the fact that eliminating affirmative action does not offer much of a financial payoff. Affirmative action is not expensive; its only direct cost to the taxpayer is the expense of maintaining civil-rights agencies like the EEOC.

Claims have been made that affirmative action does represent a major cost to the American economy, but the facts are unclear since neither the media nor scholarly researchers nor the corporations themselves have shown an interest in undertaking an investigation of its economic impact. Indeed, though affirmative action is one of the most intensely discussed social issues of the day, it is probably the least researched. Press coverage is generally limited to the political debate; seldom are stories done about the actual functioning of affirmative-action programs. Nor is there much serious scholarly investigation of such questions as affirmative action's impact on employee morale, the performance of students admitted to college on an affirmative-action track, or the degree to which contract set-asides have contributed to the establishment of stable minority businesses.

Given the truly massive amount of research devoted to racial issues over the years, the lack of attention to preferential policies raises the suspicion that what has been operating here is a deliberate decision to avoid knowing the details of affirmative action's inner workings out of fear of the public reaction.

OPPONENTS of racial preference must also contend with the widespread acceptance of the "diversity" principle within certain key institutions. Here the American university stands out for its uncritical embrace of the notion that, as one recent cliché has it, "diversity is part of excellence." When Francis Lawrence, the president of Rutgers University, came under fire for uttering the now-famous phrase which seemed to question the genetic capabilities of black students, his principal defense—indeed practically his only defense—was that he had increased minority enrollment at Rutgers and during a previous administrative stint at Tulane. True to form, no one bothered to ask how black students recruited under Lawrence's diversity initiatives had fared academically or psychologically, or how the campus racial atmosphere had been affected, or how much standards had been adjusted to achieve the quota. The body count, and the body count alone, was what mattered for Lawrence, and, it would seem, for administrators at many campuses.

The diversity principle is also firmly entrenched throughout government service. Most agencies include a diversity or affirmative-action department, headed by an official with deputy-level status, with intrusive authority to promote staff "balance" and minority participation in contract bidding. So, too, private corporations have accepted affirmative action as part of the price of doing business. Large corporations, in fact, can usually be counted on to oppose anti-quota legislation, preferring the simplicity of hiring by the numbers to the uncertainty of more flexible systems and the increased possibilities of anti-discrimination litigation brought by minorities or by whites claiming reverse bias.

But of course the most serious obstacle to change is black America's strong attachment to affirmative action. Race-conscious policies have had no demonstrable effect at all on the black poor, but they are widely perceived as having played a crucial role in creating the first mass black middle class in American history. The claim here is wildly exaggerated—to repeat, the trend was already well advanced before affirmative action got going. Nevertheless, to many blacks, affirmative action has become not a series of temporary benefits but a basic civil right, almost as fundamental as the right to eat at a restaurant or live in the neighborhood of one's choice, and certainly more important than welfare.

Accordingly, black leaders, who are always quick to condemn even the most modest changes as "turning back the clock" or as a threat to the gains of the civil-rights movement, have now escalated the counterattack in response to the more sweeping recent challenge to affirmative action. When Governor Pete Wilson made some favorable comments about the CCRI, Jesse Jackson compared him to George Wallace blocking the schoolhouse door in Jim Crow Alabama. And when congressional Republicans moved to rescind a set-aside program in the communications industry, Representative Charles Rangel, a Democrat from Harlem, declared that the move reflected a Nazi-like mindset.

It is true that many blacks are ambivalent about preferences, or even critical of them. At the same time, however, they are highly sensitive to perceptions of white assaults on civil rights, and they may well find polemics of the Jackson and Rangel variety persuasive.

CONFRONTED with all these obstacles, some opponents of affirmative action are leaning toward a compromise strategy involving a program-by-program review. This would be a serious mistake; the most desirable and politically effective course would be federal legislation modeled on the CCRI. Such a measure would leave in place the old laws against discrimination but would eliminate all federal programs which extend preference on the basis of race (as well as ethnicity or gender).

The measure could conceivably take the form of a reaffirmation of the sections of the 1964 Civil Rights Act dealing with the workplace, with special emphasis on the clauses explicitly prohibiting reverse discrimination. But whatever the specific shape of the new legislation, absolute clarity would be required on the principal issue: there would be no room for fudging, vagueness, or loopholes on the question of bringing the era

of race-conscious social policy to a close. The legislation would therefore also have to include an explicit disavowal of the disparate-impact doctrine, under which the disproportionate representation of the races (or sexes) is often regarded as evidence in itself of discrimination, and which has often led to the imposition of de-facto quota systems.

The political struggle over this kind of sweeping legislation would be angry and unpleasant. But eliminating both the practice of racial preference and the controversy surrounding it would set the stage for an ultimate improvement in the racial environment throughout American society. On the other hand, an approach focusing on a program-by-program review of the multitude of preference initiatives in an ephemeral search for compromise only guarantees the permanence both of affirmative action itself and of the affirmative-action controversy.

A less sweeping but nevertheless useful approach would be a presidential decree revoking the executive order issued by President Johnson which opened the way to federally-mandated quotas. Though (as we have seen) Johnson did not necessarily intend this to happen, the fact is that his directive became a crucial pillar of the affirmative-action structure. With the stroke of a pen it could be rescinded.

So far as the universities are concerned, the elimination of affirmative action would mean an end to lowering standards in order to fill racial quotas. No doubt this would also mean a smaller number of blacks at the elite universities, but there are perfectly decent state colleges and private institutions for every promising student whose qualifications do not meet the standards of Yale or Stanford. The notion that a degree from one of these institutions consigns the graduate to a second-class career is based on sheer prejudice and myth; for evidence to the contrary, one need look no further than the new Republican congressional delegation, which includes a number of graduates from what would be considered second- or third-tier colleges.

It hardly needs to be added that directing a student to a university for which he is educationally and culturally unprepared benefits neither the student nor the university nor the goal of integration. The results are already clear to see in the sorry state of race relations on campus. Many colleges are dominated by an environment of racial balkanization, with blacks increasingly retreating into segregated dormitories and black student unions, rejecting contacts with white students out of fear of ostracism by other blacks, and then complaining of the loneliness and isolation of campus life. Drop-out rates for those admitted on affirmative-action tracks are high, adding to black student frustration. These problems are invariably exacerbated by college administrators who respond to racial discontent with speech codes, sensitivity training, multicultural seminars, curriculum changes, and other aggressively prosecuted diversity initiatives.

Some have proposed basing affirmative action in university admissions on social class—that is, extending preferences to promising students from impoverished backgrounds, broken homes, and similar circumstances. On a superficial level, this would seem a sensible idea. Blacks would profit because they suffer disproportionately from poverty. Universities would gain from the high motivation of the students selected for the program. And real diversity would be enhanced by the presence of students whose backgrounds differed radically from the middle- and upper-class majority, and whose opinions could not be so predictably categorized along the conformist race (and gender) lines which dominate campus discussion today.

One major caveat is that college administrators, who give every indication of total commitment to the present race-based arrangements, would discover ways to circumvent a program based on color-blind standards. Indeed, they have already done so. Under the terms of the *Bakke* case (1978), which established the guidelines for affirmative action in university admissions, race could be counted as one of several factors, including social class; affirmative action based on race alone, the Supreme Court said, could not pass muster. As matters have evolved, affirmative action on many state campuses, most notably those in California, is based almost exclusively on race and ethnicity.

A similar class-based formula is difficult to envision outside the realm of university admissions. Yet there is no reason to assume that private businesses would respond to the elimination of government-enforced affirmative action by refusing to hire and promote qualified blacks. A return to race-neutral government policies would also enable black executives and professionals to shed the affirmative-action stigma, since no one would suspect that they were in their positions only as the result of pressure by a federal agency. The supporters of preferential policies may dismiss affirmative action's psychological effects on the beneficiaries as unimportant. But the evidence indicates that the image of a black professional class having risen up the career ladder through a special racial track is a source of serious workplace demoralization for members of the black middle class.

THE arguments which have lately been advanced in favor of retaining affirmative action are by and large the same arguments that were made more than twenty years ago, when the intellectual debate over preference began.

Probably the least compelling of these is the contention that the advantages extended by uni-versity admissions offices to athletes, the children of alumni, and applicants from certain regions of the country justify extending similar advantages on the basis of race. The answer to this contention is simple: race is different from other criteria. America acknowledged the unique nature of racial discrimination when it enacted the landmark civil-rights laws of the 1960's. Moreover, the suggestion cannot be sustained that outlawing preference based on race while permitting preference based on nonracial standards would leave blacks even farther behind. Blacks, in fact, benefit disproportionately from admissions preferences for athletes or those with talents in music and art. No one objects, or thinks it unusual or wrong for some groups to be overrepresented and others to be underrepresented on the basis of such criteria.

A similar, but even weaker, argument (already alluded to above) holds that America has never functioned as a strict meritocracy, and that white males have maintained their economic dominance through connections, pull, and family. Affirmative action, this theory goes, simply levels the playing field and actually strengthens meritocracy by expanding the pool of talent from which an employer draws. The problem is that those who advance this argument seem to assume that only white males rely on personal relationships or kinship. Yet as we have learned from the experience of immigrants throughout American history, every racial and ethnic group values family and group ties. Korean-American shop-owners enlist their families, Haitian-American taxi fleets hire their friends.

What about the claim that affirmative action has improved the racial climate by hastening the integration of the workplace and classroom? While the integration process has often been painful and disruptive, there is no question that more contact between the races at school and at work has made America a better society. But integration has not always succeeded, and the most signal failures have occurred under conditions of government coercion, whether through busing schemes or the imposition of workplace quotas. In case after case, the source of failed integration can be traced to white resentment over racial preference or the fears of blacks that they will be perceived as having attained their positions through the preferential track.*

There is, finally, the argument that, since black children suffer disproportionately from poor nutrition, crack-addicted parents, wrenching poverty, and outright discrimination, affirmative action rightly compensates for the burden of being born black in America. Yet affirmative action has

---

* An important exception is the military, where affirmative action is applied to promotions but where standards have not been lowered to enlarge the pool of qualified black applicants.

been almost entirely irrelevant to these children, who rarely attend college or seek a professional career. The new breed of Republican conservatives may sometimes betray a disturbing ignorance of the history of racial discrimination in America. But on one crucial issue they are most certainly right: the march toward equality begins at birth, with the structure, discipline, and love of a family. The wide array of government-sponsored compensatory programs, including affirmative action, has proved uniformly ineffective in meeting the awesome challenge of inner-city family deterioration.

To ADVOCATE a policy of strict race neutrality is not to ignore the persistence of race consciousness, racial fears, racial solidarity, racial envy, or racial prejudice. It is, rather, to declare that government should not be in the business of preferring certain groups over others. Because it got into this business, the United States has been moved dangerously close to a country with an officially-sanctioned racial spoils system. Even Justice Blackmun was concerned about this kind of thing. In his *Bakke* opinion, Blackmun made it clear that preferential remedies should be regarded as temporary, and he speculated that race-conscious policies could be eliminated in ten years—that is, by the end of the 1980's.

Affirmative action's supporters grow uncomfortable when reminded of Blackmun's stipulation, which clashes with their secret conviction that preferences will be needed forever. Despite considerable evidence to the contrary, they believe that racism (and sexism) pervade American life, and they can always find a study, a statistic, or an anecdote to justify their prejudice.

If racial preference is not eliminated now, when a powerful national momentum favors resolving the issue once and for all, the result may well be the permanent institutionalization of affirmative action, though probably at a somewhat less expansive level than is the case right now. Alternatively, a cosmetic solution, which eliminates a few minor policies while leaving the foundation of racial preference in place, could trigger a permanent and much more divisive racial debate, with a mushrooming of state referenda on preference and the growing influence of extremists of both races.

It is clear that a bipartisan majority believes that the era of racial preference should be brought to a close. It will take an unusual amount of political determination and courage to act decisively on this belief. But the consequences of a failure to act could haunt American political life for years to come.

A Twofer's Lament

Yolanda Cruz

Yolanda Cruz is an associate professor of biology at Oberlin College.

This piece was adapted from a 1993 speech delivered at Oberlin College.

I grew up and graduated college in the Philippines; I've spent the last twenty years in the United States. I see a tremendous difference between the perception of education there versus here, then versus now—of whether securing an education is viewed as an opportunity or as a privilege.

I received a bachelor of science degree from the University of the Philippines. I was an agricultural science major, but I had just as many courses in engineering as in philosophy, in language as in math, in literature as in physics, in physical education as in the arts. The five-year curriculum was extremely strict: inflexible in terms of course choices, not only rigorous but quite brutal. There was no entrance exam; your freshman year *was* the entrance exam, and it was trial by fire. Anyone who survived the thirty-six-credit requirement was permitted to continue. We took those painful but marvelously edifying years one at a time, savoring and suffering every midterm exam, sweating every horrific term paper, including the dreaded senior thesis. Every student wrote one based on original research—that is, every student who made it to senior year. Many didn't.

Courses were taught in English (in a country whose citizens speak approximately 100 non-English languages and dialects) by a faculty that was 40 percent women. These women were not merely technicians or teaching assistants but professors, deans, lecturers and research scientists, with Ph.D.s from American, Canadian, Australian and European universities, just like the men. At the time, our student body was also about 40 percent women, although in recent years, I'm told, this figure has grown to about 50 percent. We enjoyed no financial aid or student loans; we went to university the old-fashioned way—on full scholarship, paying full tuition or working. There was only one criterion for admission: academic excellence. The occasional congressman's son or niece got in, but the brutal freshman year was a great equalizer. It didn't matter that your grandfather had graduated fifty years before either, because that didn't guarantee whether or not you would do well in your courses. It didn't matter how tall you were, what ethnic group you represented, what sport you played or what sex you were; or that you came from a finishing school in Switzerland or a public school in the boonies. The only criterion for admission—and for success—was that you could do your stuff and do it well.

It struck me as extraordinary, therefore, that when I matriculated at the University of California at Berkeley, I had to identify myself by sex, ethnicity and other criteria such as financial need. I considered my Graduate Record Examination and Test of English as a Foreign Language scores as relevant; after all, I was to be a graduate student in an English-speaking country. But sex? Ethnicity? I wasn't even sure what "ethnicity" meant. (Even today, I'm not sure whether I'm Asian, Filipino or Pacific Islander. I usually end up checking the box marked "other.") Financial need? That was my concern; I intended to work my way through graduate school. I wasn't asking for privileges, only opportunities.

Imagine my shock, then, when one of the second-year grad students came up to me, shook my hand and said that he had been looking forward to meeting the "twofer" who had been accepted that year. I discovered later that "twofer" meant I was a double whammy; not only was I a woman in a male-dominated field, but I was also not white. Little did that second-year student know that I was transferring from another department and had been accepted into his department because I had aced all the courses there. I remember feeling diminished by his remark; it was as if I had somehow been accepted because my sex and skin color made up for my lack of smarts. Years later I had a similar jolt. In 1986, shortly after I took my present teaching job, I asked one of my colleagues if my sex and ethnicity had anything to do with my getting hired. He said yes: it was affirmative action. And there I was, assuming I had gotten the job because I was good.

Until recently I thought nothing of this. I figured it came with the territory of living a foreigner's life in an alien country. Then a talk with one of my research students, a Hispanic-American woman, brought back a bit of the pain. Last year this student was accepted into Ph.D. programs in molecular biology at Harvard, Cal-Tech and the University of California at San Francisco. After recounting for me the back and forth of her interviews, she asked a poignant question: Did I think she'd been admitted to these universities because she is a twofer? At that moment, I realized my experience at Berkeley had nothing to do with my being foreign. It had to do with the American perception of education as a privilege, deserved or undeserved. My student did not want an undeserved privilege. Like me, all she wanted was an opportunity. How cruel that a person so young, so bright, is made to feel that she is being given a handout, not a hand.

More recently I encountered, in an exchange with my daughter, Elsa, the confusion that seems to accompany the delineation between opportunity and privilege. After Elsa came home with a perfect eighth-grade report card, she regaled me with tales of her classmates who, after earning high marks, had received from their parents gifts, allowance increases, shopping sprees, and spring breaks in the Caribbean. "Why can't I get $20 for every A I bring home, Mama?" Elsa asked.

Smart kid. She knew she had me cornered. I searched my mind for a fitting response. Without losing my

cool, I said, "My dear, I love you very much, but in this household you do not get paid for A's. Instead, you will have to pay me for every grade of B or lower that you bring home." Elsa realized that an A was simply an opportunity to move farther in her coursework; it did not entitle her to an automatic privilege.

Being awarded a privilege and

given an opportunity are similar in that the odds are stacked in the recipient's favor. With privilege, however, the odds are handed to you; with opportunity, you stack the odds in your own favor. It is hard not to see the dignity in the latter enterprise—the sublime feeling of self-worth, self-respect and pride that it engenders.

Crisis of Community

MAKE AMERICA WORK FOR AMERICANS

WILLIAM RASPBERRY, *Columnist for* Washington Post

Delivered at the Landon Lecture Series at Kansas State University, Manhattan, Kansas, April 13, 1995

I'VE been writing a good deal of late about the violence in our streets, the apathy in our schools, and the hopelessness among our young people — the crisis in our community. But this morning, I want to talk about a deeper, more pervasive and ultimately more serious crisis. Let me call it our crisis of community.

America has a crisis of community that is as deep and wide as it is unnoticed. And it threatens to destroy our solidarity as a nation, in much the same fashion as a similar crisis in community has ripped apart the former Soviet Union and what used to be Yugoslavia.

I refer, of course, to the gender wars newly resurrected by the latest battles in the Clarence Thomas/Anita Hill holy wars; to the ethnic battles over university canons and multi-culturalism, to the political warfare that makes party advantage more important than the success of the nation, and to the racial animosities and suspicions fueled by everything from the rantings of Khalid Abdul Muhammed to the O.J. Simpson trial to Charles Murray's pseudo-intellectual call for racial abandonment.

But when I express my fear that we are coming unglued, I'm thinking about far more than these things.

I'm talking about more even than the normal give and take among the various sectors and ideologies of the society. I am talking about our growing inability to act — even to *think* — in the interest of the nation.

It's almost as though there IS no national interest, apart from the aggregate interests of the various components. The whole society seems to be disintegrating into special interests.

And not just in politics. College campuses are being ripped apart by the insistence of one group after another on proving their victimization at the hands of white males, and therefore their right to special exemptions and privileges.

One example of what I'm talking about: A few years ago, the Federal Aviation Administration adopted a rule that would bar emergency exit row seating to passengers who are blind, deaf, obese, frail or otherwise likely to inhibit movement during an emergency evacuation. Common sense? Only if you think of the common interests of all the passengers.

Surely it is reasonable to have those emergency seats occupied by people who can hear the instructions of the crew, read the directions for operating the emergency doors and assist other passengers in their escape.

But some organizations representing the deaf, blind and otherwise disabled reacted to the regulation only as a form of discrimination against their clients who, they insist, have a "right" to the emergency seats.

It is true that the majority must never be allowed to run roughshod over the rights of minorities. That is one of the tenets of the American system. But the notion of fairness to particular groups as an element of fairness to the whole has been perverted into a wholesale jockeying for group advantage.

Mutual fairness, with regard to both rights and responsibilities, can be the glue that bonds this polyglot society into a nation. Single-minded pursuit of group advantage threatens to rip us apart at the seams. The struggle for group advantage has us so preoccupied with one another's ethnicity that we are losing our ability to deal with each other as fellow humans.

What are we to make of this dismaying evidence that the relationships among us are getting worse — even among our college students? I believe two things are happening, and that they reinforce one another. The first is the racism and bigotry that never went away, even though it was relatively quiet for a time.

The second is what has been called the politics of difference. There is a pattern I have seen repeated on campuses across America. A black group, perhaps motivated by some combination of discomfort and rejection, goes looking (always successfully) for demonstrable evidence of racism.

I used to marvel at this search. Of course there was racism on campus, but what was the point of PROSPECTING for it, as though panning for gold?

I mean, where was the assay office to which one took these nuggets of racism and traded them in for something of value?

Well, it turns out that there IS such an assay office. It's called the Administration Building. Turn in enough nuggets and you get your reward: a Black Student Union, a special course offering, an African American wing in a preferred dormitory — whatever. All it takes is proof that you are a victim.

But despite the reports one hears these days, college students aren't exactly stupid. They are bright enough to see that there are rewards in the politics of difference, in demonstrated victimism. So the victories won by black students become models for similar prizes for gay students or Hispanic students or female students, all of whom gather up their nuggets of victimism and take them to the administration building for redemption.

Cornell University, one of the finest institutions in America, has a dormitory called Ujamaa College, a residence for black students; Akwe:kon, a dorm for Native Americans, and also the Latin Living Center.

That's the trend when the accent is on difference. And finally, it turns out that everybody gets something out of the politics of difference except white males, who start to feel sorry for themselves.

And if they can't find anyone to reward them for their sense of being slighted, they may turn to behavior that was once unthinkable — the "acting out" that manifests itself in incivility, reactionary politics, open bigotry and, on occasion, violence.

Every gain by minority groups justifies the sense of victimism on the part of white males, and every repugnant act of white males becomes a new nugget for a minority to take to the assay office.

Two things get lost in this sad ritual. The first is that the administration seldom gives up any of its own power: the gains of one group of students are extracted from other groups of students, who then must play up their own disadvantage to wrest some small advantage from another group. The administration's power remains intact.

The second overlooked aspect is that the process turns the campus into warring factions — each, no doubt, imagining itself as the moral successor to the heroes of the Civil Rights Movement. There's a difference, though. Dr. King's constantly repeated goal was not special advantage but unity. His dream was not of a time when blacks would finally overcome whites; his dream was that we should overcome, black and white together.

His hope was not that we should celebrate our differences but that we should recognize the relative unimportance of these differences. The differences do not *seem* unimportant, of course. Sometimes we seem to notice ONLY our differences.

That's why I find it helpful to look at what used to be the Soviet Union and what used to be Yugoslavia. From this distance, it seems clear that the similarities between the Serbs and Croats and other ethnic neighbors in Bosnia-Herzegovinia should outweigh their differences.

They share the history of a place and indeed many were intermarried. But now that Yugoslavia has broken up, even the marriages have been ripped apart.

I find myself wishing these erstwhile Yugoslavs could see for themselves what distance makes clear to us. And I wish we could learn to see ourselves as from a distance. Maybe we'd learn to appreciate how great are our similarities and how trivial our differences, and get OUR act together.

A "Star Trek" episode of some years ago makes my point. Capt. Kirk and his crew rescue a humanoid who, on his left side, is completely black. His right side, it turns out, is altogether white.

They are in the process of trying to learn the origins of this stranger — Lokai, he is called — when they are confronted by a similar humanoid named Bele — this one black on his right side and white on the left. The Enterprise crew, of course, can hardly tell them apart. But the humanoids can see themselves only as complete opposites — which, of course in one sense they are. And not just opposites. Though they are from the same planet, they are also sworn enemies.

I won't try to tell you the whole episode, but let me recall this much. Lokai is thought to be a political traitor, and Bele, an official of their home planet's Commission on Political Traitors, has been chasing him throughout the galaxy for a thousand years.

Lokai tries to convince the Enterprise crew that Bele and his kind are murderous oppressors. Bele counters that Lokai and his kind are ungrateful savages. The Enterprise crew decides to travel near the strangers' planet.

When they come within sensor range they are surprised to learn there is no sapient life there. The cities are intact, vegetation and lower animals abound, but the people are dead. They have annihilated each other. These two have survived only because they happened to be in the business of chasing each other down.

And what do they do when they learn what has happened to their planet? They lunge at each other in furious battle. Though the Enterprise crew is appalled, Kirk is unable to convince the two enemies of the futility of their war.

"To expect sense from two mentalities of such extreme viewpoints is not logical," says Spock. "They are playing out the drama of which they have become the captives, just as their compatriots did."

"But their people are dead," Sulu says slowly. "How can it matter to them now which one is right?"

"It does to them," says Spock. "And at the same time, in a sense, it doesn't. A thousand years of hating and running have become all of life."

We don't learn from this "Star Trek" episode the nature of the original problem between these warring humanoids, though we can be certain each felt fully justified in continuing the war. They had made a mistake that too many of us make in real life: They had forgotten the difference between problems and enemies.

And so have we. Virtually every issue that strikes us as urgent or important is made more intractable by our insistence on seeing it as a matter of us against them.

Give us a problem, and we'll find an enemy. Is the U.S. economy in trouble? Make the Japanese the enemy. Are we concerned about the discouraged and dangerous underclass? Blame white racists.

Members of my own profession seem unable to tell a story, no matter how significant, unless they can transform it into a case of one person, or one group, against another — unless they can make it a matter of enemies.

It is not so much that the enemies we identify are innocent as that identifying and pursuing them takes time and attention away from the search for solutions.

It was no trouble at all to come up with evidence that the Japanese were hurting the American economy through predatory pricing, product dumping and nonreciprocity, and certainly all these things merited attention.

But the U.S. auto industry improved its position relative to Japan's auto industry not when we all became expert at bashing our Japanese enemy but when Detroit started making better cars.

And that's the point. The failure to distinguish between the enemy and the problem has us looking balefully at one another instead of jointly attacking the problem which, in most cases, is as much a problem for us as for those we attack.

Take the current fight over affirmative action, for instance. Politicians who lack the imagination to address the *problem* settle for giving us each other to attack. White men — particularly those with a high school education or less — are not imagining things when they feel less secure economically than their fathers were. But they make a mistake when they suppose that their jobs have somehow been handed over to black people in the name of affirmative action. More likely those jobs are in Taiwan or Singapore or have gone up in the smoke of corporate mergers and downsizing. We've got a problem, and we waste our time assaulting enemies.

Honest communication about the problem might lead us to look for ways to restore our industrial base, expand our economy, improve the quality of our products and put our people to work. Focusing on enemies produces stirring speeches and little else.

You've heard the speeches. You've watched as communities have been ripped apart by those who deliver these speeches. There's how Teresa Heinz, widow of the late Pennsylvania senator, described them in a recent speech:

"... critical of everything, impossible to please, indifferent to nuance, incapable of compromise. They laud perfection but oddly never see it in anybody but themselves. They are right all the time, eager to say I told you so, and relentlessly unforgiving. They occasionally may mean well, but the effect of even their good intentions is to destroy. They corrode self-confidence and good will; they cultivate guilt; they rule by fear and ridicule.

"They are creatures of opportunity as much as of principles, extremists of the left and the right who feed on our fear and promote it, who dress up their opponents in ugly costumes, who drive a bitter wedge between us and the Other, the one not like us, the one who sees the world just a shade differently. ... They demonize us by our parts and tear our country into pieces."

My own formulation is less eloquent; they focus on enemies rather than on problems. They forget that, at the end of the day, when we've all taken our unfair shots at one another, this simple truth remains: The *problem* is the problem.

Our politicians and our factional leaders never miss an opportunity to list the atrocities the *enemy* has committed against us. But nothing changes.

Sometimes we're not even sure what we want to change, or what we want the people we call enemies to do. We say we want things to get better, when sometimes I think we only want to score points.

We say we want a society in which all of us can live together as brothers and sisters, and the whole time we are saying it we are busy creating another group of barriers to place between us.

It's a strange sort of progress we have made since the death of Dr. King. We have "progressed" to the point where we are embarrassed to speak of brotherhood, of black and white together, of our shared status as Americans.

That's not an accusation; it's a confession. All of us are capable of getting so caught up in the distance that remains to be run that we forget to give ourselves full credit for the distance we've come.

Yet, every now and then, we manage to overcome our embarrassment and see things as from a distance. In that spirit, I'd like to share something I wrote a while back — something I still believe but something I may have trouble saying again.

Here it is: The immigration applications, the legal and ille-

gal dodges for getting into this country, the longings you hear in virtually every other part of the world all attest to two astounding facts.

The first, widely accepted though not always with good grace, is that "everybody" wants to be an American. The second, of which we take almost no notice, is that virtually anybody can *become* an American.

To see just how extraordinary a fact that is, imagine hearing anyone — black, white or Asian — saying he wants to "become Japanese." It sounds like a joke. One can *live* in Japan (or Ghana or Sweden or Mexico) — can live there permanently, and prosper. But it's essentially impossible to imagine anyone born anywhere else becoming anything else — except American.

It's a thought that crosses my mind whenever I hear demands that the government protect the ethnic or language heritage of particular groups: when African Americans demand that the *public* schools adopt an Afrocentric curriculum, for instance, or when immigrants from Latin America are sworn in as American citizens — in Spanish.

It crossed my mind again when I came across Jim Sleeper's essay, "In Defense of Civic Culture."

I won't try to characterize Sleeper's piece or to summarize its recommendations. [the Washington-based Progressive Foundation] I won't even tell you I agree with everything Sleeper has to say on the subject of race and ethnicity.

But he says some things that echo my own feelings, especially when I ponder the extraordinary possibility of becoming American.

He acknowledges the obvious: that the America that counted my great-great-grandfather as only three-fifths of a human being has never been free of ethnic and racial bigotry, and that that bigotry has sometimes achieved the status of law, of philosophy — even of religion.

But he notes something else: that America is one of the few places on the globe where accusation of such bigotry is a serious indictment. Even when America has been at its ugliest in fact — slavery, the slaughter of Native Americans, the internment of the Japanese and the full range of private and public atrocities, "yet always America held out the promise that, as Ralph Waldo Emerson put it, 'in this asylum of all nations, the energy of ... all the European tribes [and] of the Africans, and of the Polynesians will construct a new race.'"

The civic culture Sleeper writes about includes this notion of Americans as a new and different race, but it also entails what he describes as characteristic American virtues: tolerance, optimism, self-restraint, self-reliance, reason, public-mindedness — virtues that are "taught and caught in the daily life of local institutions and in the examples set by neighbors, co-workers and public leaders."

It is, he suggests, the internalizing of these virtues that defines "becoming American."

But the transformation works both ways. If people from an awesome range of colors, cultures and ethnicities have become Americans, so has America become what it is (and continues to become) by absorbing and embracing these myriad influences.

Some of us are angry, and ought to be, that our academic texts and teachings still disregard or underestimate our part of these influences.

Some of us are disappointed that what we bring to the smorgasbord is often undervalued, even brutally rejected.

But surely the cure is in working for greater inclusion, not cultural isolation. That's what observers as different as Sleeper, Arthur Schlesinger and John Gardner have been saying. That's what Gary Trudeau was saying in that hilarious (and sobering) series of "Doonesbury" strips that ended with black students — already having attained their separate courses and dormitories — demanding, at last, separate drinking fountains. Sleeper's insight is that there is nothing "natural" or automatic about those values and attitudes that used to be called "the American way." Educators must teach them, he says, and also "teach that self-esteem is enhanced not simply through pride in one's own cultural origins but, more importantly, by taking pride in one's mastery of civic virtues and graces that all Americans share and admire in building our society."

Critics of this view will argue that Sleeper's virtuous and graceful American is a figment, that America is a deeply — perhaps irredeemably — racist society.

I prefer to think that Americans are still becoming Americans, just as America is still becoming America.

How can we accelerate that becoming? By recognizing its importance, by understanding that hating and running must not become all of life, and by working to grasp the difference between problems and enemies.

Confront a difficulty as a problem, and you have taken the first steps toward creating the climate for change.

Confront it as the work of enemies and you create the necessity for DEFEATING someone, of intimidating someone, of browbeating someone into doing something against his will.

Enemies have to be sought out, branded and punished. Which, naturally, gives them one more reason to find an opportunity to strike back at us. And the beat goes on.

Problems, on the other hand, admit of cooperative solutions that can help build community.

Searching for enemies is most often a pessimist's game, calculated less to resolve difficulties than to establish that the difficulties are someone else's fault. Identifying *problems* is by its very nature optimistic and healing. The whole point of delineating problems is to fashion solutions.

Maybe that's what President Clinton had in mind when he called on America to bring back "the old spirit of partnership, of optimism, of renewed dedication to common efforts."

"We need," he said, "an array of devoted, visionary, healing leaders throughout this nation, willing to work in their communities to end the long years of denial and neglect and divisiveness and blame, to give the American people their country back."

And that is precisely what we need. America has had enough of the politics of difference, the marketing of disadvantage, the search for enemies. It's about time we started to work on what may be the most important problem we face:

How to heal our crisis of community and make America work — not for blacks or whites or women or gays; not for ethnics; not for Christians, Moslems or Jews — but for Americans.

Cities, Urban Growth, and the Quality of Life

- **Cities (Articles 32 and 33)**
- **Quality of Life (Articles 34 and 35)**
- **Education (Articles 36–38)**
- **Drugs (Articles 39 and 40)**

Until 1965 the major problems facing cities were those associated with growth. People by the millions were abandoning rural areas and migrating to the cities. Because of a complexity of factors, this trend has been reversed. Since 1965 many U.S. cities have lost major industries and businesses as well as the people involved. These losses have produced a declining tax base and an aging infrastructure, both of which spawn a host of related social problems such as unemployment, underemployment, homelessness, crime, and gangs. But what is fascinating is that while many major cities are in trouble, others are thriving. In this issue of *Annual Editions: Social Problems,* we have created four subcategories for this unit's articles: *Cities, Quality of Life* in cities, *Education,* and *Drugs.* The last two categories reflect both the quality of life in any city and one of the major social problems, and they do have unique implications for American society as a whole, hence their own subcategory.

Answering the questions regarding how to stop the deterioration of the cities necessitates discovering the basic causes underlying the decline. The authors of the report "Can We Stop the Decline of Our Cities?" contrasted those cities in decline with those that are not and discovered that decline or growth is directly dependent on the costs and quality of services provided by the city and the size of governmental bureaucracy.

David Moberg, in his essay "Can We Save the Inner City?" examines recent attempts to stop the progressive decline of poor urban neighborhoods—which has occurred in spite of three decades of intermittent federal action on poverty and civil rights. How to save these neighborhoods is being hotly debated among academics, private foundations, and the federal government's modest urban strategies.

Rob Gurwitt observes that the practice of concentrating public housing projects in high-rise, high density areas may provide low income housing, but it also causes heightened crime, drugs, and other community blights. To correct this problem, Gurwitt argues, in the article "The Projects Come Down," that high density projects must be replaced by housing scattered throughout the community. The author reports on cities where this has happened and finds the results very encouraging.

In "Jumping Off the Fast Track," more and more individuals are discovering that life is much more than the time and stress associated with the acquisition of large salaries, power, or high-status positions. In addition, foreign competition, advanced technologies, and corporate restructuring has forced many people to reevaluate what they want out of life. More and more individuals are leaving corporate America to spend more time with their families, for home-based work, and for a chance to do something more meaningful with their lives.

Despite escalating spending, school performance and student achievement have not improved. "The Dismal State of Public Education" points out that public education in the United States is jeopardizing our ability as a nation to compete internationally. Allyson Tucker notes, "Tinkering with an inefficient and ineffective monopoly system has not improved the condition of public education. The dismal state of American public education will improve only with deregulation, decentralization, and choice."

Karen Lehrman's article, "Off Course," examines what is happening in many women's study courses around the country. Lehrman visited many campuses and discovered that "discussions run from the personal to the political and back again with mere 'pit stops' at the academic."

"Truth and Consequences: Teen Sex" explores the implications of earlier and earlier experiences of teen sexual activity. The "sexual revolution" is into its fourth decade and the results are far from positive. The authors look at the social, medical, psychological, and economic costs and what, if anything, can be done to reduce them.

"A Society of Suspects: The War on Drugs and Civil Liberties" reflects the paradoxes of trying to balance effective measures against crime with the upholding of civil rights. While trying to win the war on drugs, law enforcement personnel insist their hands are being tied. But those constraints were established by the Founding Fathers to protect the rights of every American citizen to be free from unwarranted searches, forced entry into homes, and arrest. Steven Wisotsky argues that constitutional rights are being systematically limited and redefined because of this "war."

Why don't our welfare, medical, and criminal justice systems work? "It's Drugs, Alcohol and Tobacco, Stupid!"

reiterates that until we develop workable policies concerning drugs, the rest of the system cannot function effectively. Drug abuse creates costly medical problems both for the users and their families. Drug addiction creates a demand that cannot be realized legally—which thus clogs the courts and prisons. The problem facing society cannot be addressed until we find a solution to the problem of drugs.

Looking Ahead: Challenge Questions

Describe the possibilities for rescuing our inner cities.

In countering urban decline, how effective has the infusion of federal dollars into cities been? What are the implications of tearing down substandard housing and rebuilding high-rise subsidized housing exclusively for the poor?

Why does the emergence of a nation from a totalitarian state to a democracy seem to result in rampant crime, violence, and death?

What should be the primary objective(s) of any university academic program?

Is public education failing in the United States? What can/must be done to make students in America competitive with comparable students anywhere else on Earth?

Distinguish between the harmful effects of societal approved drugs (alcohol, tobacco, and caffeine) and of those that are not (heroin, cocaine, marijuana).

What major ways can raising the fears of the members of society impact on their rights as citizens?

Why are so many people rejecting success in the corporate world?

Which of the three sociological theoretical positions do you think most clearly helps to understand the issues/problems covered in this unit?

What are the values, rights, obligations, and harms associated with each of the activities included in this unit?

Can We Stop the Decline of Our
CITIES?

Unless and until they start putting people first—
by cutting service costs and anti-growth tax rates—no amount of
Federal aid can reverse the trend.

Stephen Moore and Dean Stansel

The authors are, respectively, director of fiscal policy studies and a research assistant, Cato Institute, Washington, D.C.

FOR MORE THAN a quarter-century, Americans have been voting with their feet against the economic policies and social conditions of the inner cities. Fifteen of the largest 25 U.S. cities have lost 4,000,000 people since 1965, while the total U.S. population has risen by 60,000,000. The exodus no longer is just "white flight"—minorities also are leaving the cities in record numbers.

In recent years, the departure of businesses, jobs, and middle-income families from the old central cities has begun to resemble a stampede. For example, since the late 1970s, more than 50 Fortune 500 company headquarters have fled New York City, representing a loss of over 500,000 jobs. Cleveland, Detroit, Philadelphia, St. Louis, and other major cities also are suffering from severe out-migration of capital and people. Those once-mighty industrial centers are becoming hollow cores of poverty and crime.

Ever since the Los Angeles riots and looting, urban lobbyists—including mayors, public employee unions, urban scholars, and many members of Congress—have been arguing that the inner cities were victims of Federal neglect under Presidents Ronald Reagan and George Bush. "There was, quite literally, a massive Federal disinvestment in the cities in the 1980s," according to Congressional delegate Eleanor Holmes Norton of Washington, D.C. To revive them, the U.S. Conference of Mayors is asking for $35,000,000,000 in new Federal funds—a "Marshall Plan for the cities."

The Federal government already has tried the equivalent of some 25 Marshall Plans to revive the cities. Since 1965, it has spent an estimated 2.5 trillion dollars on the War on Poverty and urban aid. (That figure includes welfare, Medicaid, housing, education, job training, and infrastructure and direct aid to cities.) Economist Walter Williams has calculated that this is enough money to purchase all the assets of the Fortune 500 companies *plus* all of the farmland in the U.S., but it has not spurred urban revival. In 1992 alone, Federal aid to states and cities rose to $150,000,000,000. Adjusted for inflation, that is the largest amount of Federal intergovernmental aid ever extended—hardly a massive disinvestment.

Central cities' budgets on the rise

The budgets of Cleveland, Detroit, Philadelphia, New York, St. Louis, and other large central cities have not been shrinking; they have been rapidly expanding for decades. In constant 1990 dollars, local governments spent, on average, $435 per resident in 1950, $571 in 1965, and $1,004 in 1990. The largest cities saw an even faster budget rise. In real dollars, New York's budget nearly tripled from $13,000,000,000 in 1965 to $37,000,000,000 in 1990. Philadelphia, another nearly bankrupt city, allowed its budget to rise by 125% between 1965 and 1990—from $1,600,000,000 to $3,500,000,000. During the same time period, the city lost 20% of its population. In short, 25 years of doubling and even tripling city budgets have not prevented urban bleeding.

Not all U.S. cities are in decline. Among the nation's largest urban areas, there are dozens—many on the West Coast, in the Sunbelt, and in the Southeast—that have been booming financially and economically for at least the past 20 years. Las Vegas, Nev.; Phoenix, Ariz.; Arlington and Austin, Tex.; Sacramento and San Diego, Calif.; Raleigh and Charlotte, N.C.; and Jacksonville, Fla., all have rapidly rising incomes, populations, and employment and low poverty and crime rates.

What do growth cities—Phoenix, Raleigh, and San Diego, for example—do differently from shrinking cities such as Buffalo, Cleveland, and Detroit? The answer is found, at least partially, in their fiscal policies. Bureau of the Census finance data from 1965, 1980, and 1990 for the 76 largest cities reveal significant and consistent patterns of higher spending and taxes in the low-growth cities than in the high-growth ones.

• For every dollar of per capita expenditures (excluding those spent on anti-poverty programs, education, and health care) in the highest-growth cities, the shrinking cities spend $1.71.

• In 1990, a typical family of four living in one of the shrinking cities paid $1,100 per year more in taxes than it would if it lived in one of the highest-growth cities.

• Shrinking cities' bureaucracies are twice as large as those of growth cities. In 1990, the latter had, on average, 99 city employees per 10,000 residents; the former, 235.

• Cities with high spending and taxes lost

population in the 1980s; those with low spending and taxes gained. High spending and taxes are a cause, not just a consequence, of urban decline.

Expenditures are high and rising in large central cities primarily because their governments generally have above-average unit costs for educating children, collecting garbage, building roads, policing neighborhoods, and providing other basic services. In 1988, for example, the shrinking cities spent roughly $4,950 per pupil on education, whereas the high-growth cities spent $3,600. The $1,350 cost differential can not be explained by better schools in places such as Detroit and Newark.

The influence of municipal employee unions also contributes to higher costs in declining central cities. Compensation for unionized local employees tends to be roughly 30% above wages for comparably skilled private-sector workers. In New York, the average school janitor is paid $57,000 a year. In Philadelphia, the average municipal employee receives more than $50,000 a year in salary and benefits. According to the Census Bureau, cities with populations over 500,000 pay their mostly unionized workers more than 50% more than those with populations under 75,000, whose workforces are less likely to be unionized. In short, thriving cities are places where costs are lower, bureaucracies are smaller, and services are better.

Some city officials are beginning to recognize economic reality. Philadelphia Mayor Edward Rendell is challenging the entrenched municipal unions and other spending constituencies with a budget plan that calls for $1,100,000,000 in savings over five years. He has spurned more Federal aid as the poison that produced Philadelphia's near-insolvency in 1992. Chicago Mayor Richard M. Daley and Indianapolis Mayor Stephen Goldsmith have contracted out dozens of services to private providers and have slowed the growth of massive, bloated budgets to a crawl.

The decline of America's major cities is not inevitable. They can and should be saved. For generations, they have served as the nation's centers, not only of industrial might, but of culture, diversity, and intellect. Through an aggressive agenda of budget control, tax reduction, privatization, and deregulation, America's declining cities can rise again in prominence and prosperity.

The riots in Los Angeles in the spring of 1992 dramatized the social and economic deterioration of many central cities. At a rally held in Washington a month after the riots, then-New York Mayor David Dinkins aptly described the inner cities as places of "only grief and despair." Almost all quality-of-life indicators for many of the fastest shrinking cities confirm that gloomy assessment. Consider these examples:

• The 1990 census data reveal that 48% of all Detroit households are headed by a single female.
• Newark has a lower real per capita income today than it did in 1969.
• Cleveland had nearly 1,000,000 residents in the 1950s; now, it has fewer than 500,000.
• The Chicago area has averaged 10,000 manufacturing job losses annually for the past 15 years. A Feb. 14, 1992, *Chicago Tribune* headline said it all: "Factory Flight Hits Record Pace."
• St. Louis has lost more than two of every five jobs it had in 1965.
• Philadelphia has a four-year $1,000,-000,000 budget deficit. Its bond rating sunk so low that it effectively is blocked from municipal capital markets and must borrow through a state oversight agency.
• Washington, D.C., has been dubbed the "murder capital of the world."
• In Baltimore, 56% of black males between the ages of 18 and 35 were in trouble with the law in 1991, according to a study by the National Center on Institutions and Alternatives.

The root cause of almost all the social, economic, and fiscal problems of America's depressed cities is the steady flight of businesses and middle- and upper-income families. In the past quarter-century, 15 major cities combined have lost 3,800,000 people and roughly the same number of jobs. No longer is the issue just white flight. The 1990 census data suggest that middle-income minorities are fleeing to the suburbs in record numbers.

The urban crisis is not shared by all cities. The declines in the most depressed are matched by impressive gains in the highest-growth cities. Raleigh, for instance, has seen its population almost double, jobs more than double, and real per capita income grow by better than 40% since the mid 1960s. The wide diversity in the economic performance of central cities suggests that the individual policies of each play an important role in explaining urban growth and decline.

In conventional analyses of the urban crisis, cities are portrayed primarily as victims of national trends, Federal mandates, and other conditions beyond their control. Factors blamed include the recession, Reagan budget cuts, suburbanization, decline in manufacturing, rise of the automobile, immigration, an aging infrastructure, racism, AIDS, homelessness, urban gangs, guns, and drugs. Each of these can place considerable strain on municipal budgets, yet city officials are impotent to combat them.

There is some truth to this. The last recession is painful evidence that no city is immune from the impact of national economic conditions and policies. For instance, from the 1950s through the 1980s,

most California cities enjoyed spectacular rates of growth. The state widely was considered recession proof. Yet, the recession had a devastating impact on California localities—many of which are at the top of the list of growth cities. One-third of all job losses in the past two years has occurred in California. Another example is the impact that wide fluctuations in international oil prices in the 1970s and 1980s had on the economies and budgets of Texas cities.

Unquestionably, there are regional factors at play in determining relative rates of growth. Most of the declining cities are the once-mighty industrial centers in the Northeast and Midwest—the Rust Belt. Most of the growth cities are in the Sun Belt, on the West Coast, and in the Southeast. A related factor that usually correlates with the rate of economic growth is age—older cities tend to experience less economic growth, a phenomenon that often is attributed to their aging infrastructures.

Still, the fact that some cities have been flourishing for long periods of time as others have been deteriorating suggests that self-imposed policies play an important role in determining their economic fates. Regional factors can not explain fully the different growth rates of cities. Although the South has been a high-growth region, three of the fastest declining cities—Birmingham, Louisville, and New Orleans—are in that area.

Even within states, there are significant differences in the economic performance of cities. Why is Oakland declining, but Santa Ana growing? Why is Arlington doing so much better than Fort Worth, or Colorado Springs better than Denver? What explains the fact that the eighth fastest growing city, Lexington, and the ninth fastest declining city, Louisville, both are in Kentucky? An important factor is that their spending and taxing policies are very different. Growth cities have pro-growth fiscal policies; declining cities, anti-growth.

Taxes and spending. There are several potential problems in comparing spending and taxes by city. The major one is the division of responsibilities for program funding among state governments, counties, school districts, and cities differs from state to state. For example, in some, the responsibility for funding welfare assistance is delegated to the counties; in others, it is paid for by the state government; and in still others, the cities bear the cost. Another complication is that some cities are not part of independent counties, and so the city government funds all the activities of the county. By contrast, most cities are part of larger counties, which means that the costs of funding services such as hospitals and courts in the inner cities are spread to the suburbs. Finally, in some cities, school funding is handled by school districts or in large part by the state, not the city, government.

Another potential difficulty with comparing city growth rates over time is that borders change. Many cities, such as Portland, Ore., aggressively have annexed neighboring suburbs. In the case of Portland, annexation has been a major source of population growth. However, that annexation probably is as much a consequence of the city's economic success as it is an explanation. In many cases, localities have merged with central cities because it has been in their economic interests to do so. By the same token, more and more localities are attempting to secede from declining central cities because the latter's economic policies, such as tax rates and service costs, have grown too burdensome.

Population growth. The best indication of the livability of a city probably is whether people are moving to or out of it. Those that had large population losses from 1965 to 1990 spend, tax, and hire city workers at roughly twice the rates of the cities that had large population gains. For instance, the highest-growth cities (those with population gains of 100% or more) spend six percent of personal income, whereas the lowest-growth cities (those that lost at least 15% of their populations) expend 12% of personal income. The highest-growth cities had 107 employees per 10,000 residents vs. 217 in the lowest-growth cities. Those findings suggest that cities with high taxes and service costs are driving people away.

Job growth. Just as population changes are a measure of how people are voting with their feet, so are employment patterns. Firms and capital that create jobs tend to migrate to areas with pro-growth and pro-business climates. Per capita spending is roughly 50% higher in the lowest-growth cities than in those with the greatest increase in employment. The cities with the lowest growth in employment spend almost $1.40 for every $1.00 of municipal expenditures in the highest-growth cities. High taxes and spending are driving businesses and jobs away from shrinking cities.

Female-headed households. One indication of poverty and family disintegration in an area is the percentage of female-headed households. Fatherless homes are about eight times more likely to be poor than are intact families. Moreover, children who grow up in fatherless households are much more likely to commit crimes and engage in other socially unacceptable behavior of the type that plagues inner cities.

Between 1970 and 1990, the percentage of female-headed households rose at an alarming pace nationwide. The largest growth occurred in the inner cities, where

Census Bureau data indicate an increase from about 15 to 35% in fatherless homes. Cities with the largest rise in female-headed households have spending and taxes at least 50% higher than those with small increases.

Per capita income growth is one of the best measures of the economic growth rate of a city and the standard of living of its residents. The cities with the lowest growth in income (less than 10%) are characterized by per capita spending and taxes that are about 10% higher than those of cities with the highest growth in income (more than 25%). As a share of personal income, spending and taxes are about 25% higher in cities with the lowest growth.

Where the money goes

The urban lobby and scholars invariably argue that low-growth cities spend more because their needs are greater. Poor cities have to meet increased demands for anti-poverty spending, subsidized child care, homeless assistance, drug abatement and rehabilitation, crime control, job training, etc. Because declining cities have less wealth and fewer workers and businesses to pay the cost of those programs, they have to impose higher tax burdens on their residents and businesses to raise the same amount of revenue wealthy and prospering cities do.

Education is a major budget item that should not cost much more on a per student basis in a low-growth city. If per student education costs were uniform across cities, one would expect to find higher per pupil expenditures in growing and affluent areas if only because the residents have more money to devote to the schools. Indeed, the education lobby successfully has argued before several state supreme courts that school financing is inequitable because wealthy areas spend more on schools than do poor areas.

The data show that, on average, per pupil expenditures on schools in the lowest job growth cities are approximately $1,800 higher than they are in the highest job growth cities. Yet, spending on schools and student performance appear to be wholly unrelated. For example, Washington, D.C., which spent almost $6,000 per student in 1988, has among the worst inner-city schools in the nation. Conversely, San Diego spent about $3,500 per child in 1988 for schools that are considered above average for cities its size.

Low-growth cities appear to provide education, one of the major items in local budgets, much less cost-efficiently than do

high-growth cities. If declining central cities simply could lower their education costs to the national average for large cities, they could reduce their per family tax burden by hundreds of dollars.

City taxes and economic growth. A city's economic performance is influenced not only by its over-all tax burden, but by the composition of its taxes. In particular, income taxes have a consistently strong negative effect on city growth rates. Only one high-growth city—Lexington, Ky.—imposes a city income tax, whereas the low-growth cities have average per capita income taxes of approximately $100-200. The evidence suggests that imposition of a city income tax is a recipe for economic decline.

City property taxes also have a negative impact on economic growth, but not to the extent that income taxes do. Cities with high population and job growth, as well as those with low poverty rates, have substantially lower property taxes than cities in decline.

City sales taxes have no apparent positive or negative impact on economic growth. If anything, high-growth cities tend to rely heavily on sales taxes for revenue; declining cities, on income taxes.

Impact of state taxes. Workers and businesses are affected not only by local tax burdens, but by state taxes as well. High-growth cities tend to be located in states that have low combined city-state tax burdens. State and city taxes are about $360 per person higher in cities with population losses of 15% or more since 1965 than in those with population gains of 100% or more.

Even more dramatic is the destructive impact of high combined state and city income taxes on the economic performance of cities. Growth cities tend to have state and local income tax burdens that are, on average, about 60% of those of shrinking cities.

Federal aid. Cities have a multitude of problems, but too little money is not one of them. Real per capita spending escalated from $435 in 1950 to $571 in 1965 to $1,004 in 1990. At the start of that spending binge, America's largest cities were at the peak of prosperity—indeed, they had higher per capita incomes than the suburbs. Now, incomes are 50% lower than in the suburbs. A nearly 2.5-fold increase in outlays has not prevented urban bleeding; if anything, it has accelerated it.

Those figures understate the true extent of the budget buildup in cities. In the 1950s and early 1960s, cities had primary responsibility for funding welfare programs and indigent health care, whereas today the burden of funding anti-poverty programs is borne mostly by the Federal government and the states. In fact, most cities spend a much smaller share of their budgets on health and welfare than they did 40 years ago.

The cities that are least underfunded are not the smaller, more affluent communities, but the largest ones (*i.e.*, those that would be the beneficiaries of more Federal aid). Cities with populations over 500,000 spend roughly $1,200 per resident (excluding health, education, and welfare), whereas communities with populations under 75,000 spend about $550. The primary reason the expenditures of large central cities are so excessive is not that they have more responsibilities; it is that they are increasingly inefficient in providing basic services. It costs New York, Chicago, Los Angeles, Philadelphia, and other big cities twice as much to educate a child, collect garbage, build a road, police a neighborhood, and provide other basic services as it does smaller communities.

From 1980 to 1990, direct Federal aid to cities was reduced by about 50%. That reduction was made up in various ways. A 1990 study in the *American Economic Review* reports that, for every dollar the cities lost in Federal aid, they received an additional 80 cents in state aid. Moreover, while direct Federal aid to cities was cut in the Reagan years, aid to poor people living in cities increased. Federal social welfare spending—on education, training, social services, employment, low-income assistance, community development, and transportation—rose from $255,000,000,000 to $285,000,000,000 from 1980 to 1992. Those figures exclude Social Security, Medicare, and Medicaid—programs that have mushroomed in cost and significantly benefit inner-city residents as well.

Since 1989, domestic spending across the board, including outlays on urban aid, has exploded. Federal domestic spending under George Bush rose by almost 25%, the fastest rate of growth of the domestic budget under any president in 30 years. In real terms, cities and states received more Federal money in 1992 than in any previous year.

Since the late 1960s, the Federal government has spent 2.5 trillion dollars on urban renewal and the War on Poverty, or the equivalent of 25 Marshall Plans. The reason the money has not caused an urban revival is that the programs, particularly those that were abolished in the 1980s, did not work. For example, Urban Development Action Grants, which finally were abolished in 1987, subsidized the construction of major chain hotels, such as Hyatts, and luxury housing developments with rooftop tennis courts, health spas, and indoor tennis courts in Detroit.

Despite Federal grants totaling more than $50,000,000,000 for urban transit since the mid 1960s, total ridership has declined. The Federal government spent over $2,000,000,000 to build Miami's Metrorail, which the local population calls Metrofail; today, it has less than 20% of predicted ridership and its operating subsidies are in the hundreds of millions of dollars a year. A Congressional Budget Office audit of Federal wastewater treatment grants to cities found that construction costs were 30% higher when plants were built with Federal funding than when local taxpayers footed the bill.

Even cities that have received huge infusions of direct Federal aid have not been able to leverage those funds to resuscitate their economies. For instance, Gary, Ind., got more than $150,000,000 from 1968 to 1972 for urban renewal—or about $1,000 per resident—yet the city's deterioration continued.

Cuts in urban aid can not account for the Los Angeles riots, the exodus from New York City, sky-high poverty in Detroit, and other woes of the central cities. The period of catastrophic decline of population, incomes, and jobs was the 1970s, when urban aid exploded. By every meaningful measure of social and economic progress, the 1970s were the worst decade for cities since at least the 1930s.

By contrast, the Reagan years were a period of economic gains for many big cities. "The 1980s was the best decade in this century for the old central business districts," maintains *Washington Post* reporter Joel Garreau in his 1992 book on urban America, *Edge City*. "From Boston to Philadelphia to Washington to Los Angeles to San Francisco to Seattle to Houston to Dallas to Atlanta, the business districts of the downtowns thrived." Adjusted for inflation, the tax base of America's inner cities expanded by 50% in the 1980s, compared to 20% in the 1970s. The entrepreneurial explosion unleashed by Reaganomics had a very positive effect on the finances of big cities.

Medium-sized areas fared even better. More than 150 thriving new suburban cities have grown up during the past decade, such as Fairfax, Va.; Mesa, Ariz.; and Irvine, Calif. They quickly have become centers of enterprise and job creation. Until the recent recession, the problem confronting those booming cities was too much development and business investment, not too little.

An agenda for urban renaissance

Reviving America's depressed cities will require implementation of a growth-oriented agenda on the part of the Federal government, states, and cities. The overriding goal of such a strategy must be to provide incentives for people, businesses, and capital to return to the inner cities.

Federal role. A proper adherence to the constitutional principles of federalism would dictate that the Federal government have almost no direct relationship with cities. All Federal programs that give direct aid to local governments and Federal regulations that mandate local spending should be abolished. Federal aid, to the extent that it continues, should be provided to the states. If cities and other jurisdictions of the states are in need of financial aid, it should be provided by the state legislatures.

If Congress feels compelled to assist areas that have deep pockets of poverty, money should be given directly to poor people, not city bureaucracies or service providers. There seems to be a bipartisan consensus emerging on such a strategy. A 1982 Brookings Institution report on urban decline emphasized that policymakers "should consider switching more federal aid from *empowering governments* to deliver services, to *empowering individuals and households* to purchase services or provide their own."

There are practical as well as philosophical objections to Federal grants to cities. As with Federal aid to foreign countries, little of the money ever gets filtered through the city bureaucracies. For example, according to the Wisconsin Policy Research Institute, Milwaukee spends about $1,100,000,000 in Federal, state, and local money annually on poverty abatement. That money flows through 68 programs that spend almost $30,000 per poor family, but only about 35 cents of every dollar ever gets to the poor. Most of the Federal money funds a massive welfare industry.

Probably the only effective Federal agenda for aiding the cities is the promotion of national economic growth. The lesson of the past three decades is that central cities' fiscal fortunes often turn with the national economy. In the slow-growth, high-inflation 1970s, cities rapidly deteriorated; in the prosperous 1980s, they partially revived; but in the recessionary 1990s, cities again are financially strapped. Reducing Federal deficit spending through expenditure control, growth-oriented reductions in payroll and capital gains taxes, a noninflationary monetary policy, and regulatory relief will have a very positive effect on cities. It would be best to provide the stimulus of tax cuts and regulatory relief to all areas nationwide, but, if politics precludes doing so, the enterprise zone concept is viable, as long as it means tax reduction and deregulation, not a new subsidy program.

States' role. State governments substantially increased their aid to cities in the 1980s, but during the 1990s, with budget problems in statehouses, aid to localities has declined. In general, such reduction is appropriate. States should not be in the business of paying for locally provided services or acting as the cities' tax collectors. Whenever possible, local services should be paid for with local taxes. State aid to localities is defensible only when it distributes funds exclusively to lower-income jurisdictions or pays for services that provide a direct benefit for the entire state.

The principal way state governments can promote the economic growth of their cities is to reduce the over-all state tax burden on individuals and businesses. States without an income tax—such as Florida and Texas—tend to have healthy and growing cities. Northeastern cities clearly have been harmed by the high state taxes in that region. For example, New York City has estimated that a $900,000,000 tax increase proposed by the state would cost the city some 300,000 jobs.

Cutting service costs

Cities' role. The key to restoring economic vitality and capital investment to declining cities is to reduce the costs of providing municipal services and then slash the heavy tax burdens that are required to pay for them. For no justifiable reason, unit service costs are substantially higher in large cities than in small ones—whether for education, public transportation, street cleaning, park maintenance, garbage collection, or police protection.

Labor costs appear to explain much of the inefficiency. Salaries of government workers in suburbs average $2,150 a month, compared to $2,700 a month in cities with populations over 500,000. If benefits are added, the disparities are even wider. Large cities also pay their employees substantially more than comparably skilled private-sector workers receive, and the gap is growing larger.

If cities had the political will to cut service costs and taxes, they could do so without sacrificing vital services. One way to begin is through competitive contracts.

Smaller cities routinely contract out municipal services; large unionized cities seldom do. Indeed, some, such as La Mirada, Calif., contract out almost all their services and thus have tiny city bureaucracies. Several dozen studies verify that unit costs are reduced 20-50% by contracting out to the private sector. Moreover, the quality of contracted-out services is rated higher than that of services offered in-house.

However, public employee unions are so powerful in some large cities that not only is contracting out effectively prohibited, but any private-sector competition with the government monopoly service provider is forbidden by regulation. For instance, in New York City, private van and jitney services are providing fast, reliable transit for Manhattan commuters, yet the city transit agency has acted to shut such operators down. The action is contrary to the interests of residents and area workers. City provisions that prohibit private competition with the government should be ended.

Education is one of the largest items in city budgets. The declining cities tend to have much higher per-student costs, despite generally lower-quality public schools. In most large cities today, private schools provide a better education for half the cost of inner-city public schools. Central cities can cut costs significantly by recognizing that, when parents send their children to private schools, there are huge savings for the public school system. Even accounting for the fact that some school costs are fixed, if cities were to provide inner-city parents with incomes under $30,000 a voucher of, say, $2,500 per year to send each child to a private school, the public school systems significantly could reduce their operating costs and educational opportunities for children of low-income families would be improved.

There are diseconomies of scale in municipal services. Some cities, like New York, have such powerful special-interest lobbies and entrenched bureaucracies that it has become politically impossible to cut service costs, even in times of severe crisis. Large cities could reduce costs by splitting service responsibilities and conferring tax-

ing authority on city districts, villages, or even homeowner associations. If the provision of services and the levying of service taxes were closer to homeowners and businesses, taxpayers would have greater influence on decisions about which services they need and which they do not, and they could place greater pressure on the government to reduce costs by diluting the influence of special-interest groups.

An even more radical idea is for cities to acknowledge that they have become unmanageable at their current size and to split up into separate smaller jurisdictions. It would make sense, for instance, for each borough of New York City to become a separate city, as Staten Island is attempting to do. Service responsibilities that can not be divided conveniently—poverty programs perhaps—then could be borne by the county government.

Finally, cities can lure businesses and people back by changing the composition of taxes. If all cities with income taxes were to replace them and other levies on industry with sales taxes, those cities substantially could improve the business climate within their borders. City income taxes are defended by local officials as fair because they fall primarily on upper-income individuals and big business. In practice, those taxes are paid by the working poor, the middle class, and small business owners, because the wealthy have fled most cities with income taxes or have received legislative exemptions from high taxes.

Urban advocates are right when they say that America's inner cities have been victims of destructive government policies, but not those of the Federal government. The wounds of the central cities largely are self-inflicted. A 1988 private audit of nearly bankrupt Scranton, Pa., stated that "the city government appears to exist for the benefit of its employees instead of the people." Those words could describe the operating principles and skewed priorities of too many ailing cities. Unless and until America's central cities start putting people first, cutting service costs and anti-growth tax rates, no amount of Federal aid can reverse the decline of urban America.

Can we save the inner city?

Some experts are giving up hope. But the truth is, we haven't really tried.

David Moberg
CHICAGO

For several decades, starting just before World War I, the intersection of 35th and State Streets in Chicago was the heart of an African-American cultural and commercial hub known as Bronzeville. Businessmen and blueswomen alike gave vitality to a neighborhood populated by modestly paid blacks from the South who—when they had a chance—worked in the city's meatpacking plants, steel mills and railyards.

Now dreary, crime-ridden public housing high-rises stretch for several miles down the west side of State Street. Few stores of any type remain. Buildings that once housed historic black enterprises are boarded up and crumbling. Nearby multistory factory buildings are abandoned hulks with broken windows. Much housing is vacant; even more has been torn down.

The surrounding neighborhoods, where the population has plunged by two-thirds since 1950, are now among the poorest in the nation: as many as two out of every three residents live in poverty, and more than half are on public assistance. Through three decades of intermittent federal action on civil rights and poverty, these communities have progressively deteriorated.

Can a neighborhood like this still be saved? That question is being hotly debated among academics and even among the private foundations that have long bankrolled community-development projects. Journalist Nicholas Lemann, author of *The Promised Land*, argues in a recent *New York Times Magazine* article that it is folly to imagine that such urban wastelands can be economically redeveloped. These neighborhoods never had many jobs and now cannot attract business, Lemann asserts. Economic development of poor neighborhoods hasn't worked and can't work, he writes.

Sokoni Karanja disagrees. Karanja, who holds a doctorate in urban planning and has received a MacArthur Foundation "genius" grant, is the director of the Center for New Horizons, a community organization. Over the past three years, he has helped bring together more than 80 community organizations and 3,000 people to draft a plan to restore the neighborhood.

Karanja believes that redevelopment can succeed only with a grass-roots strategy that has broad support and tackles education, housing, health, jobs, recreation and much more. "It's not one thing but at least 25 to 30 things, and they're all difficult," he says. "It won't happen with a quick fix."

Karanja argues that such a development scheme has never really been tested. Mayors like the late Richard J. Daley of Chicago lobbied to change early poverty programs so that participation by the poor would be minimized, and development money would be funneled through political machines and government agencies. Since then, Karanja says, when federal funds have gone to poor communities, it has usually provoked futile squabbling among various agencies, politicians and community groups.

The South Side of Chicago would be a worthy candidate for one of the nine new "empowerment zones" that President Clinton is touting as the centerpiece of his modest urban strategy. Lemann's justifiable skepticism about what these zones can do—shared even by their advocates—does not warrant the conclusion that rebuilding historic Bronzeville is a lost cause. After all, even within the area's ravaged landscape there are pockets of rehabbed housing, a few lively shopping strips, some strong community organizations and other indications of hope for revival.

The 1993 empowerment zone legislation, an update of

the long-languishing enterprise zone idea, will provide $2.5 billion in both wage credits to employers hiring empowerment zone residents and tax incentives to businesses located in the zones. There's also $1 billion in new social service grants and a grab bag of other less targeted resources.

After years of neglect, virtually any new money for poor urban neighborhoods will be better than nothing. But even though the empowerment zones are less of a tax and deregulation bonanza for business than earlier enterprise zones, they are still anemic responses to a grave situation.

By contrast to the $3.5 billion Clinton is proposing to spend on the zones, more than half of his $23 billion crime bill would go for prisons. Spending the same amount wisely in neighborhoods like Chicago's mid-South Side could eliminate much of the supposed need for those penal facilities.

Clinton also has some low-budget initiatives, such as providing incentives for community-development financial institutions (contained in a bill now awaiting Senate action) or

changing the Community Reinvestment Act (CRA) regulations for bank lending. Both of these proposed reforms are aimed at directing more private capital into poor neighborhoods. (See *In These Times*, June 28, 1993.) Ultimately, they may prove more beneficial than the empowerment zones.

There's a simple truth behind the complex debates on poverty: poor individuals—or communities—are poor because they lack both income and capital. Yet instead of providing more money for already poor, black urban communities, our society has done just the opposite: for more than 15 years real incomes—from low-wage work or public assistance—have been plummeting. Public and private investment in poor black neighborhoods has been meager at best, as the housing stock and infrastructure have deteriorated.

Even the trickle of spending designated for the poor does not in fact end up in their hands. John McKnight of Northwestern University's Center for Urban Affairs calculated that government poverty spending is equivalent to about $20,000 a year for

Urban poverty theory comes full circle

For decades, debates have raged about the causes of the disproportionate rate of urban black poverty. In the '60s, the "culture of poverty" explanation held sway. This theory blamed the emergence of the underclass on patterns of behavior that were inconsistent with socioeconomic advancement. According to its most enlightened proponents, this culture was a coping mechanism for the chronic social immobility experienced by those living in areas of concentrated poverty.

Those socialized in such a culture were said to lack impulse control and the ability to defer gratification. The instability of their families led to early sexual initiations, lack of spousal fidelity and high levels of child abandonment.

Perhaps the most prominent proponent of this thinking was Daniel Patrick Moynihan who, as assistant secretary of labor, authored a report that labeled these characteristics "tangles of pathology."

Conservative theorists, seeking ways to discredit President Lyndon Johnson's ambitious War on Poverty, picked up on this argument and used it to blame poverty on its victims. People were poor because of self-destructive behavior patterns, they insisted. In reaction to this sophistry, liberal theorists began recasting the black family as a beleaguered but resilient institution under relentless attack by institutional racism.

By the onset of the Reagan revolution, some conservative theorists were employing a new logic. Trumpeting triumphs of a civil rights movement that they had ardently opposed, they argued that blacks now had legal access to American prosperity, but preferred the easy road of welfare dependency.

Charles Murray, in *Losing Ground: Social Policy 1950-1980*, blamed poverty on the same liberal welfare state that had been designed to eliminate it. Murray argued that federal anti-poverty programs altered the incentives governing the behavior of poor people by reducing the desirability of marriage, increasing the benefits of unwed childbearing and lessening the lure of menial labor. The welfare state effectively undermined those cultural characteristics that encouraged success, Murray and his legion of acolytes argued.

In the '90s, Murray has dusted off and reinvigorated the argument, and it has reappeared in the current debate on welfare reform. Perhaps this is Murray's way of belatedly responding to William Julius Wilson, a University of Chicago sociologist and the man most responsible for debunking *Losing Ground*. Wilson argues that macro-economic shifts were responsible for the peculiar and intractable species of urban poverty that now bedevils us.

Wilson primarily promotes liberal policies to address the problems of the ghetto poor, but he champions a race-neutral approach. This neutrality is palatable to the "new Democrat" postures of the Clinton administration.

Another University of Chicago sociologist, Douglas Massey, has recently been getting a lot of attention by arguing that racial segregation is the key structural factor responsible for the perpetuation of black poverty in the United States. Ironically, Massey's diagnosis closely echoes one made by the Kerner Commission in 1968. The commission—established to study the causes of inner-city riots—squarely placed the blame for ghetto poverty on white America. "What white Americans have never fully understood—but what the negro can never forget—is that white society is deeply implicated in the ghetto," the report read. "White institutions created it, white institutions maintain it, and white society condones it." The message was resolute, honest and well-received at the time. Ultimately, it was ignored.

—Salim Muwakkil

a family of three in Chicago. Yet the poor got only about one-third of that in cash. McKnight argues that poor people, especially if they organize themselves, would be far better off simply getting the money.

Even the best conceived, most generously funded development effort would fail, given the staggering disinvestment and income losses in many urban neighborhoods. What's stunning is not that most projects have failed, but that any have worked.

If we are going to judge whether it's possible to develop a neighborhood like Bronzeville, we need to understand how it came to its present sorry state. This sets us squarely in the midst of an academic debate between two leading University of Chicago sociologists, William Julius Wilson, author of *The Truly Disadvantaged*, and Douglas Massey, author of *American Apartheid: Segregation and the Making of the Underclass*. (See *In These Times*, Aug. 23, 1993.)

In crude terms, the question is: what most accounts for the intense urban poverty around 35th and State Streets—race or class? In other words, is discrimination to blame or the workings of the market? And should the solutions be race-specific or race-neutral?

Massey argues that the extremely high level of black residential segregation, especially in Northern cities over the past 80 years, is unique and unparalleled in American history. Despite 30 years of legislation, discriminatory practices by individuals, institutions (such banks and realtors) and the government persist, although sometimes in more subtle ways than in the past.

No ethnic group has experienced anything like the degree of social isolation that is commonplace for blacks. On a sociological scale in which 100 equals complete segregation, the index of segregation for most past and present new immigrants has been about 30 to 40 or less, according to Massey. But the average index of segregation for blacks in major Northern cities was nearly 80 in 1980 and 77 in 1990 (though slightly less in the South).

Despite the civil rights revolution, those indices of segregation have barely changed: in Chicago in 1920, the figure stood at around 90; in 1990 it had dropped only slightly, to 86. The record of progress elsewhere is similarly slow. Furthermore, affluent blacks are virtually as segregated residentially as poor blacks; the poorest Latinos typically live in more integrated neighborhoods than the most affluent blacks, Massey reports.

Numerous recent studies have demonstrated that blacks continue to suffer extreme discrimination in searching for homes and in obtaining mortgages, regardless of their income. The long history of urban renewal, public housing construction and other government policies at all levels has further contributed to concentrating blacks in the ghetto.

As Massey explained to a Chicago Urban League conference recently: "Take a group of people, segregate them, cut off capital and guess what? The neighborhoods go downhill. There's no other outcome possible."

Lemann blithely describes the loss of population in poor ghetto areas as simply the standard upward American march out of lowly neighborhoods. Yet Massey demonstrates that on the whole blacks have not had the same opportunities as other Americans to link residential mobility with social mobility. Because of segregation, they are thus denied the options—living close to better jobs, building equity in houses, pursuing safer communities or better schools—of white middle-class suburbanites. Affluent blacks move, but primarily to neighborhoods that are mainly African-American.

Residential segregation leads to an unparalleled concentration of poverty and its related social problems, intensifying the downward spiral of community destruction. Massey sees segregation as the essential creator of the underclass. Racial concentration may secure offices for a few black politicians, he argues, but in the long run it weakens blacks politically because they and their needs are isolated. The implication is that only a massive assault on this segregation, as well as discrimination by lending institutions, can undo the underclass and make it possible for Bronzeville and other such communities to be revived.

Wilson, on the other hand, has long contended that overt racial discrimination has "declining significance" in explaining black community problems. Instead, the flight of manufacturing from central cities and other economic changes has left many blacks without traditional jobs and unprepared for the new urban service and information economy, he argues. As black men were less able to support a family, marriage and family declined. Children of those single-mother families were impoverished and disadvantaged.

In a recent lecture (which was based on research for his upcoming book, *The New Urban Poverty*), Wilson acknowledged the importance of segregation, but argued that "to focus mainly on segregation is to miss dynamic aspects of social and economic change in Chicago." Today's hard-core urban poverty results from high and concentrated joblessness. Wilson used Bronzeville as an example: in 1950, 69 percent of neighborhood men over 14 were employed; in 1990 only 37 percent of those over 16 had jobs. The quality of jobs also declined. In 1970, 72 percent of young employed men worked in manufacturing and construction, but by 1987 only 28 percent of young employed men had jobs in those decently paid blue-collar occupations.

Joblessness makes a difference. Black and white youths at age 11 are equally likely to commit violent crimes but by their late 20s blacks are four times more likely to be violent offenders, Wilson says. There's one big exception: blacks and whites who are employed differ little in violent behavior.

The ghetto today may be just as segregated as ever, but it is far less stable, Wilson argues. Moreover, rapid desegregation seems impossible as long as whites can and will flee a neighborhood when the number of blacks rises. Politically, he concludes, blacks would gain most from broad policies to create demand for more workers, to provide universal health insurance and to boost low incomes. If blacks are working, they can better organize socially and politically.

Massey's work demonstrates that racial discrimination in

housing is a unique and persistent cause of the terrible poverty of inner-city blacks. Wilson's work underscores how changes in American business have contributed to hard-core joblessness. Together these forces have created the raw underclass culture that in turn is used to further legitimate racism.

Ideally, the government should both attack discrimination and stimulate job creation. Realistically, it is likely to do very little of either, although Housing and Urban Development Secretary Henry Cisneros has embraced Massey's work and shown interest in more aggressive fair housing action.

Where does all this leave Bronzeville? The community plan envisions building on the recent surge in middle-class black rehabilitation of the inexpensive but splendid old homes that remain in some areas and on building new, moderate-income housing. That in turn would support new retail centers. Karanja hopes to tap economic opportunities on the neighborhood's periphery—an expanding convention center, downtown developments, local universities—as well as within the neighborhood, such as a newly created black historic district and blues entertainment center. Some public housing would be rehabbed; other units would be razed and used for low-rise housing, schools or other new institutions.

In the shadow of the projects, the plan seems utopian. But if the federal government were willing to invest in housing and infrastructure in Bronzeville a fraction of what it spends on mortgage deductions and highways in the suburbs, then the plan might have a chance.

Even private investment could click, especially with some government cooperation. Most bankers look upon neighborhoods like Chicago's mid-South Side as a barren wasteland. Nonetheless, the 1976 CRA requires banks to make some effort to lend in all local communities.

Organized pressure over CRA compliance has generated more than $100 billion in bank loans to lower-income neighborhoods across the nation. Last year, the Woodstock Institute, a Chicago-based bank research group, reported that CRA loans for single-family homes and apartment buildings in low-income neighborhoods have proven no riskier than loans in better-off communities.

Nevertheless, most banks have dragged their feet about even minimal CRA compliance. Bank regulatory agencies, acting at Clinton's request, recently proposed new CRA regulations that would focus more on performance in lending, services and investment—and less on process and paperwork. The regulations also would force banks to reveal some data on business loans, as they now must with housing loans. This would help community watchdog groups press banks for increased inner-city business lending.

The proposed rules may never be instituted, due to Federal Reserve opposition. But even if the new rules are enacted, community-development strategists say they don't go far enough. Though the new rules would increase the pressure on the worst banks, they would also let many banks—especially the smaller banks that make up three-fourths of the industry—to escape close scrutiny.

Community advocates want the CRA to cover all financial institutions—including entities like mutual funds and insurance companies—and they want the act to impose tougher performance standards on lenders. After all, the evidence is now overwhelming that lack of credit in poor black neighborhoods represents a severe failure of the market with devastating social consequences, not the rational wisdom of the invisible hand.

Throughout many unstable but not desperately poor black Chicago neighborhoods, non-profit groups, private developers and some banks are successfully rehabbing old buildings and even building new single-family homes. Without CRA requirements, little of this would be happening; with greater federal support, much more could take place. Other local development groups are successfully retaining small manufacturing firms and even recruiting some new employers.

Yet these efforts at community economic development must contend with the much more powerful forces of continued segregation and discrimination, the mobility of capital and the restructuring of American business. Massey and Wilson clash on important points, but together their research shows that racial discrimination and market forces combine to wreak peculiarly harsh devastation on blacks.

This combined outside assault makes the resurrection of Bronzeville a tough proposition. It's hard to argue with Lemann's contention that years of scholarly theorizing about community redevelopment have had little result on the streets.

Still, advocates like Karanja are right in saying that the energies of both the government and the people within poor neighborhoods have never been fully committed to community development. If such a commitment were made, such efforts would need to focus on housing and education, supplemented by measures to link urban blacks to suburban jobs. Yet there are still inner-city industrial neighborhoods where manufacturing and other employment could be regenerated.

Wholesale residential desegregation, however desirable, seems remote, even with more aggressive fair housing action. Consequently, despite all the difficulties, it is both morally and pragmatically indefensible to abandon the hard task of economic development for neighborhoods like Bronzeville.

THE PROJECTS COME DOWN

America's worst public housing facilities are finally getting the bulldozer they deserve. That isn't a solution to inner-city decay, but it could be the beginning of one.

Rob Gurwitt

Rob Gurwitt can be reached by e-mail at robbg@well.com.

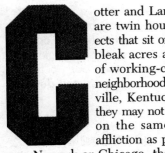

Cotter and Lang Homes are twin housing projects that sit on about 70 bleak acres amid a set of working-class black neighborhoods in Louisville, Kentucky. While they may not quite rank on the same scale of affliction as projects in, say, Newark or Chicago, they are not pleasant places to live. Two-story, barracks-style apartments built in the 1940s with flat, leaky roofs, they are planted hard by what is, not coincidentally, Louisville's most notoriously violent and drug-ridden intersection. Much like a rust-eaten chassis that threatens an otherwise serviceable car, the projects form the corrosive heart of the poorest census tracts in all of Jefferson County. So Louisville has decided to do something about them.

Until recently, that would have meant, at best, making cosmetic changes that might improve the complexes slightly— upgrading the apartments, putting in awnings, doing some landscaping—but would avoid the central problems. Now, however, it means something entirely different. Cotter and Lang are coming down. If all goes according to plan, the Louisville Housing Authority will not only bulldoze them but replace them on the same site with about 1,700 units of single-family homes, townhouses and garden apartments, only a third of which will be reserved for public housing residents. The rest will be subsidized housing for the working poor and market-rate housing for middle-class families in search of value.

Then, the city plans to take the Cotter and Lang residents who don't make it back onto the redeveloped site and scatter them in small, mixed-income multi-family units elsewhere in the city, hoping to use its own construction as a way to begin rebuilding confidence in other shaky neighborhoods. "You can use it to start turning the tide of a situation where all you see is disinvestment," says Barry Alberts, executive director of the Louisville Development Authority.

This is a moment of radical change in public housing and in the history of the ghetto, in Louisville and cities all over the country, large and small. After decades of debate, the projects are starting to come down. It is far from clear just what will ultimately replace them, or what the result will be for those who have been trapped in them for the past generation. It is not clear what the job of a public housing authority will even be five years from now. Inevitably, at the end of the decade, there will still be concentrated housing projects in large cities. Still, there is no doubt that a turning point has been reached.

In much of inner-city America, 1995 will be remembered as the year of demolition. No fewer than 32 housing projects around the country are slated for total or partial destruction before it is over. In the next few years, there will be many more. Most of the 13 cities that have big high-rise projects have made it clear they would be just as happy without them. "Just about everyone wants to get rid of the family high-rise," says Wayne Sherwood, former director of research for the Council of Large Public Housing Authorities.

But if the rush to dismantle actual buildings produces the most drama, the true revolution these days is less visible: It is a new determination to change the basic dynamics of public housing. Instead of trying to administer dense congregations of the poor, housing authorities want to "deconcentrate" their tenants.

As in Louisville, many are turning quietly but decisively to scattered-site housing, whether in blocks of a few dozen units or in single-family homes. They are beefing up their use of Section 8 vouchers, the federally administered program that subsidizes rental housing for poor families. They are experimenting with so-called "residential mobility" programs that move inner-city residents to middle-class neighborhoods. They are trying to piece together funding for mixed-income developments in an effort to transform both the physical and the social environment of what is now the ghetto. And even where they are simply tearing down projects and then rebuilding on the site, they are planning to create far less dense developments geared toward improving tenants' odds of eventually escaping the system altogether.

In Denver, for instance, the local housing authority has torn down 422 units in its Lincoln Park development, and will replace them with 206 townhouses. It plans to create a "family investment center" on the site that will provide day care and educational programs aimed at helping residents find work and become self-sufficient. In Charlotte, North Carolina, the housing authority plans to demolish the 400-unit Earle Village and replace it, in part, with what it is calling "family transition" units and a community services center.

"To participate in the program," says John Kinsey, who is coordinating the Charlotte effort, "tenants will have to identify specific goals over a five-year period of time. They will have to agree to improve their education level or take job training or whatever is required to move up and out of public housing within five years and be off all public assistance."

At the heart of all these moves is a conviction that by changing the circumstances in which tenants live, public housing will help the roughly 55 percent of residents who are neither elderly nor disabled to change their lives. "One of the reasons we're in this business," says Richard Gentry, executive director of Richmond, Virginia's housing authority, "is the belief that by changing the habitat, the surroundings, you can better their lives. We're trying to create a context within which normal life can occur."

Some skepticism is appropriate. Public housing authorities have talked this way at other times in their 60-year history. They talked this way, a generation ago, of the very projects they are now planning to level. Yet the underclass population they are dealing with today is depressingly vast: There are an estimated 4 million people across the country who live in public housing, 3.3 million of them officially and the rest off the books. As yet, deconcentration strategies have affected only a small minority of them; some of the schemes—most notably the residential mobility programs—still amount at this point to little more than boutique policies.

But none of this challenges the fundamental point. The era of massive housing projects crammed with the poor is coming to an end. "What we as public housing administrators have inherited are clearly ghettos of the very poorest people in projects that isolate them in the least desirable areas," says Andrea Duncan, executive director of the Louisville Housing Authority. "They are simply out of step with the times."

The notion that it might not, in fact, be the best social policy to sequester the poor in housing projects set outside the main currents of civic life is hardly new. Lee Rainwater, a Harvard sociologist, made the point as early as 1970 in his study of Pruitt-Igoe, the notorious St. Louis high-rise development that foreshadowed current trends when large portions of it were pulled down a few years later.

In *Behind Ghetto Walls*, Rainwater detailed the design problems that amplified the project's troubles and talked about the ruinous social effects of putting large numbers of families together who, because of welfare and housing eligibility rules, were overwhelmingly poor, disproportionately headed by women, and predominately minority and unemployed.

Rainwater was writing at a time when there was still a deep reservoir of belief in the beneficial effects even of large public housing projects. It was possible in 1970 to read without snickering what Franklin D. Roosevelt had said 35 years earlier as he dedicated Atlanta's Techwood Housing Project and launched the federal public housing program. "Within a very short time," Roosevelt told the crowd, "people who never before could get a decent roof over their heads will live here in reasonable comfort and healthful, worthwhile surroundings." By May of this year, when demolition began on Techwood, the words seemed hopelessly innocent.

At the time Roosevelt made his remarks, of course, public housing was envisioned as a place for working families to get a toehold on upward mobility. Those days are long gone. The median income of families living in public housing now is less than $6,500, compared with over $35,000 nationally. HUD has estimated that some 80 percent of nonelderly public housing residents live below the

poverty line, but that only gives a hint of the level of desperation. Most tenant households in large cities report income that is less than a fifth of the local median income, while overall, the portion of public housing residents making less than a tenth of the local median rose from just over 1 percent in 1974 to almost 20 percent in 1991. Public housing has, in short, become the place we put the very poorest of our citizens.

That policy carries a price. In the years since Rainwater published his Pruitt-Igoe study, a rich and extensive literature has grown up detailing the devastating effects of concentrating poverty, whether in public housing or simply in neighborhoods segregated by race and class. What is somewhat less familiar, although equally disturbing, is the effect the worst of the projects can have on the communities around them. A recent study of census tracts in Philadelphia by two academics at the University of Pennsylvania's

Wharton School found that public housing gradually dragged surrounding neighborhoods into the web of poverty over the course of a decade. "As the distance to a large public housing project decreases," wrote law professor Michael Schill and real estate professor Susan Wachter, "the likelihood that poverty in a census tract will rise goes up."

That is not to say that public housing need serve its tenants poorly or drag down the surrounding community. New York City's high-rises are often safer and in better shape than their surrounding neighborhoods, in no small part because the city's tight housing market has helped them—until recently, at least—to safeguard their mixed-income character.

Even the worst of large, concentrated housing projects can be rejuvenated. Boston's Commonwealth development, for instance, is "arguably the single greatest success story in the country of turning around a severely distressed develop-

Housing authorities are ready to abandon their most distressed projects, soured not just by crime and social despair but by the sheer burden of trying to keep aging buildings going.

ment," says Lawrence Vale, an associate professor of planning at MIT who has studied it. It took a determined—and $30 million—effort by the housing authority, the project's tenant organization and a private developer to make it happen, but the result, says Vale, is not just a tenant population that has the highest employment rate among public housing residents in the city, it is a housing project where suburbanites actually park their cars before taking public transit downtown.

Still, Commonwealth is an exception. In the vast majority of cities, public housing authorities are ready to abandon their most distressed projects, soured not just by the gangs, drug use, rampant unemployment and social despair but by the sheer burden of trying to keep aging buildings going. No new large-scale developments have been built in this country since the early 1970s, and much of the country's public housing stock dates from decades earlier. Estimates of the cost to modernize existing public housing range from $14 billion to $29 billion.

Small wonder, then, that any number of cities want to start over. "Our buildings make no sense in 1995," says Zack Germroth, spokesman for the Baltimore Housing Authority, which intends to tear down all of its family high-rises. "In 1948, they probably made some sense, although that's arguable to a lot of people. They just were not designed for poor people to have any amenities; they're vertical warehouses."

Until fairly recently, local authorities did not have the freedom even to consider radical change. "Not only have our residents been isolated by past housing policy and the restrictive nature of where they could live but we as entities have not been allowed to be players in our communities," says Andrea Duncan. "We had no flexibility with money; our only choice was to dump it back into projects that were poorly designed in the first place."

Now, however, those restrictions have been lifted, in large part by the changed outlook of their patron and regulator, the U.S. Department of Housing and Urban Development. For the first time, HUD is willing to countenance public housing options that don't involve simply modernizing existing buildings. In fact, it is promoting them.

"One of the major tenets of what we are trying to do is, when you have bad public housing, tear it down," says Deputy Assistant Secretary Kevin Marchman. "If you build back up on the same site, put it up in a way that will blend into the community and that will allow people pride in where they live, or disperse it into other neighborhoods of the city. And where you don't build or acquire hard units, give people opportunities by having vouchers, so they can find housing in the private market." In fact, HUD has recently made it clear that it intends Section 8 vouchers eventually to take the place of much of the existing federal housing program.

And so, driven chiefly by their own desires and by some slacking of HUD's tight hold on the reins, there is tremendous ferment among housing authorities. In San Antonio, Texas, and Pueblo, Colorado, they are moving out of the business of running traditional housing projects by buying up properties taken over after the savings and loan debacle by the Resolution Trust Corporation. In Rich-

'We learned a hard lesson from urban renewal 35 years ago,' says one expert. 'There is a risk that viable communities are going to be swept away' in the new wave of bulldozing.

mond and several other cities, they are buying existing housing with an eye toward selling it to tenants within a few years. In Baltimore, the housing authority has joined forces with the state to develop privately managed low-income rental housing scattered around the city.

In Hartford, Connecticut, Mayor Michael Peters pushed hard not just for the demolition of the sprawling Charter Oak Terrace but for redevelopment of the site for commercial uses. Instead, the city and the housing authority have reached an agreement to tear down one part of the project and replace it with about half the number of units, some single-family homes and some townhouses, with the goal of helping tenants eventually buy them. The other part of the project would mix residential and commercial development. "Everything we build from now on will be built not for housing for the poor," says Paul Capra, special assistant to housing authority director John Wardlaw, "it's going to be housing in which the poor might temporarily live, but it will be attractive to homeownership."

And then, of course, there are projects like Louisville's—or a similar proposal for a corner of Chicago's Cabrini-Green— that aim not just to reduce the number of public housing families living on a given site but essentially to develop the area economically and socially by making it attractive to working and middle-income families. No one has had much experience making such projects work, but its backers in Louisville are optimistic. An earlier project in another rundown neighborhood, overseen by the Louisville Development Authority, filled most of its market-rate units before its subsidized units. And a marketing study for the new project produced results that were surprisingly positive. "What we found," says Barry Alberts, "was that for African Americans, and particularly for some who had lived in that area before, there was an interest in returning and living in the inner city—in traditional African-American neighborhoods—if, in fact, the proj-

ects were to disappear and there was a good housing product."

There is, of course, another route that housing authorities are pursuing in their efforts to diffuse poverty, and that is to scatter it across an entire city or metropolitan area. Their thinking is that poor people will be more likely to find a way out of poverty and dependency if they can be helped to put the ghetto behind them.

One of the most extensive scattered-site programs in the country, in reach if not in absolute numbers, is Omaha's. After a modest start in 1987 buying houses around the city, housing authority President Robert Armstrong decided to push the program to the next stage by tearing down the city's worst project; then, after much controversy, he persuaded the city council to place the tenants equally throughout the city's seven council districts. In the years since, that notion has actually become overall city policy; eventually, each council district will have an equal number of public housing units spread throughout it. "Our plan," says Armstrong, "is over time to get rid of all our developments."

As Omaha's experience suggests, one clear factor in the success of scattered-site programs is how well housing officials manage to spread them out. That is not just because it would be pointless to reconstitute the ghetto in a new neighborhood; it is also because the politics of public housing become much dicier when you begin mixing public housing residents into working- and middle-class neighborhoods.

Springfield, Illinois, for instance, is just beginning to recover from a bruising fight over the housing authority's plans to build complexes in several neighborhoods. The numbers were not large by inner-city standards—mostly four to eight units—but their concentration was more than enough for the middle-class homeowners in whose neighborhoods they were to be located.

"When you put five or six units on one of our blocks, it's half the block," says

Charles Redpath, an alderman who represents one of the wards involved and a leading opponent of the authority's plans. "What you were doing was making concentrated housing in well-established neighborhoods that frankly didn't want it. The argument was we were basing our opposition on race, but that wasn't it—we had neighborhoods where some of the neighbors were black or Hispanic, and they said, 'We don't want this stuff, we worked hard to get here, we don't want concentrated housing in our neighborhood.'" In the end, the housing authority agreed to scatter the sites more broadly throughout the city.

The tangled politics of race and class have also recently put a dent in the other leading deconcentration strategy, known as residential mobility. Residential mobility programs help public housing tenants move to working-class or middle-income neighborhoods, either within the city or in the suburbs, subsidized by Section 8 vouchers. The notion is modeled after Chicago's Gautreaux program, which has placed about 5,600 public housing families around Chicago and in more than 115 suburban communities since 1976. Administered by the nonprofit Leadership Council for Metropolitan Open Communities, Gautreaux has been, in a sense, geared for success: It screens out families with poor rental records and more than three children; it avoids sending families to communities thought to be near a racial "tipping point"; and it provides its families abundant help in finding housing.

The results from Chicago and a smaller program in Cincinnati have been compelling enough that HUD set up five other programs around the country to study the impact more closely. The effort, known as Moving to Opportunity, was launched last year in Boston, Baltimore, Chicago, New York and Los Angeles. Earlier this year, however, Congress canceled the program's second year of funding after the first steps to move public housing tenants in Baltimore ran into fierce opposition in several suburban blue-collar communities that feared they would be overrun by inner-city blacks. Though the project continues to work with the first year's families in Baltimore, it will not expand as planned.

In the eyes of many housing analysts, MTO's mistake was that it operated blatantly. "Part of the success of Gautreaux and Cincinnati is they're essentially stealth programs," says Paul Fischer, a political scientist at Lake Forest College

in Illinois who studied the Cincinnati effort. "In some communities, there may be many families who have moved out of public housing, but there's no heightened identifiability. The problem in Baltimore was that the people running the program decided to have outreach in communities where some of these families were going to be going. It lent itself to a tremendous amount of demagoguery."

Indeed, says MIT's Lawrence Vale, that may be enough to limit the use of such programs. "To me, the results of Gautreaux would suggest that it's very much worth having in one's repertoire," he says, "but I would guess that the level of community resistance is so high that cities that want to do it run the risk of proposing a program that is politically not feasible to carry out." Vale's point becomes even more compelling when you reflect that Gautreaux covers only a relative handful of Chicago's public housing tenants, and the best-functioning ones at that. How it could be meaningfully applied even to the 12,000 inhabitants of Robert Taylor Homes is difficult to imagine.

In fact, all of the strategies that housing authorities are trying these days present formidable problems, though none of them are insurmountable. Scattered-site housing can not only be difficult to find, it is more difficult to administer and manage than concentrated developments. That may not be an impossible burden for well-run housing authorities, but 100 of them around the country are currently on HUD's administratively "troubled" list, and others will no doubt find effective management difficult.

Mixed-income developments have their own limits. They are, to begin with, tricky to piece together, requiring housing authorities to develop the kind of adroitness at assembling funds that nonprofit developers gained during the 1980s. And even then, they are not going to work everywhere. "It's incredibly difficult to do in most areas where there is concentrated poverty," says George Galster, director of housing research at the Urban Institute. "At Cabrini-Green, because of its proximity to the Loop, it's conceivable that non-poor individuals could be induced to live with poor individuals because it's a great location. But Robert Taylor Homes? Uh uh, I don't believe it. It's a strategy with pockets of possibility, but it can't be thought of as generalizable."

As much as we know about the baneful effects of concentrating poverty, we don't

actually know much about the impact of trying to deconcentrate it. It is more than a little ironic—bitterly so, in some cases—that renewing urban areas now involves, in part, tearing down the very places built for those who were displaced by the urban renewal of three decades ago. Nothing says that dispersing public housing residents won't carry hidden costs as well.

"We learned a hard lesson from urban renewal 35 years ago about destroying communities because of a rundown physical appearance," says Vale. "There is a risk, at least in some cases, that viable communities are going to be swept away, either intentionally or unintentionally, by deconcentration efforts."

And finally, creating new forms of public housing will undoubtedly require public housing authorities themselves to change. Already, the most forward-looking of them have abandoned their somewhat separate status as federal enclaves and begun to work far more closely than in the past with other local government agencies and service providers. "Our role has changed from being property managers to being owners of property where we must create an atmosphere that's conducive to positive learning, where we can assist, educate, help and employ individuals so they can become self-sufficient," says Omaha's Robert Armstrong. "The only way to do that is to have collaborative relationships with schools, police departments and social agencies that can provide the kinds of opportunities people need."

"What we're evolving into we still don't know," says Louisville's Andrea Duncan. "One possibility is a downsized entity that becomes more of an asset manager protecting the options for low-income people in the community—making sure that in the housing that's developed we're crafting a place for low-income people, because no one else will take that responsibility."

There is, of course, enormous risk for housing authorities as they abandon the past. If they're going to be putting up mixed-income developments, for instance, it's reasonable to ask whether they are the best qualified to take on the tasks involved. And if they are to adopt the goal of revitalizing poor communities, should they be taking the lead, or should they make way for development professionals to do so? Finding a new role may, in fact, turn out to be the greatest challenge housing authorities now face. As Lawrence Vale says, "If they aren't going to provide and manage public housing developments, who are they?"

Jumping Off The Fast Track

Career success was one a big part of the American Dream. Now, more and more people are waking up to a nightmare.

Bonnie Miller Rubin

Bonnie Miller Rubin is a Tribune staff writer.

Michael Jordan quit at his peak because the thrill was gone. So did Cubs superstar Ryne Sandberg. Gary Larson, "The Far Side" cartoonist, just retired at 44 because he feared his work would slide into mediocrity. Anna Quindlen, Pulitzer-prize winning columnist of the New York Times, recently stepped off the fast track to write novels and stay home with her kids. Harvard President Neil Rudenstine is on leave because he's "worn to a frazzle."

What's going on here? If those with some of the most glamorous jobs in America are dissatisfied—people who get six-figure salaries, limousines and thunderous ovations—what about the rest of us? How are we supposed to charge up the hill and capture the prize for the company?

We can't. We won't. We're tired.

It wasn't always this way. At one time, we came early, stayed late, worked weekends, dragged home briefcases and dutifully checked our voice mail, even on vacation. But now, what's the point?

The perks—the promotions, the raises and bonuses, the job security—are all but gone, and our ambition has evaporated right along with it. So, we'll just take a desk out of the way, even in some suburban outpost, if it means we can have a life in return.

Thanks to technology—to computers, faxes, cellular phones and laptops—the barrier between home and office has been removed, so we could be available 24 hours a day. Like some kind of Pac-Man, work devoured every waking moment until there was no time for anything else. Those were the rules. For 15, 20, even 25 years, we accepted them. But now, we'll pass on the brass ring.

"I'm squeezed dry," an IBM manager says. "Besides, if you're out of the loop, it can't be slipped around your neck."

●

An unmistakable job malaise has settled over the country like a fog, researchers say, and one need look no farther than the next cubicle to know that they are right.

With Baby Boomers getting older, organizations getting flatter and the contract between employer and employee—the one that said if you worked hard and kept your nose clean, you would be taken care of—virtually dead, driving yourself hardly seems worth it anymore.

"The signs are everywhere; people are at the end of the line in what they're willing to give up in their humanity," says Jeremy Rifkin, an economist and author of "The End of Work,"

a provocative new book that examines the changing workplace. "The mental fatigue today is every bit as significant as the physical fatigue of the early Industrial Revolution."

Indeed in numerous surveys, stress is identified as the nation's No. 1 health issue. In some two dozen interviews for this story—mostly white-collar, Chicago professionals in their 30s and 40s—the overload was palpable. Respondents used medical terms to describe themselves ("brain dead," "hemorrhaging") and their workplaces ("triage," "trauma ward").

What is significant is not the exhaustion but that it has gripped one of the most educated, driven and overachieving generation in history. Everywhere you go, the talk is about slowing things down; about sabbaticals and resigning partnerships and scaling back to part-time status. When Mickey Kaus, a columnist for The New Republic, recently flipped through Yale University's alumni report, he was struck with the fact that fellow 1974 graduates craved less, not more.

Wrote one Yalie: "As the commitment to achieve fades . . . forward momentum fueled by the desire to advance one's position has come slowly to a halt . . . I am beginning to discover the beauty of and the satisfaction in standing still."

We're in the midst of a seismic psychological shift about defining success, according to Mitchell Marks, an organizational psychologist and director of the Delta Consulting Group in New York, which advises senior executives of Fortune 500 firms.

With the first of the Baby Boomers hitting 50 this year, it is a logical time for taking stock; for reflecting on what has been done and what is left to do. As people enter the second half of life, they're asking themselves, "Is this *really* how I want to spend my valuable time?"

"There is a realization that there is more to life than where I am on the organizational chart," says Marks, author of "From Turmoil to Triumph," a book that addresses life after downsizing. "People see a workplace with scant advancement opportunities, limited pay increases and fewer resources to get the job done. It prompts them to ask, 'What's the payoff for working so hard?' "

Along with the psychological aspects, there are the physical realities of aging. Although vigor is not the sole province of the young, it is harder to sustain the frenzied pace of 25-year-olds. Rollerblading, vitamin-popping, Evian-swilling boomers may be loathe to admit it, but the days of working until 2 a.m. are over.

The voracious demands of the workplace show no signs of abating, however. Primarily because of downsizing, the amount of time spent on the job has grown by 158 hours a year—nearly a whole month—over the last two decades, according to Juliet Schor, Harvard economist and author of "The Overworked American." At the same time, the amount of paid vacation and sick leave has declined by almost four days.

In every previous period of history, increases in technology have resulted in a steady reduction in the number of hours worked. The opposite has occurred since the birth of the computer revolution, which made it possible for fewer people to do more work. "If current trends continue," Rivkin says, "by the end of the century Americans will be spending as much time at their jobs as they did back in the 1920s."

And that doesn't even take into account commuting, which in a metropolitan area such as Chicago can add two or three hours to the workday.

Not only are people working longer, they're working more intensely. As jobs have been eliminated, survivors are now doing the tasks of two or three people and living constantly with the everratcheting pressures of productivity.

In a national survey of 3,400 workers developed by the Families and Work Institute in New York, 80 percent believe their jobs require working very hard, 65 percent said their jobs require working very fast and 42 percent often feel "used up" by the end of the day. The Japanese even have a word for it, "*karoshi*," which literally means dropping dead at your desk.

At the same time, we've been all but overwhelmed by responsibilities at home. Sixty percent of all women are back in the work force before their babies are 1 year old. Fewer fathers fit "The Organization Man" profile of the 1950s, since they, too, must be available to stay home when day-care arrangements go haywire.

Everybody is stretched too thin. The only problem is that just when we need to find secure niches, where we can take it a little easier, those niches are disappearing. "The nation's economy and demography are heading in different directions," said Kaus in The New Republic.

"In the past, as people aged, it was pretty clear that they couldn't keep up with technology and hours, but they were kept around because of their wisdom and because they were carriers of the corporate culture," says David Noer, a vice president for the Center for Creative Leadership, a non-profit research and education institute in Greensboro, N.C.

"When aging Eskimos could no longer chew whale meat, they put them on an iceberg to die. Now, we're turning out our elders . . . we're turning into Eskimos."

You could hardly find a better carrier of corporate culture than Robert Reith, 53, who received his pink slip last summer, after 26 years at Amoco.

The polymer chemist was a casualty of a major restructuring, which claimed 4,500 jobs and lopped off an entire layer of management. The ways of the corporation were so deeply ingrained in Reith that when interviewed for this story, he asked to review it before it was printed, "because that's what the company always taught us."

In 1968 Reith—a newly minted Ph.D. from Carnegie Mellon University—started at Amoco and never looked back. Over the years, he had received nine promotions and had survived three reorganizations since 1992. All those accolades, along with a higher salary, were the very things that made him vulnerable this time around, when Amoco brought out the big broom. The oil company projected annual savings of $600 million as a result of the layoffs.

He chuckles nervously about his loyalty, knowing it may seem a foolish virtue in the retooled workplace of the '90s.

"Even when we were offered outplacement help, I didn't take as much advantage of it as I should have," he says. "I wanted to clear up matters before I went on to other things. . . . I believed at the last minute I would be placed somewhere else within the company."

But there were no 11th-hour reprieves. Now, he fills his days making phone calls from his Glen Ellyn home and trying to figure out what to do next. He'd like to stay in the Chicago area, even if it means limiting his job prospects, so he can be near his children and grandchildren.

"You never think it's going to happen to you," he says. "The company says it values people . . . but it's all about bottom line. I'm not bitter, but I am disappointed."

Baby Boomers, some just a few years younger than Reith, have seen the casualties and know it can happen to them. According to the Families and Work Institute study, 42 percent of the 3,718 respondents have experienced downsizing, and 1 in 5 fear they will be fired.

Even if you manage to hang on to your job, the rungs on the ladder are vanishing, making five-year plans all but obsolete, Marks says.

"I don't even know who to suck up to anymore," one copywriter said ruefully, after her advertising agency was restructured. "So, I'm giving up. It's too hard."

Instead of climbing vertically, some professionals think a better strategy is to move laterally, where broader skills—the ability to do many jobs well—may save you when the ax is wielded.

It may not have been exactly what you had in mind, but it can invigorate a career that has gone stale. You might face some challenges, learn something new, struggle a bit. But in the end, there are no guarantees.

Instead, people are bonding to their work, not to their organizations, analysts say. "It's healthier to be committed to being a good engineer or a good human resources person rather than to IBM, General Motors or Procter & Gamble," Noer says. "It's certainly safer; that way, if you're laid off, you don't lose everything."

Under the new contract—the one that says we'll keep you as long as we need you—it is more important to forge a tighter relationship with your customers than your boss, who may be of limited assistance if the company decides to cut you loose, Noer adds. Professional associations are essential, too. Not only can they help you in times of trouble, they also can furnish the social outlet that once was provided by the company.

Robin Hardman of the Families and Work Institute sums up the new contract this way: We won't promise you lifetime employment and, in exchange we won't hold you so strictly to the old rules. It has opened the door for employees to take advantage of family-friendly policies—such as job-sharing, part-time status and flex time—which used to carry heavy career consequences.

This shift has not been brought about by any moral imperative but rather the need for a work force that can expand and contract and reshape itself as economic conditions demand. Today's workplace has more temporary workers, part-time workers, even the beginnings of what is called task employment. Several corporations even offer one or two years of employment, and then you're out.

The good job, once the badge of responsibility, is now risky, and free-lance activity that was once risky is now the choice of people who want to act responsibly, according to Fortune magazine.

As Ronald Compton, CEO of Aetna Life & Casualty, puts it: "Forty years ago, we expected to be faithful and conscientious and stay together until retirement did us part. Today, on the company side, we expect to provide employees a competitive salary, interesting work and a chance to develop as individuals. Employees expect good benefits and a good salary. Rigid work rules and schedules have no place on either side of the equation. They just get in the way."

Says Noer: "The focus is more external than internal. People aren't jumping through the hoops because they don't matter anymore. You can dress right, live in the right suburb, do all the right things and be laid off anyway."

•

The lessons of people such as Robert Reith have not been lost on survivors. Given increasing job insecurity, employees are searching for ways to nurture the other areas of their lives. It's not a grand, defiant gesture but rather a series of small, subtle changes.

Perhaps it starts with reading a novel on the train instead of a trade journal. Or not bringing home work on weekends. Then it's a promise to be on the 6:08 every night. Or to stop working through lunch, and instead spend the noon hour in a Bible study group or other spiritual exercises, as one group of LaSalle Street investment bankers has done.

Then the thought of not commuting at all starts to sound pretty good. You transfer to a satellite office—away from the meetings and the company grapevine that used to be so important but also drained time from your day. Perhaps

you'll embrace telecommuting and move the whole operation to your basement. Without even realizing it, you have stepped off the track.

It's a strategy that Carrie Cochran, 44, a consulting producer for "Fox Thing in the Morning" on Fox-Ch. 32, recommends highly. She has stepped on and off the track periodically, the first time in 1980, when she left an anchor job at WBBM-Ch. 2—unheard of, especially for a woman who finally broke into the elite ranks once reserved only for men.

"I have no off switch. . . . I have a tough time saying, 'I know there is work to be done, but I'm going to go home now and be a person.' It is what drove me out of TV."

Cochran was practicing "task employment" before anyone called it that. "Since I can't control my appetite for work, I limit the length of the project."

The generation that has come up behind her doesn't have the same problem striking a balance between work and home, she says.

"We were the golden children, born into an era where the only direction was up and we could be anything as long as we were willing to work for it," she says. "People in their 20s aren't programmed for bigger, better, faster."

In an expanding economy, hitching one's identity to a career may have made some sense, but when the pie is shrinking, it's a recipe for disaster. A 30-year-old man in 1949 could expect to see real earnings rise by 63 percent by the time he turned 40; the same man in 1973 would see his income decline by 1 percent by his 40th birthday, making Baby Boomers the first American generation to be less successful than their fathers at the same age.

The outlook remains dismal, despite an improved economic picture. Wages have been depressed throughout the '90s, as ever-smaller raises barely kept pace with inflation.

Yet, at the same time, corporate profits and top executive salaries have risen rapidly. "The benefits of increased productivity and efficiency brought about by the new technology have not trickled down," Rifkin says. "They're staying at the top with stockholders and CEOs. So is it any wonder people are asking, 'Why should I kill myself?'"

It would be a mistake to take this throttling back as a sign that Americans don't care about their jobs. Indeed, the work ethic is as strong as ever. In the Families/Work survey, 99 percent of the respondents agreed with the statement, "I always try to do my job well."

They just long for more control.

They want to eat dinner as a family. They want to attend Little League games and be home to help their kids with their homework. They want to see friends.

No longer able to put their faith in careerism, they long for purpose to their lives. They'd rather invest time at a local soup kitchen or a neighborhood group than in boosting the company's bottom line.

In short, they want more time, and the average worker is willing to take a 5 percent pay cut to get it, according to a Department of Labor study.

"It's not ambition itself that is lacking," says Cheryl Heisler, a Chicago career consultant. "It is the ambition to succeed on other people's terms."

Last year, Heisler, president of Lawternatives, helped 1,000 professionals make career moves—some of them back down the ladder, such as doctors who wanted out of administrative positions.

"You can have all the trappings of success, but if they don't make you happy, what good are they?" asks Heisler, a former attorney who moved to a marketing job at Kraft and found them both an ill fit.

"For some people, the title and the prestige are not enough. Even judges—the pinnacle of the law profession—have found themselves unsatisfied. . . . They got away from what it was that attracted them to the profession in the first place. People say, 'What's wrong with me?' Nothing is wrong. The problem comes when you force yourself into an area that's not for you . . . for which you have no passion."

Mihaly Csikszentmihalyi, a psychologist at the University of Chicago, calls that passion "flow." It's that state of mind when people are completely absorbed in their work. Maybe it happens when you're painting, woodworking or gardening, when you are so engaged in the activity at hand that you're astonished to find that the hours have flown by.

Over the last 30 years, Csikszentmihalyi has interviewed more than 8,000 people on work, including a prolific 84-year-old inventor.

"He woke up every morning raring to go. He told me, 'I've been working constantly since I was a kid, but I didn't work a day in my life.' These are the people that carve out their own work life, and they're a pretty satisfied group."

The message is clear: The problem isn't work, it's fulfillment. In Csikszentmihalyi's study, people reported being in flow 54 percent of the time while working, but only 18 percent of the

Some for whom the flame still burns

Life isn't a sprint, it's a marathon. The tricky part isn't just doing it well; it's doing it well for a long time. So how do some people keep that enthusiasm and energy for years and years? Here are the secrets of the long-distance runners:

ROY CURRY, teacher and coach at Robeson High School for 29 years: "For me, it's being able to see that I've made an impact. These kids come in, and they don't know nothing; some of them have never been exposed to football. You watch that child grow and develop, and when you're done, you know he can play ball with anyone in the country. That's where I get my pleasure. That really gives me a reason to get up in the morning—and if you don't have something to wake up for, life isn't worth a thing."

ANN LANDERS, syndicated columnist for 40 years: "I'm motivated by the feeling that I am contributing something. Another reason I've been able to do this for so long is that I have a lot of energy. The personal contact that I get from readers is very energizing. If you're just a drone going through the motions, your work shows it, and you should make a change. You really have to care about what you're doing or you can't do it so well."

KIRK KLEIST, 43, supervisor, beaches and pools; 25 years with the Chicago Park District Lifeguard Service: "People who find their work mundane need to search for new ways to make it interesting. I tell the guards, 'Don't just sit there, get in the water, help people out, develop new programs, get people excited, make it fun.' Then, you'll have more fun, too.

"I also love the diversity of the job. One minute you can be working a swim meet, then you can get a call that a boat has sunk in the harbor. I've recovered hundreds of people over the years, and you always have to be mentally and physically ready. I don't ask my people to do anything I wouldn't do myself, and when I can't, I'll get out."

BILL ARNOS, 49, First District Tactical Unit for 26 years. Has been known to chase buses for blocks in pursuit of a pickpocket: "It's the thrill of the hunt, looking for pickpockets. You track them, stay out of view, watch them commit the crime and then apprehend them. . . . It's like a contest. And the criminals are always changing their methods: First, they worked the buses, then the subways, now they're stealing credit cards. You're always testing your skills against theirs.

"But when you recover someone's wallet—especially when it's a tourist or an elderly person—it makes you feel great. My paycheck would be exactly the same whether I ran after someone or not, but I wouldn't get that feeling of satisfaction."

PIRKO MILLER, coordinates patient care at the Ingalls Comprehensive Breast Center in Tinley Park. A nurse since 1957, she has worked in virtually every department, including a 10-year stint in the emergency room: "First, you have to be a participant, not a spectator. Life is a continuous journey, and you have to learn all the time. . . . For the Breast Center, I read research papers from all over the world, so I would know what's going on. You have to keep growing, and nothing grows in a stagnating pool of water. The more you do and see and experience, the richer you get. When I organized a medical mission to Ecuador, and when I started the AIDS hospice—the first in the south suburbs—I always got back more than I gave."

NATE JARVINEN, real estate developer and owner of Distant Mirror Cafe, 7007 N. Sheridan Rd., Chicago: "In real estate, everything turned tedious and negative in the late '80s and early '90s. Before, people would have tripped over one another to fund a project, but then everything changed. There was only so much negativity one person can tolerate, so I created a healthy diversion for myself: I opened a restaurant. I got to use a lot of creativity—I designed and developed a space, from the furniture to the menu.

"It gave me an opportunity to pour myself into something that could be exciting. . . . People are having a good time, they're telling you what a wonderful place you have. In real estate, you don't get that social aspect."

JONATHON BRANDMEIER, 38, radio personality, WLUP. On the air for 16 years, the last 11 in Chicago: "Listeners will say, 'Why don't you go out on the street with a phone like you used to?' I say, 'Been there, done that.' The key is to recharge it before you get into a rut. . . . That why I thought it was so cool when Michael [Jordan] quit basketball. It was the best move he could make."

—*Bonnie Miller Rubin*

time during non-working activities, such as watching TV. "Constantly look for ways to take a more artful approach to your job, master it until you can do it better than anybody and then move on to a new challenge."

That's what Jonathon Brandmeier, the WLUP radio personality, did last year. After 10 years in morning drive, he needed to shake things up. Despite pleas from management, he moved to an afternoon shift and arranged to do his show from Los Angeles on a regular basis.

"People thought I was crazy, the ratings were better than ever, and here I was messing with the formula," Brandmeier says. "But I needed to see new faces, new walls, even a different time on the clock. I needed to flex new muscles."

That may be impossible from within. For some, the only sane move is out of the corporation and into self-employment. Even Steven Spielberg, who had everyone in Hollywood clamoring for his services, embraced entrepreneurism. Why leave Universal to create a new studio with Jeffrey Katzenberg and David Geffen?

"Because," says Spielberg, "We want to be the owners of our own dreams."

So did Mary Ann Lillie, albeit on a smaller scale. A former vice president at First Chicago Bank, she endured a decade of turmoil in the '80s and had five bosses in nine years and found herself mired in monotony.

"I could have opened a file cabinet and pulled out what I'd done years ago, and no one would have known the difference. Sometimes, I just wanted to scream."

Instead, she researched business opportunities. She believed the market could support a fine-linens store and in 1988 opened a boutique called Sassparella on Wells Street, which she moved to Chicago Place two years later.

There are days, she admitted, when business is slow, and she thinks about the comfort of a regular paycheck, but she has never regretted her decision.

"You have to think about what makes you happy," she says. "For some, it's being on automatic pilot. I wanted to be in charge of my own destiny."

Since she left First Chicago, there has been yet another reorganization. "I might have been out of a job. . . . I'm glad I took action when I was just dissatisfied instead of miserable."

Sometimes, someone has to force your hand.

"I hated my job, but if Midway hadn't folded, I'd probably still be there," says Tom Beckman, a former flight attendant turned pastry chef. When the airlines went out of business in 1991, Beckman was scared—not only because he lost his job but his wife, Margie, did, too. He used his severance package for cooking lessons at the Cooking and Hospitality Institute of Chicago and is now creating confections at the Ritz-Carlton.

"Sure, there's aggravation, but I'm always there early, on my own time, trying something new. If you do something you love, you don't mind. We didn't realize it at the time, but Midway folding was the best thing that ever happened . . . it was like a blast of cold air."

Workplace gurus have even coined a phrase for it: serial careers. Anna Quindlen, however, eschewed the jargon for something simpler: "I want to do what I want to do. And what I want to do is different from what I've been doing."

That's easy for a highly paid New York Times columnist, but not for ordinary folks. Job consultants agree, however, that money—the golden handcuffs—is not the obstacle it once was. Cheryl Heisler, for example, has clients willing to cut their incomes in half to gain more intrinsic rewards.

To that end, we're doing the unthinkable, Heisler says. We're practicing some old-fashioned frugality. The big mortgage, expensive cars and designer clothes did not make us feel better. Neither did the boats, the skis or other pricey toys. What good is the $75,000 kitchen redo if you're still eating a vending-machine sandwich at the office?

"What I discovered was that I was too wrung out to enjoy the lavish lifestyle," says one Chicago accountant, who is quietly plotting his escape from a Big Six firm. "What I was really buying was the illusion of leisure. . . . That I was better off spending a summer afternoon reading a good book at home than battling traffic to get to our cottage near Lake Geneva."

So people are learning to live on less, either because they no longer want to be tied to the company or because they know that the tether can break at any time. Sometimes, the belt-tightening isn't even as painful as feared.

After 11 years with the American Hospital Association, Leslie Barnett was reorganized out of a job in 1992, along with her old boss. Together, they opened their own venture, Barnett & Miller Corporate Awards. He works from home on the North Side, while she works out of a no-frills office on the South Side, close to her Flossmoor home.

Today, the duo has some 300 accounts—including their former employer, which found it more cost-efficient to buy their services than to keep them on the payroll. Barnett says that after calculating the savings from a monthly train ticket, wardrobe, lunches, downtown health club (she now has the time to take real walks instead of using the treadmill), she is actually ahead of the game. "I can't believe how much more money I'm saving," says Barnett with astonishment.

The flexibility is just another fringe benefit, says Barnett, who has two boys, ages 8 and 11. She still puts in an eight-hour day, but now she's more available for everything from school conferences to car pools. "I loved going downtown every day, but I could never go back."

•

Can any of us go back? Are we consigned to workplaces where there is no loyalty on either side? Where people will see no merit in hard work, the virtue that has propelled countless waves of immigrants and is the cornerstone of the American dream?

Says Marks: "Employers have to accept a certain amount of distraction.

When workers wonder 'What's next?' it means a loss of focus that used to go into your job. Employers can't expect loyalty, and employees can't be naive enough to assume that loyalty will be rewarded."

Noer says that before we resuscitate that old ambition, some healing needs to take place. Employees need to let go of the anger and cynicism that has built up over the last 15 years, and executives need to acknowledge the pain.

"The ones who have empathy have already owned up to the fact," Noer says. "They've said, 'We've put you through a hellish time,' and that scores a lot of points. Employees rarely hear CEOs do a *mea culpa*."

Rifkin views the long-term implications in a more global context. "The central issue facing every nation in the years ahead is what to do with the time and labor of millions of people who will no longer be needed to produce the goods and services they once did."

The solution, he says, is the 30-hour work week, and he makes a compelling case, citing the success at some European corporations, such as Volkswagen. It not only means more jobs for more people, but it gives workers—especially parents—the time they so desperately need and want. An estimated 7 million children are home alone during some part of the day, and the loss of "family values" has been blamed for everything from the decline of our schools to violent crime. More jobs means reducing welfare, another political mandate. "This could be a powerful national crusade."

The dawn of a new postmarket era also means more people will be turning away from the private and public sectors and toward volunteerism—or what Rifkin calls the "third sector."

Not only does it provide satisfaction in a way that other jobs cannot, but it is the only sector that is expanding, Rifkin says. "It is the only area where technology can't penetrate. . . . It means using all your skills, but using them for a totally different end."

It also offers a different outlet for people's ambitions.

"Think of it as a wonderful wakeup call," Noer says, "to apply your human spirit to the world of work, to do something besides making other people wealthy, to make a real difference in this world."

The Dismal State of Public Education

Despite escalating spending, school performance and student achievement have not improved.

ALLYSON TUCKER

Allyson Tucker is manager of the Heritage Foundation's Center for Educational Law and Policy and editor of the Business/Education Insider, *a bimonthly education newsletter for business leaders.*

The education establishment claims that the answer to America's public education crisis is more money, more bureaucracy, more regulation, and greater federal intrusion. The data overwhelmingly suggest, however, that America's education crisis can be solved only by adopting structural reforms that ensure greater school choices for parents and local control and school autonomy for teachers and principals.

These reforms would change the system's fundamental incentives by replacing today's government monopoly, which is responsive to union bureaucrats, with a competitive system controlled by parents. The result would be increased options for parents and students, greatly improved school performance and student achievement, and a vastly improved working environment for teachers and principals.

The education establishment used the National Commission on Excellence in Education's report *A Nation at Risk* to lobby for substantial increases in educational spending. A spring 1994 report from the Education Commission of the States, How Much Are Schools Spending?: A Fifty State Examination of Expenditure Patterns over the Last Decade, shows that despite rhetoric to the contrary, after adjusting for inflation, state and local expenditures for education increased from about $108.4 billion a decade ago to around $210.4 billion by 1991–92.

According to the U.S. Department of Education's National Center for Educational Statistics, total spending on public elementary and secondary schools rose 396 percent, in nominal terms, from 1972 to 1992. While spending increased dramatically, enrollment actually declined by 7 percent during the same period, according to Mark Mattson in his Factbook on Elementary, Middle and Secondary Schools, 1993.

Despite escalating spending, school performance and student achievement have not improved. Scores on the Scholastic Aptitude Test (SAT), designed to predict success in the freshman year of college, have dropped nearly 80 points in the past three decades, even though, due to changes in the test over time, a person taking the same test and giving the same answers would score between 18 and 30 points higher in 1992 than in 1960.

This article originally appeared in *The World & I*, October 1994, pp. 32-39. Reprinted by permission of *The World & I*, a publication of The Washington Times Corporation. © 1994.

In 1992, the average SAT verbal score did not decline for the first time in six years, but the score was eight points lower than the average verbal score in 1986. During the same period, the average SAT math score remained fairly constant, according to the Department of Education. When taken in long-term context, however, SAT scores have declined dramatically during the past 20 years, especially on verbal aptitude. In 1972, the SAT verbal average was 453, and the SAT math average was 484. In 1991, the SAT verbal score reached a historical low of 422, while the SAT math score leveled off at 474.

The College Board, the organization that administers the SAT exam, recently announced that it would raise the average scores on the verbal and the math SAT tests to 500, making it considerably more difficult to compare the test scores of future students with those of previous years. By 1995, the average verbal SAT would rise from 424 to 500, while the average math SAT would increase from 478 to 500, thus inflating the test scores of all students who take the test in the future.

This recentering, according to a column in the *Washington Post* by Robert Samuelson, will "obscure long-term trends and make them harder to explain." He continues, "The practical effect will be to hide the lower scores and to reassure everyone. Worse, the recentering blurs the distinction between students' abilities in math and reading (and, by inference, writing). The trends on the two SATs contrast sharply." He concludes that "by raising both the verbal and math averages to 500, the College Board would obscure the crucial fact that scores have deteriorated much more in reading than in math for college-bound students."

American students are also scoring significantly lower than their international counterparts on international exams. For example, in the 1991 International Assessment of Educational Progress (IAEP), which assessed academic achievement in 11 countries, U.S. students finished last in the mathematics exam and 10th in science. In the 1990 IAEP exams, which tested student achievement in 20 countries, American 13-year-olds outscored only those from Brazil, Mozambique, Jordan, and Portugal in mathematics and only students from those countries and Ireland in science.

In an international assessment in 13 countries, the test scores of American elite 12th-grade students ranked near the bottom in biology, chemistry, and physics compared with equivalent students from other countries. When our top 1 percent of students were matched against the top 1 percent in an international mathematics study in 1988, our students received the lowest scores of any country.

Studies on literacy

Not only are our students' test scores dropping, but illiteracy has become a nationwide epidemic. A recent study by the Department of Education discovered that nearly half of America's 191 million adult citizens cannot write a coherent letter about a billing error or calculate the length of a bus trip from a bus schedule. Like other studies on literacy, the late 1993 government report discovered that 10 percent of all adult Americans admit that they have difficulty reading and writing. Needless to say, the business community was not surprised about the results of the recent study. According to Brenda Ball, vice president of

marketing for the National Alliance of Business, "only about 25 percent of the adult population is highly literate."

Our current education system is also failing America's brightest students, according to another recent report, *National Excellence: A Case for Developing America's Talent*, published by the Department of Education. It found that many smart students are not encouraged to work hard or master complex material, thereby learning less than their counterparts around the world. "The U.S. shortage of graduate students in mathematics and science," the report says, "forces many large companies—such as Texas Instruments, Bell Laboratories and IBM—to fill jobs, particularly in research, with people educated outside the United States."

Most gifted elementary schoolchildren have mastered from a third to half of the year's curriculum before the first day of class. But the education system makes few provisions for the special needs of these children. In fact, the department report found that 84 percent of assignments for gifted students were the same as those for the rest of the class. In addition, a survey of gifted high school students finds that they spend less than an hour a day doing homework. As Secretary of Education Richard Riley writes in the forward to the report, "Youngsters with gifts and talents that range from mathematical to musical are not challenged to their fullest potential."

As a result, America's schools are producing fewer top-level students. There has been a sharp drop-off of high-scoring students in the SAT verbal scores during the past 20 years. In 1972, 116,630 students scored higher than 600 on the SAT verbal exam. By 1991, that number had fallen by 35 percent to

Education's Report Card

Scholastic Aptitude Test scores have dropped nearly 80 points in the last three decades.

The school system does not encourage bright students to work hard or master complex material.

An increasing amount of what is spent on public education goes to administrators and other nonteaching staff.

74,836. The high-scoring students were 11.4 percent of the test-takers in 1972 but only 7.2 percent in 1991. These results are not due to low teacher salaries or large class sizes.

Teacher salaries rose 18 percent in constant dollars between 1982–83 and 1992–93, according to C. Emily Feistritzer's *Report Card on American Education*, published by the American Legislative Exchange Council and Empower America. *Report Card* also shows that the number of teachers increased by 16 percent in that 10-year period and that student-to-teacher ratios fell from 22:1 in 1972 to 17:1 by 1992.

American students spend less time studying and receiving classroom instruction than their international counterparts. American students do less homework than children from almost any other country in the industrialized world. Among 13-year-olds, 35 percent of British students spend two or more hours on their lessons, 59 percent of Spanish, and 62 percent of Japanese, compared with only 27 percent of American students. And American students are also spending less time on core subjects while they are at school.

In a report released in May 1994 by the National Education Commission on Time and Learn-

ing, American students were found to be spending less than half of each school day, only about three hours, on core academic subjects. The rest of the time is taken up by drivers education, AIDS and sex education, powerlifting, conversation, street law, study hall, home economics, industrial arts, and pep rallies, according to the study. The commission found that American students spend 41 percent of the school day studying core academic subjects, or less than half of the total time that their international peers spend on academics. That translates into 1,460 hours U.S. students spend on academics in the final four years of high school, compared with 3,170 hours for Japanese students, 3,280 hours for French students, and 3,528 hours for German students.

High costs

Increased government spending on education has not improved test scores or helped American students catch up with their international counterparts. Only a small percentage of the money spent on public education in America goes toward classroom instruction, the majority instead feeding the hungry education bureaucracy.

For example, a 1990 study by

scholars at Fordham University found that only 32.3 percent of the funding for New York City's high schools was spent on classroom instruction. The rest was used primarily for administrative overhead and nonclassroom support. Almost half was absorbed by the central city board of education and its staff of over 4,000, which filled eight city buildings. By contrast, the central board for New York City's Catholic schools, with enrollment of 111,000 students (or one-ninth the enrollment of the public schools) employed only 33 people.

Similarly, a 1989 study by the Wisconsin Public Policy Research Institute (WPRI), covering 110 of the state's elementary schools, found that only 33.5 percent of education dollars made it to the classroom. And a 1990 WPRI study found that Milwaukee's public elementary schools spent only 25.7 percent of their funds in the classroom. These statistics are repeated throughout the country. A study published in January 1993 by the Indiana Policy Review Foundation discovered that only 38.8 percent of that state's education dollars were spent on instruction, classrooms, and materials. That figure fell to 35.9 percent in Indianapolis.

Increased education costs can largely be attributed to the high number of administrators. For example, while the number of public school students has declined by 7 percent in the past 20 years, the number of administrators and other nonteaching staff has grown by 40 percent, according to Feistritzer's *Report Card on American Education*. New York City has more school administrators than the entire nation of France. And New York State has more than all of Europe.

New York City school custodians, for example, work part-time, are required to clean class-

Foreign Schools

by William F. Lauber

In the 1991 International Assessment of Educational Progress (IAEP), U.S. students finished dead last among 11 countries in the mathematics section and 10th in science. Yet when asked how well they think they have done, American students typically rank at the top. This false sense of confidence and poor performance signals danger ahead for the United States in its international competitiveness.

The American education system's poor performance internationally is not for lack of money. With the single exception of Switzerland, the United States spends more per pupil than any other country. In fact, the United States spends almost 50 percent more on education per student than Germany does and nearly 85 percent more than Japan does. And the spending gap continues to grow: U.S. spending per pupil grew at a rate 23 percent greater than that of Japan and over two times as fast as that of Germany throughout the 1980s.

Another frequently cited excuse for America's poor educational performance is large class sizes. However, this assertion has no basis in reality. According to a recent report by the Organization for Economic Cooperation and Development (OECD), for every teacher, there are 15.5 students in the United States, 20.3 students in Japan,

and 20.5 students in Germany.

Other apologists for the education establishment argue that the reason for America's poor educational performance is its relatively short school year compared with that of other countries such as Japan. Japanese students typically are in school for 40 days a year more than their American counterparts. However, when instructional hours per hour are taken into account, U.S. students spend more time in the classroom per year than Japanese students. As Diane Ravitch, former assistant secretary for educational research and improvement, notes, "We are the most schooled people in the world. The question remains as to whether we are the most educated people in the world."

The real problem

The real problem with the U.S. education system is that it has developed into a bureaucratic system concerned with preserving itself and promoting politically correct ideas such as self-esteem at the expense of true education.

The education bureaucracy in American public schools is much larger than that of its international competitors. According to a recent study by the OECD,

whereas teachers make up only 2.6 percent of all U.S. workers, workers in other education-related jobs (administrators, bus drivers, counselors, janitors, etc.) make up nearly 3 percent of the total U.S. work force. In comparison, nonteaching education employees in Japan make up less than 1 percent of the total national labor force.

The United States does not need to spend more money, lengthen the school year, lower the class sizes, or model itself after the Japanese or Germans. What we really need is to be, in the words of James Fallows, Washington editor of the *Atlantic*, "more like us" and open up our government-run education monopoly to competition. There is no reason why a country founded upon pluralistic ideals should have a "one size fits all" education system. We should follow in the footsteps of other countries around the world (i.e., Australia, Belgium, Canada, Chile, France, Ireland, the Netherlands, New Zealand, Sweden, and even the former Soviet Union among others) that have opened up their education system to competition through school choice.

William F. Lauber is assistant editor of Business/Education Insider, *a publication of the Center for Education Policy at the Heritage Foundation.*

rooms only every two days, and mop floors just three times a year. Yet they earn more than the city's teachers. The custodians earned on average $58,000 per year in 1990–91, compared with the teachers' starting

salary of $26,375 and maximum salary of $52,750. And while student enrollment in Washington, D.C., declined by 29 percent from 1979 to 1992, staff levels in the schools' central administrative office rose by 102.9 percent.

The evidence clearly shows that reforms based on increased spending, higher teacher salaries, smaller classes, and similar marginal changes do not work, because these factors are not related to school performance or student achievement. Only fundamental reforms including parental choice, school autonomy, and deregulation can reverse the deteriorating performance of our schools and the declining academic achievement of our students.

A comprehensive school-reform proposal would give parents choice of any public or private school for their child and deregulate the public schools. It would give principals and teachers in each local school, perhaps with parents as representatives, the authority to run their schools as they choose and select their school's curriculum, textbooks, and staff.

For 10 years since *A Nation at Risk,* the American education system has been broken. Tinkering with an inefficient and ineffective monopoly system has not improved the condition of public education. The dismal state of American public education will improve only with deregulation, decentralization, and choice.

Off course

Women's studies has empowered women to speak up in class. The problem is what they're often talking about.

Karen Lehrman

Karen Lehrman is writing a book on postideological feminism.

It's eight o'clock on a balmy Wednesday morning at the University of California at Berkeley, and Women's Studies 39, "Literature and the Question of Pornography," is about to begin. The atmosphere of the small class is relaxed. The students call the youngish professor by her first name; the banter focuses on finding a man for her to date. She puts on the board: "Write 'grade' or 'no grade' on your paper before turning it in." Students—nine women and one man—amble in sporadically for the first twenty minutes.

Today's discussion involves a previous guest speaker, feminist-socialist porn star Nina Hartley. The professor asks what insights the students gained from Hartley's talk. They respond: "She's free with her sexuality. . . . I liked when she said, 'I like to . . . my friends.' . . . No body-image problems. . . . She's dependent in that relationship. . . ." The professor tries to move the discussion onto a more serious question: have traditional feminists, in their antiporn stance, defined women out of their sexuality? After a few minutes, though, the discussion fixes on orgasms—how they're not the be-all and end-all of sexual activity, how easy it is to fake one. The lone male stares intently at a spot on the floor; occasionally he squirms.

I never took a porn class when I went to college ten years ago. In fact, I never took a women's studies class and don't even know if the universities I attended offered any. Women's studies was about a decade old at the time, but it hadn't yet become institutionalized (there are now more than six hundred programs), nor gained notoriety through debates over the canon and multiculturalism. But even if I had been aware of a program, I'm certain I would have stayed far away from it. It's not that I wasn't a feminist: I fully supported equal rights and equal opportunities for women.

But I was feminist like I was Jewish—it was a part of my identity that didn't depend on external affirmation.

Perhaps more important, as a first-generation career-woman, I felt a constant need to prove my equality. I took as many "male" courses—economics, political science, intellectual history—as I could; I wanted to be seen as a good student who happened to be a woman. There were a couple of problems, though: I didn't learn much about women or the history of feminism, and like most of my female peers, I rarely spoke in class.

Last spring I toured the world of women's studies, visiting Berkeley, the University of Iowa, Smith College, and Dartmouth College. I sat in on about twenty classes, talked to students and professors at these and other schools, amassed syllabi, and waded through the more popular reading materials. I admit to having begun with a nagging skepticism. But I was also intrigued: rumor had it that in these classes, women talked.

And they do. The problem, as I see it, is what they're often talking about. In many classes discussions alternate between the personal and the political, with mere pit stops at the academic. Sometimes they are filled with unintelligible post-structuralist jargon; sometimes they consist of consciousness-raising psychobabble, with the students' feelings and experiences valued as much as anything the professor or texts have to offer. Regardless, the guiding principle of most of the classes is oppression, and problems are almost inevitably reduced to relationships of power. "Diversity" is the mantra of both students and professors, but it doesn't apply to political opinions.

Not every women's studies course suffers from these flaws. In fact, the rigor and perspective of individual programs and classes vary widely and feminist academics have debated nearly every aspect of the field. But it seems that the vast majority of women's studies professors rely to a greater or lesser extent, on a common set of feminist theories. Put into practice,

Reprinted with permission from *Mother Jones* magazine, September/October 1993, pp. 45-51, 64, 66, 68. © 1993 by the Foundation for National Progress.

these theories have the potential to undermine the goals not only of a liberal education, but of feminism itself.

This doesn't mean, as some critics have suggested, that these programs should simply be abolished. Women's studies has played a valuable role in forcing universities to include in the curriculum women other than "witches or Ethel Rosenberg," as Iowa's Linda K. Kerber puts it. The field has generated a considerable amount of first-rate scholarship on women, breaking the age-old practice of viewing male subjects and experience as the norm and the ideal. And it has produced interdisciplinary courses that creatively tie together research from several fields.

Whether all this could have been accomplished without the creation of women's studies programs separate from the traditional departments is a moot question, especially since these programs have become so well entrenched in the academy. The present challenge is to make women's studies as good as it can be. Although the problems are significant, they're not insurmountable. And perhaps more than anything else, women's studies prides itself on its capacity for self-examination and renewal.

Berkeley was the only stop on the tour with an actual women's studies department. It is one of the largest, most established and respected programs in the country. Overall, it impressed me the least. At the other extreme was Smith, where the classes tended to be more rigorous and substantive and there was a greater awareness of the pitfalls of the field. (The students were also far more articulate, though that may have little to do with women's studies.) I found the most thoughtful professors in Iowa's program, which doesn't even offer a major. The program at Dartmouth, perhaps compensating for the school's macho image, seemed the most prone to succumbing to the latest ideological fads.

Discussions run from the personal to the political and back again, with mere pit stops at the academic.

CLASSROOM THERAPY

"Women's studies" is something of a misnomer. Most of the courses are designed not merely to study women, but also to improve the lives of women, both the individual students (the vast majority of whom are female) and women in general. Since professors believe that women have been effectively silenced throughout history, they often consider a pedagogy that "nurtures voice" just as, if not more, important than the curriculum.

Women's studies professors tend to be overtly warm, encouraging, maternal. You want to tell these women your problems—and many students do. To foster a "safe environment" where women feel comfortable talking, many teachers try to divest the classroom of power relations. They abandon their role as experts, lecturing very little and sometimes allowing decisions to be made by the group and papers to be graded by other students. An overriding value is placed on student participation and collaboration: students make joint presentations, cowrite papers, and use group journals for "exploring ideas they can't say in class" and "fostering a sense of community." Because chairs are usually arranged in a circle, in a couple of classes taught by graduate students I couldn't figure out who the teacher was until the end.

Most of the women's studies students I met were quite bright, and many argued certain points very articulately.

To give women voice, many professors encourage all discourse—no matter how personal or trivial. Indeed, since it is widely believed that knowledge is constructed and most texts have been influenced by "the patriarchy" many in women's studies consider personal experience the only real source of truth. Some professors and texts even claim that women have a way of thinking that is different from the abstract rationality of men, one based on context, emotion, and intuition. Fully "validating" women, therefore, means celebrating subjectivity over objectivity feelings over facts, instinct over logic.

The day I sat in on Berkeley's "Contemporary Global Issues for Women" (all women except for one "occasional" male), we watched a film about women organizing in Ahmadabad, India. The film was tedious, but it seemed like grist for a good political/economic/sociological discussion about the problems of women in underdeveloped countries. After the film ended, though, the professor promptly asked the class: "How do you *feel* about the film? Do you find it more sad or courageous?" Students responded to her question until the end of class, at which point she suggested, "You might think about the film in terms of your own life and the life of your mother Women are not totally free in this culture. It just might come in more subtle ways."

A previous discussion was apparently not much better. "We had to read an enormous amount of interesting material on reproductive rights, which I was very excited to discuss," Pam Wilson, a women's studies sophomore, told me. "But all she did in class was ask each of us, 'What forms of birth control have you used, and what problems have you had?' We never got to the assigned readings."

Self-revelation is not uncommon to women's studies classes. Students discover that they're lesbian or bisexual, for example, and then share it with the class. In a group journal (titled "The Fleshgoddesses") from last year's porn class, B. wrote: "There is still something about a [man] eating a [woman] out . . . that freaks me out! I guess I'm such a dyke that it seems abnormal." G. recalled that her father used to kiss her on the mouth "real hard" when she was eight or nine.

Of course, self-discovery and female bonding are important for young women, and so, one might argue, are group therapy and consciousness-raising. Indeed, I wish I had had some when I was that age; it might have given me the courage to talk in class and to deal with abusive bosses later in life. But does it belong in a university classroom?

Many of the professors I talked with (including the chair of Berkeley's women's studies department) viewed the more touchy-feely classes as just as problematic as I did. I saw a couple of teachers who were able to use personal experience, either of historical figures or students, to buttress the discussion, not as an end in itself. But even these classes were always on the verge of slipping into confession mode.

This pedagogy does get women talking. But they could do much of this type of talking in support groups at their schools' women's centers. Young women have many needs, and the college classroom can effectively address only one of them: building their intellects. As Ruth Rosen, who helped start the women's studies program at the University of California at Davis, puts it, "Students go to college to be academically challenged, not cared for."

But the problem with a therapeutic pedagogy is more than just allowing students to discuss their periods or sex lives in class. Using the emotional and subjective to "validate" women risks validating precisely the stereotypes that feminism was supposed to eviscerate: women are irrational, women must ground all knowledge in their own experiences, etc. A hundred years ago, women were fighting for the right to learn math, science, Latin—to be educated like men; today, many women are content to get their feelings heard, their personal problems aired, their instincts and intuition respected.

POLITICS, AS USUAL

"Don't worry. We've done nothing here since she forgot her notes a couple of weeks ago," Michael Williams reassures another male student. "We'll probably talk about Anita Hill again." We're waiting for Berkeley's "Gender Politics: Theory and Comparative Study" to begin. When the professor finally arrives and indicates

that, yes, we'll be talking about Anita Hill again, the second male student packs up and bolts. Williams tells me that during the first week or two, whenever a male student would comment on something, the professor would say, "What you really mean is . . ." Most men stopped speaking and then dropped out. "Other classes I walk out with eight pages of notes," says Williams. "Here, everybody just says the same thing in a different way" (He stays, though, for the "easy credits.")

Most women's studies professors seem to adhere to the following principles in formulating classes: women were and are oppressed; oppression is endemic to our patriarchal social system; men, capitalism, and Western values are responsible for women's problems. The reading material is similarly bounded in political scope (Andrea Dworkin, Catharine MacKinnon, bell hooks, Adrienne Rich, and Audre Lorde turn up a lot), and opposing viewpoints are usually presented only through a feminist critique of them. *Feminist Frontiers III*, a book widely used in intro courses, purports to show readers "how gender has shaped your life," and invites them to join in the struggle "to reform the structure and culture of male dominance."

Says one student, "The way to get A's was to write papers full of guilt and angst about how I'd bought into society's definition of womanhood."

Although most of the classes I attended stopped short of outright advocacy of specific political positions, virtually all carried strong political undercurrents. Jill Harvey, a women's studies senior at Smith, recalls a feminist anthropology course in which she "quickly discovered that the way to get A's was to write papers full of guilt and angst about how I'd bought into society's definition of womanhood and now I'm enlightened and free."

Sometimes the politicization is more subtle. "I'm not into consciousness-raising," says Linda K. Kerber, a history professor at Iowa. "Students can feel I'm grading them on their competence and not on their politics." Yet in the final project of "Gender and Society in the United States," she asked students: "Reconsider a term paper you have written for another class. How would you revise it now to ensure that it offers an analysis sensitive to gender as well as to race and class?"

Politicization is also apparent in the meager amount of time the classes devote to women who have achieved anything of note in the public sphere. Instead, students scrutinize the diaries and letters of unremarkable women who are of interest primarily because the patriarchy victimized them in one way or another.

According to professors and students, studying "women worthies" doesn't teach you much about oppression. Moreover some added, these women succeeded by male, capitalist standards. It's time for women's traditional roles and forms of expression to be valued.

This may be true, but you don't need to elevate victimized women to the status of heroes to do that. It should also be noted that over the past twenty-five years feminists have been among those who have devalued women's traditional roles most vigorously. I bet not many women's studies majors would encourage a peer's decision to forgo a career in order to stay home and raise children. More important, examples of women who succeeded in the public sphere, possibly even while caring for a family, could be quite inspiring for young women. Instead, the classes implicitly downplay individual merit and focus on the systematic forces that are undermining everything women do.

In general, "core" women's studies courses are more overtly political and less academically rigorous than those cross-listed with a department. The syllabus of Iowa's "Introduction to Women's Studies" course declares: "As we make our collective and individual journeys during this course, we will consider how to integrate our theoretical knowledge with personal and practical action in the world." "Practicums," which typically entail working in a women's organization, are a key part of many courses, often requiring thirty or more hours of a student's time.

Volunteering in a battered-women's shelter or rape crisis center may be deeply significant for both students and society. But should this be part of an undergraduate education? Students have only four years to learn the things a liberal education can offer—and the rest of their lives to put that knowledge to use.

Courses on women don't have to be taught from an orthodox feminist perspective. Smith offers a biology course that's cross-listed with women's studies. It deals with women's bodies and medical issues; feminist theory is not included. Compare that to the course description of Berkeley's "Health and Sex in America": "From sterilization to AIDS; from incest to date rape; from anorexia to breast implants: who controls women's health?" Which course would you trust to be more objective?

Many women's studies professors acknowledge their field's bias, but point out that all disciplines are biased. Still, there's a huge difference between conceding that education has political elements and intentionally politicizing, between, as Women's Studies Professor Daphne Patai puts it, "recognizing and minimizing deep biases and proclaiming and endorsing them." Patai, whose unorthodox views got her in hot water at the University of Massachusetts, is now coauthoring a book on the contradictions of women's studies. "Do they really want fundamentalist studies, in which teachers are not just studying fundamentalism but supporting it?"

A still larger problem is the degree to which politics has infected women's studies scholarship. "Feminist theory guarantees that researchers will discover male bias and oppression in every civilization and time," says Mary Lefkowitz, a classics professor at Wellesley. "A distinction has to be made between historical interpretation of the past and political reinterpretation." And, I would add, between reading novels with an awareness of racism and sexism, and reducing them entirely to constructs of race and gender.

Apparently there has always been a tug of war within the women's studies community between those who most value scholarship and those who most value ideology. Some professors feel obligated to present the work of all women scholars who call themselves feminists, no matter how questionable their methodology or conclusions.

Unfortunately women's studies students may not be as well equipped to see through shoddy feminist scholarship as they are through patriarchal myths and constructs. One reason may be the interdisciplinary nature of the programs, which offers students minimal grounding in any of the traditional disciplines. According to Mary Lefkowitz, women's studies majors who take her class exhibit an inability to amass factual material or remember details; instead of using evidence to support an argument, they use it as a remedy for their personal problems.

But teaching students how to "think critically" is one of the primary goals of women's studies, and both students and professors say that women's studies courses are more challenging than those in other departments. "Women's studies gives us tools to analyze," says Torrey Shanks, a senior women's studies and political science major at Berkeley. "We learn theories about how to look at women and men; we don't just come away with facts."

Women's studies has generated first-rate scholarship on women, but professors often consider a pedagogy that "nurtures voice" just as, if not more, important than the curriculum.

Most of the women's studies students I met were quite bright, and many argued certain points very articulately. But they seemed to have learned to think critically through only one lens. When I asked some of the sharpest students about the most basic criticisms of women's studies, they appeared not to have thought about them or gave me some of the stock women's studies rap. It seemed that they couldn't fit these questions into their way of viewing the world.

For instance, when I expressed the view that an at-times explicit anticapitalist and anti-Western bias pervades the field, a couple of majors told me they thought that being anticapitalist was part of being a feminist. When I asked whether, in the final analysis, women weren't still most free in Western capitalist societies, the seemingly programmed responses ran from "I wouldn't feel free under a glass ceiling" to "Pressures on Iranian women to wear the veil are no different from pressures on women in this country to wear heels and miniskirts."

THE STUDENT PARTY LINE

Despite the womb-like atmosphere of the classrooms, I didn't see much student questioning of the professors or the texts. Although I rarely saw teachers present or solicit divergent points of view the students' reluctance to voice alternative opinions seemed to stem more from political intolerance and conformity on the part of fellow students.

In Smith's "Gender and Politics" class, several students spoke against the ban on gays in the military before Erin O'Connor, her voice shaking, ventured: "I think there is something to the argument of keeping gays out of the military because of how people feel about it."

After several students said things like, "The military should reflect society" O'Connor rebounded: "I'm sick and tired of feeling that if I have a moral problem with something, all of a sudden it's: 'You're homophobic, you're wrong, you're behind the times, go home.' There must be someone else in this classroom who believes as I do."

Professor: "No one is saying that support of the ban is homophobic."

"I would make that assertion," offered a student.

Professor: "But you can argue against the ban from a nonhomophobic perspective."

Another student: "It's homophobic."

When class ended, another woman approached O'Connor and said: "You're absolutely right, and I'm sure there are others who felt the same way but just didn't say anything. You went out on a limb."

No one used the word homophobic until O'Connor did. Still, students, especially in this ostensible "safe environment," shouldn't have to overcome a pounding heart to voice a dissident opinion. "Women's studies creates a safe space for p.c. individuals, but doesn't maintain any space for white Christians," says O'Connor, an English and government major and member of the College Republican Club.

In a study by the Association of American Colleges, 30 percent of students taking women's studies courses at Wellesley said they felt uneasy expressing unpopular opinions; only 14 percent of non-women's studies students felt that way.

Smith's Jill Harvey told me about a "Medical Anthropology" class filled with women's studies students. The professor presented an author's view that one difference between men and women when paralyzed is that men are rendered incapable of getting an erection. "The students jumped down his throat, believing he was insinuating that all women have to do is lie back and enjoy sex," says Harvey. "It was absurd, but I didn't feel like I could speak up. I sometimes feel the other students' attitude is: if you don't agree with me, you're too stupid to understand how oppressed you are."

The pressures on professors to toe the correct feminist line can be even stronger. History Professor Elizabeth Fox-Genovese says she stepped down as chair of Emory's women's studies program because of complaints from students and faculty that she wasn't radical enough. Political theorist Jean Bethke Elshtain left the University of Massachusetts after being attacked for including men on her reading list, allowing men in class, and presenting an array of different feminist positions. She now teaches at Vanderbilt. "Most teachers of women's studies presume that if you don't see yourself as a victim, you're in a state of false consciousness, you're 'male-identified.' The professors here [at Vanderbilt] recognize that feminism is in part an argument."

Women's studies professors take little responsibility for turning female students into Angry Young Women. Yet the effect of these classes, one after another, can be quite intoxicating. (After just a few days, I found myself noticing that the sign on the women's bathroom door in the University of Iowa's library was smaller than the one on the men's room door.) The irony is not only that these students (who, at the schools I visited at least, were overwhelmingly white and upper-middle-class) probably have not come into contact with much oppression, but that they are the first generation of women who have grown up with so many options open to them.

POST-STRUCTURALISM AND MULTICULTURALISM

Perhaps the most troubling influence on women's studies in the past decade has been the collection of theories known as post-structuralism, which essentially implies that all texts are arbitrary all knowledge is biased, all standards are illegitimate, all morality is subjective. I talked to numerous women's studies professors who don't buy any of this (it's typically more popular in the humanities than in the social sciences), but nevertheless it has permeated women's studies to a significant extent, albeit in the most reductive, simplistic way.

According to Delo Mook, a Dartmouth physics professor who is part of a team teaching "Ways of Knowing: Physics, Literature, Feminism," "You can't filter other cultures through our stencil. Nothing is right or wrong."

What about cannibalism? Clitorectomies? "Nope. I can only say 'I believe it's wrong.'"

But post-structuralism is applied inconsistently in women's studies. I've yet to come across a feminist tract that "contextualizes" sexism in this country as it does in others, or acknowledges that feminism is itself a product of Western culture based on moral reasoning and the premise that some things are objectively wrong. Do feminist theorists really want the few young men who take these classes to formulate personal rationales for rape? There's a huge difference between questioning authority, truth, and knowledge and saying none of these exist, a difference between rejecting male standards and rejecting the whole concept of standards.

Like post-structuralism, the concept of multiculturalism has had a deep influence on women's studies. Professors seem under a constant burden to prove that they are presenting the requisite number of books or articles by women of color or lesbians. Issues of race came up in nearly every class I sat through. I wasn't allowed to sit in on a seminar at Dartmouth on "Racism and Feminism" because of a contract made with the students that barred outside visitors.

Terms like sexism, racism, and homophobia have bloated beyond all recognition, and the more politicized the campus, the more frequently they're thrown around. I heard both professors and students call Berkeley's women's studies department homophobic and racist, despite the fact that courses dealing with homosexuality and multiculturalism fill the catalog and quite a number of women of color and lesbians are affiliated with the department.

Although many professors try to work against it, in the prevailing ethos of women's studies, historical figures, writers, and the students themselves are viewed foremost as women, as lesbians, as white or black or Hispanic, and those with the most "oppressed" identities are the most respected. Feminist theorists now generally admit that they can't speak for all women, but some still presume to speak for all black women or all Jewish women or all lesbians. There's still little acknowledgment not only of the individuality of each woman, but of the universal, gender-blind bond shared by all human beings.

THE ROAD NOT TAKEN

Women's studies programs have clearly succeeded with at least one of their goals: whether because of the mostly female classes, the nurturing professors, or the subject matter, they have gotten women students talking.

But getting women to speak doesn't help much if they're all saying the same thing. Women's studies students may make good polemicists, but do they really learn to think independently and critically?

Elizabeth Fox-Genovese says she had envisioned Emory's women's studies program as a mini-women's college: "I thought it should be a special environment that took women seriously and asked them to be the best that they could be by the standards of a good, liberal arts education." Young women—and men—would be steeped in sound scholarship on women, but they would also be offered a variety of theories and viewpoints, feminist and otherwise.

Unfortunately, this hasn't been the perspective of most women's studies professors. Women's studies was conceived with a political purpose—to be the intellectual arm of the women's movement—and its sense of purpose has only gotten stronger through the years. The result is that the field's narrow politics have constricted the audience for nonideological feminism instead of widening it, and have reinforced the sexist notion that there is a women's viewpoint. There's a legitimate reason why two-thirds of college women don't call themselves feminists. "When I got here I thought I was a feminist," Erin O'Connor from Smith told me. "I don't want to call myself that now."

Clearly the first step is for women's studies to reopen itself to internal and external criticism. The intimidation in the field is so great that I had trouble finding dissident voices willing to talk to me on the record. The women's movement has come a long way in the past twenty-five years-feminists should feel secure enough now to take any and all lumps.

Young women should also no longer feel it necessary to shun classes devoted to women, as my friends and I did. Women today still have to work for their equality, but they don't have to prove it every second. And as the status of women in this country evolves, so should the goals of women's studies. It's for its own sake that women's studies should stop treating women as an ensemble of victimized identities. Only when the mind of each woman is considered on its own unique terms will the minds of all women be respected.

Truth and Consequences
TEEN SEX

Douglas J. Besharov with Karen N. Gardiner

Douglas J. Besharov is a resident scholar at the American Enterprise Institute. Karen Gardiner is a research assistant at the American Enterprise Institute.

Ten million teenagers will engage in about 126 million acts of sexual intercourse this year. As a result, there will be about one million pregnancies, resulting in 406,000 abortions, 134,000 miscarriages, and 490,000 live births. Of the births, about 313,000, or 64 percent, will be out of wedlock. And about three million teenagers will suffer from a sexually transmitted disease such as chlamydia, syphilis, gonorrhea, pelvic inflammatory disease, and even AIDS.

This epidemic of teen pregnancy and infection has set off firestorms of debate in school systems from Boston to San Francisco. Last May, Washington, D.C. Mayor Sharon Pratt Kelly announced that health officials would distribute condoms to high school and junior high school students. Parents immediately protested, taking to the streets with placards and angry shouts. And the New York City Board of Education was virtually paralyzed for weeks by the controversy surrounding its plans for condom distribution.

Both sides have rallied around the issue of condom distribution as if it were a referendum on teen sexuality. Proponents argue that teenagers will have sex whether contraceptives are available or not, so public policy should aim to reduce the risk of pregnancy and the spread of sexually transmitted diseases by making condoms easily available. Opponents claim that such policies implicitly endorse teen sex and will only worsen the problem.

The causes of teen pregnancy and sexually transmitted diseases, however, run much deeper than the public rhetoric that either side suggests. Achieving real change in the sexual behavior of teenagers will require action on a broader front.

Thirty Years into the Sexual Revolution

Some things are not debatable: every year, more teenagers are having more sex, they are having it with increasing frequency, and they are starting at younger ages.

There are four principal sources of information about the sexual practices of teenagers: the National Survey of Family Growth (NSFG), a national in-person survey of women ages 15–44 conducted in 1982 and again in 1988; the National Survey of Adolescent Males (NSAM), a longitudinal survey of males ages 15–19 conducted in 1988 and 1991; the National

Survey of Young Men (NSYM), a 1979 survey of 17- to 19-year-olds; and the Youth Risk Behavior Survey (YRBS), a 1990 questionnaire-based survey of 11,631 males and females in grades 9–12 conducted by the Centers for Disease Control (CDC). In addition, the Abortion Provider Survey, performed by the Alan Guttmacher Institute (AGI), collects information about abortions and those who provide them.

With minor variations caused by differences in methodology, each survey documents a sharp increase in the sexual activity of American teenagers. All these surveys, however, are based on the self-reports of young people and must be interpreted with care. For example, one should always take young males' reports about their sexual exploits with a grain of salt. In addition, the social acceptability of being a virgin may have decreased so much that this, more than any change in behavior, has led to the higher reported rates of sexual experience. The following statistics should therefore be viewed as indicative of trends rather than as precise and accurate measures of current behavior.

A cursory glance at Figure 1 shows that there was indeed a sexual revolution. The 1982 NSFG asked women ages 15–44 to recall their first premarital sexual experience. As the figure shows, teenagers in the early 1970s (that is, those born between 1953 and 1955) were twice as likely to have had sex as were teenagers in the early 1960s (that is those born 1944 to 1946).

The trend of increased sexual activity that started in the 1960s continued well into the late 1980s. According to the 1988 NSFG, rates of sexual experience increased about 45 percent between 1970 and 1980 and increased another 20 percent in just three years, from 1985–1988, but rates have now apparently plateaued. Today, over half of all unmarried teenage girls report that they have engaged in sexual intercourse at least once.

These aggregate statistics for all teenagers obscure the second remarkable aspect of this 30-year trend: sexual activity is starting at ever-younger ages. The 1988 NSFG found that the percentage of 18-year-olds who reported being sexually active increased about 75 percent between 1970 and 1988, from about 40 percent to about 70 percent. Even more startling is that the percentage of sexually experienced 15-year-old females multiplied more than fivefold in the same period, from less than 5 percent to almost 27 percent.

Moreover, the increase in sexual activity among young teens continued beyond 1988. In 1990, 32 percent of ninth-grade females (girls ages 14 and 15) reported ever having had sex, as did 49 percent of the males in the same grade. At the same time, the proportion of twelfth-grade females (ages 17 and 18) who reported ever engaging in sex remained at 1988 levels.

Teenagers are not only having sex earlier, they are also having sex with more partners. According to the NSAM, the average number of partners reported by males in the 12 months preceding the survey increased from 2.0 in 1988 to 2.6 in 1991. Almost 7 percent of ninth-grade females told the YRBS that they had had intercourse with four or more different partners, while 19 percent of males the same age reported having done so. By the twelfth grade, 17 percent of girls and 38 percent of boys reported having four or more sexual partners.

A major component of these increases has been the rise in sexual activity among middle-class teenagers. Between 1982 and 1988, the proportion of sexually active females in families with incomes equal to or greater than 200 percent of the poverty line increased from 39 percent to 50 percent. At the same time, the proportion of females from poorer families who had ever had sex remained stable at 56 percent.

Until recently, black teenagers had substantially higher rates of sexual activity than whites. Now, the differences between older teens of both races have narrowed. But once more, these aggregate figures obscure underlying age differentials. According to the 1988 NSAM, while 26 percent of white 15-year-old males reported engaging in sex compared to 67 percent of blacks, by age 18 the gap narrowed to 71 percent of whites and 83 percent of blacks. A similar trend appears among females. Twenty-four percent of white 15-year-old females have engaged in sex, compared to 33 percent of their black counterparts, reports the 1988 NSFG. By age 16, the proportions increase to 39 percent and 54 percent, respectively. Even by age 17, fewer white females have started having sex (56 percent) than have blacks (67 percent). On the other hand, white teen males reported having had almost twice as many acts of intercourse in the 12 months preceding the 1988 NSAM than did black teen males (27 versus 15). The white males, however, had fewer partners in the same period (2 versus 2.5).

The Social Costs

Among the consequences of this steady rise in teen sexuality are mounting rates of abortion, out-of-wedlock births, welfare, and sexually transmitted diseases.

Abortion. About 40 percent of all teenage pregnancies now end in abortion. (Unmarried teens account for about 97 percent.) This means that of the 1.6 million abortions in 1988, over 400,000—or a quarter of the total—were performed on teenagers. In the 11 years between 1973 and 1984, the teenage abortion rate almost doubled, from about 24 to about 44 per 1,000 females ages 15–19. (Between 1984 and 1988, the rate stabilized.)

A study by AGI's Stanley Henshaw found that between 1973 and 1988, the abortion rate for girls ages 14 and under increased 56 percent (from 5.6 to 8.6 per 1,000), 62 percent for those ages 15–17 (from 18.7 to 30.3), and among older

FIGURE ONE: TRENDS IN PREMARITAL SEXUAL ACTIVITY FOR ALL FEMALE TEENAGERS

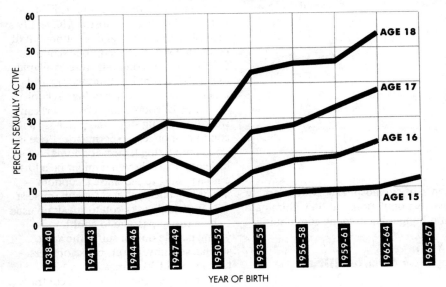

SOURCE: S. Hofferth, J. Kahn, and W. Baldwin, "Premarital Sexual Activity Among U.S. Women Over the Past Three Decades," *Family Planning Perspectives*, Vol. 19, No. 2, March/April 1987.

As Table 1 shows, welfare dependency is more a function of a mother's age and marital status than of her race. White and black unmarried adolescent mothers have about the same welfare rate one year after the birth of their first child. After five years, black unmarried mothers have a somewhat higher rate of welfare dependency than whites (84 percent versus 72 percent), but various demographic factors such as family income, educational attainment, and family structure account for this relatively small difference.

Disease. Over three million teenagers, or one out of six sexually experienced teens, become infected with sexually transmitted diseases each year, reports the Centers for Disease Control (CDC). One Philadelphia clinic administrator laments that she used to spend $3 on contraceptives for every $1 on disease screening and related health issues. Today, the ratio is reversed. Susan Davis, a contraception counselor at a Washington, D.C. area Planned Parenthood clinic, explains, "The risk of infection is greater than the risk of pregnancy for teens." These diseases can cause serious problems if left untreated. The CDC estimates that between 100,000 and 150,000 women become infertile every year because of sexually transmitted disease-related pelvic infections.

The recent explosion of these diseases is in large measure caused by the sexual activity of teenagers; sexually transmitted disease rates decline sharply with age. Take gonorrhea, for example. According to AGI, there were 24 cases per 1,000 sexually experienced females ages 15–19 in 1988. Among women ages 20–24, the rate declined to

teens, almost 120 percent (from 29 to 63.5). In absolute numbers, the youngest group had about 13,000 abortions, the middle group had 158,000, and the oldest group had 234,000.

Out-of-Wedlock Births. Over 300,000 babies were born to unwed teenagers in 1988. That's three-fifths of all births to teenagers. Although the total number of births to teenagers declined between 1970 and 1988, the percentage born out of wedlock more than doubled (from 29 percent to 65 percent), and the teenage out-of-wedlock birth rate increased from about 22 per 1,000 to 37 per

1,000. Over 11,000 babies were born to children under 15 years old in 1988.

Welfare. Few teen mothers place their children up for adoption as was often done in the past. And yet most are not able to support themselves, let alone their children. Consequently, about 50 percent of all teen mothers are on welfare within one year of the birth of their first child; 77 percent are on within five years, according to the Congressional Budget Office. Nick Zill of Child Trends, Inc., calculates that 43 percent of long-term welfare recipients (on the rolls for ten years or more) started their families as unwed teens.

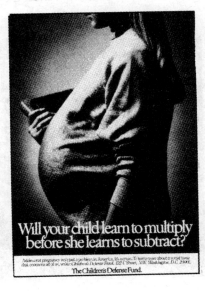

TABLE ONE: PERCENT OF ADOLESCENT MOTHERS ON AFDC

	BY FIRST BIRTH	WITHIN ONE YEAR OF BIRTH	WITHIN FIVE YEARS OF BIRTH
All	7%	28%	49%
Married	2	7	24
Unmarried	13	50	77
White	7	22	39
Black	9	44	76
White, Unmarried	17	53	72
Black, Unmarried	10	49	84

SOURCE: Congressional Budget Office, Sources of Support for Adolescent Mothers, Government Printing Office: Washington, D.C., 1990

15 and fell rapidly with age. For women ages 25–29, 30–34, and 35–39, the rates are 5, 2, and 1 per 1,000, respectively. Except for AIDS, most sexually transmitted diseases follow a similar pattern.

AIDS has not reached epidemic proportions in the teen population—yet. According to the Centers for Disease Control, fewer than 1,000 cases of AIDS are among teenagers. However, there are 9,200 cases among 20–24 year-olds and 37,200 cases among 25–29 year-olds. Given the long incubation period for the AIDS virus (8–12 years), many of these infections were probably contracted during adolescence.

According to Lawrence D'Angelo and his colleagues at the Children's National Medical Center in Washington, D.C., the rate of HIV (the virus that causes AIDS) infection among teenagers using the hospital increased rapidly between 1987 and 1991. For males, the rate increased almost sevenfold, from 2.47 per 1,000 in 1987 to 18.35 per 1,000 in 1991. The female rate more than doubled in the same period, from 4.9 to 11.05. These statistics only reflect the experience of one hospital serving a largely inner-city population, but they illuminate what is happening in many communities.

Use, Not Availability

Many people believe that there would be less teen pregnancy and sexually transmitted diseases if contraceptives were simply more available to teenagers, hence the call for sex education at younger ages, condoms in the schools, and expanded family planning programs in general. But an objective look at the data reveals that availability is not the prime factor determining contraceptive use.

Almost all young people have access to at least one form of contraception. In a national survey conducted in 1979 by Melvin Zelnik and Young Kim of the Johns Hopkins School of Hygiene and Public Health, over three-quarters of 15- to 19-year-olds reported having had a sex education course, and 75 percent of those who did remembered being told how to obtain contraception.

Condoms are freely distributed by family planning clinics and other public health services. They are often sitting in a basket in the waiting room. Edwin Delattre, acting dean of Boston University's School of Education and an opponent of condom distribution in public schools, found that free condoms were available at eight different locations within a 14-block radius of one urban high school.

And, of course, any boy or girl can walk into a drug store and purchase a condom, sponge, or spermicide. Price is not an inhibiting factor: condoms cost as little as 50¢. Although it might be a little embarrassing to purchase a condom—mumbling one's request to a pharmacist who invariably asks you to speak up used to be a rite of passage to adulthood—young people do not suffer the same stigma, scrutiny, or self-consciousness teenagers did 30 years ago.

Teenagers can also obtain contraceptives such as pills and diaphragms from family planning clinics free of charge or on a sliding fee scale. In 1992, over 4,000 federally funded clinics served 4.2 million women, some as young as 13. According to AGI, 60 percent of sexually active female teens use clinics to obtain contraceptive services, while only 20 percent of women over 30 do. In all states except Utah, teenagers can use clinic services without parental consent. To receive free services under the Medicaid program, however, a teenager must present the family's Medicaid card to prove eligibility.

In 1990, total public expenditures for family planning clinics amounted to $504 million. Adjusted for inflation, however, combined federal and state funding for clinics has declined by about one-third since 1980. But the impact of

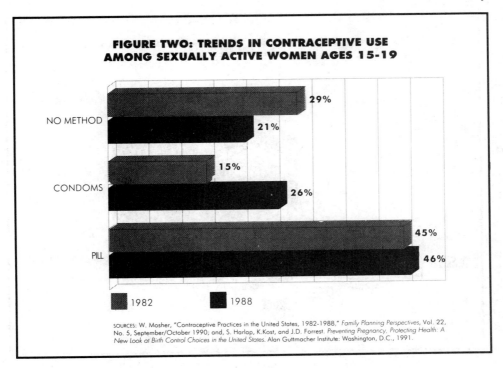

FIGURE TWO: TRENDS IN CONTRACEPTIVE USE AMONG SEXUALLY ACTIVE WOMEN AGES 15-19

NO METHOD — 29% / 21%
CONDOMS — 15% / 26%
PILL — 45% / 46%

1982   1988

SOURCES: W. Mosher, "Contraceptive Practices in the United States, 1982-1988," *Family Planning Perspectives*, Vol. 22, No. 5, September/October 1990; and, S. Harlap, K.Kost, and J.D. Forrest. *Preventing Pregnancy, Protecting Health: A New Look at Birth Control Choices in the United States.* Alan Guttmacher Institute: Washington, D.C., 1991.

these cuts is unclear. On the one hand, the U.S. Department of Health and Human Services reports that the number of women using publicly funded clinics actually rose between 1980 and 1990, from 4.0 million to 4.2 million. When William Mosher of the National Center for Health Statistics analyzed the NSFG data, however, he found a slight decline between 1982 and 1988 in the proportion of respondents who had visited a clinic in the 12 months preceding the survey (37 percent versus 35 percent).

Whatever the effect of these cuts, the evidence suggests that as with condoms, teens know how to find a clinic when they want to. When they are younger, they do not feel the need to go to a clinic since condoms tend to be their initial form of contraception.

Susan Davis of Planned Parenthood explains, "The most common reason teenagers come is because they think they are pregnant. They get worried. Or they get vaginal infections. I had a whole slew of girls coming for their first pelvic exam and they all had chlamydia." The median time between a female teenager's first sexual experience and her first visit to a clinic is one year, according to a 1981 survey of 1,200 teenagers using 31 clinics in eight cities conducted by Laurie Zabin of the School of Hygiene and Public Health at the Johns Hopkins University in Baltimore.

The Conception Index

Two pieces of evidence further dispel the notion that lack of availability of contraception is the prime problem. First, reported contraceptive use has increased even more than rates of sexual activity. By 1988, the majority of sexually experienced female teens who were at risk to have an unintended pregnancy were using contraception: 79 percent. (This represents an increase from 71 percent in 1982.) When asked what method they use, 46 percent reported using the pill, 26 percent reported using condoms, and 2 percent reported using foam (see figure 2). In addition, the proportion of teen females who reported using a method of contraception at first intercourse increased from 48 percent in 1982 to 65 percent in 1988.

The second piece of evidence is that as they grow older, teenagers shift the forms of contraception they use. Younger teens tend to rely on condoms, whereas older teens use female-oriented methods, such as a sponge, spermicide, diaphragm, or the pill, reflecting the greater likelihood that an older female will be sexually active.

A major reason for this increase in contraceptive use is the growing number of middle-class youths who are sexually active. But it's more than this. Levels of unprotected first sex have decreased among all socioeconomic groups. Among teens from wealthier families, the proportion who reported using no method at first sex decreased between 1982 and 1988 from 43 percent to 27 percent. During the same period, non-use among teens from poorer families also declined, from 60 percent to 42 percent.

Unprotected first sex also decreased among racial groups. Between 1982 and 1988, the proportion of white females who reported using a method of contraception at first intercourse increased from 55 percent to 69 percent. Among blacks, the increase was from 36 percent to 54 percent.

It's not just that teens are telling interviewers what they want to hear about contraception. Despite large increases in sexual activity, there has not been a corresponding increase in the number of conceptions. Between 1975 and 1988, when about 1.3 million more teen females reported engaging in sex (a 39 percent increase), the absolute number of pregnancies increased by less than 21 percent (see figure 3).

In fact, one could create a crude "teen conception index" to measure the changing rate of conception (composed of abortions, miscarriages, and births) among sexually active but unmarried teenagers. If we did so, the 1988 index would stand at .87, representing a decline of 13 percent from 1975 (down from 210 to 182 per 1,000 sexually active, unmarried teens). Most of this decline

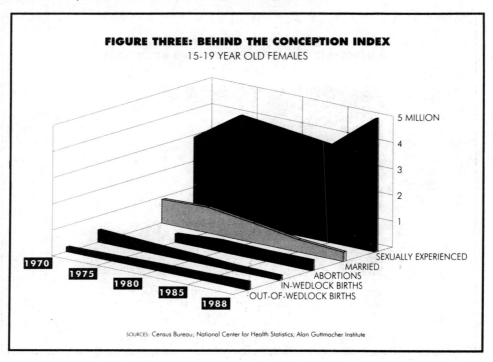

FIGURE THREE: BEHIND THE CONCEPTION INDEX
15-19 YEAR OLD FEMALES

SOURCES: Census Bureau; National Center for Health Statistics; Alan Guttmacher Institute

occurred between 1985 and 1988 as more middle-class teenagers had sex.

The Challenge

Although the conception index among teens is declining, the enormous increase in sexual activity has created a much larger base against which the rate is multiplied. Thus, as we have seen, there have been sharp increases in the rates of abortion, out-of-wedlock births, welfare dependency, and sexually transmitted diseases as measured within the whole teen population.

Teenage sexuality does not have to translate into pregnancy, abortion, out-of-wedlock births, or sexually transmitted diseases. Western Europe, with roughly equivalent rates of teen sexuality, has dramatically lower rates of unwanted pregnancy. According to a 1987 AGI study, the pregnancy rate among American teens (96 per 1,000 women) was twice as high as that in Canada (44), England and Wales (45), and France (43). It was almost three times higher than Sweden's (35) and more than six times higher than in the Netherlands (14). The answer, of course, is effective contraception.

The magnitude of the problem is illustrated by data about reported condom use. Between 1979 and 1988, the reported use of a condom at last intercourse for males ages 17–19 almost

tripled, from 21 percent to 58 percent. A decade of heightened concern about AIDS and other sexually transmitted diseases probably explains this tripling. According to Freya Sonenstein and her colleagues at the Urban Institute, over 90 percent of males in their sample knew how AIDS could be transmitted. Eighty-two percent disagreed "a lot" with the statement, "Even though AIDS is a fatal disease, it is so uncommon that it's not a big worry."

As impressive as this progress was, 40 percent did not use a condom at last intercourse. In fact, the 1991 NASM found that there has been no increase in condom use since 1988—even as the threat of AIDS has escalated.

The roots of too-early and too-often unprotected teen sex reach deeply into our society. Robin Williams reportedly asked a girlfriend, "You don't have anything I can take home to my wife, do you?" She said no, so he didn't use a condom. Now both Williams and the girlfriend have herpes, and she's suing him for infecting her. (She claims that he contracted herpes in high school.) When fabulously successful personalities behave this way, should we be surprised to hear about an inner-city youth who refuses his social worker's entreaties to wear a condom when having sex with his AIDS-infected girlfriend?

This is the challenge before us: How to change the behavior of these

young men as well as the one in five sexually active female teens who report using no method of contraception. First, all the programs in the world cannot deal with one vital aspect of the problem: many teenagers are simply not ready for sexual relationships. They do not have the requisite emotional and cognitive maturity. Adolescents who cannot remember to hang up their bath towels may be just as unlikely to remember to use contraceptives. Current policies and programs do not sufficiently recognize this fundamental truth.

At the same time, the clock cannot be turned all the way back to the innocent 1950s. Sexual mores have probably been permanently changed, especially for older teens—those who are out of high school, living on their own or off at college. For them, and ultimately all of us, the question is: How to limit the harm being done?

The challenge for public policy is to pursue two simultaneous goals: to lower the rate of sexual activity, especially among young teens, and to raise the level of contraceptive use. Other than abstinence, the best way to prevent pregnancy is to use a contraceptive, and the best way to prevent sexually transmitted diseases is to use a barrier form of contraception. Meeting this challenge will take moral clarity, social honesty, and political courage—three commodities in short supply these days.

A Society of Suspects:
THE WAR ON DRUGS AND CIVIL LIBERTIES

Property seized in drug raids, including large amounts of money, may be forfeited to the government without proof of the owner's guilt.

A decade after Pres. Reagan launched the War on Drugs, all we have to show for it are city streets ruled by gangs, a doubled prison population, and a substantial erosion of constitutional protections.

Steven Wisotsky

Mr. Wisotsky, professor of law, Nova University, Ft. Lauderdale, Fla., is a member of the advisory board of the Drug Policy Foundation, Washington, D.C., and author of Beyond the War on Drugs. *This article is based on a Cato Institute Policy Analysis.*

ON DEC. 15, 1991, America celebrated the 200th anniversary of the Bill of Rights. On Oct. 2, 1992, it marked the 10th anniversary of an antithetical undertaking—the War on Drugs, declared by Pres. Ronald Reagan in 1982 and aggressively escalated by Pres. George Bush in 1989. The nation's Founders would be disappointed with what has been done to their legacy of liberty. The War on Drugs, by its very nature, is a war on the Bill of Rights.

In their shortsighted zeal to create a drug-free America, political leaders—state and Federal, elected and appointed—have acted as though the end justifies the means. They have repudiated the heritage of limited government and individual freedoms while endowing the bureaucratic state with unprecedented powers.

That the danger to freedom is real and not just a case of crying wolf is confirmed by the warnings of a few judges, liberals and conservatives alike, who, insulated from elective politics, have the independence to be critical. Supreme Court Justice Antonin Scalia, for example, denounced compulsory urinalysis of Customs Service employees "in the front line" of the War on Drugs as an "invasion of their privacy and an affront to their dignity." In another case, Justice John Paul Stevens lamented that "this Court has become a loyal foot soldier" in the War on Drugs. The late Justice Thur-

good Marshall was moved to remind the Court that there is "no drug exception" to the Constitution.

In 1991, the Court of Appeals for the Ninth Circuit declared that "The drug crisis does not license the aggrandizement of governmental power in lieu of civil liberties. Despite the devastation wrought by drug trafficking in communities nationwide, we cannot suspend the precious rights guaranteed by the Constitution in an effort to fight the 'War on Drugs.'" In that observation, the court echoed a 1990 ringing dissent by the chief justice of the Florida Supreme Court: "If the zeal to eliminate drugs leads this state and nation to forsake its ancient heritage of constitutional liberty, then we will have suffered a far greater injury than drugs ever inflict upon us. Drugs injure some of us. The loss of liberty injures us all."

Those warnings are cries in the wilderness, however, unable to stop the relentless buildup of law enforcement authority at every level of government. In fact, the trend toward greater police powers has accelerated. One summary of the Supreme Court's 1990-91 term observed that its criminal law decisions "mark the beginning of significant change in the relationship between the citizens of this country and its police."

Despite such warnings, most Americans have yet to appreciate that the War on Drugs is a war on the rights of all of us. It could not be otherwise, for it is directed not against inanimate drugs, but against people—those who are suspected of using, dealing in, or otherwise being involved with illegal substances. Because the drug industry arises from the voluntary transactions of tens of millions of individuals—

all of whom try to keep their actions secret—the aggressive law enforcement schemes that constitute the war must aim at penetrating their private lives. Because nearly anyone may be a drug user or seller of drugs or an aider and abettor of the drug industry, virtually everyone has become a suspect. All must be observed, checked, screened, tested, and admonished—the guilty and innocent alike.

The tragic irony is that, while the War on Drugs has failed completely to halt the influx of cocaine and heroin—which are cheaper, purer, and more abundant than ever—the one success it can claim is in curtailing the liberty and privacy of the American people. In little over a decade, Americans have suffered a marked reduction in their freedoms in ways both obvious and subtle.

Among the grossest of indicators is that the war leads to the arrest of an estimated 1,200,000 suspected drug offenders each year, most for simple possession or petty sale. Because arrest and incarceration rates rose for drug offenders throughout the 1980s, the war has succeeded dramatically in increasing the full-time prison population. That has doubled since 1982 to more than 800,000, giving the U.S. the highest rate of incarceration in the industrialized world.

It has been established that law enforcement officials—joined by U.S. military forces—have the power, with few limits, to snoop, sniff, survey, and detain, without warrant or probable cause, in the war against drug trafficking. Property may be seized on slight evidence and forfeited to the state or Federal government without proof of the personal guilt of the owner.

From *USA Today Magazine*, July 1993, pp. 17-21. © 1993 by the Society for the Advancement of Education. Reprinted by permission.

Finally, to leverage its power, an increasingly imperial Federal government has applied intimidating pressures to shop owners and others in the private sector to help implement its drug policy.

Ironically, just as the winds of freedom are blowing throughout central and eastern Europe, most Americans and the nation's politicians maintain that the solution to the drug problem is more repression—and the Bill of Rights be damned. As Peter Rodino, former chairman of the House Judiciary Committee, said in expressing his anger at the excesses of the Anti-Drug Abuse Act of 1986, "We have been fighting the war on drugs, but now it seems to me the attack is on the Constitution of the United States."

In the beginning, the War on Drugs focused primarily on supplies and suppliers. Control at the source was the first thrust of anti-drug policy—destruction of coca and marijuana plants in South America, crop substitution programs, and aid to law enforcement agencies in Colombia, Peru, Bolivia, and Mexico.

Because this had no discernible, lasting success, a second initiative aimed to improve the efficiency of border interdiction of drug shipments that had escaped control at the source. There, too, success was elusive. Record numbers of drug seizures—up to 22 tons of cocaine in a single raid on a Los Angeles warehouse, for instance—seemed only to mirror a record volume of shipments to the U.S. By 1991, the amount of cocaine seized by Federal authorities had risen to 134 metric tons, with an additional amount estimated at between 263 and 443 tons escaping into the American market per year.

A reasonable search and seizure in the War on Drugs is interpreted very broadly and favors local police and Federal drug agents.

As source control and border interdiction proved futile, a third prong of the attack was undertaken: long-term, proactive conspiracy investigations targeted at suspected high-level drug traffickers and their adjuncts in the professional and financial worlds—lawyers, accountants, bankers, and currency exchange operators. This has involved repeated and systematic attacks by the Federal government on the criminal defense bar, raising dark implications for the integrity of the adversarial system of justice. Defense lawyers have been subjected to grand jury subpoenas, under threat of criminal contempt, to compel disclosures about their clients. Informants have been placed in the defense camp to obtain confidential information. In each instance, the effect has been to undermine the protections traditionally afforded by the attorney/client relationship. This demonstrates the anything-goes-in-the-War-on-Drugs attitude of the Department of Justice, which publicly defended using lawyers as informants as "a perfectly valid" law enforcement tool.

As these expanding efforts yielded only marginal results, the war was widened to the general populace. In effect, the government opened up a domestic front in the War on Drugs, invading the privacy of people through the use of investigative techniques such as urine testing, roadblocks, bus boardings, and helicopter overflights. Those are dragnet methods; to catch the guilty, everyone has to be watched and screened.

Invading privacy

Drug testing in the workplace. Perhaps the most widespread intrusion on privacy arises from pre- or post-employment drug screening, practiced by 80% of Fortune 500 companies and 43% of firms employing 1,000 people or more. Strictly speaking, drug testing by a private employer does not violate the Fourth Amendment, which protects only against government action. Nevertheless, much of the private drug testing has come about through government example and pressure. The 1988 Anti-Drug Abuse Act, for instance, prohibits the award of a Federal grant or contract to an employer who does not take specified steps to provide a drug-free workplace. As a result of these and other pressures, tens of millions of job applicants and employees are subjected to the indignities of urinating into a bottle, sometimes under the eyes of a monitor watching to ensure that clean urine is not smuggled surreptitiously into the toilet.

In the arena of public employment, where Fourth Amendment protections apply, the courts largely have rejected constitutional challenges to drug testing programs. In two cases to reach the U.S. Supreme Court, the testing programs substantially were upheld despite, as Justice Scalia wrote in dissent in one of them, a complete absence of "real evidence of a real problem that will be solved by urine testing of customs service employees." In that case, the Customs Service had implemented a drug testing program to screen all job applicants and employees engaged in drug interdiction activities, carrying firearms, or handling classified material. The Court held that the testing of such applicants and employees is "reasonable" even without probable cause or individualized suspicion against any particular person, the Fourth Amendment standard.

For Scalia, the testing of Customs Service employees was quite different from that of railroad employees involved in train accidents, which had been found constitutional. In that case, there was substantial evidence over the course of many years that the use of alcohol had been implicated in causing railroad accidents, including a 1979 study finding that 23% of the operating personnel were problem drinkers. Commenting on the Customs case, Scalia maintained that "What is absent in the government's justifications—notably absent, revealingly absent, and as far as I am concerned dispositively absent—is the recitation of even a single instance in which any of the speculated horribles actually occurred: an instance, that is, in which the cause of bribe-taking, or of poor aim, or of unsympathetic law enforcement, or of compromise of classified information, was drug use."

Searches and seizures. Other dragnet techniques that invade the privacy of the innocent as well as the guilty have been upheld by the Supreme Court. In the tug-of-war between the government's search and seizure powers and the privacy rights of individuals, the Court throughout the 1980s almost always upheld the government's assertion of the right of drug agents to use the airport drug courier profile to stop, detain, and question people without warrant or probable cause; subject a traveler's luggage to a sniffing examination by a drug-detecting dog without warrant or probable cause; search without warrant or probable cause the purse of a public school student; and search at will ships in inland waterways.

The right of privacy in the home seriously was curtailed in decisions permitting police to obtain a search warrant of a home based on an anonymous informant's tip; use illegally seized evidence under a "good faith exception" to the exclusionary rule (for searches of a home made pursuant to a defective warrant issued without probable cause); make a trespassory search, without a warrant, in "open fields" surrounded by fences and no trespassing signs and of a barn adjacent to a residence; and conduct a warrantless search of a motor home occupied as a residence, a home on the consent of an occasional visitor lacking legal authority over the premises, and the foreign residence of a person held for trial in the U.S. The Court also validated warrantless aerial surveillance over private property—by fixed-wing aircraft at an altitude of 1,000 feet and by helicopter at 400 feet.

Similarly, it significantly enlarged the powers of police to stop, question, and detain drivers of vehicles on the highways on suspicion with less than probable cause or with no suspicion at all at fixed checkpoints or roadblocks; make warrantless searches of automobiles and of closed containers therein; and conduct surveillance of suspects by placing transmitters or beepers on vehicles or in containers therein.

The foregoing list is by no means comprehensive, but it does indicate the sweeping expansions the Court has permitted in the investigative powers of government. Indeed, from 1982 through the end of the 1991 term, the Supreme Court upheld government search and seizure authority in approximately 90% of the cases. The message is unmistakable—the Fourth Amendment prohibits only "unreasonable" searches and seizures, and what is reasonable in the milieu of a War on Drugs is construed very broadly in favor of local police and Federal drug agents.

Surveillance of U.S. mail. Another casualty of the War on Drugs is the privacy of the mail. With the Anti-Drug Abuse Act of 1988, the Postal Service was given broad law enforcement authority. Using a profile, investigators identify what they deem to be suspicious packages and place them before drug-sniffing dogs. A dog alert is deemed probable cause to apply for a Federal search warrant. If an opened package does not contain drugs, it is resealed and sent to its destination with a copy of the search warrant. Since January, 1990, using this technique, the Postal Service has arrested more than 2,500 persons for sending drugs through the mail. The number of innocent packages opened has not been reported.

Wiretapping. As a result of the War on Drugs, Americans increasingly are being overheard. Although human monitors are supposed to minimize the interception of calls unrelated to the purpose of their investigation by listening only long enough to determine the relevance of the conversation, wiretaps open all conversations on the wiretapped line to scrutiny.

Court-authorized wiretaps doubtless are necessary in some criminal cases. In drug cases, though, they are made necessary because the "crimes" arise from voluntary transactions, in which there are no complainants to assist detection. The potential is great, therefore, for abuse and illegal overuse.

Stopping cars on public highways. It is commonplace for police patrols to stop "suspicious" vehicles on the highway in the hope that interrogation of the driver or passengers will turn up enough to escalate the initial detention into a full-blown search. Because the required "articulable suspicion" rarely can be achieved by observation on the road, police often rely on a minor traffic violation—a burned-out taillight, a tire touching the white line—to supply a pretext for the initial stop. In the Alice-in-Wonderland world of roving drug patrols, however, even lawful behavior can be used to justify a stop. The Florida Highway Patrol Drug Courier Profile, for example, cautioned troopers to be suspicious of "scrupulous obedience to traffic laws."

Another tactic sometimes used is the roadblock. Police set up a barrier, stop every vehicle at a given location, and check each driver's license and registration. While one checks the paperwork, another walks around the car with a trained drug-detector dog. The law does not regard the dog's sniffing as the equivalent of a search on the theory that there is no legitimate expectation of privacy in the odor of contraband, an exterior olfactory clue in the public domain. As a result, no right of privacy is invaded by the sniff, so the police do not need a search warrant or even probable cause to use the dog on a citizen. Moreover, if the dog "alerts," that supplies the cause requirement for further investigation of the driver or vehicle for drugs.

Monitoring and stigmatizing. In the world of anti-drug investigations, a large role is played by rumors, tips, and suspicions. The Drug Enforcement Administration (DEA) keeps computer files on U.S. Congressmen, entertainers, clergymen, industry leaders, and foreign dignitaries. Many persons named in the computerized Narcotics and Dangerous Drug Information System (NADDIS) are the subject of "unsubstantiated allegations of illegal activity." Of the 1,500,000 persons whose names have been added to NADDIS since 1974, less than five percent, or 7,500, are under investigation by DEA as suspected narcotic traffickers. Nevertheless, NADDIS maintains data from all such informants, surveillance, and intelligence reports compiled by DEA and other agencies.

The information on NADDIS is available to Federal drug enforcement officials in other agencies, such as the Federal Bureau of Investigation, the Customs Service, and the Internal Revenue Service. State law enforcement officials probably also can gain access on request. Obviously, this method of oversight has troubling implications for privacy and good reputation, especially for the 95% named who are not under active investigation.

Another creative enforcement tactic sought to bring about public embarrassment by publishing a list of people caught bringing small amounts of drugs into the U.S. The punish-by-publishing list, supplied to news organizations, included only small-scale smugglers who neither were arrested nor prosecuted for their alleged crimes.

Military surveillance. Further surveillance of the citizenry comes from the increasing militarization of drug law enforcement. The process began in 1981, when Congress relaxed the Civil War-era restrictions of the Posse Comitatus Act on the use of the armed forces as a police agency. The military "support" role for the Coast Guard, Customs Service, and other anti-drug agencies created by the 1981 amendments expanded throughout the 1980s to the point that the U.S. Navy was using large military vessels—including, in one case, a nuclear-powered aircraft carrier—to interdict suspected drug smuggling ships on the high seas.

By 1989, Congress designated the Department of Defense (DOD) as the single lead agency of the Federal government for the detection and monitoring of aerial and maritime smuggling into the U.S. DOD employs its vast radar network in an attempt to identify drug smugglers among the 300,000,000 people who enter the country each year in 94,000,000 vehicles and 600,000 aircraft. Joint task forces of military and civilian personnel were established and equipped with high-tech computer systems that provide instantaneous communication among all Federal agencies tracking or apprehending drug traffickers.

The enlarged anti-drug mission of the military sets a dangerous precedent. The point of the Posse Comitatus Act was to make clear that the military and police are very different institutions with distinct roles to play. The purpose of the military is to prevent or defend against attack by a foreign power and to wage war where necessary. The Constitution makes the president commander-in-chief, thus centralizing control of all the armed forces in one person. Police, by contrast, are supposed to enforce the law, primarily against domestic threats at the city, county, and state levels. They thus are subject to local control by the tens of thousands of communities throughout the nation.

Since the 1987 enactment of the Uniform Sentencing Guidelines, the penalties for drug crimes have become extreme and mandatory.

To the extent that the drug enforcement role of the armed forces is expanded, there is a direct increase in the concentration of political power in the president who commands them and the Congress that authorizes and funds their police activities. This arrangement is a severe injury to the Federal structure of our democratic institutions. Indeed, the deployment of national military forces as domestic police embarrasses the U.S. in the international arena by likening it to a Third World country, whose soldiers stand guard in city streets, rifles at the ready, for ordinary security purposes.

The dual military/policing role also is a danger to the liberties of all citizens. A likely military approach to the drug problem would be to set up roadblocks, checkpoints, and roving patrols on the highways, railroads, and coastal waters, and to carry out search-and-destroy missions of domestic drug agriculture or laboratory production. What could be more destructive to the people's sense of personal privacy and mobility than to see such deployments by Big Brother?

Excessive punishment

These are some of the many ways the War on Drugs has cut deeply—and threatens to cut deeper still—into Americans' privacy, eroding what Justice Louis D. Brandeis described as "the right to be let alone—the most comprehensive of rights and the right most valued by civilized men." Working hand-in-hand with the political branches, the courts have diminished constitutional restraints on the exercise of law enforcement power. In addition to expanded powers of surveillance, investigation, and prosecution, punishment has been loosed with a vengeance, against enemy and bystander alike.

Punishments have become draconian in part because of permission conferred by Justice William Rehnquist's 1981 circular dictum: "the question of what punishments are constitutionally permissible is not different from the question of what punishments the Legislative Branch intended to be imposed." The penalties have become so extreme, especially since the 1987 enactment of the Uniform Sentencing Guidelines, that many Federal judges have begun to recoil. U.S. district court Judge J. Lawrence Irving of San Diego, a Reagan appointee, announced his resignation in protest over the excessive mandatory penalties he was required to mete out to low-level offenders, most of them poor young minorities. Complaining of "unconscionable" sentences, the judge said that "Congress has dehumanized the sentencing process. I can't in good conscience sit on the bench and mete out sentences that are unfair."

Judge Harold Greene of the District of Columbia went so far as to refuse to impose the minimum guideline sentence of 17.5 years on a defendant convicted of the street sale of a single Dilaudid tablet, pointing to the "enormous disparity" between the crime and the penalty. In the judge's view, the minimum was "cruel and unusual" and "barbaric." Fourth circuit Judge William W. Wilkins objected to mandatory penalties because "they do not permit consideration of an offender's possibly limited peripheral role in the offense." Agreeing with that thinking, the judicial conferences of the District of Columbia, Second, Third, Seventh, Eighth, Ninth, and Tenth circuits have adopted resolutions opposing mandatory minimums.

As drug control policymakers came to realize that the drug dealers were, in an economic sense, merely entrepreneurs responding to market opportunities, they learned that attacks on dealers and their supplies never could succeed as long as there was demand for the products. Thus, they would have to focus on consumers as well as on suppliers. Pres. Reagan's 1986 Executive Order encouraging or requiring widespread urine testing marked a step in that direction. By 1988, Administration policy was being conducted under the rubric of "zero tolerance." In that spirit, Attorney General Edwin Meese sent a memorandum to all U.S. Attorneys on March 30, 1988, encouraging the selective prosecution of "middle and upper class users" in order to "send the message that there is no such thing as 'recreational' drug use. . . . "

Because of the volume of more serious trafficking cases, however, it was not remotely realistic, as the Attorney General must have known, to implement such a policy. Indeed, in the offices of many U.S. Attorneys, there were minimum weight or money-volume standards for prosecution, and the possession and small-scale drug cases routinely were shunted off to state authorities. In fact, in many districts, the crush of drug cases was so great that the adjudication of ordinary civil cases virtually had ceased. The courthouse doors were all but closed to civil litigants.

In the name of zero tolerance, Congress purposely began enacting legislation that did not have to meet the constitutional standard of proof beyond a reasonable doubt in criminal proceedings. In 1988, it authorized a system of fines of up to $10,000, imposed administratively under the authority of the Attorney General, without the necessity of a trial, although the individual may request an administrative hearing. To soften the blow to due process, judicial review of an adverse administrative finding is permitted, but the individual bears the burden of retaining counsel and paying court filing fees. For those unable to finance a court challenge, this system will amount to punishment without trial. Moreover, it has been augmented by a provision in the Anti-Drug Abuse Act of 1988 that may suspend for one year an offender's Federal benefits, contracts, grants, student loans, mortgage guarantees, and licenses upon conviction for a first offense.

Both sanctions are a form of legal piling on. The legislative intent is to punish the minor offender more severely than is authorized by the criminal law alone. Thus, the maximum penalty under Federal criminal law for a first offense of simple possession of a controlled substance is one year in prison and a $5,000 fine, with a minimum fine of $1,000. Fines up to $10,000 plus loss of Federal benefits obviously exceed those guidelines.

The most recent innovation of this kind is a form of greenmail, a law that cuts off highway funds to states that do not suspend the driver's licenses of those convicted of possession of illegal drugs. The potential loss of work for those so punished and the adverse consequences on their families are not considered. The suspension is mandatory.

Seizure and forfeiture

The War on Drugs not only punishes drug users, it also penalizes those who are innocent and others who are on the periphery of wrongdoing. The most notable example is the widespread and accelerating practice, Federal and state, of seizing and forfeiting cars, planes, boats, houses, money, or property of any other kind carrying even minute amounts of illegal drugs, used to facilitate a transaction in narcotics, or representing the proceeds of drugs. Forfeiture is authorized, and enforced, without regard to the personal guilt of the owner. It matters not whether a person is tried and acquitted; the owner need not even be arrested. The property nonetheless is forfeitable because of a centuries-old legal fiction that says the property itself is "guilty." Relying on it, in March, 1988, the Federal government initiated highly publicized zero tolerance seizures of property that included the following:

● On April 30, 1988, the Coast Guard boarded and seized the motor yacht *Ark Royal,* valued at $2,500,000, because 10 marijuana seeds and two stems were found on board. Public criticism prompted a return of the boat, but not before payment of $1,600 in fines and fees by the owner.

● The 52-foot *Mindy* was impounded for a week because cocaine dust in a rolled up dollar bill was found on board.

● The $80,000,000 oceanographic research ship *Atlantis II* was seized in San Diego when the Coast Guard found 0.01 ounce of marijuana in a crewman's shaving kit. The vessel eventually was returned.

● A Michigan couple returning from a Canadian vacation lost a 1987 Mercury Cougar when customs agents found two marijuana cigarettes in one of their pockets. No criminal charges were filed, but the car was kept by the government.

● In Key West, Fla., a shrimp fisherman lost his boat to the Coast Guard, which found three grams of cannabis seeds and stems on board. Under the law, the craft was forfeitable whether or not he had any responsibility for the drugs.

Not surprisingly, cases like the foregoing generated a public backlash—perhaps the only significant one since the War on Drugs was declared in 1982. It pressured Congress into creating what is known as the "innocent owner defense" to such *in rem* forfeitures, but even that gesture of reasonableness is largely illusory.

First, the defense does not redress the gross imbalance between the value of property forfeited and the personal culpability of the owner. For example, a Vermont man was found guilty of growing six marijuana plants. He received a suspended sentence, but he and his family lost their 49-acre farm. Similarly, a New York man forfeited his $145,000 condominium because he sold cocaine to an informant for $250. The law provides no limit to the value of property subject to forfeiture, even for very minor drug offenses.

Second, the innocent owner defense places the burden on the property claimant to demonstrate that he or she acted or failed to act without "knowledge, consent or willful blindness" of the drug activities of the offender. Thus, the Federal government instituted forfeiture proceedings in the Delray Beach, Fla., area against numerous properties containing convenience stores or other businesses where drug transactions took place, claiming that the owners "made insufficient efforts to prevent drug dealings."

Placing the burden on the claimant imposes expense and inconvenience because the claimant must hire a lawyer to mount a challenge to the seizure. Moreover, many cases involve the family house or car, and it often is difficult to prove that one family member had no knowledge of or did not consent to the illegal activities of another. For instance, a Florida court held that a claimant did not use reasonable care to prevent her husband from using her automobile in criminal activity; thus, she was not entitled to the innocent owner defense.

A particularly cruel application of this kind of vicarious responsibility for the wrongs of another is seen in the government's policy of evicting impoverished families from public housing because of the drug activities of one unruly child. The Anti-Drug Abuse Act of 1988 specifically states that a tenant's lease is a forfeitable property interest and that public housing agencies have the authority to hire investigators to determine whether drug laws are being broken. The act authorizes eviction if a tenant, member of his or her household, guest, or other person under his or her control is engaged in drug-related activity on or near public housing premises.

To carry out these provisions, the act funded a pilot enforcement program. In 1990, the Departments of Justice and Housing and Urban Development announced a Public Housing Asset Forfeiture Demonstration Project in 23 states. The project pursued lease forfeitures and generated considerable publicity.

In passing this law, it must have been obvious to Congress that many innocent family members would suffer along with the guilty. Perhaps it was thought vital, nonetheless, as a way of protecting other families from drugs in public housing projects. As experience proves, however, even evicted dealers continue to deal in and around the projects. It is hard to take public housing lease forfeitures very seriously, therefore, other than as a symbolic statement of the government's tough stand against illegal drugs.

Destructive consequences

A policy that destroys families, takes property from the innocent, and tramples the basic criminal law principles of personal responsibility, proportionality, and fairness has spillover effects into other public policy domains. One area in which the fanaticism of the drug warriors perhaps is most evident is public health. Drugs such as marijuana and heroin have well-known medical applications. Yet, so zealous are the antidrug forces that even these therapeutic uses effectively have been banned.

Marijuana, for instance, has many applications as a safe and effective therapeutic agent. Among them are relief of the intraocular pressure caused by glaucoma and alleviating the nausea caused by chemotherapy. Some AIDS patients also have obtained relief from using cannabis.

Yet, marijuana is classified by the Attorney General of the U.S., not the Surgeon General, as a Schedule I drug—one having a high potential for abuse, no currently accepted medicinal use, and lack of accepted safety for utilization. It thereby is deemed beyond the scope of legitimate medical practice and thus is not generally available to medical practitioners.

The only exception was an extremely limited program of compassionate treatment of the terminally or seriously ill, but even that has been eliminated for political

---

The intensive pursuit of drug offenders has generated an enormous population of convicts held in prison for very long mandatory periods of time; so much so that violent criminals (murders, robbers, and rapists) often serve less time than the drug offenders.

---

reasons. Assistant Secretary James O. Mason of the Department of Health and Human Services announced in 1991 that the Public Health Service's provision of marijuana to patients seriously ill with AIDS would be discontinued because it would create a public perception that "this stuff can't be so bad." After a review caused by protests from AIDS activists, the Public Health Service decided in March, 1992, to stop supplying marijuana to any patients save the 13 then receiving it.

There also are beneficial uses for heroin. Terminal cancer patients suffering from intractable pain generally obtain quicker analgesic relief from heroin than from morphine. Many doctors believe that heroin should be an option in the pharmacopeia. Accordingly, in 1981, the American Medical Association House of Delegates adopted a resolution stating that "the management of pain relief in terminal cancer patients should be a medical decision and should take priority over concerns about drug dependence." Various bills to accomplish that goal were introduced in the 96th, 97th, and 98th Congresses. The Compassionate Pain Relief Act was brought to the House floor for a vote on Sept. 19, 1984, but was defeated by 355 to 55. Although there were some concerns voiced about thefts from hospital pharmacies, the overwhelming concern was political and symbolic—a heroin legalization bill could not be passed in an election year and, in any event, would send the public the "wrong message."

The final and perhaps most outrageous example in this catalog of wrongs against public health care is the nearly universal American refusal to permit established addicts to exchange used needles for sterile ones in order to prevent AIDS transmission among intravenous drug users. In 1991, the National Commission on AIDS recommended the removal of legal barriers to the purchase and possession of intravenous drug injection equipment. It found that 32% of all adult and adolescent AIDS cases were related to intravenous drug use and that 70% of mother-to-child AIDS infections resulted from intravenous drug use by the mother or her sexual partner. Moreover, the commission found no evidence that denial of access to sterile needles reduced drug abuse, but concluded that it did encourage the sharing of contaminated needles and the spread of the AIDS virus. Notwithstanding the commission's criticism of the government's "myopic criminal justice approach" to the drug situation, the prevailing view is that needle exchange programs encourage drug abuse by sending the wrong message.

Public safety is sacrificed when, nationwide, more than 18,000 local, sheriff's, and state police officers, in addition to thousands of Federal agents, are devoted full time to special drug units. As a result, countless hours and dollars are diverted from detecting and preventing more serious violent crimes. Thirty percent of an estimated 1,100,000 drug-related arrests made during 1990 were marijuana offenses, nearly four out of five for mere possession. Tax dollars would be spent better if the resources it took to make approximately 264,000 arrests for possession of marijuana were dedicated to protecting the general public from violent crime.

The intensive pursuit of drug offenders has generated an enormous population of convicts held in prison for very long periods of time as a result of excessive and/or mandatory jail terms. It is estimated that the operating cost of maintaining a prisoner ranges from $20,000 to $40,000 per year, depending upon the location and level of security at a particular prison. With more than 800,000 men and women in American correctional facilities today, the nationwide cost approaches $30,000,000,000 per year. This is a major diversion of scarce resources.

These financial burdens are only part of the price incurred as a result of the relentless drive to achieve higher and higher arrest records. More frightening and damaging are the injuries and losses caused by the early release of violent criminals owing to prison overcrowding. Commonly, court orders impose population caps, so prison authorities accelerate release of violent felons serving non-mandatory sentences in order to free up beds for non-violent drug offenders serving mandatory, non-parolable terms.

For example, to stay abreast of its rapidly growing inmate population, Florida launched one of the nation's most ambitious early release programs. However, prisoners serving mandatory terms—most of them drug offenders, who now comprise 36% of the total prison population—are ineligible. As a result, the average length of sentence declined dramatically for violent criminals, while it rose for drug offenders. Murderers, robbers, and rapists often serve less time than a "cocaine mule" carrying a kilo on a bus, who gets a mandatory 15-year term.

A Department of Justice survey showed that 43% of state felons on probation were rearrested for a crime within three years of sentencing. In short, violent criminals are released early to commit more crimes so that their beds can be occupied by non-violent drug offenders. Civil libertarians are not heard often defending a societal right to be secure from violent criminals, much less a right of victims to see just punishment meted out to offenders. In this they are as shortsighted as their law-and-order counterparts. The War on Drugs is a public safety disaster, making victims of us all.

However uncomfortable it may be to admit, the undeniable reality is that drugs always have been and always will be a presence in society. Americans have been paying too high a price for the government's War on Drugs. As Federal judge William Schwarzer has said, "It behooves us to think that it may profit us very little to win the war on drugs if in the process we lose our soul."

It's Drugs, Alcohol and Tobacco, Stupid!

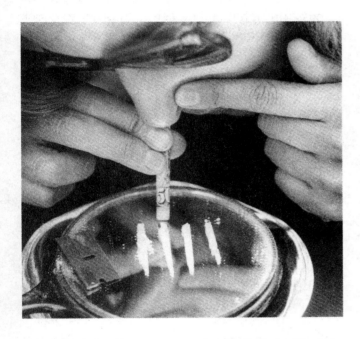

As the new generation of political leaders in Washington, state capitals and city halls grapples with America's collapsing judicial systems, rising medical costs, persistent poverty amid plenty and the defiant federal budget deficit that looms over future generations, they confront the same 800-pound gorilla: drug, alcohol and tobacco abuse and addiction. The sooner these leaders see how substance abuse has fundamentally changed the nature of the pressing social and economic problems they face, the sooner they'll deal with them effectively.

For 30 years, we've tried to curb crime and renew our ailing court system with tougher punishments,

bigger prisons, and more cops and judges; rein in health costs by manipulating payments to doctors and hospitals for delivering sick care; wage war on poverty with a welfare system that encourages dependence and drives families apart; and reduce the deficit by cooking the federal books. Trying to reform our court and criminal justice systems, restrain health care spending, reduce welfare rolls, trim the deficit and nourish the American family without confronting, front and center, substance abuse and addiction is like trying to clean coastal waters without stopping the flow of oil from the ruptured offshore well. It can't be done.

Criminals and Courts

Congress and state legislatures have been passing laws designed for celluloid gangsters and inmates played in classic 1930s movies by James Cagney and Humphrey Bogart. But today's prisons are wall to wall with drug dealers, addicts, alcohol abusers and the mentally ill (often related to drug and alcohol abuse).

In 1960, less than 30,000 Americans were arrested for drug offenses; by 1991, the number had soared to more than a million. Since 1989, more individuals have been incarcerated for drug offenses than for all violent crimes—and most violent crime is committed by drug and alcohol abusers. Alcohol and drug abuse are implicated in

From the Center on Addiction and Substance Abuse at Columbia University, *1994 Annual Report,* pp. 6-11. Reprinted by permission.

three-quarters of all spouse abuse, rapes, child molestations, suicides and homicides.

In 1994, the number of Americans in prison broke the one million barrier and, on its current trajectory, will double soon after the turn of the century. The United States is second only to Russia in the rate of citizens it imprisons: 519 per 100,000, compared to 558 in Russia, 368 in third-place South Africa, 116 in Canada and 36 in Japan.

Probation and parole are sick jokes in most American cities. With so many parolees needing drug treatment and aftercare as essential first steps to rehabilitation, they demand far more monitoring than their drug-free predecessors of a generation ago. Yet in Los Angeles, for example, probation officers must handle as many as 1,000 cases at a time. With most offenders committing drug- or alcohol-related crimes, it's no wonder so many of them go right back to jail: 80 percent of prisoners have prior convictions and more than 60 percent have served time before.

Drugs have turned the private security industry from a less than four-billion-dollar weakling in 1970 into a 70-billion-dollar behemoth in 1994, as office

buildings and homes install sophisticated protection systems and commercial properties post guards around the clock.

Judges and prosecutors are demoralized as they juggle caseloads more than double the

recommended maximums. The rush of drug-related criminal cases has created intolerable delays for civil litigants: four years in Newark, five in Philadelphia, up to ten in Cook County, Illinois. In many jurisdictions, divorce and separation cases languish for years, as splitting parents and their children struggle to survive in a limbo of nasty uncertainty.

The safety and civility of urban life have been shattered by alcohol- and drug-related crimes. Children kill children and innocents are downed by random gunfire from warring drug gangs. Elementary and high school students are required to pass through metal detectors in order to check for weapons, the deadly companions of the drug trade, and teachers are locked in classrooms for their own protection.

City dwellers can no longer buy out of the mess. Individuals walking Wisconsin Avenue in Washington D.C.'s Georgetown, Madison Avenue in New York, Newbury Street in Boston and the Miracle Mile in Chicago are accosted by angry, aggressive panhandlers, many seeking money for their next fix. The ugly scrawls of graffiti on city buildings mark not only the arrival of spray paint, but also the widespread abuse of drugs and alcohol.

Substance abuse is an equal opportunity killer, snaring addicts in every social and economic class. Store owners lock their doors during daytime business hours in fear of robbery by alcohol- and drug-crazed criminals. Office managers bolt computers to desks to prevent theft. Customers and employees warily read headlines about murders and assaults, often committed under the influence of alcohol and drugs, that have torn apart the comfortable routines where America works, eats and shops—post offices, fast-food restaurants, banks and supermarkets. Two-thirds of illegal drug users are employed, adding an element of Russian roulette to going to work each day.

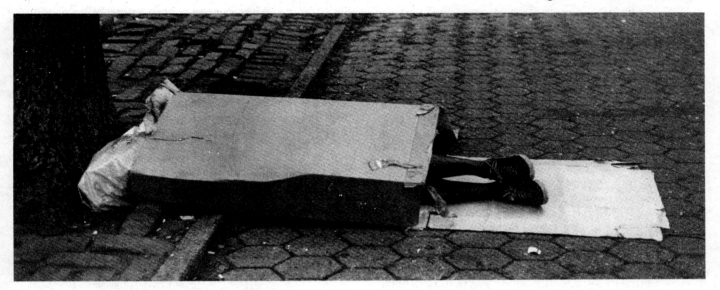

Health care Costs

In 1995, drugs, alcohol and tobacco will trigger some $200 billion in health care costs.

Hospital emergency rooms are piled high with the debris of drug use on city streets. From Boston to Baton Rouge, hospitals teem with the victims of gunshot wounds and other violence caused by alcohol abusers, drug addicts and dealers, and of a variety of medical conditions, such as cancer, emphysema and cardiac arrest, caused by alcohol, tobacco, cocaine and other drugs.

AIDS and tuberculosis spread rapidly and not just among intravenous drug users and crack addicts. Beyond sharing dirty needles and trading sex for drugs, individuals high on beer, other alcohol and pot are far more likely to have sex and to have it without a condom.

The more than 500,000 newborns exposed each year to drugs and/or alcohol during pregnancy is a slaughter of innocents of biblical proportions. Crack babies, a rarity a decade ago, crowd $2,000-a-day neonatal wards. Many die. Each survivor can cost one million dollars to bring to adulthood. Fetal alcohol syndrome is a top cause of birth defects.

Even where prenatal care is available, women on drugs and alcohol are not likely to take advantage of it. Those who do seek help must often wait in line for scarce treatment slots. Mothers abusing drugs during pregnancy account for most of the $3 billion that Medicaid spent in 1994 on inpatient hospital care for illness and injury due to drug abuse.

Poverty in History's Most Affluent Society

Drugs have changed the nature of poverty in America. Nowhere is this more striking than in the persistent problem of welfare dependency.

At least 20 percent of Chicago and Maryland's Montgomery County adults on welfare have drug problems. And that may be low compared to other urban areas. Many of the million teenagers who get pregnant each year are high on alcohol or drugs at the time they conceive, and one of the surest ways to get locked in poverty is to become an unwed mother before graduating from high school. At least half the homeless men and women—some say 80 to 90 percent—are alcohol and drug abusers.

The American electorate is hell-bent on putting welfare mothers to work. But all the financial sticks and carrots and all the job training in the world will do precious little to make employable the hundreds of thousands of welfare recipients who are drug and alcohol abusers. For too long, reformers have had their heads in the sand about this unpleasant reality. Liberals fear that acknowledging the extent of alcohol and drug use among welfare recipients will incite even more punitive reactions than those currently in fashion. Conservatives don't want to face up to the cost of treatment.

This political denial ensures failure. Any reform that will move individuals from welfare to work must provide funds to treat drug and alcohol abuse.

Supplemental Security Income, the welfare program that provides monthly checks to blind, disabled and poor adults, reveals the grim and expensive consequence of the alternative. Of 90,000 individuals receiving SSI primarily because of substance abuse, fewer than ten percent are in treatment. Not surprisingly, the U.S. Department of Health and Human Services found that thousands of these addicts and alcoholics receive benefits until they die.

Illegal drugs have added a vicious strain of intractability to urban poverty. Drugs are the greatest threat to family stability, decent housing, public schools and even minimal social amenities. Widespread drug use derails the emotional, social and intellectual development not only of the children who abuse them, but also of their peers and neighbors who must grapple with the violent consequences of rampant drugs in housing projects and schools. It becomes difficult—sometimes

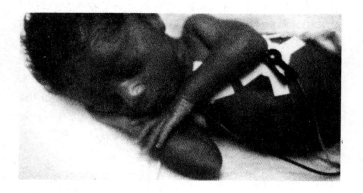

impossible—for children in this sordid environment to acquire the basic educational and social skills they need to get out of poverty.

The Federal Budget Deficit

In fiscal 1995, tobacco, alcohol and drug abuse will account for at least $77.6 billion in entitlement expenditures, an amount equivalent to 40 percent of the 1995 federal budget deficit.

Of that amount, $66.4 billion are costs to health and disability programs, such as Medicare, Medicaid and veterans' health and disability. Cigarette smoking is by far the biggest culprit. Two-thirds of the $66.4 billion—$44 billion—is attributable to tobacco. Alcohol accounts for 18 percent and drugs for 16 percent.

Substance abuse takes its biggest slice from the veterans' health care program. Nearly 30 percent of the dollars spent on veterans' health is due to substance abuse, more than half of that as a result of alcohol and drug abuse. Welfare payments to illegal drug addicts and alcoholics draw the rhetorical fire of legislators. But American taxpayers fork over $4.6 billion a year to individuals on Social Security disability as a result of smoking cigarettes.

Of the $77.6 billion, the remaining $11.2 billion is spent on welfare, food stamp and Supplemental Security Income recipients who regularly use alcohol and drugs and are unlikely to get off the rolls without treatment and aftercare.

Any honest attack by the President and the Congress on entitlement programs—from Medicare and veterans' health and disability to Medicaid and welfare—has to confront substance abuse and addiction. That means a significant investment in prevention and treatment of all abuse. Simply removing individuals who abuse alcohol and drugs from disability, welfare and health care programs will only shift costs to the states, cities and counties, which will then have to deal with the resulting illness, hunger, homelessness and crime. Indeed, a wholesale denial of benefits to alcoholics and drug addicts without providing treatment and aftercare will push up the crime rate and scatter thousands more homeless individuals on America's streets.

Is There Anything We Can Do?

We can begin by ending our national and personal denial of the tough truth that the common **denominator of the nation's hot buttons—crime and violence, health care costs, welfare reform and the budget deficit—is substance abuse. Our denial keeps our sights on the wrong targets. Indeed, 92 percent of federal health entitlement program costs attributable to substance abuse is spent to treat the *consequences* of tobacco, alco-**

hol and drugs; only eight percent is spent to treat the tobacco, alcohol or drug dependence itself.

Our leaders and citizens focus on the top killers: heart disease (720,000 deaths in 1990), cancer (505,000), stroke (144,000), accidents (92,000), emphysema (87,000), pneumonia and influenza (80,000), diabetes (48,000), suicide (31,000), chronic liver disease and cirrhosis (26,000), and AIDS (25,000). But they give scant attention to the *causes* of these killers, which, according to a 1993 *Journal of the American Medical Association* study, include tobacco (435,000 deaths), alcohol (100,000) and illicit drug use (20,000).

Our obsession with the consequences and neglect of the causes is not limited to health care. We pump billions into combatting crime—cops, courts, prisons and punishment—and pennies into preventing the drug and alcohol abuse and addiction that spawn so much criminal activity. We pour resources into shoveling up city slums—rebuilding gutted housing, putting more cops on unsafe streets and barbed wire around housing projects—and little into curbing drug and alcohol abuse. And we often use our hefty budget-cutting axes to chop down prevention and treatment programs, which are most likely to reduce the deficit over the long run.

Dealing effectively with the causes requires up-front investments—the kind that corporations make every day to produce long-term results for their stockholders, the kind that parents make to give their children the best education they can get. It also requires that we scrub the stigma off drug and alcohol abuse and devote the kind of energy and resources to research on addiction and its prevention that we have committed to cancer and heart disease. And it requires common sense.

Here are a few starter suggestions:

• Provide federal funds to state and federal prison systems only if they provide drug and alcohol treatment and aftercare for all inmates who need such care.

• Instead of across-the-board mandatory sentences, keep inmates in jails, boot camps or halfway houses until they demonstrate at least one year of sobriety after treatment.

• Require drug and alcohol addicts to go regularly to treatment and aftercare, like Alcoholics Anonymous, while on parole or probation.

• Provide federal funds for police only to cities that agree to enforce drug laws throughout their jurisdictions. End acceptance of drug bazaars in Harlem, southeast Washington, D.C., and south-central Los Angeles, which would not be tolerated on the streets of New York's Upper East Side, Georgetown or Beverly Hills.

• Encourage judges with lots of drug cases to employ public health professionals, just as they hire economists to assist with anti-trust cases. Drug cases present far more complex human and medical problems than the economic issues posed by commercial litigation.

• Charge higher Medicare premiums to individuals who smoke.

• Cut off welfare payments to drug addicts and alcoholics who refuse to seek treatment and pursue aftercare. As employers and health professionals know, addicts from CEOs to chambermaids need lots of carrots and sticks, including the threat of losing their jobs and incomes, to get the monkey off their backs.

• Subject inmates, parolees and welfare recipients with a history of drug or alcohol abuse to random tests and fund the treatment they need. Conservatives who preach an end to recidivism and welfare dependency must recognize that reincarceration and removal from the welfare rolls for those who test positive is a cruel catch-22 unless treatment is available. Liberals must recognize that getting off drugs is the only chance these individuals (and their babies) have to enjoy their civil rights.

• Identify parents who abuse their children by their own drug and alcohol abuse and place those children in decent orphanages and foster care until the parents go into treatment and shape up.

These are only a few suggestions. The overriding point is that addiction and abuse—involving heroin, cocaine, hallucinogens, amphetamines, inhalants, marijuana, alcohol and tobacco—have fundamentally changed the nature of America's pressing social and economic challenges, and we must rethink how we address them. If a mainstream disease like diabetes or cancer affected as many individuals and families as drug, alcohol and tobacco abuse and addiction do, this nation would mount an effort on the scale of the Manhattan Project to deal with it.

Joseph A. Califano Jr.

Global Issues

Many of the social problems facing Americans today are shared by people worldwide, such as the environment, pollution, and inflation. Some problems facing the entire world are fueled by the consumerism of Americans, and some problems facing the United States are the product of other nations' improvements in production and their desire to improve their economic conditions. The world is no longer the exclusive marketplace for U.S. goods. What Americans do impacts on the world, and what happens around the world impacts on the United States.

The first unit article, "The Mirage of Sustainable Development," refers to the belief that international government's regulations or ownership of environmentally sensitive resources is necessary if the world's environment is to be protected effectively. Through the use of data and examples, the author demonstrates that the world's environment is better protected through private rather than public ownership.

In "The Civil Rights Issue of the '90s," Nancie Marzulla examines the social factors encouraging people to band together to protect their property rights. Legislation to protect the environment, provide flood control, and protect endangered species is often implemented at the expense of private property owners.

Rensselaer Lee, in "Global Reach: The Threat of International Drug Trafficking," documents that the flow of drugs between nations has become a critical issue in global security. While in the short run the economies of some developing nations are benefited (thus explaining their reluctance to eliminate the problem), their long-range stability is jeopardized. Resistance to multinational cooperation is compromised by concerns over national sovereignty.

"The West's Deepening Cultural Crisis" is reflected in its growing crime rate, increasing drug problems, rampant violence, and widespread depressive illnesses. Richard Eckersley argues that Western culture has failed to provide a sense of meaning, belonging, and purpose to life. Without these, individuals feel impotent, insecure, and vulnerable.

In "A Decade of Discontinuity," Lester Brown points out that humankind can no longer expect a future of ever-increasing productivity. World population growth is increasingly outstripping its food production and fossil fuel capacity. Scientists are concerned that the technological innovations that kept pace in the past may not be capable of doing so in the future.

In "Earth Is Running Out of Room," Lester Brown points out scientists' are concerned that the continuation of destructive human activities may interrupt and limit the world's ability to sustain life as we know it.

Looking Ahead: Challenge Questions

Which is the most effective strategy to use in protecting the world's environment, public or private ownership? Explain.

Can the United States continue to be the police force and/or savior of the world?

Can technological innovation continue to meet the world's ever-increasing demand for food, fuel, and security?

Just how far should the government go in creating and implementing laws designed to protect the environment?

What should be done to nations that not only do not discourage drug production within their borders but sometimes may even actively promote it?

What are the possible implications for world peace of increasing populations and shrinking resources?

In what significantly different ways would the three major sociological theoretical perspectives argue that we should study global issues?

What are the major values, rights, obligations, and harms associated with each of the issues covered in this unit?

THE MIRAGE OF SUSTAINABLE DEVELOPMENT

HOW DO WE ACHIEVE BOTH ECONOMIC GROWTH AND ENVIRONMENTAL

PROTECTION? AN ECONOMIST ARGUES THAT PRIVATE-PROPERTY RIGHTS

WILL WORK BETTER THAN INTERNATIONAL BUREAUCRACIES.

THOMAS J. DILORENZO

Thomas J. DiLorenzo is professor of economics in the Sellinger School of Business and Management, Loyola College, Baltimore, Maryland 21210. He has written and lectured extensively on public finance and public-policy-oriented issues and is an editorial referee for 15 academic journals.

A longer version of this article was published by The Center for the Study of American Business (CSAB), a nonpartisan research organization at Washington University in St. Louis. Copies of "The Mirage of Sustainable Development," Contemporary Issues Series 56 (January 1993), are available from CSAB, Washington University, Campus Box 1208, One Brookings Drive, St. Louis, Missouri 63130-4899, telephone 314/935-5630.

There is no precise definition of sustainable development. To some, it simply means balancing economic growth with environmental-protection goals, a relatively uncontroversial position. But to others, it means something different: dramatic reductions in economic growth in the industrialized countries coupled with massive international income redistribution.

According to advocates of the latter viewpoint, there are not enough resources left worldwide to sustain current economic growth rates, and these growth rates are also too damaging to the environment. Consequently, these advocates argue for government regulation of virtually all human behavior on a national and international scale and for governmental control of privately owned resources throughout the world. Such controls may be enforced by national governments or by international bureaucracies such as the United Nations. The "lesson" to be learned from the tragic failures of socialism, the sustainability advocates apparently believe, is that the world needs more socialism.

Such views would be dismissed as bizarre and irrational if they were not held by someone as influential as Norway's Prime Minister Gro Harlem Brundtland, who also chairs the United Nations World Commission on Environment and Development. This Commission published its views in a 1987 book, *Our Common Future*, which laid the groundwork for the June 1992 "Earth Summit" held in Rio de Janeiro.

But the policy proposals advocated by *Our Common Future* and the Earth Summit fail to recognize the many inherent flaws of governmental planning and regulation, and they ignore the important role of private-property rights, technology, and the market system in alleviating environmental problems.

What Role for Property Rights And Free Markets?

The final collapse of communism in 1989 revealed a dirty secret: that pollution in the communist world was far, far worse than virtually anywhere else on the planet. In theory, this should not have been the case, for it has long been held that the profit motive and the failure of unregulated markets to provide incentives to internalize external costs were the primary causes of pollution. Government regulation or ownership of resources was thought to be a necessary condition for environmental protection.

But that was just a theory. The reality is that, in those countries where profit seeking was outlawed for decades and where government claimed ownership of virtually all resources, pollution and other forms of environmental degradation were

From *The Futurist*, September/October 1993, pp. 14-19. © 1993 by the World Future Society. Reprinted by permission of *The Futurist*, 7910 Woodmont Avenue, Suite 450, Bethesda, MD 20814.

COURTESY OF GERMAN INFORMATION CENTER

devastating. According to the United Nations' Global Environment Monitoring Program, pollution in central and eastern Europe "is among the worst on the Earth's surface."

In Poland, for example, acid rain has so corroded railroad tracks that trains are not allowed to exceed 24 miles an hour. Ninety-five percent of the water is unfit for human consumption, and most of it is even unfit for industrial use, so toxic that it will dissolve heavy metals. Industrial dust rains down on towns, depositing cadmium, lead, zinc, and iron. Half of Poland's cities do not even treat their wastes, and life expectancy for males is lower than it was 20 years ago.

The landscape is similar in other parts of central and eastern Europe, in the former Soviet Union, and in China. Eighty percent of the surface waters in former East Germany are classified unsuitable for fishing, sports, or drinking. One out of three lakes has been declared biologically dead because of decades of dumping untreated chemical waste. Some cities are so polluted that cars must use their headlights during the day. Bulgaria, Hungary, Romania, the former Yugoslavia, and the former

Czechoslovakia suffered similar environmental damage during the decades of communism.

These sad facts teach important lessons that the sustainable development theorists have not learned. The root cause of pollution in the former communist world, and worldwide, is not the profit motive and unregulated markets, but the absence of property rights and sound liability laws that hold polluters responsible for their actions. The environmental degradation of the former communist world is an example of one massive "tragedy of the commons," to borrow the phrase coined by biologist Garrett Hardin. Where property is communally or governmentally owned and treated as a free resource, resources will inevitably be overused with little regard for future consequences.

But when people have ownership rights in resources, there is a stronger incentive to protect the value of those resources. Furthermore, when individuals are not held liable for damages inflicted on others—including environmental damages—then there is little hope that responsible behavior will result. Needless to say, the state did not

Industrial effluents pour into river near Bitterfeld in eastern Germany. Decades of dumping untreated chemical wastes in the former East Germany have left one out of three lakes biologically dead and 80% of all surface waters unsuitable for human use.

hold itself responsible for the environmental damage it was causing in the former communist countries. Thus, far from being the answer to environmental problems, pervasive governmental control of natural resources was the cause.

Our Common Future's Misinterpretations

Our Common Future neglects the role of property rights, and, consequently, it grants entirely too much credence to the efficacy of greater governmental controls and regulations as solutions to environmental problems. Several examples stand out.

• **Deforestation.** International economic relationships "pose a particular problem for poor countries trying to manage their environments," says *Our Common Future.* For example, "the trade in tropical timber . . . is one factor underlying tropical deforestation. Needs for foreign exchange encourage many developing countries to cut timber faster than forests can be regenerated."

But the need for foreign exchange is not unique to people in developing countries. All individuals prefer more to less, but they do not all cut down and sell all the trees in sight for economic gain. Deforestation was also a massive problem in the former communist countries, but the main reason was that the forests were communally owned. Consequently, anyone could cut them down, and there were virtually no incentives to replant because of the absence of property rights.

Deforestation has also taken place in democratic countries, primarily on government-owned land that is leased to timber companies who, since they do not own the land, have weak incentives to replant and protect its future value. Some of these same timber companies are very careful indeed not to overharvest or neglect replanting their own private forest preserves. They do so not so much out of a desire to protect the environment as to protect the value of their assets. Well-enforced property rights and the existence of a market for forest products will assure that forests are likely to be used wisely, not exploited.

• **Desertification.** The sustainable development theorists also misdiagnose the problem of desertification—the process whereby "productive arid and semiarid land is rendered economically unproductive," as *Our Common Future* defines it. They blame capitalism for desertification, particularly "the pressures of subsistence food production, commercial crops, and meat production in arid and semiarid areas." Their "solution" is greater governmental controls on agriculture.

Desertification is undoubtedly a problem throughout the world—including parts of the United States. The primary cause is not commercial agriculture, however, but the tragedy of the commons.

A particularly telling example of the importance of private property to desertification was reported in *Science* magazine in a 1974 article on desertification in the Sahel area of Africa. At the time, this area was suffering from a five-year drought. NASA satellite photographs showed a curiously shaped green pentagon that was in sharp contrast to the rest of the African desert. Upon investigation, scientists discovered that the green blotch was a 25,000-acre ranch, fenced in with barbed wire, divided into five sectors, with the cattle allowed to graze only one sector a year. The ranch was started at the same time the drought began, but the protection afforded the land was enough to make the difference between pasture and desert.

• **Wildlife management.** The Earth Summit advocated a "biodiversity treaty" whereby national governments would establish policies aimed at slowing the loss of plant and animal species. The type of policies most preferred by sustainable development theorists include prohibition of commercial uses of various plants and animals, such as the ban on ivory from African elephants, and the listing of more "endangered species," which may then be "protected" by governments on game preserves or elsewhere.

There is growing evidence, however, that the best way to save truly endangered species is not to socialize them, but to allow people to own them. As conservationist Ike Sugg has written:

[W]here governments allow individuals to reap the economic benefits of conserving and protecting their wildlife stocks—wildlife flourish. Where individuals are denied the opportunity to profit from wildlife legally, they do so illegally and without the sense of responsibility that comes with stewardship.

One particularly telling example that illustrates Sugg's point is the African elephant. Kenya outlawed elephant hunting in the 1970s; its elephant population quickly *dropped* from 140,000 in 1970 to an estimated 16,000 today as illegal poaching proliferated.

In contrast, Zimbabwe had only 30,000 elephants in 1979 but has over 65,000 today. The main reason for these differences, according to Sugg, is that in 1984 the government of Zimbabwe granted citizens ownership rights over elephants on communal lands—a large step in the direction of defining property rights. As expressed by one tribal chief who implicitly understood the value of property rights and the commercialization of elephants:

For a long time the government told us that wildlife was their resource. But I see how live animals can be our resources. Our wealth. Our way to improve the standard of living without waiting for the government to decide things. A poacher is only stealing from us.

The preservation of endangered wildlife through private-property rights and free markets is also prevalent in parts of the United States in the form of game ranching, which typically involves "exotic" or non-native animals. Game rancher David Bamberger of Texas, for example, has preserved 29 of the 31 remaining bloodlines of the Scimitar-horned Oryx, a rare antelope that is virtually extinct in its native Africa. Despite such successes, several states have outlawed game ranching because the notion of privatizing wildlife is blasphemy to the "religion" of environmentalism (not to mention "animal rights"), which holds that markets and property rights decimate species.

The principle of using property rights and market incentives to protect global resources and the environment applies to a wide range of problems, including the exploitation of water resources in the American West, the mismanagement of government-owned forest lands, the overfishing of public lakes and streams, and even the ocean commons: The Law of the Sea Treaty, which the United States has thus far refused to sign, would establish the oceans as the largest government-owned and regulated commons on Earth—and, inevitably, the largest tragedy of the commons.

This elementary principle, however, is not even acknowledged by the United Nations' sustainable development theorists. In answering the question, "How are individuals . . . to be persuaded or made to act in the common interest?," the Brundtland Commission answered with "education," undefined "law enforcement," and eliminating "disparities in economic and political power." No mention was made of

African elephants are protected by bans on ivory trade and other government measures. But there is growing evidence that private-property rights over wildlife may be more effective than "socialization" in protecting endangered species, according to DiLorenzo.

the role of property rights in shaping incentives.

Sustainable Delusions

Sustainable development—as it is defined by the Brundtland Commission and the planners of the Earth Summit—can best be understood as a euphemism for environmental socialism—granting governments more and more control over the allocation of resources in the name of environmental protection. But if any lesson can be learned from the collapse of socialism in the former communist countries, it is that government ownership and control of resources is a recipe for economic collapse and environmental degradation. Socialism is no more effective in protecting the environment than it is in creating wealth.

Government ownership of natural resources inevitably leads to the tragedy of the commons, but that is all too often the "solution" offered by the Brundtland Commission. The Commission recommends government control of everything from outer space to energy, which is supposedly "too important for its development to continue in such a manner" as the free market allows.

Perhaps the top priority of sustainable development theorists is to expand the international welfare state by agitating for wealth transfers from "the rich" countries to the developing. But the whole history of development aid is government-to-government—most of it is typically used to finance the expansion of governmental bureaucracies in the recipient countries—which can be adverse to economic development. Even if most of the aid did make it into the hands of the citizens of the recipient countries, sustainable development theorists do not explain how that will translate into savings, investment, capital formation, and entrepreneurial activity—the ingredients of economic development.

Finally, the theory of sustainable development commits in grand fashion the mistake of what Nobel laureate Friedrich von Hayek called "the pretense of knowledge." The detailed and constantly changing "information of time and place" required to produce even the simplest of items efficiently is so immense and so widely dispersed that no one human mind or group of minds with the largest computer in existence could imitate to any degree the efficiency of a decentralized market system. This, after all, is the principal lesson to be learned from the world-wide collapse of socialism.

Moreover, the larger and more complex an economy becomes, the more remote the likelihood that governmental planning could be anything but guess work. As Hayek states in his 1988 book, *The Fatal Conceit,*

By following the spontaneously generated moral traditions underlying the competitive market order . . . we generate and garner greater knowledge and wealth than could ever be obtained or utilized in a centrally directed economy. . . . Thus socialist aims and programs are factually impossible to achieve or execute.

The theory of sustainable development calls for myriad varieties of *international* central planning of economic activity. If the "pretense of knowledge" is fatal to attempts at governmental planning at the national level, the belief that international or global planning could possibly succeed is untenable.

The Brundtland Commission's recommendation that every government agency in the world engage in economic planning and regulation in the name of environmental protection would lead to a massive bureaucratization of society and, consequently, a sharp drop in living standards. The image of millions of "green" bureaucrats interfering in every aspect of our social and economic lives is frightening.

The irony of it all is that the wealthier economies are typically healthier and cleaner than the poorer ones. By impoverishing the world economy, "sustainable development" would, in fact, also be harmful to the environment. Private property, free markets, and sound liability laws—anathemas to the theory of sustainable development—are essential for a clean environment and for economic growth.

The Civil Rights Issue of the '90s

Nancie G. Marzulla

Nancie G. Marzulla is president and chief legal counsel of Defenders of Property Rights in Washington, D.C.

When people think of civil rights, they tend to conjure up images of segregated schools in the 1950s or the fight we had in the 1960s (indeed, are still having) in this country to ensure that all people—regardless of their skin color or nationality—can enjoy the same privileges of living under the rule of law in a free society. That right to equality regardless of race, color, or creed is guaranteed by the Fourteenth Amendment to the U.S. Constitution.

Today, however, another civil rights revolution is under way. At issue is another guaranteed right, that of obtaining payment of just compensation whenever one's private property is taken by the government for public use. As specified in the Fifth Amendment to the Constitution, "No person shall be . . . deprived of life, liberty or property, without due process of law; nor shall private property be taken for public use, without just compensation."

Just as segregation led to the racially based civil rights movement, so it is that incursions on property rights, largely in the name of protecting the environment, have sparked the property rights movement now, some 30 years later. Starting in the 1960s, federal, state, and local governments increasingly began to regulate property rights through environmental protection policies.

Today, environmental regulations touch every conceivable aspect of property use and ownership, often infringing directly upon private-property rights protected by the Constitution. Through its ability to regulate, the government has steadily and increasingly tended to "take" whatever uses and benefits of property it wishes rather than condemning the property outright and paying for what it has taken.

The property rights movement comprises thousands upon thousands of individuals across America who are being singled out by the government to bear the unfair burden of implementing land use and environmental policies the government itself is simply not prepared to pay for. The complaint of the property owner is not so much what the government is trying to achieve through its policies but the means by which it is achieving them.

THE COURT TAKES A STAND

A case in point is last June's decision by the U.S. Supreme Court in *Dolan v. City of Tigard*. At issue was whether the city could demand from Florence Dolan approximately 10 percent of her land—which the city planned to use for a bicycle/pedestrian pathway and public greenway—in exchange for being granted permission to enlarge her plumbing-supply store. No one, including the Dolans, objected to the city's plans for a bike path or greenway. Clearly, the fair thing for the city to do—the constitutionally mandated way of achieving its objectives—was to buy the land necessary to complete the project rather than hold Dolan's planned use of her property hostage, as the city did.

Such infringements have provoked people to unite to form the property rights movement. These people are objecting to an environmental regulatory regime that by 1993, according to a report from the American Enterprise Institute, was costing Americans $140 billion a year in compliance costs and that ranks even the most insignificant snail's welfare as more important than human interests.

They are objecting to a wetlands program that delineates one to two hundred million acres of land—75 percent of which is privately owned—as "wet" and stipulates that it must be maintained untouched by human hands. They are objecting to a criminal enforcement program that puts innocent people in jail for simply placing dry sand on existing dry sand, all on land that is privately owned, because it violates the government's policy of no net loss of wetlands.

Until recently, the Supreme Court showed little interest in property rights law. In 1922, Justice Oliver Wendell Holmes declared the bedrock principle of takings law: "The general rule at least is, that while property may be regulated to a certain extent, if regulation goes too far it will be recognized as a taking." After this ruling, however, the Court did not select any cases that would advance this doctrine. This was apparent in 1978, when Justice William Brennan expressed his dismay over the Court's inability to "develop any 'set formula' for determining when 'justice and fairness' require that economic injuries caused by public action be compensated by the government rather than remain disproportionately concentrated on a few persons."

In 1987, however, the Court showed a renewed interest in property rights, ruling on three cases. In *First English Evangelical Church v. County of Los Angeles*, the Court held the county could be required to compensate

Property Rights in America

■ **They are protected** under the Fifth Amendment.

■ **They have been under assault** from local, state, and federal governments for at least 30 years.

■ **They have been aided** by the Supreme Court's proproperty decision in the Dolan case, handed down this June.

a church barred by a flood-control ordinance from reconstructing summer camp buildings destroyed during a 1978 flood. In *Nollan v. California Coastal Commission*, the justices ruled the public could not require that the owner of a home next to a beach donate a third of his land to the state in order to obtain a permit to rebuild the house without paying just compensation. *Hodel v. Irving* invalidated a regulation eliminating Native Americans' right to devise reservation lands to their heirs.

In 1992, the Supreme Court again ruled for the plaintiff in *Lucas v. South Carolina Coastal Council*. The case involved two beachfront lots the owner planned to develop that were rendered useless by a beachfront protection statute. The central holding of *Lucas* is that

regulations that deny the property owner of all 'economically viable use of his land' constitute one of the discrete categories of regulatory deprivations that require compensation without the usual case-specific inquiry into the public interest advanced in support of the restraint.

The state was forced to purchase the property from Lucas.

The state then put the property up for sale to potential developers: the very activity from which Lucas had been barred. This shows how the government's attitude changes when it is forced to bear the cost of its regulations, at least when the Fifth Amendment is applied.

In his opinion in the *Dolan* case, Chief Justice William Rehnquist noted, "We see no reason why the Takings Clause of the Fifth Amendment, as much a part of the Bill of Rights as the First Amendment, should be relegated to the status of a poor relation in these comparable circumstances." The high court reversed the decision of the lower court, sending it back to be retried. This time, the burden is on the city to prove why it needs to take the Dolan property.

CONGRESS GOING IN THE RIGHT DIRECTION

The courts, however, are not the only place where the muscle of the property rights movement is being felt. The 103rd Congress has been active on three fronts—unfunded mandates, risk-assessment analyses of regulations, and property rights bills—which environmentalists collectively refer to as the "unholy trinity." These three reforms have become dreaded amendments to regulatory reauthorizations in the eyes of the environmentalist movement.

In a memo to environmental leaders, a Natural Resources Defense Council lobbyist warned that regulations long overdue for reauthorization could not be passed during this session of Congress without one or more of the trinity amendments attached. The strategy the lobbyist offered was to keep most of the reauthorization bills off the table, allowing the environmental movement to focus on just one or two pieces of legislation. Regulations that have not been reauthorized are in no danger of expiring because they remain valid until reauthorized.

Property rights were the focus early in the session, when Interior Secretary Bruce Babbitt's National Biological Survey—a plan to map the entire

■

Today, environmental regulations touch every conceivable aspect of property use and ownership, often infringing directly upon private property rights protected by the Constitution.

■

nation by ecosystems—was saddled with property rights amendments when it passed the House. The bill was never introduced in the Senate.

The importance of risk-assessment analyses led to the downfall of the bill that would

have elevated the EPA to cabinet-level status. When the bill arrived on the House floor for debate, the leadership would not allow consideration of a risk-assessment amendment that had already passed by an overwhelming margin in the Senate. Angered over this move, congressmen sent it back to committee, effectively stopping the bill.

Lawmakers with political ideologies as divergent as Sens. Dirk Kempthorne (R-Idaho) and Carol Moseley-Braun (D-Illinois) have come to agreement on the issue of curbing unfunded mandates, with each sponsoring bills to reduce or even eliminate them completely. An unfunded mandate is federal legislation that seeks to achieve its goal by compelling states and localities to pick up the bill for enforcement.

These mandates are the bane of mayors and governors

■ *The current justices:* The Court's decision in *Dolan v. City of Tigard* has given a boost to private property rights.

across America, and the Clinton administration has been forced to take notice of the problem. Environmentalists are particularly concerned about this because so many environmental regulations passed at the federal level compel the states to pay for their compliance and fiscal outlay. In some cases, they are forced to set up their own programs.

The property rights issue has gained such prominence that the Senate has established a property rights caucus led by Sens. Bob Dole (R-Kansas) and Howell Heflin (D-Alabama), a former chief justice of the Alabama Supreme Court. In the House, Louisiana Democrat Billy Tauzin is finding himself at odds with his party colleagues in the House leadership as he circulates a discharge petition to bring his "Property Owner's Bill of Rights" to the floor for debate. Sen. Phil Gramm (R-Texas), an oft-mentioned Republican candidate for the White House in 1996, has also introduced property rights legislation, and he has expressed interest in using it as a campaign issue in this fall's elections. (Gramm is the head of the National Republican Senatorial Campaign Committee.)

Property rights are also becoming a major issue in the states. Over the past legislative session, 37 state legislatures introduced almost 100 bills to protect property rights. Ten of these states have turned the bills into law. At the American Legislative Exchange Council's 1994 conference, a whole morning was set aside to discuss the issue of property rights. Many states are eagerly awaiting the results of a vote to take place in Arizona in November, where voters will be asked to decide the fate of property rights legislation.

After a petition campaign rife with deceitful allegations that property rights legislation would ruin Arizona's economy and ecology, environmentalists were able to force a referendum on property rights legislation already passed by the legislature and signed by the governor. Proposition 300, as it is now known, "would require state agencies, before a taking results, to examine their activities, including rules and other regulatory actions that effect the use of property, to determine if an action requires compensation from the state." In addition to this important election battle, Massachusetts and Florida are also putting property rights to a vote in referendums this fall.

From the very beginning of our republic, property rights have been considered sacred. The Founding Fathers envisioned a strong system of property rights as a means of protecting individual liberty. John Adams, in his *Defense of the Constitutions of Government*, said, "The moment the idea is admitted into society that property is not as sacred as the laws of God, and there is not force of law and public justice to protect it, anarchy and tyranny commence." The founders believed property rights to be of overreaching importance. Indeed, the Constitution provides that money be awarded to citizens for incurred damages in only one case. As stipulated in the Fifth Amendment, "Nor shall private property be taken for public use, without just compensation."

Property rights are the true linchpin of all the rights we hold dear. If the government possesses the ability to take away our land at any given time for any given reason, our rights to speak freely, associate with whom we choose, and other individual freedoms are at risk. It has taken the American people over two decades to take serious notice of this erosion, but they are making up for lost time. Property rights, like any civil rights movement, is strong at the grass roots.

■

John Adams said: "The moment the idea is admitted into society that property is not as sacred as the laws of God, and there is not force of law and public justice to protect it, anarchy and tyranny commence."

■

Facing the equally strong and well-funded environmental establishment, it is shaping up as one of the biggest battles of this decade—and beyond.

ADDITIONAL READING

Terry Anderson and Donald Leal, *Free Market Environmentalism*, Pacific Research Institute, San Francisco, Calif., 1991.

Richard Epstein, *Takings: Property Rights and the Power of Eminent Domain*, Harvard University Press, Cambridge, Mass., 1985.

"The Pocket Guide to Your Property Rights," Defenders of Property Rights, Washington, D.C., 1994.

Dixy Lee Ray, *Trashing the Planet*, Regnery Gateway, Washington, D.C., 1991.

———, *Environmental Overkill*, Regnery Gateway, Washington, D.C., 1993.

The international trade in drugs has become an increasingly important issue in global security. It is a problem, however, that falls outside traditional national security concerns, even though it threatens the political stability of many states.

Global Reach:
The Threat of International Drug Trafficking

Rensselaer W. Lee III

RENSSELAER W. LEE III, *president of Global Advisory Services in Alexandria, Virginia, and associate scholar at the Foreign Policy Research Institute in Philadelphia, is the author of* The White Labyrinth: Cocaine and Political Power *(New Brunswick, N.J.: Transaction Press, 1989).*

Narcotics industries rank as the world's most successful illegal enterprises, generating annual profits of roughly $200 billion to $300 billion. Major production and trafficking complexes in the Andes, Southwest Asia, and the Golden Triangle of Southeast Asia thrive, impervious to international enforcement programs. Indeed, between 1982 and 1994, worldwide opium production more than doubled, and the global output of coca leaves rose by 300 percent. Opium cultivation is expanding rapidly in several communist or former communist states, primarily China, Vietnam, Uzbekistan, Tajikistan, and Turkmenistan. (In China, the revolutionary government claimed four decades ago that the once pervasive problem of opiate addiction was all but obliterated, but poppy plantings have been reported in at least 17 of the nation's 30 provinces, and drug use is escalating rapidly.)

China currently serves as an important transit country for Burmese heroin, and entrepreneurial North Koreans are entering the heroin business, possibly with the backing of their government. Colombia, which produces an estimated 70 to 80 percent of the world's refined cocaine, is the world's third largest opium producer, with an estimated 20,000 hectares under poppy cultivation. Moreover, the distinctive signature of Colombian-refined heroin is increasingly appearing in United States retail markets. A similar trend toward diversification in the industry is also seen in Peru, the world's largest producer of coca leaf, where low levels of poppy cultivation are being recorded. In addition, several communist or former communist countries—Poland, China, Russia, Azerbaijan, and the Baltic states—are emerging as important producers and exporters of sophisticated amphetamines. And narcotics such as LSD, Ecstasy, and trimethylphentanil (a powerful synthetic opiate) are marketed with increasing frequency in former Soviet states.

Narcotics industries are becoming larger, more powerful, and more entrenched in the global economy and in the economies and societies of individual producing states, although they differ significantly in organizational sophistication and systematic effects. For example, trafficking organizations in China are at a rudimentary stage of development, with small staffs that often disband after one or two deals. Furthermore, the profits generated by smuggling opium or heroin out of China flow primarily to overseas Chinese, not mainlanders. Consequently, Chinese drug organizations exert little influence on China's economic system and are generally not viewed as a threat to state authority. (Virtually no reports of high-level drug corruption in China have surfaced.)

At the other extreme, Colombia's highly developed trafficking enterprises employ hundreds of specialized personnel—pilots, shippers, chemists, accountants, lawyers, financial managers, and assassins—directly or on contract, and earn an estimated $4 billion to $7 billion annually, mainly from cocaine sales in the United States and Europe. These revenues endow the narcotraffickers with a significant capability to bribe or otherwise influence the behavior of key Colombian officials and political leaders. (United States law enforcement officials estimate that the Colombian cartels spend more than $100 million annually on bribes in the country.) Colombia constitutes a model of advanced or mature narcotics enterprises that have the economic and political problems associated with a large criminal sector.

Some worrisome trends have arisen in narcotic industry strategies: widening economic influence, that is, the impact of the illicit drug trade on illegal economic structures and processes in major producing or transit countries; the increasing political corruption in such countries; the growing intrusion of narcocriminal enterprises into the realm of the state and the law, a process that some scholars associate with the delegitimation of government; the successes of narcotics businesses in innovation, avoiding detection, and increasing operating efficiency; and, especially apparent since the late 1980s, the growing transnational cooperation among criminal empires that deal in drugs and other black market items. All these trends suggest that narcotics industries are enhancing their power and reach, developing new and advanced capabilities, and establishing new bases of support. At the same time, the leaders and citizens of some trafficking countries are exhibiting clear signs of drug war fatigue. Much to the dismay of the United States, support is growing for peaceful resolutions of the drug trade issue, ranging from negotiated surrenders that treat drug kingpins leniently to the outright legalization of narcotics.

DRUG ECONOMICS

The economic effects of the drug trade stem mainly from the processes of legitimizing narcotics earnings in the country or countries of origin. Different nations display different patterns. For example, officials in the Chinese Ministry of Public Security believe that opium and heroin smugglers invest few of their earnings in ventures that benefit the Chinese economy. Most drug proceeds are banked in noncommunist Asian countries and the little money that does return to the country tends to be used to buy luxury housing, furniture, electronic equipment, and gold jewelry. In Russia the sales of illicit drugs total an estimated $800 million each year, and law enforcement officials contend that much of the startup capital for small, legitimate businesses, such as stores, restaurants, and fruit stands, is supplied by the narcotics trade. (However, the economic effect of drugs in Russia is difficult to separate from the effect of organized crime groups in general, which operate many profitable illegal enterprises.) Colombia is probably suffering from the most advanced case of narcoeconomic penetration; traffickers annually repatriate an estimated $2 billion to $5 billion from narcotics exports, or approximately 4 to 9 percent of Colombia's GDP of $55 billion. One Colombian economist, Francesco Thoumi, has calculated that accumulated trafficker assets in Colombia and abroad reached anywhere from $39 billion to $66 billion between 1989 and 1990, a scale of narcowealth so immense that it could easily alter Colombia's economic and political status quo.

Indeed, drug money pervades the Colombian economy. For example, according to the Colombian Institute of Agrarian Reform and the Colombian Farmers Association, drug dealers expanded their direct or intermediary ownership of agricultural land from 1 million hectares in the late 1980s to an estimated 4 million hectares in 1994. Today, traffickers own or control between 8 and 11 percent of agriculturally usable land in at least 250 of 1,060 Colombian

municipalities, making them a powerful force in the rural Colombian economy. Technological improvements in cattle raising and commercial agriculture sometimes accompanied narco land investments, strengthening traffickers as rural leaders in some areas. Furthermore, as the so-called Cali cartel gained ascendancy, the infiltration of legitimate businesses by drug dealers reached significant new levels. Earlier generations of traffickers, such as the leaders of the Medellín cartel of the 1980s (then the dominant trafficking group in Colombia), were relatively unsophisticated economic actors who were more concerned with laundering drug earnings than realizing adequate returns on their investments. However, these earlier traffickers clearly spent to enhance their status. Conspicuous examples abound. Jose Gonzalo Rodriguez Gacha accumulated 140 country estates, collectively worth an estimated $100 million; some of these residences were lavishly furnished with items such as pillows stuffed with ostrich feathers, gold-plated bathroom fixtures, and imported Italian toilet paper stamped with likenesses of Botticelli's The Birth of Venus.

In contrast, the Cali group cultivated an image of business respectability by investing in a wide range of economic activities. According to a recent report by the Colombian Department of Administrative Security, Cali drug money has "infiltrated the construction industry, drugstore chains, radio stations, automobile dealerships, department stores, factories, banks, sports clubs, and investment firms." Agribusiness enterprises such as cut flowers, tropical fruit production, and poultry farms can be added to this list. "In what sectors of the economy has the Cali cartel not invested?" asked Gabriel de Vega Pinzon, the head of the Colombian National Drug Directorate, in a December 1994 interview with this writer.

DRUG POLITICS

Drug trafficking also has wide-ranging effects on political and administrative systems in developing countries. Narcotics industries in countries such as Myanmar, Afghanistan, and Colombia (especially between 1989 and 1991) are associated with extreme antistate violence or with the disintegration of national authority. However, most drug dealers are not pursuing independent political initiatives, preferring to coexist with and manipulate the state authority. "We don't kill judges or ministers, we buy them," remarked Cali cartel leader Gilberto Rodriguez Orejuela on one occasion. Indeed, corruption has assumed outlandish proportions in Colombia. In 1994 police and judicial investigations detected evidence of trafficker payoffs to: a former president of the Colombian national congress, a former comptroller general, a recently elected congressman, 12 retired army officers (communication and security specialists "decorated for their outstanding service to the army"), more than 150 Cali police officers, almost the entire contingent of Cali airport police, employees of the El Valle telephone system, the Cali regional prosecutor, 6 of 22 Cali city councillors, and the mayors of 4 Colombian cities, among them Medellín.

The pattern of corruption in Latin America also includes attempts by traffickers to purchase influence at the highest political levels. During the 1980s, narcocorruption involving top national leaders or their closest associates was documented in Bolivia, Panama, the Bahamas, and the Turks and Caicos Islands. One drug informant claims that Fidel Castro's brother Raúl personally authorized the shipment of 6 tons of cocaine through Cuba between 1987 and 1989. Traffickers have also indirectly sought political leverage by contributing to presidential election campaigns. Trafficker support of the 1989 Bolivian campaign of President Jaime Paz Zamora prompted Paz in 1991 to appoint a known drug dealer, Faustino Rico Toro, to head the Bolivian Special Narcotics Force, although pressure from the United States subsequently forced Paz to dismiss Rico Toro from that post; in early 1995 the Bolivian Supreme Court authorized the extradition of Rico Toro to the United States on drug charges. In Colombia a major scandal erupted in June 1994 when a taped telephone conversation leaked to the press showed Gilberto Rodriguez Orejuela and his brother discussing a possible donation of $3.8 million to the presidential campaign of Ernesto Samper Pizano. Some Colombian and United States observers—among them Jose Toft, the United States Drug Enforcement Agency (DEA) representative in Colombia at the time—contend that the Samper campaign did in fact receive millions of dollars from the Cali cartel. Toft, who resigned from the DEA last September, summarized a widely held belief about the state of Colombian politics when he commented to a Colombian television news station that, "I cannot think of a single political or judicial institution that has not been penetrated by the narco-traffickers—I know that people don't like to hear the term 'narcodemocracy,' but the truth is it's very real and it's here."

Modern narcotics enterprises have also helped criminal authority grow at the expense of legitimate state authority. In Latin America this encroachment spans issues such as social welfare, counterinsurgency, and (ironically) the maintenance of law and order. For example, in Mexico, Colombia, and Bolivia, traffickers have cultivated a Robin Hood image by devoting vast resources to community development projects such as roads, schools, airport repairs, and housing, or by donating money and gifts to the poor. Such activities cemented political support for the drug capos among marginalized social groups such as Medellín slum dwellers and poor farmers in the Bolivian Beni—populations that governments and legitimate nongovernment organizations cannot serve. In Colombia a weak government presence in the countryside, an

ongoing rural insurgency, and the acquisition of landed estates by drug lords in the 1980s created new political opportunities and roles for narcotics dealers. For example, paramilitary organizations financed by trafficking interests emerged, supplanting an impotent Colombian state by furnishing local security against predatory guerrilla groups. Curbed somewhat by the Colombian government's 1990 crackdown on the Medellín cartel, narco-backed paramilitaries nonetheless pursue their mission in the middle Magdalena Valley, Cordoba, Uraba, and other guerrilla-infested regions. (Of course, paramilitary operations to root out and exterminate leftist guerrilla sympathizers pose serious human rights challenges for Colombia.) Legitimate private groups conducting business in the Colombian hinterlands—coffee growers, cattlemen associations, and foreign oil companies, for example—admittedly provide public welfare and security protection functions. However, the assumption of such roles by the narcotraffickers generates particularly ominous overtones for the Colombian political process.

Traffickers tend to support their local police on law and order issues such as the defense of property rights and maintenance of basic community services; police who spearhead government narcotics crackdowns or work for rival trafficking organizations, however, stand a good chance of being murdered. The Cali cartel supported a perverted and socially regressive form of law enforcement, the so-called social cleansing groups, which targeted marginal urban dwellers such as prostitutes, thieves, beggars and drug addicts. In some regions of Latin America and Asia, trafficking interests for all practical purposes are the law, since the government does not exercise real sovereignty in those areas. (Drug trafficker Khun Sa's Shan state enclave in Myanmar represents perhaps the most egregious modern example of narcowarlordism.) Yet, opportunistic traffickers also assist or form alliances with governments that persecute rival criminal organizations. For example, in Myanmar, the Wa insurgent trafficking groups are enlisting government help to fight Khun Sa's Shan United Army—and managing to broaden their territorial base in the process.

In Colombia the Cali cartel found it politically and commercially expedient to furnish "valuable information" to the government for its ultimately successful manhunt for Pablo Escobar and some of his lieutenants, a contribution recently acknowledged by Colombian prosecutor general Alfonso Valdivieso (according to the Cali regional prosecutor's office, the Cali group hired Japanese communication experts to track Escobar's movements in the months before his demise). Moreover, in a June 1994 interview with this writer, Valdivieso's predecessor, Gustavo de Grieff, referred to a report that a special government search force in Medellín received a $10 million payment from Cali traffickers shortly after Escobar was killed last December and allegedly distributed the funds among ranking members of the force. "Apparently, [the force] was an instrument of Escobar's enemies, not of the government," de Grieff commented.

Such scattered examples confirm the ability of traffickers, who command enormous power and resources, to pirate government functions or inherit them by default. In surrender negotiations with the Colombian government, the Cali traffickers surprised no one by wielding their contributions to the anti-Escobar campaign as leverage against the government. In a letter to President Cesar Gaviría in January 1994, Gilberto Rodriguez Orejuela petitioned for house arrest rather than a jail cell, in part on grounds of his "collaboration with the prosecutor general's office and the search group to achieve the well-known results."

Finally, new patterns of domestic and international cooperation have spawned among criminal empires that deal in illicit drugs. Such cooperation connects criminal groups such as the Colombian cartels, Mexican smuggling organizations, Japanese *yakuza*, Hong Kong Chinese syndicates, Sicilian mafia, and Russian organized crime. Central issues of common concern include the organization of markets, trade deals (for example, exchanges of drugs for weapons, drugs for cash, and drugs for drugs), smuggling logistics, and laundering or repatriation of trafficking proceeds.

Cooperation between Colombian traffickers and Italian organized crime groups to sell cocaine in Italy and the rest of Europe apparently stands at a particularly advanced stage. The Cali cartel and the Sicilian mafia are experimenting with franchise arrangements that would allow the mafia to distribute large consignments of Cali cocaine to European buyers outside Italy. The Cali group has also established working relationships with organized crime figures in Poland, the Czech Republic, and Russia. The Cali traffickers' strategic design uses these countries as a back door to deliver cocaine to western Europe. Such relationships are underscored by Russian government seizures of 1.1 tons of cocaine in Vyborg in February 1993, and 400 kilograms of the drug in St. Petersburg in April 1994; both shipments could be traced to Cali trafficking organizations. In general, international narcocooperation opens new markets for narcotics and other illegal products, exploits economies of scale for selling in those markets, enhances organized crime's penetration of legal economic and financial systems, and generally increases the power of criminal formations relative to national governments.

TREATING THE DRUG PROBLEM

Confronting powerful narcotics lobbies and publics weary of drug wars, government commitment to suppress narcotrafficking is waning perceptibly in some source countries. One manifestation of this trend is rising political support to legalize drugs. Bolivia's president, Gonzalo Sanchez de Losada, openly favors this; he declared to a Spanish newspaper in 1993 that "The antidrug fight is the politician's tomb—prohibition has achieved nothing but making vices extremely profitable for traffickers. It is terrible to say it, but some tax on drugs should be created." The Bolivian government promised coca farmers in September 1994 that it would mount an international campaign to decriminalize the coca leaf (but not the products derived from it). Colombian President Ernesto Samper recently canceled plans for a popular referendum to overturn a May 1994 decision by the Colombian constitutional court that legalized personal drug use.

The legalization or selective decriminalization of drugs is gaining ground elsewhere in the world. Poland, Russia, and Italy have lifted criminal penalties for personal drug use, and cannabis products are openly sold to adults in coffeehouses in the Netherlands. In China, where drug dealers are routinely executed with great public fanfare, some local cadres advocate removing restrictions on poppy growing to help isolated mountain areas "get rid of poverty"—possibly a sign of the significant proportions of the private opium trade in that country.

In the Andean countries, governments have not legalized drug production—an action that would spur certain retaliation by the United States—but they have attempted to diminish conflicts with the cocaine industry by negotiating with participants and leaders in the trafficking chain. Colombia's negotiations with Medellín cartel leaders date to May 1984, when former President Alfonso Lopez Michelson and Attorney General Carlos Jimenez Gomez held separate meetings with Pablo Escobar and other kingpins in Panama. Since 1990, Colombia has offered reduced sentences and other legal inducements to traffickers who surrender, confess, and turn state's evidence.

Colombian officials see negotiations as a tool of social policy that can subdue the power of individual trafficking organizations. Negotiations doubtless helped reduce narcoterrorist violence in the 1990s, but produced few successes against cocaine trafficking. Important traffickers negotiated relatively short sentences that ranged from 4 to 8 years, but furnished little information on the workings of cocaine enterprises. Ivan Urdinola, for example, refused to name major accomplices, averring that such disclosures would place him in mortal danger, and liberally laced his confessions with fatuous statements. (At one point, he informed a judge, "Aside from being a drug trafficker, I am an admirable person."). Perhaps the late Pablo Escobar abused the surrender policy most notoriously. After negotiating a deal with the government in mid-1991, Escobar was incarcerated in the La Catedral prison near Medellín, where he continued to manage his cocaine business until his escape 13 months later. (Subsequent revelations indicated that Escobar paid $2 million for construction of the facility, which was equipped with cellular telephones, fax machines, and computers.) In Bolivia, the government's repentance program produced similarly disappointing results. Repenters characterized themselves as simple cattle farmers who only dabbled in cocaine or lent money to traffickers; the three most important traffickers who surrendered under the Bolivian program received sentences of only 4 to 6 years.

Cali cartel leaders recently offered to implement a plan that would reduce cocaine exports from Colombia by 60 percent (their estimate of their share of the business) if they spent little or no time in jail. Of course, such an offer invites skepticism, since the Cali dons might not control or directly influence a sufficiently large percentage of Colombian refining and exporting capacity to fulfill such a commitment. Recent information suggests that the Colombian cocaine industry is more decentralized and balkanized than during the 1980s. Gilberto Rodriguez Orejuela himself noted in a November 1994 letter to *El Tiempo* that "there are many cartels"; moreover, the industry depends on a multitude of subcontractors and freelancers. Of course, drug kingpins possess considerable leverage over lower level operators; they can stop purchasing products and services or simply withhold protection from laboratories, transport companies, distribution cells, laundering operations, and other key trafficking entities. But, in putting forth their offer, the Cali traffickers provided no blueprint or timetable for dismantling their multibillion-dollar enterprises. Also, a number of factors—the size of the illicit drug industry, the prevalence of official corruption, and the weakness of the Colombian criminal justice and judicial institutions—indicate that Colombia could not successfully implement such a deal.

Debates over legalization, democratization, and negotiated accords with traffickers in key source countries have produced consternation in Washington. Yet, disillusionment with overseas narcotics control and with drug prohibition in general is also widespread in the United States. Many Americans favor scrapping supply-side programs altogether, shifting resources to education and prevention programs, or even legalizing the production and use of some drugs. United States international initiatives, including the roughly $1 billion allocated to counternarcotics operations in the Andes since 1989, certainly have had few long-term effects on the availability or purity of drugs in America's major urban markets. Some United States policies are wasteful, counterproductive, or worse. For example, the Bolivian government spent $48.1 million in American aid between 1987 and 1993 to pay farmers to eradicate 26,000 hectares of coca. Farmers, however, planted more than 35,000 new hectares of coca during the same period. The planned compensation for eradication transformed into little more than a coca support program.

At least in the short term, the objective of restricting internationally the suppliers of illegal drugs is probably not attainable. The number of potential drug suppliers is virtually unlimited; few geographical, organizational, or technological barriers obstruct entry into narcotics industries, and crops, laboratories, drug shipments, planes, money, chemicals, and routes can be easily replaced if destroyed. Of course, the value of international drug control does not necessarily lie solely in controlling narcotics. The war on narcotrafficking can be justified as a moral imperative even if it is a practical failure. Furthermore, the United States has staked its prestige and predicated its diplomatic relations with several countries on combating the drug scourge.

More important, however, is the fact that enterprises such as the Colombian cartels and counterpart groups in Europe and Asia dangerously aggregate power that can destabilize governments and facilitate global breakdowns in law and order. (For example, some United States intelligence officials believe that drug-trafficking networks and routes can be easily reconfigured to smuggle chemical weapons, plutonium, or tactical nuclear weapons to terrorist nations and groups.) Demolishing such power can stand alone as a worthwhile objective. Similarly, United States policy expresses legitimate concerns when helping governments curb the political and economic reach of the drug lords, contain narcoterrorist violence, and in general cope with the divisive effects of the drug business. Between 1989 and 1993, the United States supported a crackdown on the Medellín cartel that decimated the group's leadership (all the Medellín founding fathers are either dead or in jail) and removed a lethal threat to the Colombian political order. American pressure or intervention prompted the ouster of narcotics-linked military regimes in Bolivia in 1980 and 1981, and in Panama in 1989, two countries where narcotics trafficking interests had built cozy relationships with the military, giving them de facto control of the national government apparatus for controlling drug crime. In Bolivia, United States pressure on the Paz administration in 1991 prevented the appointment of Bolivians apparently linked to the cocaine trade to head the Ministry of Interior, the National Police, and the Special Narcotics Force.

In a number of countries—such as Bolivia, Thailand, and Laos—United States foreign assistance has fostered positive economic growth, widened income opportunities for farmers who cultivate drugs, and weakened the relative economic clout of narcotics industries. Perhaps international drug policy cannot substantially control entrenched drug trafficking, but supply-side programs can be reconfigured to target criminal organizations, promote stability and growth in drug-torn countries, and enhance positive United States influence.

The West's Deepening Cultural Crisis

Growing crime rates, increasing drug problems, rampant violence, and widespread depressive illness are all signs of Western culture's deepening crisis.

Richard Eckersley

Richard Eckersley is a science writer, social analyst, and policy consultant. He has written several major reports for the Australian Commission for the Future on youth, the future, science, technology, and society. His address is 23 Goble Street, Hughes ACT 2605, Australia.

A striking feature of Western civilization is that, for all our success in reducing the toll of lives taken by disease, we have failed to diminish that exacted by despair. According to the World Health Organization, suicide has steadily increased for both males and females in the developed world since the early 1950s.

What makes the trend particularly tragic is that the increase in suicide is occurring mainly among teenagers and young adults, especially males. In several countries, including the United States, Australia, and New Zealand, the suicide rate among young males has more than tripled since 1950.

We have also seen a dramatic deterioration in many indicators of the psychological well-being of youth over this period:

• Authorities and experts worldwide admit the war against illicit drugs is being lost, despite the expenditure of billions of dollars on law enforcement and education programs. Alcohol abuse among the young has become a major problem.

• There is a growing body of research suggesting that major depressive illness is becoming more widespread in Western societies, especially among teenagers and young adults.

• Obsessive dieting has become commonplace among teenage girls, and the incidence of eating disorders is rising. Recent U.S. research indicates that the incidence of anorexia nervosa among girls aged 10 to 19 has increased more than fivefold since the 1950s.

• Rates of crime, mainly an activity of teenage youths and young men, have risen sharply in most, if not all, Western societies since World War II, after a long decline from the high levels of the early 1800s.

The social reality reflected by these statistics is evident in any large Western city. One writer described a walk that he and his wife took through Sydney to "enjoy" the sights of the city:

We didn't. It was as if William Hogarth's *Gin Lane* stretched for blocks. The streets were littered with drunks, some vomiting where they stood. The footpaths outside the hotels were strewn with broken glass. People argued with and hurled abuse at one another. Others with vacant eyes stood mumbling soundlessly to themselves, arms whirling like aimless windmills. Through the streets surged packs of feral teenagers with brutish faces and foul, mindless mouths.

The reference to Hogarth's famous eighteenth-century engraving is apt: Then, the social upheaval and destruction of jobs during the Industrial Revolution, together with a booming population, produced soaring drunkenness, child abuse, and crime.

If the problems I have mentioned were limited to a small fraction of the population, while the vast majority of people were enjoying a richer and fuller life than ever before because of the changes that have taken place in recent decades—and I am not denying that there have been many positive changes—then we could conceivably argue that the problems are a price worth paying.

Yet, this is clearly not the case. Some of the problems, such as mental illness and eating disorders, are now affecting a significant proportion of the population of Western nations. The impact of increasing crime reaches far beyond the victims and perpetrators, tainting all our lives with fear and suspicion and limiting our freedom. Furthermore, surveys of public attitudes show these problems are just the tip of an iceberg of disillusion, discontent, and disaffection.

A Breakdown in Values

The modern scourges of Western civilization, such as youth suicide, drug abuse, and crime, are usually explained in personal, social, and economic terms: unemployment, poverty, child abuse, family breakdown, and so on. And yet my own and other research suggests the trends appear to be, at least to some extent, independent of such factors. They seem to reflect something more fundamental in the nature of Western societies.

I believe this "something" is a profound and growing failure of Western culture—a failure to provide a sense of meaning, belonging, and purpose in our lives, as well as a framework of values. People need to have something to believe in and live for, to feel they are part of a community and a valued member of society, and to have a sense of spiritual fulfillment—that is, a sense of relatedness and connectedness to the world and the universe in which they exist.

The young are most vulnerable to peculiar hazards of our times. They face the difficult metamorphosis from child into adult, deciding who they are and what they believe, and accepting responsibility for their own lives. Yet, modern Western culture offers no firm guidance, no coherent or consistent world view, and no clear moral structure to help them make this transition.

The cultural failing may be more apparent in the "new" Western societies such as the United States, Canada, Australia, and New Zealand than in other Western societies because they are young, heterogeneous nations, without a long, shared cultural heritage or a strong sense of identity, and hence something to anchor them in these turbulent times. Older societies may offer a sense of permanence and continuity that can be very reassuring.

Interestingly, youth suicide rates have not risen in countries such as Spain and Italy, where traditional family and religious ties remain strong. And in Japan, despite the persistent myth of high levels of youth suicide, the rates have plummeted since the 1960s to be among the lowest in the industrial world.

The United States, the pacesetter of the Western world, shows many signs of a society under immense strain, even falling apart. Recent reports and surveys reveal a nation that is confused, divided, and scared. America is said to be suffering its worst crisis of confidence in 30 years and to be coming unglued culturally—the once-successful ethnic melting pot that the United States represented now coagulating into a lumpy mix of minorities and other groups who share few if any common values and beliefs. Most Americans, one survey found, no longer know right from wrong, and most believe there are no national heroes.

Although the symptoms may not be as dramatic, Australians are suffering a similar malaise. Surveys suggest a people who, beneath a professed personal optimism, nonchalance, and hedonism, are fearful, pessimistic, bewildered, cynical, and insecure; who feel destabilized and powerless in the face of accelerating cultural, economic, and technological change; and who are deeply alienated from the country's major institutions, especially government.

Children's Views of the Future

The most chilling of such surveys, in their bleakness, are the studies of how children and adolescents in Western nations see the future of the world. To cite just one example, *The Sydney Morning Herald* in 1990 conducted a survey in which about 120 eleven-year-old Sydney schoolchildren were asked to write down their perceptions of Australia's future and how their country would fare in the new millennium. The idea was to publish a cheerful view of Australia's future. The newspaper chose bright, healthy youngsters, young enough to be untarnished by cynicism, yet this is what the *Herald* said of the results:

Yes, we expected a little economic pessimism, some gloom about the environment and job prospects and perhaps even a continuing fear of nuclear war. But nothing prepared us for the depth of the children's fear of the future, their despair about the state of our planet and their bleak predictions for their own nation, Australia.

In any other culture, at any other time, children this age would be having stories told to them that would help them to construct a world view, a cultural context, to define who they are and what they believe—a context that would give them a positive, confident outlook on life, or at least the fortitude to endure what life held in store for them.

Our children are not hearing these stories.

It may be, then, that the greatest wrong we are doing to our children is not the fractured families or the scarcity of jobs (damaging though these are), but the creation of a culture that gives them little more than themselves to believe in—and no cause for hope or optimism.

At the social level, this absence of faith grievously weakens community cohesion; at the level of the individual, it undermines our resilience, our capacity to cope with the more-personal difficulties and hardships of everyday life.

We can see clearly the consequences for indigenous people, such as American Indians, Innuits (Eskimos), and Australian Aborigines, when their culture is undermined by sustained contact with Western industrial society: the social apathy, the high incidence of suicide, crime, and drug abuse. We are seeing all these things increase among youth in Western societies. Other young people—the majority—may be coping and outwardly happy, but they often suggest a cynicism, hesitancy, and social passivity that reveal their uncertainty and confusion.

In making the individual the focus of Western culture, it seems we have only succeeded in making the individual feel more impotent and insecure. Not surprisingly, the more we feel diminished as individuals, the more insistently we stand up for our rights—producing, as commentators such as Robert Hughes have said of America, a nation of victims, a society pervaded by a culture of complaint.

The evidence strongly suggests that, robbed of a broader meaning to our lives, we have entered an era of often pathological self-preoccupation: with our looks, careers, sex lives, personal development, health and fitness, our children, and so on. Alternatively, the desperate search for meaning and belonging ends in the total subjugation of the self—in, for example, fanatical nationalism and religious fundamentalism. The suicidal deaths earlier this year of more than 80 followers of the Branch Davidian cult in the siege of its Waco, Texas, compound—like the Jonestown massacre in Guyana in 1978—have provided sad evidence of this social sickness.

The harm that modern Western culture is doing to our psychic well-being provides reason enough to forge a new system of values and beliefs. However, the need is made even more critical by the relationship between modern Western culture and the many other serious problems that Western societies face: the seemingly intractable economic difficulties, the widening social gulf, the worsening environmental degradation.

Fundamentally, these are problems of culture, of beliefs, and of moral priorities, not of economics. Furthermore, addressing these problems will require good management; good management requires clarity and strength of purpose and direction. How can we know what to do if we don't know what we believe in and where we want to go?

The Sources of Cultural Decay

There is a range of possible sources of the cultural decay of the West, all linked to the domination of our way of life by science.

The first source is the way science has changed the way we see ourselves and our place in the world through its objective, rational, analytical, quantitative, reductionist focus. Science, its critics say, has caused the crisis of meaning in Western culture by separating fact from value and destroying the "magic" and "enchantment" that gave a spiritual texture to our lives.

A second is the accelerating rate and nature of the changes driven by the growth in science and technology since World War II. These changes have torn us from our past and from the cultural heritage that provided the moral framework to our lives. Science undermined our faith in "God, King, and Country" by replacing it with faith in

"progress": the belief that the life of each individual would always continue to get better—wealthier, healthier, safer, more comfortable, more exciting.

A third source, then, is the collapse of this belief as the limits and costs of progress become ever more apparent: Economic, social, and environmental problems pile up around us; expectations are raised, but remain unmet. We are now failing even by the standard measure of progress: For the first time in many generations, today's youth cannot assume that their material standard of living will be higher than their parents'.

A fourth source of our cultural malaise is one specific set of products of our scientific and technological virtuosity—the mass media. The media have become the most-powerful determinants of our culture, yet we make little attempt to control or direct the media in our best long-term interests. Indeed, the style of public culture dictated by the popular media virtually guarantees that we will fail to address effectively the many serious problems we have.

For all their value and power as instruments of mass education and entertainment, the media:

• Fail to project a coherent and internally consistent world view.

• Divide rather than unite us, fashioning public debate into a battle waged between extremes—a delineation of conflict rather than a search for consensus.

• Heighten our anxieties and intimidate us by depicting the world outside our personal experience as one of turmoil, exploitation, and violence.

• Debase our values and fuel our dissatisfaction by promoting a superficial, materialistic, self-centered, and self-indulgent lifestyle—a way of life that is beyond the reach of a growing number of citizens.

• Erode our sense of self-worth and promote a sense of inadequacy by constantly confronting us with images of lives more powerful, more beautiful, more successful, more exciting.

Science and technology may not be the sole source of the cultural flaws that mar Western civilization. But they have certainly magnified cultural weaknesses to the point where they now threaten our culture—just as, for example, the October 1987 stock-market crash was

caused, in the words of one analyst, by "the emotions that drive a trader, magnified a millionfold by the technology at his disposal."

Creating a More Harmonious Society

If those who see science as intrinsically hostile to human psychic well-being are right, then we could be in for the mother of upheavals as Western civilization falls apart. But I believe that the problem rests more with our immaturity in using a cultural tool as powerful as science, and I remain hopeful that, with growing experience and wisdom, we can create a more benign and complete culture, and so a more equitable and harmonious society.

Aldous Huxley once said that if he had rewritten *Brave New World*—with its vision of a scientifically controlled society in which babies were grown in bottles, free will was abolished by methodical conditioning, and regular doses of chemically induced happiness made servitude tolerable—he would have included a sane alternative, a society in which "science and technology would be used as though, like the Sabbath, they had been made for man, not (as at present and still more so in the Brave New World) as though man were to be adapted and enslaved to them."

Paradoxically, given its role in creating the situation we are in, science can, I believe, provide the impetus for the changes that are required, both through the knowledge it is providing about the human predicament and also, perhaps, through its increasing compatibility with spiritual beliefs.

Having inspired the overemphasis on the individual and the material, science is now leading us back to a world view that pays closer attention to the communal and the spiritual by revealing the extent of our interrelationship and interdependence with the world around us. This is evident in the "spiritual" dimensions of current cosmology, with its suggestion that the emergence of consciousness or mind is written into the laws of nature; in the primary role science has played—through its discovery and elucidation of global warming, ozone depletion, and other global environmental problems—in the "greening" of public consciousness and political agendas in recent years; and in the part that scientists (such as David Suzuki and David Maybury-Lewis) are playing in validating to Westerners the holistic and spiritually rich world view of indigenous peoples.

But science, in effecting change, must itself be changed. While remaining intellectually rigorous, science must become intellectually less arrogant, culturally better integrated, and politically more influential. Science must become more tolerant of other views of reality, other ways of seeing the world. It must become more involved in the processes of public culture. And it must contribute more to setting political agendas.

Arguably, only science is powerful enough to persuade us to redirect its power—to convince us of the seriousness of our situation, to strengthen our resolve to do something about it, and to guide what we do. Science can be the main (but by no means the only) source of knowledge and understanding that we need to remake our culture.

So I am not pessimistic about our prospects, despite the grim trends. Nor do I underestimate the immensity of the challenge. I sometimes do feel, in contemplating what is happening, that we are in the grip of powerful historical currents whose origins go back centuries, perhaps millennia, and against which individuals and even governments can only struggle punily.

Yet, it is also true that people, collectively and individually, can stand against those currents—and even change their course.

A DECADE OF DISCONTINUITY

The 1980s may have been the last decade in which humankind could anticipate a future of ever-increasing productivity on all fronts. By one measure after another, the boom we have experienced since mid-century is coming to an end.

LESTER R. BROWN

When the history of the late 20th century is written, the 1990s will be seen as a decade of discontinuity—a time when familiar trends that had seemed likely to go on forever, like smooth straight roads climbing toward an ever-receding horizon, came to abrupt bends or junctures and began descending abruptly. The world's production of steel, for example, had risen almost as reliably each year as the sun rises in the morning. The amount of coal extracted had risen almost uninterruptedly ever since the Industrial Revolution began. Since the middle of this century, the harvest of grain had grown even faster than population, steadily increasing the amount available both for direct consumption and for conversion into livestock products. The oceanic fish catch, likewise, had more than quadrupled during this period, doubling the consumption of seafood per person.

These rising curves were seen as basic measures of human progress; we *expected* them to rise. But now, within just a few years, these trends have reversed—and with consequences we have yet to grasp. Meanwhile, other trends that were going nowhere, or at most rising slowly, are suddenly soaring.

That such basic agricultural and industrial outputs should begin to decline, while population continues to grow, has engendered disquieting doubts about the future. These reversals, and others likely to follow, are dwarfing the discontinuities that occurred during the 1970s in the wake of the 1973 rise in oil prices. At that time, an overnight tripling of oil prices boosted energy prices across the board, slowed the growth in automobile production, and spurred investment in energy-efficient technologies, creating a whole new industry.

The discontinuities of the 1990s are far more profound, originating not with a handful of national political leaders as with the OPEC ministers of the 1970s, but in the collision between expanding human numbers and needs on the one hand and the constraints of the earth's natural systems on the other. Among these constraints are the capacity of the oceans to yield seafood, of grasslands to produce beef and mutton, of the hydrological cycle to produce fresh water, of crops to use fertilizer, of the atmosphere to absorb CFCs, carbon dioxide, and other greenhouse gases, of people to breathe polluted air, and of forests to withstand acid rain.

Though we may not have noticed them,

these constraints drew dramatically closer between 1950 and 1990, as the global economy expanded nearly fivefold. Expansion on this scale inevitably put excessive pressure on the earth's natural systems, upsetting the natural balances that had lent some stability to historical economic trends. The trends were driven, in part by unprecedented population growth. Those of us born before 1950 have seen world population double. In 1950, 37 million people were added to the world's population. Last year, it was 91 million.

Against the Grain

The production of grain, perhaps the most basic economic measure of human well-being, increased 2.6 fold from 1950 to 1984. Expanding at nearly 3 percent per year, it outstripped population growth, raising per capita grain consumption by 40 percent over the 34-year period, improving nutrition and boosting consumption of livestock products—meat, milk, eggs, and cheese—throughout the world.

That period came to an end, ironically, around the time the United States withdrew its funding from the United Nations Population Fund. During the eight years since 1984, world grain output has expanded perhaps one percent per year. In per capita terms, this means grain production has shifted from its steady rise over the previous 34 years to a *decline* of one percent per year since then—a particularly troubling change both because grain is a basic source of human sustenance and because of the likely difficulty in reversing it (see Figure 1).

This faltering of basic foodstuffs was triggered by other, earlier discontinuities of growth—in the supply of cropland, irrigation water, and agricultural technologies. Cropland, measured in terms of grain harvested area, expanded more or less continuously from the beginning of agriculture until 1981. The spread of agriculture, initially from valley to valley and eventually from continent to continent, had come to a halt. Since 1981, it has not increased. Gains of cropland in some countries have been offset by losses in others, as land is converted to nonfarm uses and abandoned because of erosion.

Irrigation, which set the stage for the emergence of early civilization, expanded gradually over a span of at least 5,000 years. After the middle of this century, the growth in irrigated area accelerated, averaging

nearly 3 percent per year until 1978. Around that time, however, as the number of prime dam construction sites diminished and underground aquifers were depleted by overpumping, the growth of irrigated area fell behind that of population. Faced with a steady shrinkage of cropland area per person from mid-century onward, the world's farmers since 1978 have faced a shrinking irrigated area per person as well.

Although there was little new land to plow from mid-century onward, the world's farmers were able to achieve the largest expansion of food output in history by dramatically raising land productivity. The engine of growth was fertilizer use, which increased ninefold in three decades—from 14 million tons in 1950 to 126 million tons in 1984—before starting to slow (see Figure 2).

In 1990, the rise in fertilizer use—what had been one of the most predictable trends in the world economy—was abruptly reversed. It has fallen some 10 percent during the three years since the 1989 peak of 146 million tons. Economic reforms in the former Soviet Union, which removed heavy fertilizer subsidies, account for most of the decline. Letting fertilizer prices move up to world market levels, combined with weakened demand for farm products, dropped fertilizer use in the former Soviet Union by exactly half between 1988 and 1992. This was an anomalous decline, from which there should eventually be at least a partial recovery.

More broadly, however, growth in world fertilizer use has slowed simply because existing grain varieties in the United States, Western Europe, and Japan cannot economically use much more fertilizer. U.S. farmers, matching applications more precisely to crop needs, actually used nearly one-tenth less fertilizer from 1990 to 1992 than they did a decade earlier. Using more fertilizer in agriculturally advanced countries does not have much effect on production with available varieties.

The backlog of unused agricultural technology that began to expand rapidly in the mid-19th century now appears to be diminishing. In 1847, German agricultural chemist Justus von Leibig discovered that all the nutrients removed by plants could be returned to the soil in their pure form. A decade later, Gregor Mendel discovered the basic principles of genetics, setting the stage for the eventual development of high-yielding, fertilizer-responsive crop varieties.

Falling Capacities: *With human population growing by the equivalent of 12 New York Cities or 11 Somalias a year, the world's food-producing capacity has been seriously strained—and the amount per person now shows signs of reversing its historic growth.*

Figure 1. Grain, the basic staple of both direct human consumption and livestock feed, is now falling in per-person production after decades of growth.

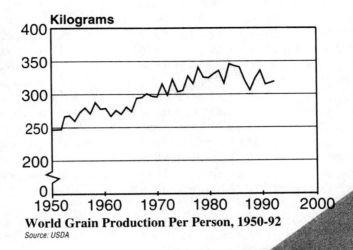

World Grain Production Per Person, 1950-92
Source: USDA

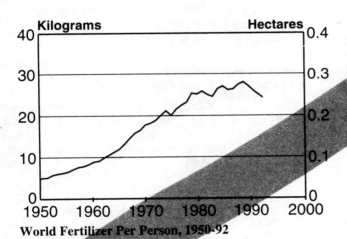

World Fertilizer Per Person, 1950-92
Source: USDA, FAO, IFA

Figure 2. Fertilizer use, the engine that drove up farm productivity worldwide, is sputtering—and in per-capita terms, is falling.

Figure 3: Fish from the oceans, once thought virtually limitless in supply, may already have reached its global limit—launching a decline in the catch per person that will continue to worsen as long as human population grows.

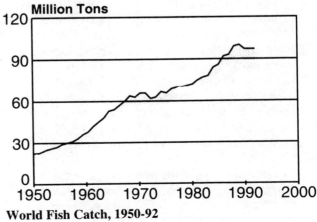

World Fish Catch, 1950-92
Source: FAO

As the geographic frontiers of agricultural expansion disappeared in the mid-20th century, the adoption of high-yielding varieties and rapid growth in fertilizer use boosted land productivity dramatically. In the 1960s, an array of advanced technologies for both wheat and rice producers was introduced into the Third World—giving rise to a growth in grain output that was more rapid than anything that had occurred earlier, even in the industrial countries.

Although it cannot be precisely charted, the backlog of unused agricultural technology must have peaked at least a decade ago. Most of the known means of raising food output are in wide use. The highest-yielding rice variety available to farmers in Asia in 1993 was released in 1966—more than a quarter-century ago. Today, the more progressive farmers are peering over the shoulders of agricultural scientists looking for new help in boosting production, only to find that not much is forthcoming. Agricultural scientists are worried that the rapid advance in technology characterizing the middle decades of this century may not be sustainable.

Less Meat *and* Less Fish

The growth in meat production, like that of grain, is slowing. Between 1950 and 1987, world meat production increased from 46 million tons to 161 million tons—boosting the amount per person from 18 kilograms in 1980 to 32 kilograms (about 70 pounds) in 1987. Since then, however, it has not increased at all. The one percent decline in per capita production in 1992 may be the beginning of a gradual world decline in per capita meat production, another major discontinuity.

Underlying this slowdown in overall meat production is a rather dramatic slowdown in the production of beef and mutton, resulting from the inability of grasslands to support more cattle and sheep. From 1950 to 1990, world beef output increased 2.5-fold. Now, with grasslands almost fully used—or overused—on every continent, this growth may be nearing an end. From 1990 to 1992, per capita beef production for the world fell 6 percent.

The supply of fish, like that of meat, no longer keeps pace with increases in human numbers. Here, too, there has been a reversal of the historic trend. Between 1950 and 1989, the global catch expanded from 22 million tons to 100 million tons. The per capita seafood supply increased from 9 to 19 kilograms during this period. Since 1989, the catch has actually declined slightly, totalling an estimated 97 million tons in 1992 (see Figure 3). United Nations marine biologists believe that the oceans have reached their limit and may not be able to sustain a yield of more than 100 million tons per year.

Throughout this century, it has been possible to increase the fish take by sending out more ships, using more sophisticated fishing technologies, and going, literally, to the farthest reaches of the ocean. That expansion has now come to an end. The world's ocean catch per capita declined 7 percent from 1989 until 1992, and is likely to continue declining as long as population continues to grow. As a result, seafood prices are rising steadily.

Getting more animal protein, whether it be in the form of beef or farm-raised fish, now depends on feeding grain and soybean meal. Those desiring to maintain animal protein intake now compete with those trying to consume more grain directly.

Table 1. Growth and Decline in Production of Fossil Fuels, 1950-92

Fossil Fuel	Growth Period Years	Growth Period Annual Rate (percent)	Decline Period Years	Decline Period Annual Rate (percent)
Oil	1950-79	+ 6.4	1979-92	- 0.5
Coal	1950-89	+ 2.2	1989-92	- 0.6
Natural Gas	1950-92	+ 6.2		

Fossil Fuels: The Beginning of the End

While biological constraints are forcing discontinuities in agriculture and oceanic fisheries, it is atmospheric constraints—the mounting risks associated with pollution and global warming—that are altering energy trends. Throughout the world energy economy, there are signs that a major restructuring is imminent. On the broadest level, this will entail a shifting of investment from fossil fuels and nuclear power toward renewables—and toward greater energy efficiency in every human activity.

We cannot yet see the end of the fossil fuel age, but we can see the beginning of its decline. World oil production peaked in 1979 (see Table 1). Output in 1992 was four percent below that historical high. World coal production dropped in 1990, in 1991, and again in 1992 (partly because of the recession), interrupting a growth trend that had spanned two centuries. If strong global warming policies are implemented, this could be the beginning of a long-term decline in coal dependence.

Of the three fossil fuels, only natural gas is expanding output rapidly and is assured of substantial future growth. Gas burns cleanly and produces less carbon dioxide than the others, and is therefore less likely to be constrained by stricter environmental policies. While oil production has fallen since 1979, gas production has risen by one-third.

With oil, it was the higher price that initially arrested growth. More recently, it has been the pall of automotive air pollution in cities like Los Angeles, Mexico City, and Rome that has slowed the once-unrestrained growth in motor vehicle use and, therefore, in oil use. With coal, it was neither supply nor price (the world has at least a few centuries of coal reserves left), but the effects of air pollution on human health, of acid rain on forests and crops, and of rising CO_2 concentrations on the earth's climate that have sent the industry into decline. Several industrial countries have committed themselves to reducing carbon emissions. Germany, for example, plans to cut carbon emissions 25 percent by 2005. Switzerland is shooting for a 10 percent cut by 2000, and Australia for 20 percent by 2005. Others, including the United States, may soon join them.

With the beginning of the end of the fossil fuel age in sight, what then will be used to power the world economy? Fifteen years ago, many would have said, with little hesitation, that nuclear power will. Once widely thought to be the energy source of the future, it has failed to live up to its promise (the problems of waste disposal and safety have proved expensive and intractable) and is being challenged on economic grounds in most of the countries where it is produced.

Nuclear generating capacity reached its historical peak in 1990. Though it has declined only slightly since then, it now seems unlikely that there will be much, if any, additional growth in nuclear generating capacity during this decade—and perhaps ever.

The Winds of Change

Even as the nuclear and fossil fuel industries have faltered, three new technologies that harness energy directly or indirectly from the sun to produce electricity—solar thermal power plants, photovoltaic cells, and wind generators—are surging. In wind power, particularly, breakthroughs in turbine technol-

ogy are setting the stage for rapid expansion in the years ahead. Wind electricity generated in California already produces enough electricity to satisfy the residential needs of San Francisco and Washington, D.C. Indeed, it now seems likely that during the 1990s, the growth in wind generating capacity will exceed that in nuclear generating capacity. Three countries—Denmark, the Netherlands, and Germany—have plans to develop a minimum of a thousand megawatts of wind

Table 2. World Economic Growth by Decade, 1950-93

Decade	Annual Growth of World Economy	Annual Growth Per Person
1950-60	4.9	3.1
1960-70	5.2	3.2
1970-80	3.4	1.6
1980-90	2.9	1.1
1990-93 (prel.)	0.9	−0.8

generating capacity by 2005. China aims to reach the same goal by 2000. Given the rapid advances in the efficiency of wind generating machines and the falling costs of wind generated electricity, the growth in wind power over the remainder of this decade could dwarf even current expectations.

The potential for wind power far exceeds that of hydropower, which currently supplies the world with one-fifth of its electricity. England and Scotland alone have enough wind generating potential to satisfy half of Europe's electricity needs. Two U.S. states—Montana and Texas—each have enough wind to satisfy the whole country's electricity needs. The upper Midwest (the Dakotas east through Ohio) could supply the country's electricity without siting any wind turbines in either densely populated or environmentally sensitive areas. And wind resource assessments by the government of China have documented 472,000 megawatts of wind generating potential, enough to raise China's electricity supply threefold.

For Third World villages not yet connected to a grid, a more practical source is photovoltaic arrays, which may already have a competitive advantage. With the World Bank beginning to support this technology, costs will fall fast, making photovoltaic cells even more competitive. Wind, photovoltaic cells, and solar thermal power plants all promise inexpensive electricity as the technologies continue to advance and as the economies of scale expand. Over the longer term, cheap solar electricity in various forms will permit the conversion of electricity into hydrogen, which will offer an efficient means of energy transportation and storage.

Technological advances that increase the *efficiency* of energy use are in some ways even more dramatic than the advances in harnessing solar and wind resources. Striking gains have been made in the energy efficiency of electric lighting, electric motors, the thermal efficiency of windows, and cogenerating technologies that produce both electricity and heat. One of the most dramatic, as recently noted in *World Watch* (May/June 1993), is the new compact fluorescent light bulb—which can supply the same amount of light as an incandescent bulb while using only one-fourth as much electricity. The 134 million compact fluorescent bulbs sold worldwide in 1992 saved enough electricity to close 10 large coal-fired power plants.

The discontinuities that have wreaked havoc with once-reliable trends are not random, but reflect an escalating awareness of the need to transform the global economy into one that is sustainable. They reflect the unavoidable reality that we have entered an era in which satisfying the needs of the 91 million people being added each year depends on reducing consumption among those already here. At this rate, by the year 2010, this growth will amount to a net addition equal to nearly 200 cities the size of New York, or 100 countries the size of Iraq—dramatically reducing the per capita availability of cropland and irrigation water. At some point, as people begin to grasp the implications of this new reality, population policy will become a central concern of national governments.

Economic Entropy

Whether in basic foodstuffs and fresh water, or in overall economic output, the decade of discontinuity has begun. Growth in the world economy reached its historical high at 5.2 percent per year during the 1960s (see Table 2). It then slowed to 3.4 percent per year in the 1970s, and 2.9 percent in the 1980s. Despite this slowdown, the per capita output of goods and services rose as overall economic growth stayed ahead of population growth. Now that, too, may be reversing.

From 1990 to 1992, the world economy expanded at 0.6 percent per year. If the International Monetary Fund's recent projection of 2.2 percent in world economic growth for 1993 materializes, we will find ourselves three years into this decade with an income per person nearly 2 percent lower than it was when the decade began. Even using an economic accounting system that overstates progress because it omits environmental degradation and the depletion of natural capital, living standards are falling.

Evidence is accumulating that the world economy is not growing as easily in the 1990s as it once did. The conventional economic wisdom concerning the recession of the early 1990s attributes it to economic mismanagement in the advanced industrial countries (particularly the United States, Germany, and Japan) and to the disruption associated with economic reform in the centrally planned economies. These are obviously the dominant forces slowing world economic growth, but they are not the only ones. As noted above, growth in the fishing industry, which supplies much of the world's animal protein, may have stopped. Growth in the production of beef, mutton, and other livestock products from the world's rangelands may also be close to an end. The world grain harvest shows little prospect of being able to keep pace with population, much less to eliminate hunger. And scarcities of fresh water are limiting economic expansion in many countries. With constraints emerging in these primary economic sectors—sectors on which much of the Third World depends—we may be moving into an era of slower economic growth overall.

The popular question of "growth or no growth" now seems largely irrelevant. A more fundamental question is how to satisfy the basic needs of the world's people without further disrupting or destroying the economy's support systems. The real challenge for the 1990s is that of deciding how the basic needs of all people can be satisfied without jeopardizing the prospects of future generations.

Of all the discontinuities that have become apparent in the past few years, however, it is an upward shift in the population growth trend itself that may be most disturbing. The progress in slowing human population growth so evident in the 1970s has stalled—with alarming implications for the long-term population trajectory. Throughout the 1960s and 1970s, declining fertility held out hope for getting the brakes on population growth before it began to undermine living standards. The 1980s, however, turned out to be a lost decade, one in which the United States not only abdicated its leadership role, but also withdrew all financial support from the U.N. Population Fund and the International Planned Parenthood Federation. This deprived millions of couples in the Third World of access to the family planning services needed to control the number or timing of their children.

The concern that population growth could undermine living standards has become a reality in this decade of discontinuity. There is now a distinct possibility that the grain supply per person will be lower at the end of this decade than at the beginning, that the amount of seafood per person will be substantially less, and that the amount of meat per person will also be far less than it is today.

The absence of any technology to reestablish the rapid growth in food production that existed from 1950 to 1984 is a matter of deepening concern. In early 1992, the U.S. National Academy of Sciences and the Royal Society of London together issued a report that warned: "If current predictions of population growth prove accurate and patterns of human activity on the planet remain unchanged, science and technology may not be able to prevent either irreversible degradation of the environment or continued poverty for much of the world."

Later in the year, the Union of Concerned Scientists issued a statement signed by nearly 1,600 of the world's leading scientists, including 96 Nobel Prize recipients, noting that the continuation of destructive human activities "may so alter the living world that it will be unable to sustain life in the manner that we know." The statement warned: "A great change in our stewardship of the earth and the life on it is required, if vast human misery is to be avoided and our global home on this planet is not to be irretrievably mutilated."

The discontinuities reshaping the global economy define the challenge facing humanity in the next few years. It is a challenge not to the survival of our species, but to civilization as we know it. The question we can no longer avoid asking is whether our social institutions are capable of quickly slowing and stabilizing population growth without infringing on human rights. Even as that effort gets underway, the same institutions face the complex issue of how to distribute those resources that are no longer expanding, among a population that is continuing to grow by record numbers each year.

This article is adapted from the overview chapter of Vital Signs 1993: The Trends That Are Shaping Our Future, *by Lester R. Brown, Hal Kane, and Ed Ayres, published by W.W. Norton and the Worldwatch Institute in July.*

EARTH is Running Out of Room

Brazilian children searching garbage dump for food.

UNICEF / Claudio Edinger

*Food scarcity, not military aggression, is the principal
threat to the planet's future.*

Lester R. Brown

*Mr. Brown is president, Worldwatch Institute, Washington, D.C.,
and co-author of* Full House: Reassessing the Earth's Population
Carrying Capacity.

THE WORLD is entering a new era, one in which
it is far more difficult to expand food output.
Many knew that this time would come eventually;
that, at some point, the limits of the Earth's natural
systems, cumulative effects of environmental degradation on cropland productivity, and shrinking
backlog of yield-raising technologies would slow the
record increase in food production of recent decades. Because no one knew exactly when or how
this would happen, food prospects were debated
widely. Now, several constraints are emerging

simultaneously to slow that growth.

After nearly four decades of unprecedented expansion in both land-based and oceanic food supplies, the world is experiencing a massive loss of momentum. Between 1950 and 1984, grain production expanded 2.6-fold, outstripping population growth by a wide margin and raising the grain harvested per person by 40%. Growth in the fish catch was even more spectacular—a 4.6-fold increase between 1950 and 1989, thereby doubling seafood consumption per person. Together, these developments reduced hunger and malnutrition throughout the world, offering hope that these biblical scourges would be eliminated one day.

In recent years, these trends suddenly have been reversed. After expanding at three percent a year from 1950 to 1984, the growth in grain production has slowed abruptly, rising at scarcely one percent annually from 1984 until 1993. As a result, grain production per person fell 12% during this time.

With fish catch, it is not merely a slowing of growth, but a limit imposed by nature. From a high of 100,000,000 tons, believed to be close to the maximum oceanic fisheries can sustain, the catch has fluctuated between 96,000,000 and 98,000,000 tons. As a result, the 1993 per capita seafood catch was nine percent below that of 1988. Marine biologists at the United Nations Food and Agriculture Organization report that the 17 major oceanic fisheries are being fished at or beyond capacity and that nine are in a state of decline.

Rangelands, a major source of animal protein, also are under excessive pressure, being grazed at or beyond capacity on every continent. This means that rangeland production of beef and mutton may not increase much, if at all, in the future. Here, too, availability per person will decline indefinitely as population expands.

With both fisheries and rangelands being pressed to the limits of their carrying capacity, future growth in food demand can be satisfied only by expanding output from croplands. The increase in demand for food that was satisfied by three food systems must now be satisfied by one.

Until recently, grain output projections for the most part were simple extrapolations of trends. The past was a reliable guide to the future. However, in a world of limits, this is changing. In projecting food supply trends now, at least six new constraints must be taken into account:

● The backlog of unused agricultural technology is shrinking, leaving the more progressive farmers fewer agronomic options for expanding food output.

● Growing human demands are pressing against the limits of fisheries to supply seafood and rangelands to supply beef, mutton, and milk.

● Demands for water are nearing limits of the hydrological cycle to supply irrigation water in key food-growing regions.

● In many countries, the use of additional fertilizer on currently available crop varieties has little or no effect on yields.

● Nations that already are densely populated risk losing cropland when they begin to industrialize at a rate that exceeds the rise in land productivity, initiating a long-term decline in food production.

● Social disintegration by rapid population growth and environmental degradation often is undermining many national governments and their efforts to expand food production.

New technologies are not enough

In terms of agricultural technology, the contrast between the middle of the 20th century and today could not be more striking. When the 1950s began, a great deal of technology was waiting to be used. Except for irrigation, which goes back several thousand years, all the basic advances were made between 1840 and 1940. Chemist Justus von Liebig discovered in 1847 that all nutrients taken from the soil by crops could be replaced in mineral form. Biologist Gregor Mendel's work establishing the basic principles of heredity, which laid the groundwork for future crop breeding advances, was done in the 1860s. Hybrid corn varieties were commercialized in the U.S. during the 1920s, and dwarfing of wheat and rice plants in Japan to boost fertilizer responsiveness dates back a century.

These long-standing technologies have been enhanced and modified for wide use through agricultural research and exploited by farmers during the last four decades. Although new developments continue to appear, none promise to lead to quantum leaps in world food output. The relatively easy gains have been made. Moreover, public funding for international agricultural research has begun to decline. As a result, the more progressive farmers are looking over the shoulders of agricultural scientists seeking new yield-raising technologies, but discovering that they have less and less to offer. The pipeline has not run dry, but the flow has slowed to a trickle.

In Asia, rice crops on maximum-yield experimental plots have not increased for more than two decades. Some countries appear to be "hitting the wall" as their yields approach those on the research plots. Japan reached this point with a rice yield in 1984 at 4.7 tons per hectare (2.47 acres), a level it has been unable to top in nine harvests since then. South Korea, with similar growing conditions, may have run into the same barrier in 1988, when its rice yield stopped rising. Indonesia, with a crop that has increased little since 1988, may be the first tropical rice-growing nation to see its yield rise lose momentum. Other countries could hit the wall before the end of the century.

Farmers and policymakers search in vain for new advances, perhaps from biotechnology, that will lift food output quickly to a new level. However, biotechnology has not produced any yield-raising technologies that will lead to quantum jumps in output, nor do many researchers expect it to. Donald Duvick, for many years the director of research at Iowa-based Pioneer Hi-Bred International, one of the world's largest seed suppliers, makes this point all too clearly: "No breakthroughs are in sight. Biotechnology, while essential to progress, will not produce sharp upward swings in yield potential except for isolated crops in certain situations."

The productivity of oceanic fisheries and rangelands, both natural systems, is determined by nature. It can be reduced by overfishing and overgrazing or other forms of mismanagement, but once sustainable yield limits are reached, the contribution of these systems to world food supply can not be expanded. The decline in fisheries is not limited to developing countries. By early 1994, the U.S. was experiencing precipitous drops in fishery stocks off the coast of New England, off the West Coast, and in the Gulf of Mexico.

With water—the third constraint—the overpumping that is so widespread eventually will be curbed to bring it into balance with aquifer recharge. This reduction, combined with the growing diversion of irrigation water to residential and industrial uses, limits the amount of water available to produce food. Where farmers depend on fossil aquifers for their irrigation water—in the southern U.S. Great Plains, for instance, or the wheat fields of Saudi Arabia—aquifer depletion means an end to irrigated agriculture. In the U.S., where more than one-fourth of irrigated cropland is watered by drawing down underground water tables, the downward adjustment in irrigation pumping will be substantial. Major food-producing regions where overpumping is commonplace include the southern Great Plains, India's Punjab, and the North China Plain. For many farmers, the best hope for more water is from gains in efficiency.

Perhaps the most worrisome emerging constraint on food production is the limited capacity of grain varieties to respond to the use of additional fertilizer. In the U.S., Western Europe, and Japan, usage has increased little if at all during the last decade. Utilizing additional amounts on existing crop varieties has little or no effect on yield in these nations. After a tenfold increase in world fertilizer use from 1950 to 1989—from 14,000,000 to 146,000,000 tons—use declined to the following four years.

A little-recognized threat to the future world food balance is the heavy loss of cropland that occurs when countries that already are densely populated begin to industrialize. The experience in Japan, South Korea, and Taiwan gives a sense of what to expect. The conversion of grainland to nonfarm uses and to high-value specialty crops has cost Japan 52% of its grainland; South Korea, 42%; and Taiwan, 35%.

As the loss of land proceeded, it began to override the rise in land productivity, leading to declines in production. From its peak, Japan's grain output has dropped 33%; South Korea's, 31%; and Taiwan's, 19%. These declines occurred at a time when population growth and rapidly rising incomes were driving up the demand for grain. The result is that, by 1993, Japan was importing 77% of its grain; South Korea, 68%; and Taiwan, 74%.

Asia's densely populated giants, China and India, are going through the same stages that led to the extraordinarily heavy dependence on imported grain in the three smaller countries that industrialized earlier. In both, the shrinkage in grainland has begun. It is one thing for Japan, a country of 120,000,000 people, to import 77% of its grain, but quite another if China, with 1,200,000,000, moves in this direction.

Further complicating efforts to achieve an acceptable balance between food and people is social disintegration. In an article in the February 1994 *Atlantic* entitled "The Coming Anarchy," writer and political analyst Robert Kaplan observed that unprecedented population growth and environmental degradation were driving people from the countryside into cities and across national borders at a record rate. This, in turn, was leading to social disintegration and political fragmentation. In parts of Africa, he argues, nation-states no longer exist in any meaningful sense. In their place are fragmented tribal and ethnic groups.

The sequence of events that leads to environmental degradation is all too familiar to environmentalists. It begins when the firewood demands of a growing population exceed the sustainable yield of local forests, leading to deforestation. As firewood become scarce, cow dung and crop residues are burned for fuel, depriving the land of nutrients and organic matter. Livestock numbers expand more or less apace with the human population, eventually exceeding grazing capacity. The combination of deforestation and overgrazing increases rainfall runoff and soil erosion, simultaneously reducing aquifer recharge and soil fertility. No longer able to feed themselves, people become refugees, heading for the nearest city or food relief center.

Crop reports for Africa now regularly cite weather and civil disorder as the key variables affecting harvest prospects. Not only is agricultural progress difficult, even providing food aid can be a challenge under these circumstances. In Somalia, getting food to the starving in late 1992 required a UN peacekeeping force and military expenditures that probably cost 10 times as much as what was distributed.

As political fragmentation and instability spread, national governments no longer can provide the physical and economic infrastructure for development. Countries in this category include Afghanistan, Haiti, Liberia, Sierra Leone, and Somalia. To the extent that nation-states become dysfunctional, the prospects for humanely slowing population growth, reversing environmental degradation, and systematically expanding food production are diminished.

Other negative influences exist, but they have emerged more gradually. Among those that affect food production more directly are soil erosion, the waterlogging and salting of irrigated land, and air pollution. For example, a substantial share of the world's cropland is losing topsoil at a rate that exceeds natural soil formation. On newly cleared land that is sloping steeply, soil losses can lead to cropland abandonment in a matter of years. In other situations, the loss is slow and has a measurable effect on land productivity only over many decades.

Growing pessimism

Until recently, concerns about the Earth's capacity to feed ever-growing numbers of people adequately was confined largely to the environmental and population communities and a few scientists. During the 1990s, however, these issues are arousing the concerns of the mainstream scientific community. In early 1992, the U.S. National Academy of Sciences and the Royal Society of London issued a report that began: "If current predictions of population growth prove accurate and patterns of human activity on the planet remain unchanged, science and technology may not be able to prevent either irreversible degradation of the environment or continued poverty for much of the world."

It was a remarkable statement, an admission that science and technology no longer can ensure a better future unless population growth slows quickly and the economy is restructured. This abandonment of the technological optimism that has permeated so much of the 20th century by two of the world's leading scientific bodies represents a major shift, though perhaps not a surprising one, given the deteriorating state of the planet. That they chose to issue a joint statement, their first ever, reflects the deepening concern about the future within the scientific establishment.

Later in 1992, the Union of Concerned Scientists issued a "World Scientists' Warning to Humanity," signed by some 1,600 of the planet's leading scientists, including 102 Nobel Prize winners. It observes that the continuation of destructive human activities "may so alter the living world that it will be unable to sustain life in the manner that we know." The scientists indicated that "A great change in our stewardship of the earth and the life on it is required, if vast human misery is to be avoided and our global home on this planet is not to be irretrievably mutilated."

In November, 1993, representatives of 56 national science academies convened in New Delhi, India, to discuss population. At the end of their conference, they issued a statement in which they urged zero population growth during the lifetimes of their children.

Between 1950 and 1990, the world added 2,800,000,000 people, an average of 70,000,000 a year. Between 1990 and 2030, it is projected to add 3,600,000,000, or 90,000,000 a year. Even more troubling, nearly all this increase is projected for the developing countries, where life-support systems already are deteriorating. Such population growth in a finite ecosystem raises questions about the Earth's carrying capacity. Will the planet's natural support systems sustain such growth indefinitely? How many people can the Earth support at a given level of consumption?

Underlying this assessment of population carrying capacity is the assumption that the food supply will be the most immediate constraint on population growth. Water scarcity could limit population growth in some locations, but it is unlikely to do so for the world as a whole in the foreseeable future. A buildup of environmental pollutants could interfere with human reproduction, much as DDT reduced the reproductive capacity of bald eagles, peregrine falcons, and other birds at the top of the food chain. In the extreme, accumulating pollutants in the environment could boost death rates to the point where they would exceed birth rates, leading to a gradual decline in human numbers, but this does not seem likely. For now, it appears that the food supply will be the most immediate, and therefore the controlling, determinant of how many people the Earth can support.

Grain supply and demand projections for the 13 most populous countries—accounting for two-thirds of world population and food production—show much slower growth in output than the official projections by the Food and Agriculture Organization and the World Bank. If those projections of relative abundance and a continuing decline of food prices materialize, governments can get by with business as usual. If, on the other hand, the constraints discussed above continue, the world needs to reorder priorities.

The population-driven environmental deterioration/political disintegration scenario described by Robert Kaplan not only is possible, it is likely in a business-as-usual world. However, it is not inevitable. This future can be averted if security is redefined, recognizing that food scarcity, not military aggression, is the principal threat to the future. Government must give immediate attention to filling the family planning gap; attacking the underlying causes of high fertility, such as illiteracy and poverty; protecting soil and water resources; and raising investment in agriculture.

Credits/ Acknowledgments

Cover design by Charles Vitelli

Introduction
Facing overview—United Nations photo by John Isaac.

1. Parenting and Family Issues
Facing overview—United Nations photo by John Isaac.

2. Crime, Terrorism, and Violence
Facing overview—Source unknown.

3. Health and Health Care Issues
Facing overview—United Nations photo by John Isaac.

4. Poverty and Inequality
Facing overview—Photo by Pamela Carley.

5. Cultural Pluralism and Affirmative Action
Facing overview—Click/Chicago photo by Jim Pickerell.

6. Cities, Urban Growth, and the Quality of Life
Facing overview—United Nations photo by B. Grunzweig.

7. Global Issues
Facing overview—United Nations photo by Witlin.

ANNUAL EDITIONS ARTICLE REVIEW FORM

■ NAME: _____ DATE: _____

■ TITLE AND NUMBER OF ARTICLE: _____

■ BRIEFLY STATE THE MAIN IDEA OF THIS ARTICLE: _____

_____

■ LIST THREE IMPORTANT FACTS THAT THE AUTHOR USES TO SUPPORT THE MAIN IDEA:

_____

_____

_____

_____

_____

_____

■ WHAT INFORMATION OR IDEAS DISCUSSED IN THIS ARTICLE ARE ALSO DISCUSSED IN YOUR TEXTBOOK OR OTHER READING YOU HAVE DONE? LIST THE TEXTBOOK CHAPTERS AND PAGE NUMBERS:

_____

_____

_____

_____

_____

_____

■ LIST ANY EXAMPLES OF BIAS OR FAULTY REASONING THAT YOU FOUND IN THE ARTICLE:

_____

_____

_____

_____

■ LIST ANY NEW TERMS/CONCEPTS THAT WERE DISCUSSED IN THE ARTICLE AND WRITE A SHORT DEFINITION:

_____

_____

_____

_____

_____